RUNNING

Microsoft®
PowerPoint® 2000

Stephen W. Sagman

PUBLISHED BY
Microsoft Press
A Division of Microsoft Corporation
One Microsoft Way
Redmond, Washington 98052-6399

Library of Congress Cataloging-in-Publication Data
   Running Microsoft PowerPoint 2000 / Stephen W. Sagman.
        p.   cm.
   Includes index.
   ISBN 1-57231-941-0
   1. Microsoft PowerPoint (Computer file) 2. Computer graphics.
   I. Title.   II. Title: Running Microsoft PowerPoint two thousand.
   T385.S23545 1999
   006.6'869--dc21   98-48195
                                                          CIP

Printed and bound in the United States of America.

1 2 3 4 5 6 7 8 9 QMQM 3 2 1 0 9 8

Distributed in Canada by ITP Nelson, a division of Thomson Canada Limited.

A CIP catalogue record for this book is available from the British Library.

Microsoft Press books are available through booksellers and distributors worldwide. For further information about international editions, contact your local Microsoft Corporation office or contact
Microsoft Press International directly at fax (425) 936-7329. Visit our Web site at mspress.microsoft.com.

Acquisitions Editor: Christey Bahn
Project Editor: Sandra Haynes
Copy Editor: Gail Taylor
Technical Editor: Jean Hollis Weber

Chapters at a Glance

Table of Contents

Part III Fine-Tuning the Presentation   261

Acknowledgments

I am deeply grateful to the fine people at Microsoft Press who have shepherded this book through four editions, including Lucinda Rowley, Kim Fryer, Sandra Haynes, Kristen Weatherby, Joel Panchot, Stuart Stuple, Mary DeJong, Bill Teel, Kim Eggleston, Jim Kramer, Travis Beaven, Judith Bloch, Peggy McCauley, and Ina Chang.

For this edition, I'd like to thank the fine writer Teresa Stover for her work in revising much of the material from the previous edition. Gail Taylor skillfully copy edited the manuscript, Jean Hollis Weber carefully checked everything technically, and Sharon Bell labored tirelessly, preparing the lovely layouts with extraordinary care.

Thanks also to Christine Solomon, who provided the original chapter entitled "Automating PowerPoint with Visual Basic for Applications," and to the other editors and writers who have contributed to previous editions, including Mary Deaton, Lynn Van Deventer, Polly Fox Urban, Deb Fenwick, Christina Dudley, and Ken Sanchez.

Among the Microsoft Graphics folks, I'd like to thank Jolene Carlsen and Shawn Villaron for their great cooperation and willingness to review portions of the manuscript.

And finally, as always, a special thanks to Eric for being patient and to my little love Lola for her support, too.

Introduction

S ince its introduction in 1987, Microsoft PowerPoint has pioneered new ways of working with presentation graphics. PowerPoint introduced the concept of a presentation as a single entity rather than discrete slides, and it has introduced innovations with each new release.

Microsoft PowerPoint 2000 carries on the tradition, adding dozens of features designed to make creating presentations even easier, and rich new capabilities for collaborating on presentations and publishing them to the Web. At the same time, it has become more like its colleagues in the Microsoft Office 2000 suite of applications, sharing on-screen controls like menus and dialog boxes, and techniques like drag-and-drop editing. PowerPoint has even mastered the common language of communication that is shared by the Office applications, so you can now effortlessly pass text, numbers, and graphics among the applications using the drag-and-drop feature.

What's New in PowerPoint 2000

Whether you're a new user or a veteran, you'll appreciate PowerPoint's many new features. And if you're already familiar with other Microsoft Office applications, such as Microsoft Word or Microsoft Excel, you'll recognize many of these innovations. Here is a partial list of the new features in PowerPoint 2000:

- Dozens of enhancements that make PowerPoint easier to use. PowerPoint's improved Open and Save dialog boxes with their Places Bars, makes it easier to get to the presentations you use most. PowerPoint's new adaptive menus and toolbars give you a cleaner, simpler screen by revealing only the commands and buttons you use most often and temporarily hiding those you rarely use.

- PowerPoint's new Normal view simultaneously displays the outline for the entire presentation, a slide, and notes for the slide so you can see everything you need at once.

- An improved Office Assistant that takes up less space on the screen and offers suggestions for creating better presentations based on the tasks you are in the midst of carrying out.

- Graphical bullets and numbered lists add pizzazz to slides and allow you to created ordered lists that automatically renumber when you add or remove items.

- New Design and Content templates give you more choices for both the appearance of presentations and the content. Some new templates even include animated templates and preset animations.

- The new Clip Gallery is easier to use, takes up less screen space, and organizes its thousands of images into useful categories. You can simply drag images from the gallery onto slides, and you can use the gallery to store sounds and motion clips, too.

- You can now scan a picture directly into PowerPoint if you have a TWAIN-compatible scanner. You can even download a picture directly onto a slide from a TWAIN-based digital camera.

- PowerPoint slide shows can now display animated GIFs, the popular and easy-to-create animation files that are used on Web pages.

- You can now save a presentation as a Web page and easily save the page to a Web server. You can post the presentation on the Web for others to view, or you can use any computer with a Web browser to display a presentation from a Web server on your corporate intranet or on the Internet.

- You can save and reopen an HTML version of a presentation and work with it as though you were working on the original PowerPoint file. The HTML version preserves all the formatting and contents, even charts, tables, and other elements on slides.

- PowerPoint's Online Meetings allow you to collaborate with others and share and exchange information in real time with people at other sites. During an online meeting, you can share a whiteboard on which everyone can draw, you can participate in a chat, and you can transfer files to the meeting participants.

- PowerPoint's new Presentation Broadcasting allows you to schedule and deliver a presentation over a corporate intranet or over the Internet. Viewers can visit the broadcast's Web page and watch and hear the presentation. Those who miss the presentation can replay the presentation later by visiting the broadcast's Web page.

- When a Web presentation is posted to a Web server, colleagues and associates can view the presentation and contribute comments about it to an online written discussion.

About This Book

The object of this book is to give you the broadest possible under-standing of PowerPoint in the shortest possible time. It serves as a tutorial as you're learning PowerPoint and as a reference for looking up topics. This book assumes that you have a working knowledge of Windows.

The parts and chapters of this book deliver information in the order you'll need it as you create presentations.

Part I, which includes Chapters 1 and 2, introduces PowerPoint. You learn the basics of the PowerPoint environment, and you get off on the right footing by learning the essential steps to follow whenever you create a presentation.

Part II, which includes Chapters 3 through 9, provides guidelines for creating the basic elements of a presentation. You learn how to start a presentation and how to work in Normal view, Outline view, and Slide view to enter and organize the text and add graphic charts, organization charts, and tables.

Part III, which consists of Chapters 10 through 14, offers important information on adapting the basic presentation to your specific needs. You learn how to reorganize the presentation, change its design, draw on slides, add photos and clip art, and print copies of the presentation on paper or 35-mm slides.

Part IV, which includes Chapters 15 through 17, shows you how to create lively slide shows, save slide shows as Web presentations, collaborate with others in online meetings and discussions, and deliver presentations in person or in a broadcast over a corporate intranet or the Internet.

Part V, which consists of Chapters 18, 19, and 20, covers advanced topics such as using PowerPoint with other Office applications, customizing PowerPoint to suit the way you like to work, and using Visual Basic for Applications to automate PowerPoint.

Using This Book

In this book, when you see a key combination with a plus sign, like this: Ctrl+Z, it means "Hold down the first key and then press the second key." For example, Ctrl+Z means "Hold down the Ctrl key and then press the Z key."

 TIP

Tips that contain helpful suggestions for getting more out of PowerPoint or for enhancing the visual appeal of your presentations look like this.

 NOTE

Notes about PowerPoint features, commands, or techniques look like this.

 WARNING

A heavy, black border surrounds Warnings so you will find them hard to ignore.

SEE ALSO

Finally, whenever you see the "See Also" icon, you'll find references to other sections in the book that provide additional, related information.

PART I

Introducing PowerPoint

CHAPTER 1

PowerPoint Basics (Read This!)

A word processor prepares the text in your everyday life. A spreadsheet calculates the numbers you need. And a database stores the text and numeric information you've compiled. But to communicate your knowledge, information, and achievements, and to persuade others with your opinions, you need a powerful presentation processor.

What Is PowerPoint?

PowerPoint 2000 is the newest version of Microsoft's presentation graphics program and an integral part of the Microsoft Office 2000 suite. It's a world leader in the presentation graphics category because no other program lets you convert your ideas so easily to a set of slides with the professional polish that today's sophisticated audiences demand. The ease with which you can use PowerPoint is particularly important because a presentation graphics program just doesn't get pulled off the electronic shelf and used as often as a word processor, spreadsheet, or even database.

PowerPoint takes you by the hand from the very first screen and gently guides you through the process of creating a presentation. It asks for the text and numbers it needs—you can type them in or import them from other applications—and it asks you to select from a palette of designs for the presentation. Then PowerPoint produces the kind of vivid graphics and dazzling images you'd expect from a professional artist.

After the presentation is complete, PowerPoint can produce pages to hand out at a meeting, bright, crisp slides, speaker notes, or even transparencies that you can use with an overhead projector. And that's not all. More and more people are foregoing slides and transparencies and showing a PowerPoint slide show right on the screen, instead. Electronic presentations like these, with their TV-like special effects, sound, music, animation, and even video clips, are the hottest thing today, and PowerPoint's capabilities for creating and controlling electronic presentations are state of the art. And if your audience is widely dispersed geographically, you can use PowerPoint's ability to create Web presentations that can play across a corporate intranet or even across the Internet.

Best of all, to create professional-quality visuals in PowerPoint, you don't have to be an artist. The program's built-in design templates take care of the presentation's appearance. And you don't have to be a computer expert to use all of PowerPoint's features. There's always an on-screen prompt to lead you to the next task, and often, when you have choices to make, one of PowerPoint's "wizards" appears to guide you through the preliminary decisions. About the only thing PowerPoint cannot do is help you enunciate while speaking, but the professional quality of the visuals will help give you the confidence to be at your very best.

PowerPoint's special presentation-making features can make your work easier no matter what your presentation needs:

You need quick and easy, high-impact visuals to accompany a talk. PowerPoint's AutoContent Wizard and templates not only help you design a presentation, but they give you a basic presentation outline to follow. You simply select a theme and design, and watch as PowerPoint generates eye-catching slides that are organized, consistent, and professional.

You need a fact-filled presentation with plenty of graphs and charts. PowerPoint's Chart, Organization Chart, and Table programs help you create elaborate visuals that depict numeric information, detail the structure of an organization, and make comparisons among ideas.

You need a sophisticated electronic presentation with lots of razzle-dazzle. PowerPoint's slide shows serve up the most sophisticated special effects you can get, including animated charts, sound, music and audio tracks, embedded video, and those famous, between-slide transitions. Slide shows can also be interactive—you can branch to a subtopic or call up hidden detail to respond to a viewer's question.

You need team-spirit presentations that display your group's logo and colors. Easily customizable slide backgrounds and color schemes are all part of PowerPoint's repertoire. You can place a logo on the background of every slide or select colors to match your corporate color scheme.

You need to assemble existing text and graphics from other programs. PowerPoint can easily integrate text, charts, numbers, and diagrams from other Microsoft Office applications (such as Microsoft Word and Microsoft Excel) into presentation materials. You can even edit any of these from within PowerPoint just as though you were working in the original program you used to create them.

You need to deliver your presentation on the road, across the network, or even on the Internet. Presentation Broadcasting lets you share a presentation across a company network or even across the Internet and have colleagues review it with you. While the presentation is still in development, you can post a Web version of a presentation on an organization's intranet and allow others to collaborate on the presentation using their Web browser. And with Stage Manager, Meeting Minder and the Slide Meter, you can preview slides, take notes, read your script, and keep track of the presentation's pace while PowerPoint presents your show to the audience.

Program Basics

Although PowerPoint is extremely friendly and easy to use, you still need to know just a few basics before you can master the program. The rest of this chapter covers the little bit of groundwork you need. But don't worry; you'll soon start creating an actual presentation.

PowerPoint Views

PowerPoint creates entire presentations of slides, all similar in appearance and all stored in a single file on your system. PowerPoint uses the word "slide" to refer to each page of visuals in a presentation, even though you might show the presentation onscreen, post the presentation on a Web site, or print the presentation on paper or transparencies rather than create 35-mm slides.

PowerPoint offers multiple views on a presentation in progress: Normal view, Slide view, Outline view, Slide Sorter view, Notes Page view, and Slide Show view. Each view lets you work on a different aspect of the presentation, and the changes you make in one view show up in all the other views as well.

Normal View

In Normal view, shown in Figure 1-1, you can see three separate panes. The left pane displays the presentation's text content as an

FIGURE 1-1.

Normal view.

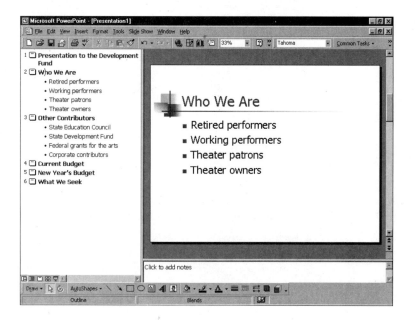

outline. The right pane displays the current slide with all its content and design elements. A third pane below the right pane displays notes you've entered about the current slide for use while the speaker is giving the presentation.

Slide View

In Slide view, you refine and embellish individual slides in a presentation. You can enter and edit text and add charts, tables, and media elements to slides. You can also dress up a slide with drawings, pictures, and text annotations. Figure 1-2 shows a slide in Slide view.

FIGURE 1-2.
Slide view.

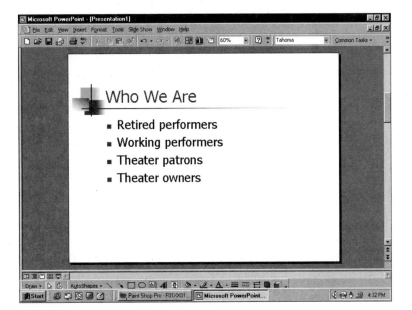

Outline View

In Outline view, PowerPoint helps you focus on the text of the presentation. Figure 1-3 on the next page shows a sample presentation in Outline view. Because you work primarily with the text content of a presentation in Outline view, you can concentrate on the words of the presentation and the flow of ideas through the slides. Outline view provides an excellent environment for organizing your thoughts and materials before you switch to a different view, where you can focus on the look of the presentation.

FIGURE 1-3.
Outline view.

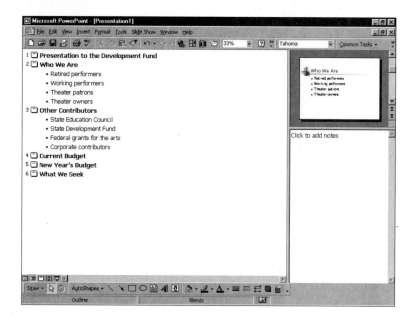

Slide Sorter View

In Slide Sorter view, you see the slides of the presentation laid out in neat rows and columns, as in Figure 1-4. Here you can see the results of sweeping changes to the appearance of the entire presentation, such as a change to the background design and color scheme. You cannot make changes to the content of individual slides in Slide Sorter view, but you can duplicate slides, cut extraneous slides, and shuffle the order of slides just as if you had laid out real 35-mm slides on a light table.

By using Slide Sorter view before you print a presentation or generate slides, you can check for inconsistencies among slides and gross errors such as a chart that is positioned on the wrong part of a page. You can also give your presentation a design overhaul by switching to a different template. When you change templates, virtually everything about your presentation's appearance changes too. As a result, a lively, colorful presentation for the sales force can become a stately, elegant presentation for the board of directors. Slide Sorter view is also the place to add and edit the transition and animation effects that appear on slides during a slide show.

FIGURE 1-4.

Slide Sorter view.

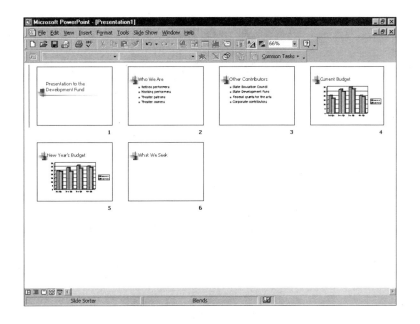

Notes Page View

The fifth PowerPoint view is dedicated to creating speaker notes that the presenter can use at the podium. Notes Page view produces a smaller version of the slide on the top part of a page and leaves the bottom part free for notes to use during the presentation. While in Notes Page view, you can view a reduced version of each slide and type in the accompanying notes. Figure 1-5 shows a slide in Notes Page view.

FIGURE 1-5.

Notes Page view.

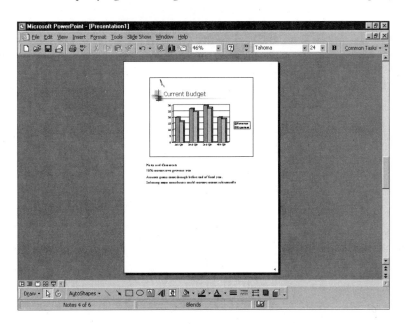

Introducing PowerPoint

Slide Show View

The sixth PowerPoint view, Slide Show view, does not display a single, static image. Instead, it shows the presentation progressing from slide to slide just like a real slide show using projected 35-mm slides. However, unlike a real slide show, which at best can only fade out on one slide before fading in on the next, a PowerPoint slide show can use eye-popping special effects to make the transition from slide to slide and to introduce new elements to the current slide. As one slide dissolves off the screen, for example, the next slide can reveal itself gradually from top to bottom, and its bulleted lines of text can glide in one by one from the side. Figure 1-6 shows a chart during the slide show as a third set of columns fades into view.

FIGURE 1-6.

Slide Show view showing a third set of columns in a chart as it fades into view.

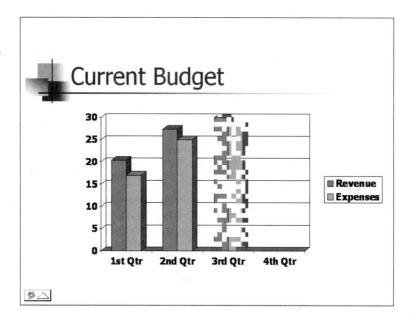

Starting PowerPoint

Before you can see how easy it is to switch from one view to another, you must get PowerPoint up and running. After PowerPoint is installed, its name is added to the Programs menu. To begin using PowerPoint, click the Start button at the end of the taskbar, point to Programs to display a menu of the programs on your system (at this point, your screen should be similar to that shown in Figure 1-7), and then click Microsoft PowerPoint.

FIGURE 1-7.

Opening PowerPoint from the Start menu on the Windows Taskbar.

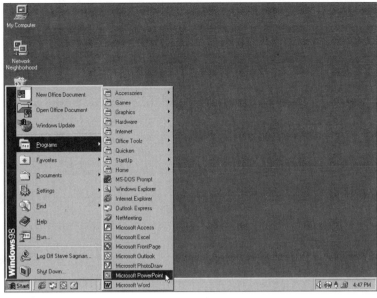

 TIP

How to Place a PowerPoint Shortcut on the Windows Desktop.
If you're using Microsoft Internet Explorer 4.0 or later, here's an easy way to put a copy of the PowerPoint icon directly on the Windows desktop so that it is within easy reach. Click the Start button and then point to Programs to open the Programs submenu. Point to Microsoft PowerPoint, hold down the Control key, and drag a copy of the entry to the Windows desktop. To remove the Microsoft PowerPoint icon from the Windows desktop (or to remove any program icon that you have added to the desktop), point to the icon and press the Delete key on the keyboard or right-click the icon and choose Delete.

When you start PowerPoint for the first time, you will see the Office Assistant, an animated little figure who's ready and all too eager to help you work. For now, you can dismiss the Assistant by clicking the Close button at the upper right corner of the Assistant window. With the Assistant out of the way, you can see the PowerPoint dialog box shown in Figure 1-8 on the next page. You use this dialog box to select a method for creating a new presentation.

FIGURE 1-8.

The PowerPoint dialog box appears whenever you start PowerPoint.

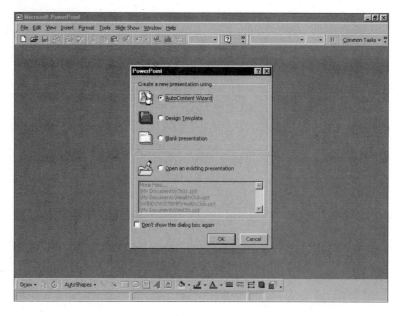

To follow along with the rest of this brief tour, start PowerPoint (if you haven't already), select the Blank Presentation option and then click OK, or simply double-click Blank Presentation. As shown in Figure 1-9, the next dialog box to appear is labeled New Slide. You use this dialog box to select a slide layout for your presentation. PowerPoint offers 24 slide layouts, called *AutoLayouts*. For now, click OK to create the first slide with the default Title Slide AutoLayout, which is the appropriate slide for the opening of a presentation.

FIGURE 1-9.

Select an AutoLayout in the New Slide dialog box.

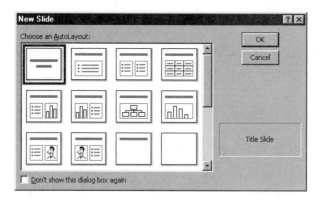

Switching Views

If you have successfully started a blank presentation and selected the Title Slide AutoLayout, you are now in Normal view, looking at the beginnings of a presentation outline in the pane at the left and a blank first slide in the pane at the right. Getting to a different view is simply a matter of clicking one of the five buttons in the lower left corner of the presentation window, as shown in Figure 1-10.

FIGURE 1-10.

To switch views, click one of the view buttons near the lower left corner of the PowerPoint window.

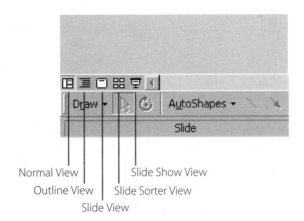

Normal View
Outline View
Slide View
Slide Show View
Slide Sorter View

Go ahead and click the first four buttons one by one. When you click the fifth button, the blank first slide of the presentation appears full-screen as a Slide Show. No, your system hasn't crashed. You just haven't created any slides to present in Slide Show view yet. Simply press the Esc key to return to the previous view.

Another way to switch between views is to use the View menu—click the word View on the menu bar, as shown in Figure 1-11 on the next page, or hold down the Alt key and then press the underlined letter in the menu name, in this case V. The first three entries on the View menu lead you to various views (Outline view is not listed) and the fourth entry, Slide Show, starts up an electronic presentation without any further ado.

If a command on a menu appears dimmed, the command is currently unavailable. If a command is followed by an ellipsis (three dots), a dialog box appears when you choose the command. If a command is preceded by a check mark, the command is currently active and can be toggled on and off. If a command is followed by an arrowhead, choosing the command displays a submenu of additional commands. And finally, commands that have toolbar equivalents are preceded by a picture of the toolbar button.

FIGURE 1-11.
You can also change
views by choosing
from the options on
the View menu.

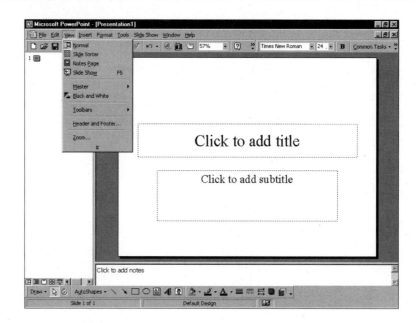

Controlling the PowerPoint Window

Like all windows, the PowerPoint window has Minimize, Maximize, and Close buttons in its upper right corner. Clicking the Minimize button shrinks the PowerPoint window to the Taskbar, and clicking the Maximize button expands it to fill the screen. Clicking the Close button shuts down PowerPoint and closes all open windows. Clicking the Control button in the upper left corner displays a menu with additional commands for restoring the PowerPoint window to its previous size, for moving and sizing the window, and for closing PowerPoint.

> When the PowerPoint window is maximized, the Maximize button becomes the Restore button. If you click this button, the window is restored to its previous size. To return the window to full size, click the Maximize button or choose Maximize from the Control menu.

How to Use the Mouse to Adjust the PowerPoint Window

When the PowerPoint window is not maximized, you can use the mouse to move and resize the window. For example, click and drag the window's title bar to move the window to a new location. To change the window's size, position the mouse pointer on one side of the window's frame, and when the pointer changes to a double-headed arrow, hold down the left mouse button and drag the frame in the desired direction.

Manipulating the Presentation Window

When you create a new presentation in PowerPoint or edit an existing presentation, the presentation window occupies most of the PowerPoint window. To change the presentation window's location or size, you can use its buttons and Control menu commands just the way you use the PowerPoint window's buttons and commands.

You can have more than one presentation open at a time so that you can compare presentations or copy graphics or text from one presentation to another. To open more than one presentation, choose Open from the File menu, and when the Open dialog box appears, locate the presentation you want to open and click the Open button. The new presentation window covers any windows that are open, but you can use the commands on the Window menu to rearrange the windows. For example, the Arrange All command places the open windows side by side, as shown in Figure 1-12.

FIGURE 1-12.

Two presentations arranged side by side using the Arrange All command on the Window menu.

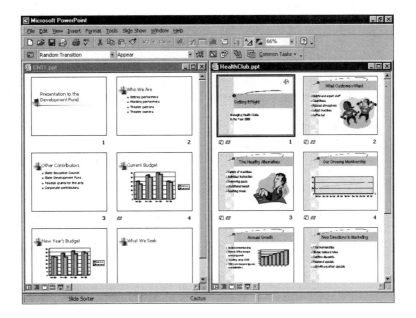

The Cascade command on the Window menu arranges open presentation windows in sequence so that you can see all their title bars. You can then click any title bar to bring that presentation window to the front. The Fit To Page command sizes the currently selected window so that it neatly fits the presentation slide. The Next Pane command on the Window moves the center of attention from one pane to the next when you are working in Normal view, which has multiple panes.

After you use any of the commands on the Window menu, you can still manipulate each window individually by using the window's buttons and Control menu commands.

 ## Using the Adaptive Menus and Toolbars

Every command in PowerPoint resides on one of PowerPoint's menus. This fact isn't very comforting, however, when you're in a rush and you'd rather not have to rummage through all the menus. Fortunately, to make life a little less complicated, PowerPoint adapts to your usage of the program. When you use menu commands infrequently, Power-Point hides them and displays only the commands you use most. When there are more commands on a menu than you can see, you can click the double-arrow button at the bottom of the menu. And if you pause in consternation, wondering where a menu command has disappeared to, PowerPoint will reveal all the commands on the menu after a few seconds.

Seeing Full Menus at All Times
If you'd like to see full menus at all times, choose Customize from the Tools menu, and then, on the Options tab of the Customize dialog box, clear the Menus Show Recently Used Commands First box.

In addition to menus, PowerPoint displays toolbars so that you can access the most often-used commands by clicking buttons right on the screen. As shown in Figure 1-13, the default PowerPoint window displays three toolbars: the Standard, Formatting, and Drawing toolbars. In addition to these toolbars, PowerPoint provides others, which often appear automatically whenever they would be helpful as you use the program.

Depending on how your system is set up, you may find that the Standard and Formatting toolbars share a single row within the Power-Point window. This conserves screen space, but it can hide some toolbar buttons. When buttons on a toolbar are hidden, a double-arrow button appears at the right end of the toolbar. You can click this button to reveal the rest of the toolbar's buttons. The buttons that you use most frequently stay visible on the toolbar.

How to Get Toolbars Quickly
A neat little shortcut is to click any toolbar with the right mouse button. Then you can choose the toolbars you want from the shortcut menu.

FIGURE 1-13.

The Standard, Formatting, and Drawing toolbars.

Standard toolbar   Drawing toolbar   Formatting toolbar

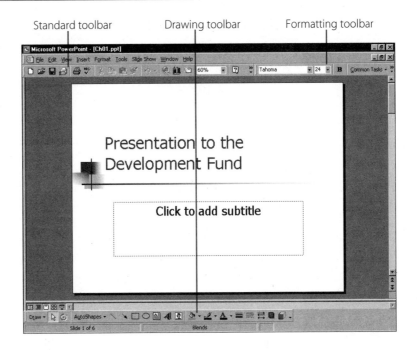

Introducing PowerPoint

Displaying Toolbars

To display a toolbar that does not appear by default, choose the Toolbars command from the View menu; when the list of main toolbars appears, as shown in Figure 1-14 on the next page, click the toolbars you want. Menu items like these act as toggles—you click once to turn on the option (add the check), and you click again to turn off the option (remove the check).

Try turning on an additional toolbar now by clicking WordArt on the list. The WordArt toolbar appears as a floating toolbar within the PowerPoint window. It contains buttons that you can use to add fancy text logos and text effects. To remove the WordArt toolbar, return to the Toolbars list and clear the WordArt check box by clicking it again.

To see even more toolbar choices, click Customize at the bottom of the toolbar list. In the Customize dialog box, you see all the toolbars that are available.

All of PowerPoint's toolbars can be customized to include only the buttons you want. You can also move buttons from one toolbar to another. And you can make the toolbar buttons large or small and display them with or without color.

FIGURE 1-14.

The Toolbars menu.

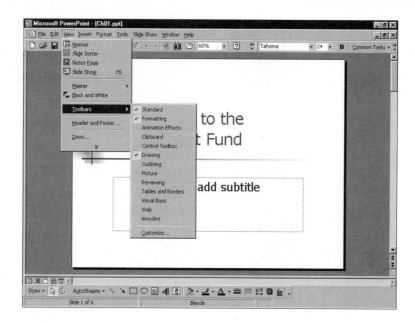

Positioning Toolbars

By default, PowerPoint arranges its toolbars where they fit best on the screen, but you can change this arrangement to create a workspace that you find more comfortable. A toolbar can be located along one of the four sides of the PowerPoint window, or it can be free-floating within the window. You might want to keep the default arrangement of toolbars for now. When you become more familiar with PowerPoint, you can position the toolbars to suit your needs.

To move a toolbar, first place the mouse pointer within the borders of the toolbar, but not on top of any button. Then hold down the left mouse button and drag the toolbar to a new location on the screen. When you release the mouse button, the toolbar drops into its new position, and, if necessary, the presentation window inside the PowerPoint window adjusts to make room.

If you drag a toolbar to one side of the PowerPoint window, the toolbar automatically changes shape to fit the space. If you drag the toolbar toward the middle of the screen, the toolbar becomes a "floating" box. After you drop a toolbar into place, you can reshape it by dragging its borders just as you reshape a window. Figure 1-15 shows the Drawing toolbar as a box within the PowerPoint window.

FIGURE 1-15.

The floating Drawing toolbar.

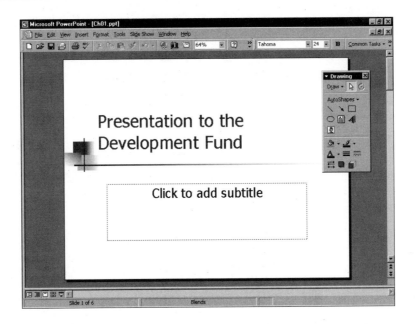

ScreenTips

PowerPoint provides a handy feature called ScreenTips to help you keep track of all those toolbar buttons and other items on the screen. To see a description of any toolbar button or of any button on the screen, simply place the mouse pointer on the button and pause. A small ScreenTip box pops up nearby, displaying the button's name; a brief description of the button appears in the status bar at the bottom of the PowerPoint window. Whenever you display a new toolbar in PowerPoint, use ScreenTips to get acquainted with its buttons. To turn off ScreenTips, choose Toolbars from the View menu, select Customize on the Toolbars menu, and then clear the Show ScreenTips On Toolbars option on the Options tab of the Customize dialog box.

Moving Through Slides

In Normal and Slide views, you see only one slide at a time, but the presentation may contain many slides. To move to another slide in your presentation, use any of the following methods:

- Press the Page Down key to move forward one slide, or press the Page Up key to move back one slide.

- Click the Next Slide button at the bottom of the presentation window's vertical scroll bar to move forward one slide, or click the Previous Slide button to move back one slide (see Figure 1-16 on the next page).

■ Drag the scroll box up or down in the presentation window's vertical scroll bar (see Figure 1-16) to move backward or forward through the presentation. As you drag the scroll box, the current slide number and title appear next to the scroll bar.

FIGURE 1-16.

The vertical scroll bar and scroll box and the Previous Slide and Next Slide buttons in Slide view.

Scroll box as it is dragged with the slide number and title display

Next Slide button
Previous Slide button

Saving Your Work

You've heard it before, but it always bears repeating: Save your work often. Don't wait until you've finished a presentation to save it. Save a presentation after you create the first slide. Save it again a little while later. The more frequently you save your work, the less you stand to lose if you fall victim to a power failure, a coffee spill, or a rambunctious child who decides to play piano on your keyboard.

To save a file, click the Save button on the Standard toolbar (that little picture on the button is a disk) or choose Save from the File menu. If you have not yet named the file (if the presentation title bar still displays the name Presentation), the Save As dialog box appears. As shown in Figure 1-17, you enter a file name in the File Name edit box. The file name can be one word, a few words, or up to 255 letters and spaces. Use something that will make sense to you later when you want to find this presentation. The Save In box at the top of the dialog box indicates where PowerPoint will save the file. You can change where the file is saved by clicking the arrow at the right end of the Save In box and opening the folder you want. You can also click one of the five large buttons at the left side of the Save As dialog box, such as My Documents or Favorites, to choose a popular destination.

FIGURE 1-17.

The Save As dialog box.

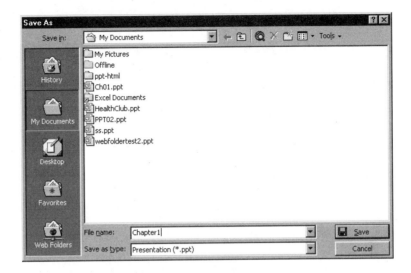

After you enter a file name and click Save, PowerPoint may display the Summary tab of the Properties dialog box for the presentation. As shown in Figure 1-18, you can enter information in this dialog box to help you search for files later. For example, if you always enter the project name for all presentations belonging to a particular project in the Keywords edit box, you can later use these keywords to extract a list of those presentations. You can also save a preview picture of your presentation, in case you find it easier to remember faces than names.

FIGURE 1-18.

You can use the information in the Properties dialog box to search for specific files.

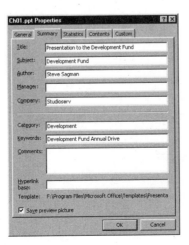

Turning On the Properties Dialog Box

When you save a presentation, the Properties dialog box opens only if the Prompt For File Properties option is turned on. You can reach this option by choosing Options from the Tools menu and then clicking the Save tab.

Searching for a Presentation

To search for a presentation, click the Open button on the Standard toolbar or choose Open from the File menu. In the Open dialog box, click the Tools button on the toolbar and choose Find from the drop-down menu.

In the Find dialog box, shown in Figure 1-19, a single criterion has already been applied; Files Of Type Is All PowerPoint Presentations, which filters out only PowerPoint files. To find a specific PowerPoint file, you can add additional criteria by clicking the arrow buttons next to Property and Criterion and choosing entries from the two drop-down lists. To complete the criterion and add it to the list, you must enter a text item, date, or time in the Value box and then click Add To List. For example, to find a presentation that includes the words "Project X" on a slide, you'd choose Contents from the Property list, Includes Words from the Criterion list, and type *Project X* in the Value box. The completed expression you've built is "Contents Includes Project X" and it appears in the list of criteria. To carry out the search, click Find Now.

FIGURE 1-19.

The Find dialog box.

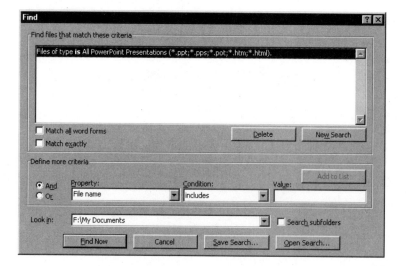

Getting Help

PowerPoint's online Help system is extensive and easy to use. To access Help, press F1 while PowerPoint is displayed, or choose Microsoft PowerPoint Help from the Help menu. The Help Topics window shown in Figure 1-20 appears.

FIGURE 1-20.

The PowerPoint Help window.

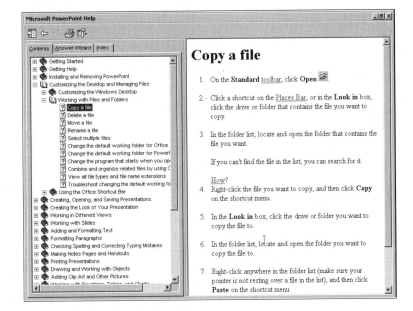

Clicking the Contents tab displays a list of book icons, and double-clicking a book icon displays its contents—either more book icons or topic icons that look like a page with a question mark. When you find the topic you want, double-click the topic icon to open it.

You can also type a question in the What Would You Like To Do box on the Answer Wizard tab. For example, you can type in the question *How do I delete a slide?* The Answer Wizard interprets your question and displays help topics that it thinks will provide relevant answers.

Clicking the Index tab in the Help Topics window displays a list of keywords associated with PowerPoint Help topics. Type the first few letters of the keyword you are looking for or select a keyword from the keyword list. As you type, the list of words advances to match the letters you type. You can also scroll through the word list until you find the word you want. Once you find the desired word, select it and click Search to find related topics. From the topics list, click the topic that seems most relevant to display its contents in the right pane of the Help window.

As you read a Help topic, you'll see underlined words. Clicking an underlined word either displays a definition of the word or takes you to a related help topic. To see other related topics, click the More Information topics at the end of a topic.

Within a Help topic, you might see a picture of a toolbar button or other object that you can click for more information. Within an instruction, you might see a shortcut button that you can click to open the dialog box you need to complete that step. Some topics might also have a small button that you can click to open another topic with more details.

While in the Help system, you can click the Back button at the top of the Help window to return to the previous topic, or you can click the Print button to print the current topic for reference.

The Office Assistant

Always ready to serve, the Office Assistant is an animated character that pops up whenever it thinks it has a way to help you. If the Office Assistant is installed in your machine (it's a custom option during the setup process) you'll see it appear, usually at the lower right corner of the PowerPoint window. Whenever the Assistant thinks it can help, a light bulb appears in its window. Click the Assistant to find out what it has to offer. You can also click the Assistant any time you need help while using PowerPoint. The Assistant will offer help options related to the work you are doing in PowerPoint at the moment, as shown in Figure 1-21.

FIGURE 1-21.

The Office Assistant.

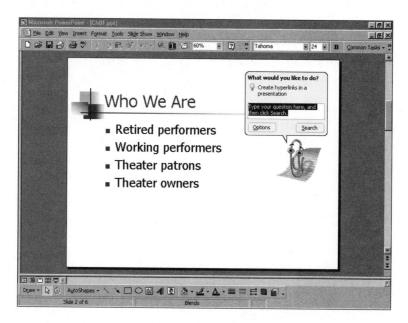

If the Assistant does not appear, you can click Show The Office Assistant on the Help menu.

Visiting Microsoft on the Web

Microsoft offers extensive online help and a number of additional resources for PowerPoint on its Web site. If you can connect to the Internet, you can choose Office on the Web from the Help menu. This opens Internet Explorer and jumps to the Microsoft Office site on the Microsoft Web site.

Other Ways of Getting Help

To get help about a button or a menu command, choose What's This from the Help menu or press Shift+F1. When the pointer displays a question mark, click the button or menu command you want information on. Help then displays the corresponding topic for the button or menu command you've chosen.

With these few indispensables out of the way, you're now just about ready to begin making presentations. Before you start, though, the next chapter gives you a brief overview of the quick and easy ten steps that will always lead you to presentation success.

CHAPTER 2

A Presentation in Ten Easy Steps

Like any good software, Microsoft PowerPoint offers a cornucopia of resources designed for a broad range of needs. Uses for the software are limited only by your time and imagination. Yet there's one well-trodden path that most users follow, taking excursions into the finer points of the program only when required. This chapter focuses on a set of steps that will guide you through the basic presentation-making processes. These general steps are also the basis for the organization of the rest of the chapters in the book. Follow these footsteps, and you'll never get lost in the woods.

As you learn to use PowerPoint, you'll discover the different ways it helps you through the process of creating a presentation. After you start a new slide, for example, PowerPoint displays a prompt that tells you to "Click here to add a title." Simply follow PowerPoint's lead. Remember, the software was written with ease of use in mind. Whenever PowerPoint's designers could anticipate your next logical move, they instructed the software to do the same.

Step 1: Starting the Presentation

The presentation process gets under way as soon as you launch PowerPoint. After the PowerPoint banner, the PowerPoint dialog box, shown in Figure 2-1, displays a set of starting options.

FIGURE 2-1.

The PowerPoint dialog box.

The AutoContent Wizard, the first option, helps you select a presentation type from a list of predefined types and then it loads a set of slides with relevant text already in place. Of course, the text is generic, such as "Details about this topic," yet it provides a useful structure for a presentation. Figure 2-2 shows the list of presentation types from which you can select.

FIGURE 2-2.

You can select a type of presentation at the first step of the AutoContent Wizard.

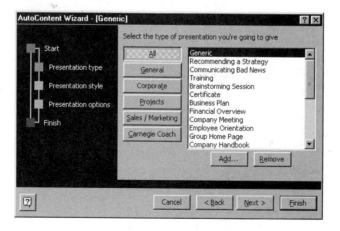

The second option, labeled Design Template, displays a list of design templates from which you can choose. These templates format everything in the presentation, giving every slide a consistent look. You'll want to use this option when you're more familiar with PowerPoint.

The third option, Blank Presentation, starts a blank presentation devoid of any design or sample text. You will, however, be prompted to select a slide layout to get started.

If you've already used PowerPoint to create a presentation, you can select the last option, Open An Existing Presentation. When you select this option, PowerPoint displays the Open dialog box so that you can open a presentation that you've already created and filed away.

If you are already working in PowerPoint, you can always click the New button on the Standard toolbar or choose New from the File menu to start a new presentation.

Step 2: Creating the Text Framework

At this step, you concentrate on the text content of the presentation, generating a series of text slides that hit all your main points and serve as a framework for the presentation. Even if you use the AutoContent Wizard rather than type in your own text, you still need to replace the wizard's generic text with your own, stepping through the presentation slide by slide and substituting your own words for PowerPoint's.

You can create a series of titled slides, one per topic, and then go back and add bulleted statements to those topics that can be expressed in words. For other topics that you know will require graphs, tables, drawings, and other visual aids, you can leave only the slide title. You'll enter chart, organization chart, and table slides at the next step.

You can create and work on individual slides one at a time or you can work in the Outline pane of the PowerPoint window as shown in Figure 2-3 on the next page, where you can focus on the overall sequence of slides as well as the text on individual slides. Working in the Outline pane, or working in Outline view, where the Outline fills the screen, is the easiest place to enter and edit text, rearrange text, and copy or move text from slide to slide.

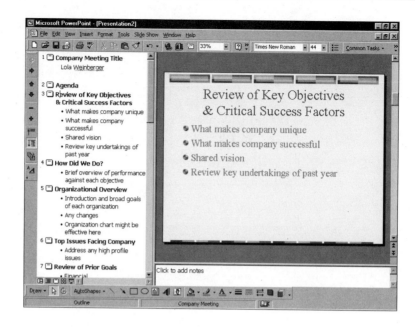

Step 3: Adding Charts, Organization Charts, and Table Slides

Not every topic is best communicated with written statements. Sometimes pictures or charts are the ticket, and sometimes tables are most effective. You can add a chart or table to a text slide, or you can create a new slide devoted to a chart or table.

When you start a new slide, PowerPoint displays the Slide Layout dialog box, which offers a variety of slide AutoLayouts, as shown in Figure 2-4. Some slide AutoLayouts have text only—a slide title and a block of text below, usually with bulleted lines of text—and others have charts, organization charts, and tables in addition to a title. Some even have combinations of text, graphics, pictures, and media on the same slide. You simply click the AutoLayout you want, and then click OK. The selected AutoLayout appears in Normal view, as shown in Figure 2-5.

FIGURE 2-4.

Select an AutoLayout from the Slide Layout dialog box.

FIGURE 2-5.

A new slide in Normal view.

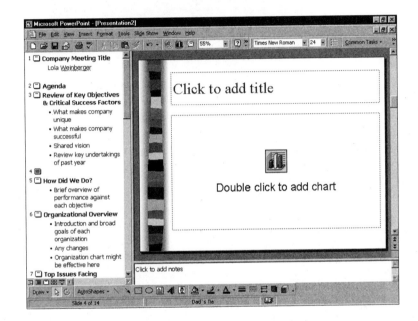

As you can see, an AutoLayout contains a combination of placeholders, which are rectangular boxes with text prompts. Some placeholders, such as chart placeholders, contain icons as well as text prompts. The text prompt in each placeholder tells you how to use the placeholder. For example, in Figure 2-5 above, one placeholder tells you to *Click To Add Title*. Another tells you to *Double Click To Add Chart*. The Auto-Layout shown in Figure 2-6 on the next page has three placeholders: one for a title, one for bulleted text, and one for a chart. With place-holders, you can't go wrong. When you click a text placeholder, such as *Click To Add Title*, PowerPoint displays an insertion point so that you can type text directly in the placeholder. If you double-click a chart placeholder, PowerPoint loads the special program within a program that you use to create charts.

FIGURE 2-6.

Bulleted text and
chart placeholder.

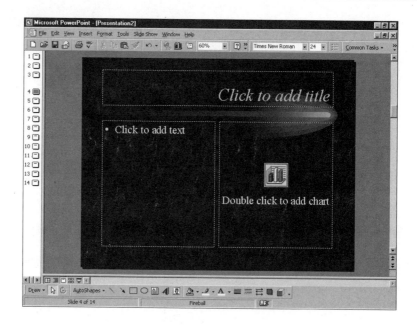

AutoLayouts and placeholders are the keys to making your way through
a presentation. When you select an AutoLayout and then click one of
its placeholders, PowerPoint displays all the tools you need so that you
don't have to hunt around for specific commands or toolbars.

Step 4: Adding Embellishments

By now, you're ready to add the finishing touches to your presentation.
The text and charts are complete, but you should take a moment to
review each slide before continuing. On some slides, a little additional
explanation might help the audience. With the Text Box tool on the
Drawing toolbar, you can add free-floating blocks of text as annotations
that highlight or explain a special feature. You can also use the Drawing
toolbar to add graphics to accompany an image or text on a slide. The
simplest case is a line that connects a text annotation to the subject it
describes, such as the line connecting the label to the pie chart in the
slide shown in Figure 2-7. But you can also draw more complex images
with PowerPoint's drawing tools.

FIGURE 2-7.

A pie chart with an annotation added.

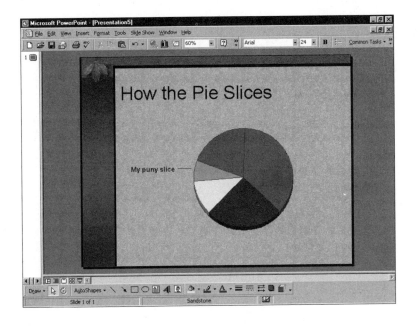

If drawing is not your thing, you can take advantage of the Clip Gallery, PowerPoint's extensive library of ready-made images that you can insert in slides. PowerPoint organizes the images by category in the Clip Gallery, as shown in Figure 2-8.

FIGURE 2-8.

The categories in the Clip Gallery.

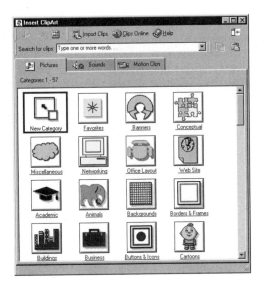

As Figure 2-9 shows, you can increase the effectiveness of a slide by adding a clip art image to the text.

FIGURE 2-9.

A slide with a clip art image.

In addition to using clip art, you can incorporate pictures you've drawn in other programs and display photos you've scanned with a scanner or captured with a digital camera. PowerPoint can import and display both drawings and pictures from many applications.

If you plan to display the slide show on screen or on the Web, you can add sound and movie files from the Clip Gallery, too.

Step 5: Tweaking the Presentation

What would you do with all that extra time if it weren't for last-minute changes? Because your presentation is stored electronically in Power-Point rather than drawn on paper, you can make changes as easily as you edit a document in a word processor or update numbers in a spreadsheet. You can also try out a different design template to see if your presentation would benefit from a different look.

PowerPoint's Slide Sorter view, shown in Figure 2-10, is the best place to see your slides and make sweeping changes to them, because you can view an entire segment of the presentation at once. While in Slide Sorter view, you can also adjust the order of the slides or delete extraneous slides.

FIGURE 2-10.

A presentation in Slide Sorter view.

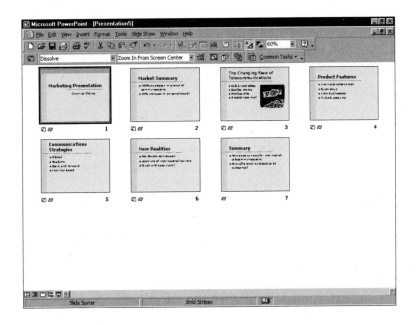

Step 6: Preparing a Slide Show

Slide Sorter view is also the place to animate the transitions between slides if you plan to give the presentation as an electronic slide show on a computer monitor or projection system, or if you're preparing a presentation that will be viewed on a corporate intranet or on the Internet.

In a slide show, you can incorporate fancy fades and slick transitions between slides and play sound and video, too. In addition to choosing from a palette of premade transitions for the switch from one slide to the next, you can also animate the individual elements on slides just as easily. You can have text fly in line by line and charts appear bar by bar, and with each element, you can add a sound effect so your audience will never have the chance to slumber off.

If you are connected to a corporate intranet or the Internet, you can deliver a slide show to others who "tune in." Slide shows can also be interactive, so you can control their flow during the presentation, stepping back to a previous slide, advancing to an additional topic, or even branching to a special set of slides that cover a topic that's raised by an audience question. What's more, in a slide show, you can click through to the spreadsheet file that contains the figures for a graph so you can try some what-if scenarios on the numbers in the spreadsheet right before an audience. Best of all, slide shows can be updated at the very last second.

Step 7: Saving Your Work

To store the completed presentation, you save it in a file. Each PowerPoint file holds an entire presentation of slides, so you don't have to worry about lost slides the next time you display a presentation. At this point, you can also save a PowerPoint presentation as the content for a Web site by choosing Save As Web Page. Of course, you shouldn't wait long to save for the first time. Remember—save early and save often.

Step 8: Soliciting Contributions from Others

If you're representing a team or workgroup, you can post a presentation on a Web page, either on the Internet or within your company, and solicit the opinions and contributions of others. Those who have access to the site can either make direct changes to slides or they can attach comments the same way they'd attach a sticky note to a paper presentation routed through internal mail.

You can even establish a discussion so people can contribute to a threaded conversation about slides, adding their own input or responding to the questions and comments of others. If you've used Internet newsgroups, you'll find that discussions are very similar.

Step 9: Generating Printed Output and Slides

Even if it's just for immediate gratification, you'll probably want to print a set of slides as soon as they're complete. PowerPoint can print slides on paper using any printer you've installed in your system. Laser printers and color ink-jet printers, today's business standards, produce especially attractive printouts.

PowerPoint is equally adept at generating 35-mm slides. Unfortunately, slides do not pop out of a slide-making device the same way that pages come out of a printer. You must either attach a film recorder, which records your slides onto slide film that must then be developed, or send the presentation file to a service bureau that can create and develop the slides for you.

Step 10: Collecting Accolades

The final step is the easiest. Leave your phone line clear, your e-mail box empty, and your door open for the flood of praise that will come your way. With a PowerPoint presentation, you'll not only enlighten your audience but entertain them as well.

In the next chapter, you'll get an opportunity to try the procedures you've learned about here.

PART II

The Basic Presentation

Starting a Presentation

I f you are new to preparing presentations, you'll find Microsoft PowerPoint ready to help you through the process step by step. If you're a presentation veteran, on the other hand, PowerPoint provides easy-to-use tools for performing familiar tasks. If you're somewhere in between, PowerPoint offers only as much assistance as you need.

PowerPoint recognizes that creating a professional presentation involves two initial tasks: drafting the content and creating a consistent design. Amazingly, PowerPoint can help you with both of these tasks. It's easy to find a presentation graphics program that comes with a selection of professionally designed templates. But it's a rare program that helps you work out what to say and how to say it.

In this chapter, you'll learn how to start a new presentation and determine how much assistance you want from Power-Point as you work. In the following chapters of this section, you will also learn to work with the sample content PowerPoint provides, enter your own text, and add graphs, organization charts, and fancy visual effects.

Starting with the Presentation Content

When you already know the general content of your presentation, you can translate your thoughts into a concrete PowerPoint presentation in three ways:

■ You can use the AutoContent Wizard to select a ready-made presentation, complete with sample slides, which suggest topics and presentation approaches. The rest of the job—replacing the sample text with your own; dropping in graphs, charts, and other elements; and customizing the generic design—is up to you.

■ If you've drafted a presentation outline in Microsoft Word, you can bring it into PowerPoint's Outline view in one step. With this option, you start your work in PowerPoint with your own content rather than a generic sample. The topics in the outline become the slides of the presentation. Later, you can add graphs, pictures, and other elements to complete the content.

■ You can start from scratch in PowerPoint, laying out the text in Outline view or entering it right onto slides, and then dropping in graphs, pictures, and annotations wherever you need them.

The first part of this chapter explains each of these options in detail.

Using the AutoContent Wizard

PowerPoint can't possibly know what you need to say, but it does know how successful communicators organize their presentations. So, with the AutoContent Wizard, PowerPoint offers a few handfuls of tried-and-true predefined outlines as starting points for your own presentation. You can select outlines to fit any of these needs:

■ General

■ Corporate

■ Projects

■ Sales and Marketing

To set up a presentation, the AutoContent Wizard asks you to choose from the following:

■ A presentation type, specifying the overall theme and subject matter of the presentation

- The presentation style, indicating the type of output you'll need (an onscreen electronic presentation, a Web presentation, or slides, for example)

- General information to be included on the opening slide and each succeeding slide

The AutoContent Wizard then displays the presentation in Normal view, which shows the outline as well as the slides themselves.

You can activate the AutoContent Wizard in two ways:

- Start PowerPoint, and when the PowerPoint dialog box (shown in Figure 2-1 on page 28) appears, double-click the AutoContent Wizard option.

- Or, if PowerPoint is already running, choose New from the File menu to open the New Presentation dialog box. On the General tab, double-click AutoContent Wizard.

No matter how you activate the AutoContent Wizard, you see this dialog box.

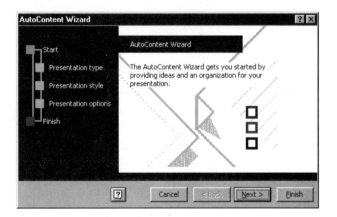

The AutoContent Wizard has three screens of queries for you. Use the wizard by following these instructions:

1 The first screen introduces you to the AutoContent Wizard. Click Next or press N to move to the next screen.

2 The Presentation Type screen in the AutoContent Wizard asks you to choose a presentation type. Click one of the presentation category buttons, for example, General or Projects. Then choose a presentation type from the list, for example, Recommending a Strategy, or Brainstorming Session. Click Next to move on.

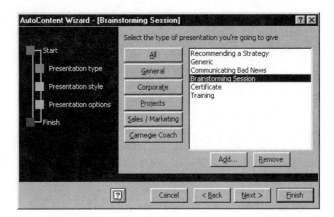

3   The Presentation Style screen asks you to choose an output type (for example, a presentation displayed on your computer, a Web presentation, overheads, or 35-mm slides). Click the option you want and click Next.

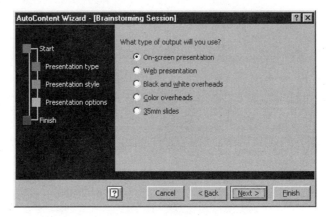

4   The final screen, Presentation Options, asks you for the presentation title and any information to be included as a footer on each slide. You can also select whether you want the date of the presentation and the slide number to be included on each slide. Specify the information you want and then click Next.

🅿 **SEE ALSO**

For more information
about Outline view
and Normal view, see
Chapter 4, "Under-
standing Outline
View," page 54.

5 When the Finish screen of the AutoContent Wizard appears,
click Finish. The new presentation appears in Normal view,
which shows the outline on the left and the slides on the right.

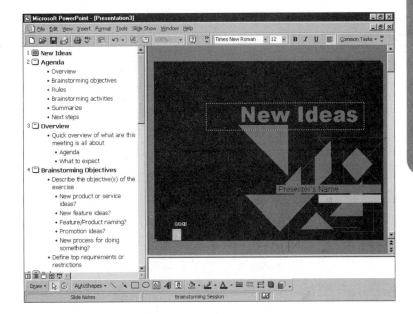

Notice that the presentation includes suggestions for the content of
each slide as well as the slide titles themselves.

Adding Custom Presentations

In addition to the standard set of presentations that come as part of the AutoContent Wizard, you can add presentations you've created. Not only does this make your own custom presentations easily available in the future, but it also helps categorize commonly used presentations because you must place each custom presentation into one of four categories in the wizard.

To add a custom presentation to the AutoContent Wizard, you first save your presentation as a template, and then you add it to the AutoContent Wizard list. Follow these steps:

1 Open the presentation you want to add to the AutoContent Wizard.

2 Choose Save As from the File menu, and then in the Save As dialog box, select Design Template from the Save As Type drop-down list.

3 Enter a file name for the presentation and click Save.

   Your presentation is now saved as a template.

4 Start the AutoContent Wizard. You can do this by choosing New from the File menu and then, on the General tab of the New Presentation dialog box, double-click AutoContent Wizard.

5 Click Next to open the Presentation Type screen.

6 Click the button that represents the category your presentation falls under.

   Don't choose the first (All) because that displays the presentations uncategorized.

7 Click the Add button.

8 In the Select Presentation Template dialog box, double-click the presentation template you just saved.

   Your presentation is added to the list of presentation types available for the category you selected.

9 Click Finish.

To remove a presentation from the AutoContent Wizard, open the AutoContent Wizard, click the presentation name in the list on the AutoContent Wizard Presentation Type screen, and then click the Remove button. The presentation is not deleted from your computer; it is simply no longer listed in the AutoContent Wizard.

Using a Predesigned Presentation

If you prefer, you can directly open and use the predesigned AutoContent Wizard presentation and make the presentation style and options changes yourself later.

1 Start PowerPoint, and when the PowerPoint dialog box (shown in Figure 2-1 on page 28) appears, double-click the Design Template option. In the New Presentation dialog box, click the Presentations tab.

Or, if PowerPoint is already running, choose New from the File menu to open the New Presentation dialog box. Click the Presentations tab.

The list of predesigned presentations appears. If you click a presentation, a preview showing the title page and design appears in the Preview box.

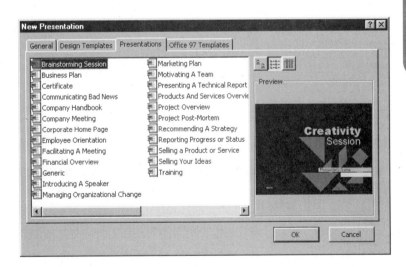

2 Double-click the predesigned presentation you want.

Customizing an AutoContent Presentation

(?) **SEE ALSO**
For more information about changing the style of a predesigned presentation, see Chapter 11, "Changing the Look," page 275.

Whether you choose a predesigned presentation with the AutoContent Wizard or directly from the Presentations tab in the New Presentations dialog box, you can customize the content or design of the presentation by modifying text on the slides or changing the template that gives the presentation its design.

1 From the File menu, choose New, and then click the Presentations tab.

2 Double-click the presentation you want to customize.

3 Make any changes you want; for example, edit the text or change the design template.

4 From the File menu, choose Save As to open the Save As dialog box.

5 In the Save As Type drop-down list, select Design Template.

6 If necessary, use the Up One Level button or the Look In drop-down list to browse for the location of the AutoContent presentation templates.

This folder is typically located in the \Program Files\Microsoft Office\Templates*number* subfolder.

7 Click the name of the presentation file you have customized, click Save, and then click Yes.

The next time you use the AutoContent Wizard or choose the presentation from the Presentations tab in the New Presentation dialog box, you'll get the same presentation types, but they'll reflect your customized changes.

Using an Outline from Microsoft Word

(?) **SEE ALSO**
For more information about using existing outlines, see Chapter 4, "Importing Outlines," page 82.

If you've prepared an outline for your presentation in Microsoft Word, you can easily send the outline to PowerPoint and use that as the starting point for your presentation.

1 In Word, prepare the presentation with appropriate heading styles. Only information tagged with a heading style will be transferred to the PowerPoint presentation. Viewing the document in Outline View is helpful to see how your slides will appear in PowerPoint.

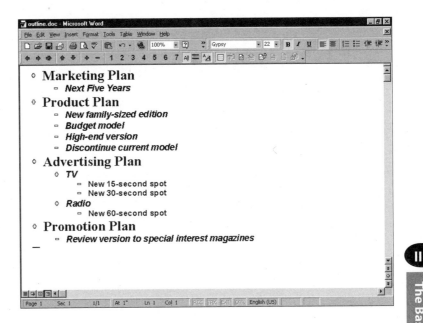

2 From the File menu, choose Send To, and then choose Microsoft PowerPoint.

PowerPoint starts, showing the content of the Word outline in a PowerPoint presentation, including outline and slides in Normal view. Level 1 headings become slide titles, and lower-level headings become indented, bulleted items on the slides.

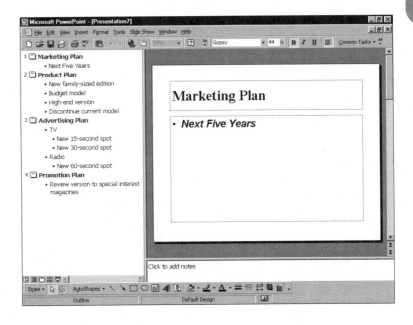

II

The Basic Presentation

Entering the Text from Scratch

When you know what you want to say and you just want to create the slides, you can always jump right into a new presentation and start entering the text from scratch. Simply start PowerPoint and select Blank Presentation in the PowerPoint dialog box. Then select an AutoLayout in the New Slide dialog box. Or, if PowerPoint is already on your screen, do one of the following:

The New
button

■ On the Standard toolbar, click the New button, and then select an AutoLayout in the New Slide dialog box.

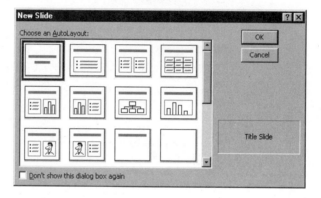

■ From the File menu, choose New, double-click Blank Presentation on the General tab of the New Presentation dialog box, and select an AutoLayout in the New Slide dialog box.

■ From the File menu, choose New, click the Design Templates tab, double-click one of the design templates, and then select an AutoLayout in the New Slide dialog box. You'll learn more about design templates in the next section.

No matter which procedure you follow, PowerPoint displays the first slide of a new presentation in Normal view. From there you can adjust your view options as needed:

■ Switch to Outline view and concentrate on the text and organization.

■ Switch to Slide view and add slides one by one, entering text and graphics as you go.

■ Stay in Normal view and work on the outline and slides at the same time.

Starting with the Presentation Design

If you want to see the presentation's design while working on its content, you can select a design template first. Each slide you create picks up the design of the template so that your presentation has a consistent look. You can choose from among PowerPoint's many ready-made design templates, or, if you're feeling creative, you can make your own design.

To select one of PowerPoint's ready-made design templates, follow these steps.

1   On the File menu, choose New. In the New Presentation dialog box, click the Design Templates tab to display template options similar to those shown here:

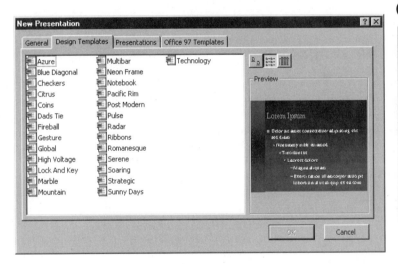

2   Click each template to see a sample of the template design in the Preview box on the right. (You can also use the arrow keys to move from one template to the next.) When you find the template you want, click it once and then click OK, or double-click it.

To store an existing presentation as a template to use as the design of a new presentation, follow this procedure:

1   Open the existing presentation and make any changes you want to the design. You can change the color scheme, background, and fonts.

2   From the File menu, choose Save As to open the Save As dialog box.

II

The Basic Presentation

For more information about creating a template, see Chapter 11, "Applying a Different Template," page 276.

3 In the Save As Type drop-down list, select Design Template.

4 If necessary, use the Up One Level button or the Look In drop-down list to browse for the location of the design templates.

This folder is typically located in the \Program Files\Microsoft Office\Templates\Presentation Designs subfolder.

5 Open the Presentation Designs folder, type a name for the new template in the File Name box, and click Save.

All you have to do to use the new template is double-click it on the Design Templates tab of the New Presentation dialog box.

How to Place Your Own Templates on the General Tab

If you want your template to appear on the General tab of the New Presentation dialog box, save it in your Templates folder, which is typically located in the \Windows\Profiles*your name*\Application Data\Microsoft folder. If you save a template in a new folder in the Templates folder, the name of the new folder appears as a separate tab in the New Presentation dialog box. For example, you can create a special folder to hold your company-specific templates.

Creating a Design from Scratch

For more information about creating a template, changing the background, color scheme, and fonts of your presentation, see Chapter 11, "Changing the Look," page 275.

If none of the templates suits your fancy or if you want to create a special presentation with a unique appearance, you can start with a blank presentation and then custom design the background, color scheme, and font choices.

To start with a blank presentation, follow these steps:

1 From the File menu, choose New. The New Presentation dialog box appears.

2 On the General tab, click Blank Presentation and then click OK, or double-click Blank Presentation.

3 In the New Slide dialog box, select an AutoLayout format for the first slide and click OK.

No matter what choices you make when starting a presentation, your next stop will probably be Outline view, where you can enter and edit the text that will form the backbone of your presentation. Chapter 4, "Writing the Text in Outline View," is devoted to this next, logical step. But if you want, you can skip Outline view and head straight to Slide view, where you can work on slides one by one. In that case, Chapter 5, "Creating Slides in Slide View," will give you the guidance you need.

Writing the Text in Outline View

C hapter 3 introduced the three ways of producing the text of a presentation: using the AutoContent Wizard, importing an outline created in Microsoft Word (or another application), and creating an outline from scratch in Outline view. The second and third methods are the topics of this chapter.

Starting a presentation in Outline view lets you mull over the themes and topics of the presentation, hone the flow of your arguments before you worry about how the presentation will look, and build a case that will be overwhelmingly persuasive. That, after all, is one of the main purposes of a presentation.

Understanding Outline View

Outline view offers these advantages:

- In Outline view, you see only the presentation text—you don't see graphs, tables, or the design elements of the presentation, such as the background design. This way you can concentrate on the content of the presentation—what it says—without being distracted by its appearance.

- In Outline view, you can easily enter the list of main topics of your presentation. Entering the main topics generates all the presentation slides you need, because each main topic becomes the title of a new slide.

- In Outline view, you can easily rearrange the topics, thereby changing the order in which you will address issues in the presentation. You can enter supporting text that will become bulleted items on the slides, and you can move the text from topic to topic until you are sure a discussion point is addressed in just the right spot during the presentation.

Figure 4-1 shows the topics and supporting items of a presentation in Outline view.

FIGURE 4-1.

A presentation outline in Outline view.

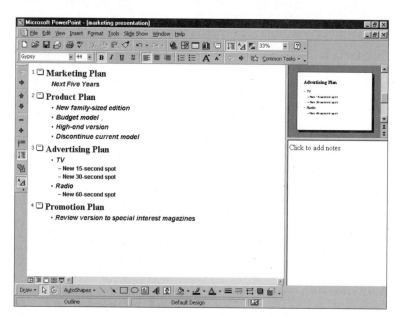

Figure 4-2 shows the resulting titles and bulleted items on slides in Slide Sorter view.

FIGURE 4-2.

The slides in Slide Sorter view.

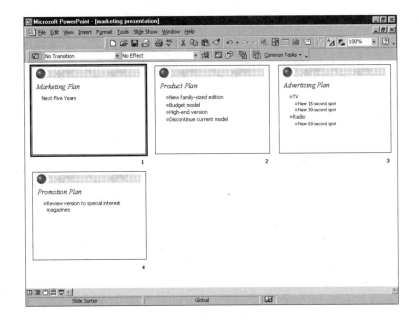

Switching to Outline View

When you start a new presentation, PowerPoint automatically opens the presentation in Normal view, as shown in Figure 4-3 on the next page. Normal view gives you the best of both worlds. You can view and work on the presentation outline on the left side of the window. If you click an outline topic, the corresponding slide appears in the slide view on the right side of the window. If you change the text or organization of an outline topic, you can see the effect of your changes immediately in the slides. Likewise, any text changes you make in the slide view are also instantly reflected in the outline. With Normal view, you can always see the overview of your presentation as well as the content details and look of each slide. You can also add and review notes for each slide.

However, if you want to concentrate on the topics you'll cover in the presentation and enter text to support each topic, you can easily switch to Outline view. You might find this useful when you want to focus on the content and organization of the presentation, without being distracted by the look of the slides themselves. After you finish with the text in Outline view, you can return to Slide or Normal view and add graphs and tables for information that is more effectively communicated with pictures or charts.

FIGURE 4-3.

Starting a new presentation in Normal view.

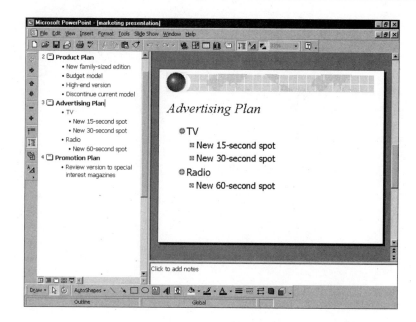

Once you start PowerPoint and open a new or existing presentation, you can switch to Outline view at any time by clicking the Outline View button in the lower left corner of the presentation window.

Click the Outline View button.

If you are beginning a new presentation and switch to Outline view, the insertion point is positioned beside blank slide number 1, as shown in Figure 4-4. When you begin typing, PowerPoint inserts your text at the insertion point. Also, when Outline view is active, the Outlining toolbar appears on the left side of the presentation window, also shown in Figure 4-4.

> NOTE

If you don't see the Outlining toolbar on the left side of your outline, you need to show it. From the View menu, point to Toolbars, and then click Outlining.

Just remember, you can make the same changes in Outline view and in the outline pane of Normal view. Which view you work in is purely a matter of personal preference.

FIGURE 4-4.

Starting a new presentation in Outline view.

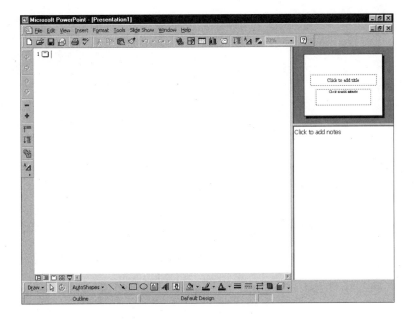

Entering the Main Topics

? SEE ALSO

For more information about reordering topics in your presentation, see "Reorganizing Text in Outline View," page 74.

You can enter a title for the presentation and a list of the topics you plan to discuss in Outline view. The title and topics become your preliminary slide titles. Don't worry about entering the topics in the exact order you plan to present them. You can always rearrange them later. This way, you can feel free to brainstorm topics at this point and organize later.

To enter the topics for your presentation, follow these steps:

1 Type the presentation title and press Enter.

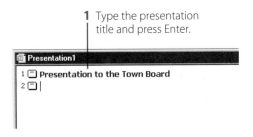

2 In slide 2, type the first topic, and press Enter. If you don't yet have a topic precisely pinned down, type a two- or three-word placeholder. You can always edit it later.

3 Type the next topic, and press Enter.

4 Type the topic for each successive slide, pressing Enter after each one except the last.

Figure 4-5 shows a completed list of topics for a presentation about the construction of a new store.

FIGURE 4-5.
A list of topics for the slides of a new presentation.

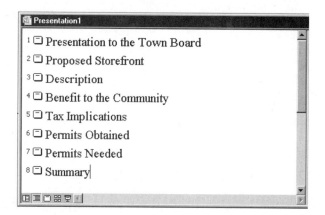

TIP

Use Fewer Words for a More Powerful Presentation
On each slide, use the fewest words possible to communicate your message. The fewer words used, the more impact the text has, and the larger and more readable it can be. Try to write newspaper-like headlines, not whole sentences. For example, write *Profits up 26%* rather than *Our profits increased by 26%*.

Next, examine your list of topics to determine the best way to communicate them to your audience. Some topics are best conveyed with a few bulleted items added below the topic titles. Other topics involve numeric data. Later, you can switch to Slide view and add graphs or tables to these slides to bring the numbers to life. You can also add organization charts and drawings.

The Outline View–Slide View Connection

Each main topic entered in a presentation in Outline view becomes a title on a slide in Slide view. Similarly, each supporting item entered under a main topic in Outline view becomes a bulleted item on a slide in Slide view. This connection between Outline view and Slide view is a two-way street. If you edit a title or bulleted item in Slide view, the changes you make show up in Outline view as well. And of course, in Normal view, you can change the outline or the slide while viewing both sides.

> **See More Text on the Screen**
>
> If your presentation outline has many topics, you can "zoom out" (reduce the magnification of the text) so that more of the outline fits on the screen. To do this, use the Zoom box on the Standard toolbar. Or, from the View menu, choose the Zoom command. *For more information about zooming, see the sidebar titled "Zooming In and Out," page 69.*

Adding Bulleted Text

After entering a list of topics, you're ready to enter the supporting items for those topic titles.

To add bulleted items under a topic, follow these steps:

1 Move the insertion point to the end of the topic title under which you want to add supporting bullets.

2 Press Enter to create a new line. PowerPoint adds a slide icon and renumbers the existing topics.

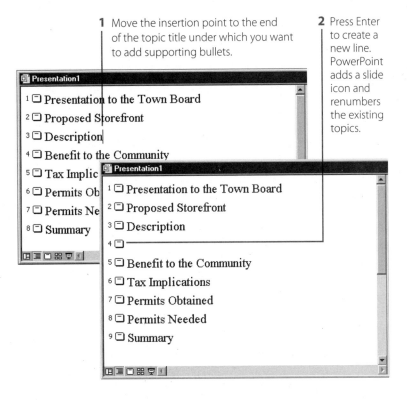

The Demote button

3 Click the Demote button on the Outlining or Formatting toolbar or press the Tab key to move the insertion point one level to the right. PowerPoint removes the slide icon, readjusts the numbers, and inserts a bullet.

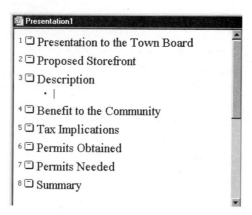

4   Type the first supporting item. If you type more text than will fit on one line, the text wraps to the next line.

5   Press Enter to add another bulleted item.

6   Repeat steps 4 and 5 until you've added all the bulleted items you need.

Figure 4-6 shows the complete set of supporting bulleted items for a slide in the store-construction presentation.

FIGURE 4-6.

A complete set of bulleted items.

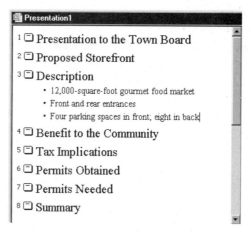

NOTE

Any text added under the slide 1 presentation title is not formatted as bulleted text; instead, it is formatted as a subtitle. If you want to add a bullet to a subtitle on slide 1, click the subtitle, and then click the Bullets button on the Formatting toolbar. Likewise, if you want to remove the bullet formatting from an item on a succeeding slide, click the item, and then click the Bullets button.

The Bullets
button

The Promote
button

If you add bulleted text below a topic of your outline and then you want to add a new topic in a new slide after them, press Enter at the end of the last bulleted item. A new bullet is created. Click the - Promote button on the Outlining or Formatting toolbar or press Shift+Tab to move the insertion point one level to the left. Then type the title for the new topic. For example, Figure 4-7 shows the store proposal presentation with a new topic added after the bulleted items.

FIGURE 4-7.

After typing in bulleted text, press Enter and click the Promote button to add another slide.

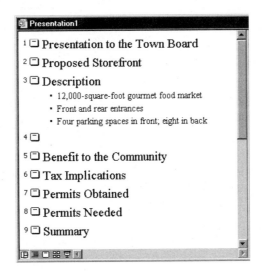

You can have five levels of supporting items on a slide, as shown in Figure 4-8 on the next page. Each level is indented from the preceding level. With five indent levels, you can have points under the main topics, subpoints under the points, and so on. Each level has its own default bullet style, which you can see by clicking the Show Formatting button on the Standard toolbar.

SEE ALSO

For information about changing the outline order, see "Reorganizing Text in Outline View," page 74.

To demote a bulleted item by one level, thereby indenting it farther to the right, click the item, click the Demote button on the Outlining or Formatting toolbar, or press the Tab key. To promote a bulleted item by one level, click the Promote button on the Outlining or Formatting toolbar, or press Shift+Tab. But don't get carried away. Remember, when it comes to presentations, less is more.

The Basic Presentation

FIGURE 4-8.

The five levels of bulleted items.

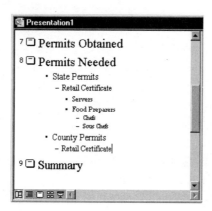

 TIP

A Sequential Approach to Creating Outlines

Typing all the topics and then adding bulleted items is one approach to creating the outline. This way, you can brainstorm and organize the list of main topics before adding any detail to the presentation. Another approach is to type a topic, press Enter, and then press the Tab key to enter the topic's supporting bulleted items. Then, after typing the last bulleted item for the topic, press Enter, and then press Shift+Tab and type the next topic title. When you finish the last topic, you can still reorganize the presentation.

Creating a Summary Slide

 SEE ALSO

For more information about selecting slides, see "Selecting Text for Editing," page 64.

You can create a summary slide from a series of slides quickly and easily. A summary slide shows the slide titles of other slides as bulleted text items. You can place a summary slide at the beginning of a series of slides to create an agenda for the presentation or a lead-in for a segment of the presentation. Or, you can place a summary slide after the series to wrap up your main points.

To create a summary slide, follow the steps on the next page.

1 Select the slides to be summarized.

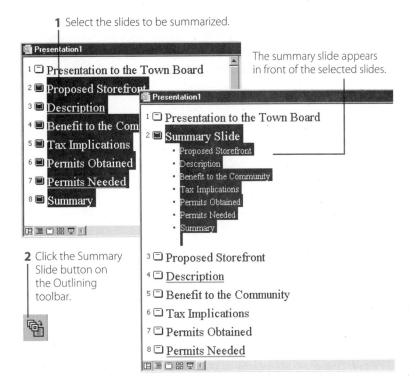

The summary slide appears in front of the selected slides.

2 Click the Summary Slide button on the Outlining toolbar.

Editing Text in Outline View

After you've entered topic titles and supporting bulleted text, you can revise the text to reword entries or make corrections. To edit text in Outline view, you first move the insertion point to the spot that needs editing. The simplest way is to click where you want the insertion point to be in the text. For example, clicking to the left of the *B* in *Board* places the insertion point as shown in Figure 4-9.

FIGURE 4-9.

An insertion point appears where you click.

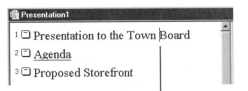

Click to place an insertion point in the text.

You can also move the insertion point with the keyboard by using one of the keys or key combinations listed in Table 4-1 on the next page.

II

The Basic Presentation

TABLE 4-1. Keyboard Shortcuts for Moving the Insertion Point

Keys	Moves the Insertion Point
Left, Right, Up, or Down	One character left/right or one line up/down
Ctrl+Left arrow key	To the beginning of the previous word
Ctrl+Right arrow key	To the beginning of the next word
Ctrl+Up arrow key	To the beginning of the current topic (or to the beginning of the previous topic if the insertion point is already at the top of a topic)
Ctrl+Down arrow key	To the beginning of the next topic
Home	To the beginning of the current line
End	To the end of the current line
Ctrl+Home	To the top of the outline
Ctrl+End	To the bottom of the outline

After positioning the insertion point, simply start typing to insert text. You can press the Backspace key to delete the character to the left of the insertion point or press the Delete key to delete the character to the right of the insertion point. You can also press Ctrl+Backspace to delete the word to the left or press Ctrl+Delete to delete the word to the right.

NOTE

> Unlike Microsoft Word, PowerPoint is always in Insert mode; that is, anything you type is inserted at the insertion point. You will not switch to Overtype mode if you press the Insert key.

Selecting Text for Editing

In PowerPoint, the easiest way to make more drastic editing changes is to select the text you want to modify so your changes affect the entire selection rather than single characters.

To select a block of text with the mouse, click to the left of the first character in the block, hold down the left mouse button, and then drag across the text past the last character in the block. PowerPoint highlights the text as you drag across it, as shown in Figure 4-10. To select more than one line, drag down to the next line. Note that if you select a single word in one topic and then drag down to the next line, the entire first topic is selected.

FIGURE 4-10.

Selected text.

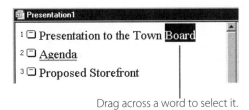

Drag across a word to select it.

Shortcuts for Selecting Text with the Mouse

You can select a single word and its trailing space by double-clicking the word. You can select a series of words by double-clicking the first word, holding down the mouse button on the second click, and dragging across the remaining words. To select all the text that follows a bullet, click the bullet character once. To select a topic and all of its bulleted items, click the slide icon to the left of the topic text. To select the entire presentation, choose Select All from the Edit menu or press Ctrl+A.

Table 4-2 summarizes how to quickly select text with the mouse.

TABLE 4-2.   Mouse Shortcuts for Selecting Outline Text

To Select	Do This
A word	Double-click the word.
A series of words	Double-click the first word, and then drag to the last word in the series. Or, click in the first word, hold down the Shift key, and click in the last word.
All text in a bulleted item	Click the bullet character.
All text in a topic	Click the slide icon.
All text in a presentation	From the Edit menu, choose Select All. Or, press Ctrl+A.

The automatic word selection option makes it easy to select multiple words with the mouse. With this option, when you drag across any part of a word and continue to drag to the next word, PowerPoint selects both the first and second words in their entirety. If you want to select an entire sentence, just click anywhere in the first word and then drag to anywhere within the last word. PowerPoint highlights the first and last words of the sentence, along with all the words in between. This word selection option is on by default.

II

The Basic Presentation

> If you want more control over selecting individual characters, you can turn off the automatic word selection option. From the Tools menu, choose the Options command, and then on the Edit tab, clear the When Selecting, Automatically Select Entire Word check box.

If you have trouble dragging across the text without also selecting part of the line above or below, you're not alone. You may want to use this technique instead: Click anywhere in the first word you want to select, hold down the Shift key, and then click anywhere in the last word of the block you want to select. PowerPoint highlights the first word, the last word, and all of the text in between. If the automatic word selection option is turned off, this technique selects the characters (instead of words) between the clicks.

> **Using the Keyboard to Select Text**
>
> You can select text with the keyboard by moving the insertion point to the beginning of the text block, holding down the Shift key, and then using the keys and key combinations listed earlier in Table 4-1 to move the insertion point to the end of the text block.

To practice selecting and editing text, try the following: Start a new presentation, and use the AutoContent Wizard to load the presentation titled *Selling a Product or Service* (a *Sales/Marketing* presentation). When the presentation appears, switch to Outline view. Click in the *Objective* topic title. Press the End key to move the insertion point to the end of the line, and then type an *s* to change the title of the slide to *Objectives*. Next, click the bullet character in front of *State the desired objective* to select the entire line, and then type *To make you happy* to replace the selected text.

Later in this chapter, you'll make further changes to the outline, so you might want to save the presentation now by choosing Save As from the File menu and entering a filename.

Moving and Copying Text

Want to take the easiest and most direct approach to moving or copying selected text to another position within the outline? Then drag-and-drop editing is for you.

To move text using drag-and-drop editing, follow these steps:

1 Select the text you want to move or copy.

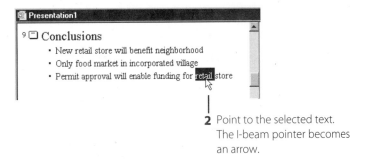

2 Point to the selected text. The I-beam pointer becomes an arrow.

3 Hold down the mouse button, drag the pointer to the destination for the selected text, and release the mouse button. The text appears in its new location, as shown here:

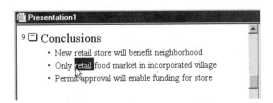

To copy text using drag-and-drop editing, follow the same procedure, but hold down the Ctrl key while dragging. Using this feature, you can even drag text to another topic's slide in the outline.

In addition to using the drag-and-drop techniques, you can move or copy selected text using the following methods:

The Cut button

- To *move* selected text, first click the Cut button on the Standard toolbar, choose Cut from the Edit menu, or press Ctrl+X. Then move the insertion point to the destination for the text (even if it's on another topic), and click the Paste button on the Standard toolbar, choose Paste from the Edit menu, or press Ctrl+V.

The Paste button

The Copy button

- To *copy* selected text, start by clicking the Copy button on the Standard toolbar, choosing Copy from the Edit menu, or pressing Ctrl+C. Then move the insertion point to the destination for the text, and click the Paste button, choose Paste from the Edit menu, or press Ctrl+V.

The Cut, Copy, and Paste commands are available on the text shortcut menu as well as on the Edit menu. To use a shortcut menu, select text with the right mouse button or point to selected text and click the right mouse button. A menu pops up with options that are relevant to the object or text.

The Basic Presentation

For example, to use the shortcut menu to move or copy a selected text, follow these steps:

1 Hold down the right mouse button and select the text you want to move or copy.

2 From the shortcut menu, choose Cut or Copy.

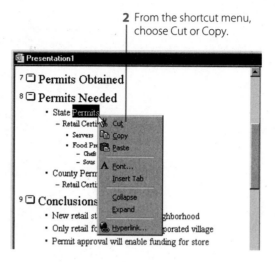

3 Move the insertion point to the destination for the text.

4 Click the right mouse button to open the shortcut menu again, and then choose Paste.

Deleting Text

To delete selected text, simply press the Delete key or the Backspace key. You can also delete selected text by clicking the Cut button on the Standard toolbar, by choosing Cut or Clear from the Edit menu, or by pressing Ctrl+X.

Undoing Editing

The Undo button

Retrieving something you've deleted is as simple as clicking the Undo button on the Standard toolbar, choosing Undo from the Edit menu, or pressing Ctrl+Z.

By repeatedly clicking the Undo button, you can undo up to your last 20 actions in PowerPoint. (If you want to increase—up to 150—or decrease this number, from the Tools menu, choose Options. On the Edit tab, change the Maximum Number Of Undos setting.)

Zooming In and Out

While working in Outline view, you can use the Zoom box on the Standard toolbar to change the magnification level, or zoom percentage, of your view of the outline. When you use a higher zoom percentage, the text appears larger. Use a smaller zoom percentage to fit more text on the screen.

To change the zoom percentage, first be sure that the outline is in the Show Formatting mode. Otherwise, the Zoom command is not available. On the Outlining or Standard toolbar, click the Show Formatting button.

Show Formatting   Zoom box

Click the arrow to the right of the Zoom box on the Standard toolbar, and then select one of the preset zoom percentages from the drop-down list. To enter a custom zoom percentage, click the current percentage in the Zoom box, type a new zoom percentage, and press Enter.

You can also change the zoom percentage by choosing Zoom from the View menu to display this Zoom dialog box:

Then select one of the Zoom To percentages or edit the number in the Percent edit box. You can also click the arrows to the right of the Percent edit box to adjust the percentage up or down by one.

By default, Outline view uses a smaller zoom percentage than Slide view so you can see more of your outline on the screen at one time. If you make Outline view's zoom percentage the same as Slide view's, the text size is identical in both views.

The Redo button

When you use the Undo button or command to reverse an action, the Redo button on the Standard toolbar and the Redo command on the Edit menu become available. You can then quickly redo the last change you made in a presentation by clicking the Redo button or choosing the Redo command. For example, after applying bold formatting and then clicking the Undo button to remove it, you can click the Redo button to reapply the bold formatting.

Repeating Actions

You can repeat many of the actions you take in PowerPoint—editing, formatting, or checking spelling, for example—by choosing the Repeat command from the Edit menu. The name of the command changes depending on your last action—for example, Repeat Typing or Repeat Bold. If you cannot repeat your last action, the Repeat command changes to Can't Repeat.

Finding and Replacing Text

While editing an outline, you can search for a word or any series of characters and replace it with another. For example, you can search for a former client's name in a presentation and replace that name with a new client's name throughout the presentation.

To search for specific text, follow these steps:

1   From the Edit menu, choose Find, or press Ctrl+F. PowerPoint displays the Find dialog box.

2   Enter the text you want to find in the Find What edit box.

3   Click Find Next or press Enter.

To have PowerPoint find only those words or strings of characters that match the capitalization entered in the Find What box, select the Match Case check box. (Then PowerPoint will not find *Man* when you enter *man*.) To have PowerPoint find the text you've entered only when it is a whole word rather than part of a word, select the Find Whole Words

Only check box. (Then PowerPoint will not find *constitutional* when you enter *constitution*.)

To replace text, follow these steps:

1 From the Edit menu, choose Replace, or press Ctrl+H. (If the Find dialog box is already open, you can just click the Replace button.) PowerPoint displays the Replace dialog box:

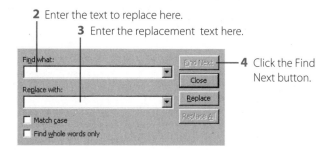

2 Enter the text to replace here.

3 Enter the replacement text here.

4 Click the Find Next button.

5 After PowerPoint locates the text you entered in the Find What box, click the Replace button to substitute it with the text entered in the Replace With box.

To replace every occurrence of the text in the Find What box throughout the presentation, click the Replace All button instead of the Find Next and Replace buttons. You may want to use the Match Case option and the Find Whole Words Only option to be sure you do not replace text that does not exactly match the Find What text.

PowerPoint remembers text you have searched for or used as a replacement. To search or replace the same text again, open the Find dialog box or the Replace dialog box, click the down arrow next to the Find What box or Replace With box, and then select a previous entry from the drop-down list.

Checking the Spelling of Presentation Text

Before your presentation goes public, take a moment to use PowerPoint's very capable spelling checker. Nothing looms larger than a silly little typo when it is projected full-screen.

The Spelling button

To check the spelling in a presentation, follow these steps:

1 Click the Spelling button on the Standard toolbar, choose Spelling from the Tools menu, or press F7. PowerPoint checks each word

The Basic Presentation

against two dictionaries: the main dictionary and a supplemental dictionary named CUSTOM.DIC, which is empty until you add words to it. When PowerPoint finds a word it considers misspelled, it displays the dialog box shown here:

The questionable word is displayed in the Not In Dictionary box. The first and most strongly suggested replacement is highlighted in the Suggestions list and appears in the Change To box.

2 Indicate what you want PowerPoint to do next:

- If you know that the word is spelled correctly—if the word is a company name, for example—click the Ignore button.

- If the word is spelled correctly and occurs frequently in this presentation, you may want to click Ignore All instead of Ignore.

- If the word is spelled correctly and occurs frequently in other presentations, you can click Add to add the word to a custom dictionary. The word will not be flagged as a misspelling when you check the spelling in the future.

- If the word is misspelled and you want to change it to the word in the Change To box, click Change.

- If the word is misspelled and you want to make the same change throughout the entire presentation, click Change All.

- If the word is misspelled and you want to change a suggested word that is not in the Change To box, click the word you want in the Suggestions list. It moves to the Change To box. Click Change or Change All.

- If the word is misspelled and you want to edit the word yourself, change the word in the Change To edit box, and then click Change.

- If the word is misspelled, or if you see other changes you want to make to the text, you can click in the outline and edit the text. When you finish editing and want to continue checking the rest of the document, click Resume in the Spelling dialog box.

Using Custom Dictionaries

When you click the Add button to add a word to a custom dictionary, the word is added to the dictionary file listed in the Add Words To box in the Spelling dialog box. The default custom dictionary is CUSTOM.DIC, the same custom dictionary file used by Microsoft Word and other Microsoft Office applications. If you have created custom dictionaries in another Microsoft Office application, you can select one of those dictionaries from the Add Words To drop-down list. If you enter words in a custom dictionary while working in another Microsoft Office application, those words won't be flagged as incorrect in PowerPoint either.

When the spell checker has completed checking the outline, PowerPoint displays a message. Click OK.

WARNING

PowerPoint cannot check the spelling of text in charts, organization charts, and tables. It also cannot check the spelling of text in embedded objects created in other applications.

Using AutoCorrect

If you frequently transpose the same letters in the same words while typing, you can use the AutoCorrect feature to recognize and then correct your mistakes. For example, if you regularly type *captial* instead of *capital*, AutoCorrect can change the incorrect spelling to the correct one. In addition, you can use AutoCorrect to change two consecutive capital letters to one, to correct the accidental use of the Caps Lock key, and to capitalize the names of the days of the week. Best of all, PowerPoint's AutoCorrect feature already contains a large list of commonly misspelled words (such as *teh*), which are corrected when you press the Spacebar or type punctuation.

To add a word to the AutoCorrect list, follow these steps:

1 From the Tools menu, choose AutoCorrect. The AutoCorrect dialog box appears as shown on the next page.

II

The Basic Presentation

2 Be sure the Replace Text As You Type check box is checked.

AutoCorrect: English (US)

AutoCorrect

☑ Correct TWo INitial CApitals   Exceptions...
☑ Capitalize first letter of sentence
☑ Capitalize names of days
☑ Correct accidental use of cAPS LOCK key
☑ Replace text as you type

Replace: With:

(c)	©
(r)	®
(tm)	™
...	...
abbout	about

Add   Delete

OK   Cancel

3 Enter the misspelled word in the Replace box, enter the correctly spelled word in the With box, and then click OK.

The next time you type the word incorrectly, PowerPoint will correct the misspelling as soon as you press the Spacebar or type punctuation. If you want to add more than one word to the list in the AutoCorrect dialog box, click the Add button after you fill in the Replace and With text boxes for each entry. If you want to delete a word in the AutoCorrect list because the feature regularly corrects text that you don't want changed, select the word and then click Delete.

 **NOTE**

> If AutoCorrect changes text that you don't want changed, immediately click the Undo button on the Standard toolbar or press Ctrl+Z.

Reorganizing Text in Outline View

The power of Outline view becomes obvious as soon as you need to reorganize the text of a presentation. You can change the order of the topics covered in the presentation, change the order of bulleted items under individual topics, and even move bulleted items from one topic to another. You can also delete topics, duplicate topics, and insert new topics.

Selecting Topics and Bulleted Text

Before you can reorganize a presentation, you must select the element you want to work with. You can select an entire topic (the topic text and its bulleted items), several topics, or one or more bulleted items within a topic.

To select an entire topic, you can use any of the following methods:

- Click the slide number.

- Click the slide icon to the left of the topic.

- Triple-click the topic title.

- Click the topic title and then press Ctrl+Shift+Down arrow key.

Whichever method you use, the result is similar to that shown in Figure 4-11.

FIGURE 4-11.

A selected topic.

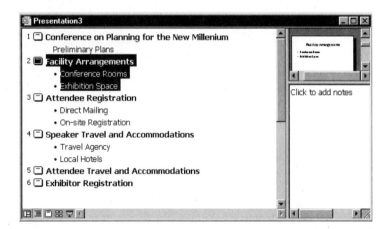

To select multiple consecutive slides, you can use one of these methods:

- Hold down the Shift key while clicking each slide's icon.

- Click the first slide in the series, hold down the Shift key, and then click the last slide in the series.

- On the first slide, point between the slide icon and the title, hold down the mouse button, and drag downward to select all the slides you want.

To select a bulleted item, as shown in Figure 4-12, do one of the following:

- Click the bullet character. This selects the bulleted item and any succeeding item indented below it.

- Triple-click a word in the bulleted item. This also selects the entire bulleted item along with any succeeding items indented below it.

- Use the mouse to drag from the beginning to end of the bulleted item.

- Click the first word of the bulleted item, hold down the Shift key, and then click the last word.

- Position the insertion point at the beginning of the bulleted item, hold down the Shift key, and press the End key to move the insertion point to the end of the bulleted item.

FIGURE 4-12.

A selected bulleted item.

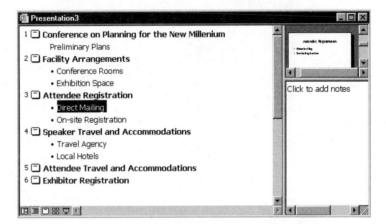

Reordering Topics and Bulleted Text

You can move a selected topic or bulleted item up or down in the outline to solidify the logic or sequence of your presentation. For example, you can move a touchy topic to the front of a presentation to get it over with early. Then move some good news to the end so that your audience can leave on a high note.

To move an entire topic, follow these steps:

1 Point to the slide icon for the selected topic.

2 Hold down the mouse button, and drag up or down. When you drag, the pointer becomes a double-headed arrow, and a horizontal line indicates where the topic will drop when you release the mouse button.

3 Release the mouse button. The topic and its bulleted items move to the new position.

For example, Figure 4-13 shows the result after the *Attendee Registration* topic was moved down in the New Millennium Conference presentation.

FIGURE 4-13.

Dragging a selected topic's slide icon moves the topic within the presentation.

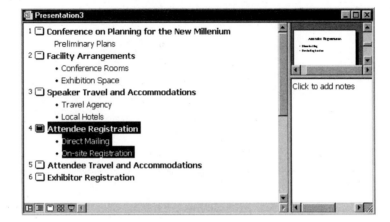

You can also move the selected topic or bulleted item up or down by clicking the Move Up or Move Down button on the Outlining toolbar.

You can change the order of entire topics just as easily in Slide Sorter view. But what makes Outline view special is that you can reorder bulleted items under a topic and move them from topic to topic, as well as reorder entire topics. To move a bulleted item up or down, follow these steps:

1 Select the bulleted item.

The Move Up button

The Move Down button

2 On the Outlining toolbar, click the Move Up button or the Move Down button until the bulleted item is positioned where you want. Or, point in the area to the left of the bullet character, hold down the mouse button, and drag up or down in the outline. When you drag, the pointer becomes a double-headed arrow, and a horizontal line indicates where the topic will drop when you release the mouse button.

3 Release the mouse button. The bulleted text moves to the new position.

Using this technique, you can quickly move the selected bulleted text all the way to another topic if you want. Working this way in Outline view saves you from having to cut and paste text from one slide to another in Slide view.

> **Use the Keyboard to Organize an Outline**
> You can press Alt+Shift+Up arrow to move selected text up and Alt+Shift+Down arrow to move selected text down, one line at a time. This works for bulleted items as well as for entire topics.

Now try reorganizing the outline for the presentation you started earlier in this chapter. Display the *Selling a Product or Service* presentation you created earlier in this chapter, and be sure you're in Outline view. Click the slide icon for slide 2. All the text related to the *Objectives* topic is now selected. Point to the slide icon, hold down the mouse button, and drag down to just below the last bulleted item on slide 3. As you drag, a horizontal line shows where the text will drop. Release the mouse button. *Objectives* becomes slide 3, and *Customer Requirements* becomes slide 2.

Now try moving a bulleted item from one topic to another. On slide 4, click the bullet at the beginning of *This section may require multiple slides*. Drag the bullet up and drop it under *Customer Requirements* on slide 2. Save the presentation again, because you'll have the opportunity to make further changes later in this chapter.

Promoting and Demoting Topics and Bulleted Text

Earlier in this chapter, you learned that promoting text moves it one level to the left and demoting text moves it one level to the right. If you need to split a topic into two slides, you can promote one of the bulleted items to the main topic level to create a new slide. Likewise, when an existing topic should be a supporting item for the previous topic, you can demote it to a bulleted item.

To promote a bulleted item, select it and then take one of the following actions:

- Click the Promote button.

- Press Shift+Tab or Alt+Shift+Left arrow.

- Click the bullet character or to its left, hold down the mouse button, and drag to the left. With this technique, you promote not only the selected bulleted item, but any subpoints indented below the selected text.

Figure 4-14 shows the result after the second bulleted item under *Facility Arrangements* in the *New Millennium Conference* presentation is promoted to a topic. As you can see, a new slide number and slide icon appear to the left of the promoted text, which becomes the title of a new slide in Slide view.

FIGURE 4-14.

Promoting a bulleted item creates a new topic on a new slide.

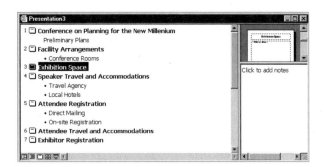

To demote a topic or a bulleted item, select it and take one of the following actions:

- Click the Demote button.

- Press the Tab key or Alt+Shift+Right arrow.

- Click the bullet character or to its left, hold down the mouse button, and drag to the right. With this technique, you demote not only the selected bulleted item, but also any subpoints indented below the selected text.

When organizing topics and bulleted items, be aware that you can fit only a certain amount of text on any one slide. For example, on the next page, in the presentation on the left in Figure 4-15, the list of bulleted items under the topic *What I Love About New York* is far too long. To get all these points across, move the insertion point to the end of *The action*, and press Enter to start a new bulleted item. Then type *What I Love to Do in New York* as a new bulleted item. Finally, drag the bullet in front of the new bulleted item one level to the left so that the bulleted item becomes a new main topic. The outline then looks as shown on the right in Figure 4-15.

II

The Basic Presentation

FIGURE 4-15.

A long list of bulleted items (left) divided between two slides for greater impact (right).

Hiding and Revealing Detail

Sometimes you need to step back to see the big picture while working on a presentation outline. If the entire outline is displayed, the volume of detail can muddle the larger themes. By collapsing bulleted items, you can temporarily hide them from view and show only the major topics. To redisplay the bulleted items, you expand them. You can collapse and expand outlines using the Collapse and Expand buttons on the Outlining toolbar.

To collapse bulleted items under a topic, follow these steps:

1 Click anywhere in the topic.

The Collapse button

2 Click the Collapse button or press Alt+Shift+Minus. PowerPoint draws a gray line under the topic to indicate the presence of collapsed bulleted items.

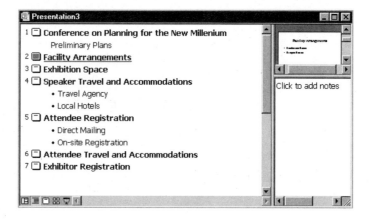

TIP

> **Why Collapse Bulleted Items**
> When you collapse bulleted items under a topic, they remain an intrinsic part of the topic. If you move that topic, the collapsed bulleted items also move. In fact, you may find it easier to reorganize a presentation with many bulleted items if you collapse them under their topics and then reorder the topics.

To expand the collapsed bulleted items, follow these steps:

1   Click anywhere in the topic.

2   Click the Expand button or press Alt+Shift+Plus.

The Expand button

To quickly collapse all bulleted items under all topics in the presentation, click the Collapse All button or press Alt+Shift+1. To expand all the bulleted items again, click the Expand All button or press Alt+Shift+A.

The Collapse All button

Try hiding detail in this chapter's sample presentation. With the *Selling a Product or Service* presentation displayed on your screen in Outline view, click the Collapse All button on the Outlining toolbar to show only the main topics. Drag topic 2, *Customer Requirements*, to just after topic 3, *Objectives*. Then click the Expand button on the Outlining toolbar to see that the collapsed bulleted items have come along for the ride. Finally, on the Outlining toolbar, click the Expand All button to redisplay all the presentation text.

The Expand All button

You may want to save the sample presentation you've made for posterity, but you'll be making no further changes to it in this chapter.

II

The Basic Presentation

Formatting Text in Outline View

Slide view is usually the best place to format the text of a presentation because you can see how the text fits with the background design. However, while entering and editing the presentation in Outline view, you can format any words or characters that are sure to need it. For example, you can italicize a special term or add superscript characters in a formula name.

 **SEE ALSO**

For more information about selecting text, see "Selecting Text for Editing," page 64.

To format text in Outline view, you first select it. Then you can use the character formatting buttons on the Formatting toolbar or the commands from the Format menu or the shortcut menu. For example, choosing the Font command from the Format menu or the shortcut menu displays the Font dialog box shown in Figure 4-16 on the next page. The character formatting buttons and commands work the same way in both Outline view and Slide view.

FIGURE 4-16.

The Font dialog box.

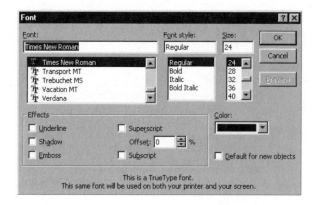

? SEE ALSO

For more information about formatting text, see "Formatting Text in Slide View," page 96.

Whether you apply character formatting in Outline view or in Slide view, you can display the outline in Outline view without character formatting. Just click the Show Formatting button on the Outlining toolbar. On the Formatting toolbar, the Font box and the Font Size box still show accurate information about the selected text, but the entire outline is displayed in a standard font and size (Arial, 28 points). To redisplay the character formatting in Outline view, click the Show Formatting button again.

Importing Outlines

If you have already created a perfectly good outline in another application, it would be tedious to have to recreate it in PowerPoint. And you don't have to. You can import the outline as a starting point for your presentation.

Importing an Outline from Microsoft Word

You can generate a presentation outline in Microsoft Word and then easily export the outline to PowerPoint. Developing the outline in Word lets you take advantage of Word's sophisticated text capabilities. For example, you can use the thesaurus to replace ordinary outline words with vibrant, vigorous, pulsating, dynamic, energetic words.

Because PowerPoint imports Word outlines so easily, someone else can generate an entire text presentation in Word and hand the file over to you. You can then import the outline, give the presentation a distinctive look, and generate slides in no time.

To import a Word outline:

1 Open the outline in Word.

2 Be sure that the outline includes appropriate heading styles. Only information tagged with a heading style will be transferred to the PowerPoint presentation. Viewing the document in Word's Outline view is helpful to see how your slides will appear in PowerPoint.

3 From Word's File menu, point to Send To, and then choose Microsoft PowerPoint. Word opens PowerPoint if necessary, opens a new presentation in Normal view, and exports the Word outline to PowerPoint. Level 1 headings become slide titles, and lower-level headings become the indented bulleted items for the topics.

Figure 4-17 shows an outline in Word. On the next page, Figure 4-18 shows the same outline after it has been imported into PowerPoint.

FIGURE 4-17.
An outline in Microsoft Word.

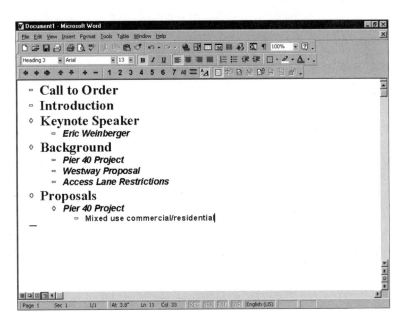

The Basic Presentation

Distribute Bullets Across Slides
If the Word outline contains a lot of detail, the PowerPoint slides you get may be too crowded for your liking. If the Office Assistant is installed, it will recognize the excess and display a light bulb. Click the light bulb for help splitting the slide into two slides.

FIGURE 4-18.
The Word outline
in PowerPoint.

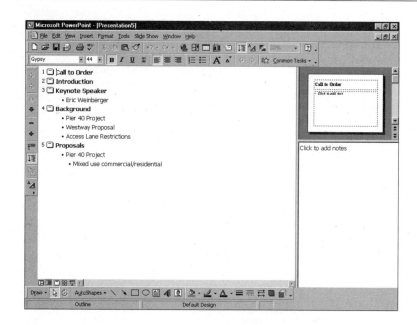

> ⭐ **TIP**
>
> **The Best Way to Copy a Word Outline to PowerPoint**
> A super-slick method you can use to create a new PowerPoint presentation
> from a Word outline is to use drag-and-drop editing to bring the Word outline
> file from Windows Explorer to the PowerPoint window. A new presentation
> opens in PowerPoint with the Word outline in place.

> ▶ **NOTE**
>
> Word outlines can have up to nine indent levels, but PowerPoint has five levels.
> When you import an outline into PowerPoint, any outline levels beyond the
> fifth are all converted to fifth-level entries.

Importing an Outline from Another Application

You can import an outline from most word processing programs as
well as from other presentation applications that can export their
presentation outlines. If the application can generate an RTF (Rich
Text Format) file, you should use that format when saving the outline
to disk. When you import the file, PowerPoint uses the styles in the
file to determine the outline structure. For example, a Heading 1 style
becomes a slide title, a Heading 2 style becomes an indented bulleted
item, and so on. If the file contains no styles, PowerPoint uses the
paragraph indents to determine the outline structure.

If the application cannot generate an RTF file, generate a plain ASCII text file. PowerPoint then picks up the outline structure from the tabs at the beginning of paragraphs. A paragraph preceded by no tabs becomes a slide title, a paragraph preceded by one tab becomes an indented bulleted item, and so on.

To import an outline file, follow these steps:

1 On the Standard toolbar, click the Open button. Or, from the File menu, choose Open. The File Open dialog box appears.

2 In the Files Of Type drop-down list, select All Outlines.

3 Navigate through the folders list, select the file you want to import, and then click Open. PowerPoint opens the file and displays it as a PowerPoint outline.

Inserting an Outline in an Existing Presentation

In addition to importing an outline created in an application such as Word, you can also insert an outline file created with another application into an existing PowerPoint presentation.

To supplement a PowerPoint outline with an imported outline, follow these steps:

1 In Outline view, click the topic after which you want the imported outline to appear.

2 From the Insert menu, choose Slides From Outline. PowerPoint displays the Insert Outline dialog box:

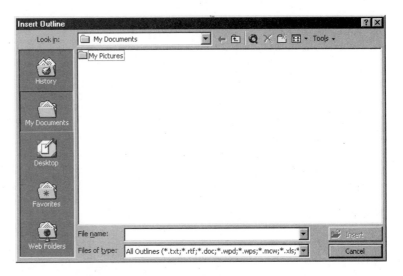

II

The Basic Presentation

3 In the Insert Outline dialog box, navigate through the folders and filenames, select the outline file you want to insert, and then click Insert. PowerPoint inserts the imported outline in the current outline, assigning numbers, slide icons, and indent levels to create a seamless presentation. If you import an outline with more than five levels, PowerPoint converts all levels beyond five to fifth-level entries.

NOTE

You can also import an outline in Slide view. First move to the slide after which you want the outline to appear, and then follow steps 2 and 3. PowerPoint imports the outline into the presentation as slides.

After you import an outline from another application as a new presentation or insert an imported outline in an existing PowerPoint presentation, you can manipulate it just as if you created it from scratch in Outline view.

In this chapter, you learned how to develop and modify a presentation outline in Outline view—the best place for concentrating on the text and the flow of ideas. In the next chapter, you'll learn how to create the text for a presentation in Slide view, where you can see and modify the design and format of each individual slide.

CHAPTER 5

Creating Slides in Slide View

While creating and organizing a presentation in Outline view is a great way to focus on the text of your presentation, you may prefer to devote your creative energy to crafting a single slide at a time in Slide view. Slide view may also be the best place to start when your job is not to conceive the presentation but to produce slides for someone else from handwritten notes and napkin sketches. Figure 5-1 on the next page shows a completed slide as it appears in Slide view.

In this chapter, you'll learn how to create text slides in Slide view. By the time you finish, you'll be just as far along as if you'd entered the presentation text in Outline view and then switched to Slide view. The task still remaining is to drop in the charts, tables, and drawings you want to include in the presentation. You'll learn how to do this in the next several chapters.

FIGURE 5-1.

A slide in Slide view.

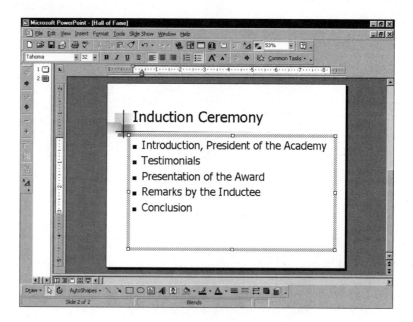

Creating a New Presentation in Slide View

If you do not use the AutoContent Wizard to start a new presentation, that is, if you start a new presentation with a design template, with a predesigned presentation, or completely from scratch, the New Slide dialog box is displayed. The Title Slide AutoLayout is selected so you can simply click OK or press Enter to have a blank title slide displayed. If PowerPoint is correct in assuming that you plan to create a complete presentation, complete this title slide.

> NOTE

> If you're using PowerPoint to create a single slide, you may want to use a slide layout other than the Title Slide layout. To work with a chart layout or organization chart layout, for example, on the Formatting toolbar, click Common Tasks, and then click Slide Layout. Select the slide layout you want. *For more information about selecting a slide layout, see "Adding a New Slide," page 92.*

Whenever you start a new presentation, PowerPoint opens it in Normal view. In Normal view, you can work on the outline on the left side of the window and work on the slides on the right side of the window. This shows you an overview of the presentation at the same time you see the detail on each slide. You can also add and review notes in a separate pane in the PowerPoint window.

But if you want to focus on the layout and look of each individual slide without worrying about the organization of the entire presentation, work in Slide view. In Slide view, you have more screen "real estate" because the outline is not showing and you can see a larger view of the slide you're working on.

To switch to Slide view from Normal view or any other view, click the Slide View button in the lower left corner of the presentation window.

Slide View

Creating the Title Slide

As shown in Figure 5-2, the Title Slide layout displays two text *placeholders*—dashed boxes that show the location for an *object* on a slide. All placeholders tell you to click to add text, a chart, or another presentation element. In this case, you're prompted for a title and a subtitle for the new presentation.

FIGURE 5-2.

The Title Slide layout that appears when you create a new presentation.

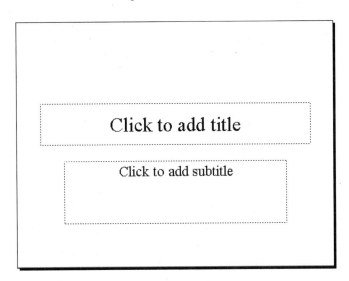

Click to add title

Click to add subtitle

To enter a presentation title in the Title Slide layout, follow these steps:

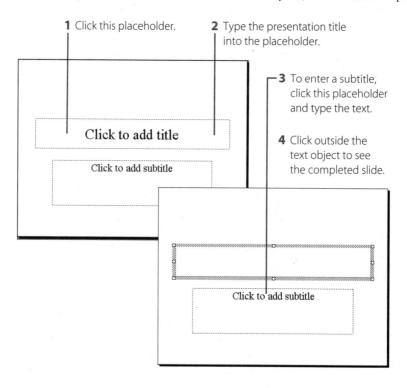

1 Click this placeholder.

2 Type the presentation title into the placeholder.

3 To enter a subtitle, click this placeholder and type the text.

4 Click outside the text object to see the completed slide.

Click to add title

Click to add subtitle

Click to add subtitle

Figure 5-3 shows an example of a completed slide.

FIGURE 5-3.
A completed
title slide.

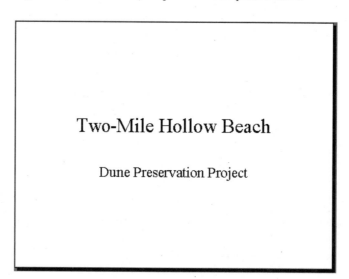

Two-Mile Hollow Beach

Dune Preservation Project

TIP

Start Typing Immediately

When you add a new slide, you can start typing without clicking the *Click To Add Title* placeholder. The first text you type is automatically entered in the placeholder. *For more information, see "Formatting Text in Slide View," page 96.*

NOTE

The formatting of the text (its font, size, color, and so on) is determined by the formatting of the text on the title master and slide master. To change the appearance of the text on any single slide, you can apply your own formatting, which overrides the title master and slide master formatting. To change the appearance of the text on all the slides of a presentation, you might want to change the formatting of the title master or slide master, instead. *For more information, see "Editing the Title Master or Slide Master," page 286.*

If you want to try creating the sample title slide shown in Figure 5-4 on the next page, start a new presentation by choosing New from the File menu. In the New Presentation dialog box, click the Design Templates tab, and then double-click the Multibar template. When the New Slide dialog box appears, select the Title Slide AutoLayout, and click OK. If you want, switch to Slide view. Then click the *Click To Add Title* placeholder, and type *Person to Person*. Click the *Click To Add Subtitle* placeholder or press Ctrl+Enter, and type *Our New Care-Giving Partnership*. Finally, click anywhere outside the subtitle's border to see the completed title slide.

TIP

Work Quickly Using the Keyboard

After typing text in one placeholder, you can press Ctrl+Enter to move to the next placeholder. If the current slide has no more placeholders, PowerPoint creates a new slide and puts the insertion point in the *Click To Add Title* placeholder on that slide.

II

The Basic Presentation

FIGURE 5-4.
A sample title slide.

Adding a New Slide

After completing the title slide, you are ready to add the next slide. When you add a slide, you select an AutoLayout from the New Slide dialog box. Like the Title Slide AutoLayout, PowerPoint's other autolayouts contain placeholders. For example, the Bulleted List AutoLayout has a *Click To Add Title* placeholder and a *Click To Add Text* placeholder, the Chart AutoLayout has a *Click To Add Title* placeholder and a *Double Click To Add Chart* placeholder, and so on. PowerPoint offers 24 autolayouts that should meet nearly all of your presentation needs.

To add a new slide to your presentation, follow these steps:

1 On the Formatting toolbar, click Common Tasks, and then click New Slide. Or, from the Insert menu, click New Slide. The New Slide dialog box appears, as shown here:

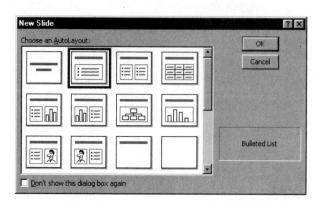

You can scroll through the display of autolayouts using the scroll bar. To see the name of an AutoLayout, click the AutoLayout once.

2 When you've decided which AutoLayout you want, either double-click it or click it once and then click OK. A new slide with the selected AutoLayout appears on the screen.

The rest of this chapter focuses on entering text in text slides. When you finish one slide, you can repeat the previous steps to create the next one. If you need to look at a slide you've already completed, you can move back to the slide by pressing the Page Up key. Press the Page Down key to move forward through your slides. You can also move from one slide to another by dragging the scroll box in the vertical scroll bar up or down.

Entering Text in a Bulleted List AutoLayout

If you add a new slide with a layout that has bulleted text, such as the Bulleted List AutoLayout or the Two-Column Text AutoLayout, a *Click To Add Title* placeholder appears on the new slide along with one or more *Click To Add Text* placeholders.

To complete a slide with bulleted items, follow these steps:

1 Type a slide title. (You don't have to click the *Click To Add Title* placeholder first.)

2 Click this placeholder or press Ctrl+Enter.

3 Type the first bulleted item, press Enter, type the next item, and so forth.

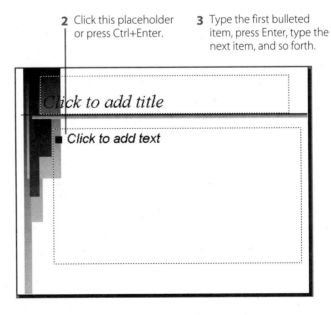

Click to add title

Click to add text

The Basic Presentation

4 After typing the last bulleted item, click outside the object border (the heavy gray border surrounding the bulleted list) to see the completed slide.

> If you want text without bullets (for a paragraph that is a quote, for example), never fear. You can turn off the bullets at any time. *For more information about turning off bullets, see "Adding and Removing Bullets," page 104.*

As an example, try adding the bulleted slide shown in Figure 5-5 to the presentation you created earlier using the Multibar template. On the Formatting toolbar, click Common Tasks, and then click New Slide. In the New Slide dialog box, double-click the Bulleted List AutoLayout— the second layout in the first row. Type *Activities* in the title place-holder. Then click the *Click To Add Text* placeholder or press Ctrl+Enter, type *Home visits*, and press Enter. Type *Hospital bedside visits*, and press Enter. Finally, type *County Community Center work*, and click outside the object border.

FIGURE 5-5.

A sample slide with bulleted statements.

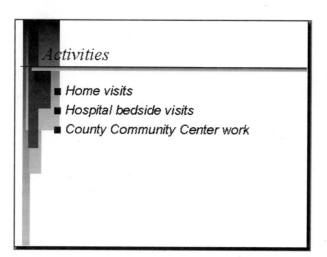

As in Outline view, you can create up to five levels of bulleted statements in Slide view using the same buttons and keystrokes you use in Outline view. Even though you're in Slide view, the Outline toolbar still shows on the left edge of the screen. The Demote and Promote buttons are available there, as well as on the Formatting toolbar. You can also press the Tab key at the beginning of a line to demote an item or Shift+Tab to promote it.

SEE ALSO

For more information about changing levels of bulleted statements, see "Promoting and Demoting Topics and Bulleted Text," page 78.

Editing Text in Slide View

While creating presentation text in Slide view, you can use all the text editing techniques available in Outline view. In fact, everything you type flows through to the presentation outline; you see the presentation as an outline if you switch to Outline view.

To edit text directly on a slide in Slide view, first position the insertion point in the spot you want to edit. The keyboard methods for moving the insertion point in Slide view are nearly the same as those used in Outline view. There are three notable exceptions:

- Pressing Ctrl+Up arrow or Ctrl+Down arrow moves the insertion point to the previous or next paragraph, respectively, rather than to the previous or next topic.

- Pressing Ctrl+Home or Ctrl+End moves the insertion point to the beginning or end of the current *text object* (all the text in a single placeholder) rather than to the beginning or end of the entire outline.

- If no object is selected, Ctrl+Home takes you to the first slide, and Ctrl+End takes you to the last slide.

? SEE ALSO
For more information about editing text, see "Editing Text in Outline View," page 63.

After clicking an insertion point or positioning the insertion point with the keyboard, you can type to insert text, press the Backspace key to delete characters that are to the left of the insertion point, or press Delete to delete characters to the right of the insertion point. As in Outline view, you can make larger edits most efficiently by first selecting the text you want to edit.

? SEE ALSO
For more information about selecting text, see "Selecting Text for Editing," page 64.

Selecting text with the mouse is the same as it is in Outline view: position the insertion point at the beginning of the text, hold down the left mouse button, and drag to the end of the text. (Remember, as long as the Automatic Word Selection option is selected, the entire word will be selected when you drag across any part of a word.) Selecting text with the keyboard is also the same: Move the insertion point to the beginning of the text, hold down the Shift key, and then use the appropriate keys to move the insertion point to the end of the text.

To select an entire text object, click the border of the object. The object border changes from fine diagonal stripes to a fine pattern of dots as shown on the right side of Figure 5-6 on the next page.

FIGURE 5-6.

A selected bulleted statement (left) and a selected text object (right).

A border of diagonal stripes surrounds the object when you select text.

A border of dots surrounds the object when you select the object itself.

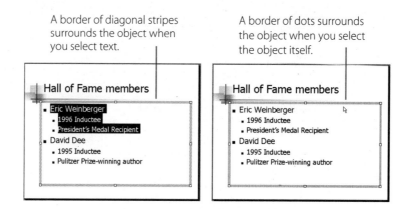

After you select text on a slide, you can delete, move, or copy it using the same buttons, commands, and key combinations you use in Outline view. You can also use drag-and-drop editing to move text within one object or to move text between objects.

Reorganizing bulleted statements is just as easy in Slide view as it is in Outline view. Because the Outlining toolbar is present even in Slide view, you can select bulleted statements and then click the Move Up and Move Down buttons. You can also press Alt+Shift+Up arrow or Alt+Shift+Down arrow to move them.

 NOTE

> If you don't see the Outlining toolbar on the left side of your outline, you need to show it. From the View menu, point to Toolbars, and then click Outlining.

Formatting Text in Slide View

 SEE ALSO

For more information about changing the slide master, see "Editing the Title Master or Slide Master," page 286.

The appearance of the text on all text slides is determined by the slide master for that particular presentation. By editing the slide master, you can change the formatting of text throughout the presentation. You can also override the slide master's control of the text on any individual slide by applying your own formatting. This section discusses formatting that you apply to individual slides.

Many of PowerPoint's text formatting options are available as buttons on the Formatting toolbar or as key combinations. Others are available only as menu commands. You'll soon get a feel for the quickest way to apply specific types of formatting.

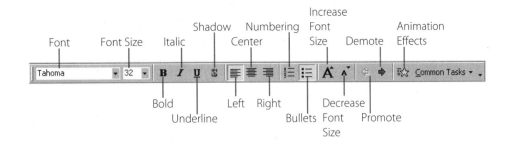

Selecting Text for Formatting

You can apply two types of formatting to the text on your slides: - character formatting that affects individual characters, and the more global object formatting that affects an entire text object. Selecting text for character formatting is just like selecting text for editing. You drag across characters to select them, and then make your formatting changes.

You can also drag to select entire text objects, but you might want to use a special technique to select all the text in the object containing the insertion point. Either press Ctrl+A to highlight all the text within the object, as shown on the left side of Figure 5-7, or press F2 to select the text object itself, as shown on the right side of Figure 5-7. When you press F2 to select a text object, the object is surrounded by handles. Press F2 again to select the text within the object. After you select a text object, you can press the Tab key to select the next text object on the slide either before or after you make formatting changes. (You can select the previous text object by pressing Shift+Tab.)

FIGURE 5-7.

Selected text within a text object (left) and a selected text object (right).

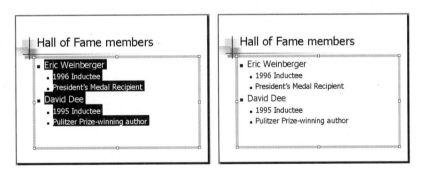

> **NOTE**
>
> Instead of pressing F2 to select the object, you can also click the gray object border that surrounds it.

Changing the Font,
Font Style, Size, Color, and Font Effects

You can emphasize individual characters, words, or phrases by changing their font, font style, size, or color. You can even apply special font effects, such as shadows or embossing. All of these options are available in the Font dialog box.

To make formatting changes using the Font dialog box:

1 Select the text you want to format. You can select an individual character, you can select a word to format the entire word, or you can select several words or sentences.

2 From the Format menu, choose Font. Or, point to the selection, press the right mouse button, and choose Font from the shortcut menu. The Font dialog box appears as shown below:

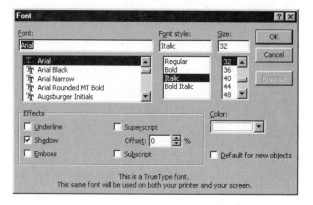

3 Select a Font, Font Style, and Size from the lists in the Font dialog box. The Font list includes the fonts installed on your Windows system. The sizes are measured in points (with 10 through 12 points being a standard book font size, and 72 points being a headline or title 1-inch tall).

4 Specify any combination of Effects options by selecting the appropriate check boxes. If you select Superscript or Subscript, you can change the percentage by which the text is set above or below the line by increasing or decreasing the value in the Offset box.

5 To change the color of the selected text, first click the down arrow next to the Color box. Then click one of the eight colors available for the current color scheme, or click More Colors to select from the full palette of available colors.

6 Click the Preview button if you want to see the changes you've made. (If necessary, drag the title bar of the Font dialog box to move the box out of the way.)

7 Click OK to implement the changes.

⭐ TIP

> **Keep Your Presentation Legible**
>
> Limiting the number of fonts on a slide is as important as limiting the number of fonts in a document. Try to stick to two fonts. Also, remember to use a light text color against a dark background and vice versa for legibility.

Try formatting some text on the bulleted slide you created earlier in this chapter. Select *County Community Center work*, press the right mouse button, and choose Font from the shortcut menu to display the Font dialog box. Under Font Style, select Bold Italic, and then click OK.

The choices you make for the selected text in the Font dialog box are cumulative. You might make certain changes during one pass, such as changing the font and font style, and then come back later and make more changes, such as changing the color. When you select already-formatted text and return to the Font dialog box, all the changes you've made to the formatting up to that point are reflected in the dialog box's settings.

After you select the text you want to format, you can also change the font and font size by using the Font and Font Size drop-down lists on the Formatting toolbar. The Increase Font Size or Decrease Font Size button increases or decreases the font size by specific increments. The increments become larger as the font size increases. (The largest theoretical font size is 4000 points, but you will probably run out of paper long before you can print a character that large!)

You can apply the bold or italic font styles by clicking the Bold button or the Italic button on the Formatting toolbar, and you can apply the underline or shadow effects by clicking the Underline button or the Text Shadow button. Clicking the down arrow next to the Font Color button on the Drawing toolbar shows a palette of the eight colors available with the current color scheme. Most text formatting options are available as keyboard shortcuts, too. Rather than using menus or the Formatting toolbar, you can select the text and then use one of the keyboard shortcuts listed in Table 5-1 on the next page.

II

The Basic Presentation

TABLE 5-1. Keyboard Shortcuts for Formatting Text

Text Formatting	Keyboard Shortcut
Change font	Ctrl+Shift+F
Change font size	Ctrl+Shift+P
Increase font size	Ctrl+Shift+>
Decrease font size	Ctrl+Shift+<
Bold	Ctrl+B
Underline	Ctrl+U or Ctrl+Shift+U
Italic	Ctrl+I or Ctrl+Shift+I
Subscript	Ctrl+=
Superscript	Ctrl+Shift+=
Plain text	Ctrl+Shift+Z
Restore default formatting	Ctrl+Spacebar

 TIP

Replace All Fonts

You can replace all instances of a certain font with another font—for example, replacing Times New Roman with Arial—by using the Replace Fonts command on the Format menu. In the Replace Font dialog box, select the font you want to replace. In the With box, select the font you want to use instead. Click the Replace button, and all the instances of the Replace font are immediately changed to the With font throughout the presentation.

Changing Indents, Alignment, and Spacing

You can perform certain types of text formatting only on entire text objects, rather than individual characters or words. These formatting types include changing the left and first-line indents of paragraphs, changing the alignment of paragraphs, and changing the spacing between and within paragraphs.

Remember, a text object includes all the text within a single placeholder. For example, a bulleted list slide has only two text objects: the title and the bulleted list, even though the bulleted list probably consists of more than one paragraph.

Changing the Left Indent and First-Line Indent

Increasing the left indent of a bulleted list text object pushes all the text to the right, increasing the space between the bullets and the text for each bullet. To change the indents of a text object, click anywhere in the text object and then drag the corresponding markers in the top ruler.

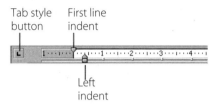

If the ruler is not visible, you can display it in one of the following ways:

■ From the View menu, choose Ruler.

■ Point to the slide background, press the right mouse button, and choose Ruler from the shortcut menu.

 NOTE

> If a text object has bulleted statements at two or more levels, the ruler contains a pair of markers (a left indent marker and a first-line indent marker) for each level.

To increase the space to the right of the bullets, follow these steps:

1 Click any of the text in the object.

2 Drag the left indent marker to the right.

NOTE

> Be sure to drag the lower, triangular marker that points upward. Dragging the rectangular marker located below the left indent marker moves the first-line indent marker and the left indent marker at the same time.

Dragging the first-line indent marker (the upper, triangular marker that points downward) to the left or the right changes the starting position of the first line of the paragraph. Because a bullet starts the first line of a bulleted list paragraph, dragging the first-line indent marker to the right moves the bullet to the right. On the next page, Figure 5-8 shows the indent settings on several rulers and the corresponding indents of the text below. If a text object contains paragraphs that have no bullets, dragging the first-line indent marker to the left creates a *hanging indent*, as shown in Figure 5-9 on page 103.

II

The Basic Presentation

FIGURE 5-8.
Notice how the ruler settings correspond to the text on these three slides.

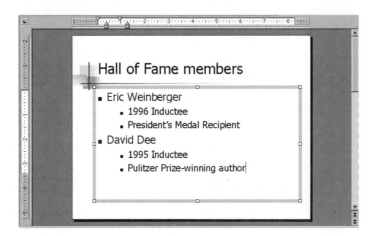

FIGURE 5-9.

Paragraphs with
hanging indents.

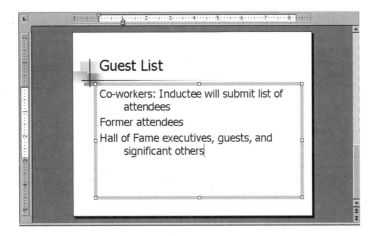

Changing Paragraph Alignment

The *alignment* of a text object determines the horizontal placement of
its lines. The alignment options are shown in Table 5-2.

TABLE 5-2.   Alignment Options

Button	Option	Keystroke	Effect
≡	Left	Ctrl+L	Text within an object is flush with the left edge of the object.
≡	Center	Ctrl+E	Text within an object is centered horizontally within the object.
≡	Right	Ctrl+R	Text within an object is flush with the right edge of the object.
None	Justify	Ctrl+J	Extra spaces are added between words to make the text flush with both the left and right edges of the object.

The alignment options for the paragraphs of a text object can also be
found on the Alignment submenu. To align text using this submenu,
follow these steps:

1   Select the text object by clicking the object border.

2   From the Format menu, point to Alignment.

3   From the Alignment submenu, select the alignment option you want.

To left-align, center, or right-align text, you can click the Align Left,
Center, or Align Right buttons on the Formatting toolbar. You can also

use one of the keyboard shortcuts listed in Table 5-2 to align text in the various ways.

Changing Line and Paragraph Spacing

The *line spacing* value determines the amount of vertical space between lines in a paragraph, and the *paragraph spacing* value determines the amount of space between paragraphs in a text object. You may want to add extra space between lines or paragraphs to separate them, to increase slide legibility, to fill more vertical space on the page, or even for a nice design effect.

To change the line spacing in a text object, follow these steps:

1   Click anywhere in the text object.

2   From the Format menu, choose Line Spacing. The Line Spacing dialog box, shown below, appears:

3 Enter a number or click the arrow buttons to change the spacing.

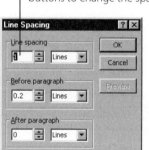

The other two options in the Line Spacing dialog box allow you to add extra space before or after each paragraph, in terms of either lines or points. By specifying values in the Before Paragraph and After Paragraph options, you can spread out the paragraphs vertically.

Adding and Removing Bullets

The Bullets button

Each bullet that appears at the beginning of a text line emphasizes the statement that follows. Bullets are only appropriate when a slide contains a series of statements of equal value. Because of this, there may be times when you don't need bulleted text, such as when a slide contains a single phrase. Fortunately, you can easily add and remove bullets in PowerPoint by using the Bullets button on the Formatting toolbar to toggle a bullet on or off.

To remove the bullet from a line of text:

1 Click anywhere in the line.

2 On the Formatting toolbar, click the Bullets button.

For example, in Figure 5-10, the bullet has been removed from the second of two text statements.

FIGURE 5-10.

The bullet has been removed from the second text statement.

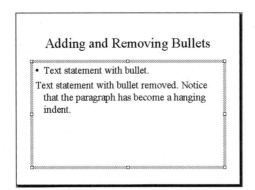

To remove the bullets from all the text in a text object, first select the text by pressing Ctrl+A. Or, select all text by pressing F2 or by clicking the gray object border so that it's selected. Click the Bullets button. The Bullets button is a toggle, so if you select the text and click the Bullets button again, PowerPoint restores the bullets.

Another way to add or remove bullets is to select the text, and choose Bullets And Numbering from the Format menu or the shortcut menu. Then, when the Bullets And Numbering dialog box appears, click the bullet style to add bullets, or click None to remove bullets.

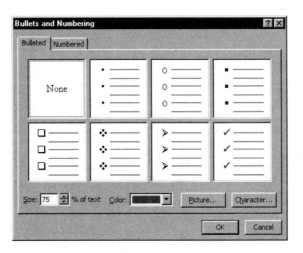

The Basic Presentation

II

When you remove the bullet from a bulleted paragraph that contains more than one line of text, you'll notice that the first line of text shifts to the left. The paragraph's hanging indent is still present, as you can see in the second text statement in Figure 5-10. To remove the hanging indent in a nonbulleted paragraph, follow these steps:

1 Check that the ruler is visible. (If it is not, choose Ruler from the View menu or the shortcut menu.)

2 Drag the left indent marker to the left so that it aligns with the first-line indent marker, as shown below. Be careful to drag the triangular part of the left indent marker, not the rectangular part, which moves both the first-line and left indent markers simultaneously.

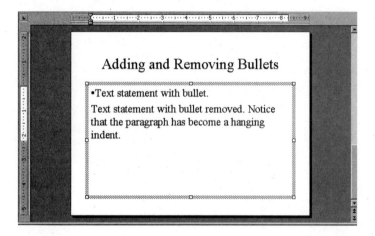

Notice that the text in the second bulleted statement is now properly left-aligned, but the top bulleted statement has been affected as well. Changes to indents affect all paragraphs in a text object.

Changing the Bullet Shape, Color, and Size

The default bullets that precede the text on your slides are only one of the almost limitless options for bullet shape, color, and size. You can use any character from any TrueType font on your system, and you can change the color and size of the bullets on any slide. There are certain fonts (for example, Symbol and Wingdings) that are completely made up of symbols, rather than letters or numbers. These symbol fonts provide a lot more choices for the bullet characters you can use.

To select a special bullet character, follow these steps:

1 Select the text following the bullet or bullets you want to change.

2 From the Format menu, choose Bullets And Numbering. Or, point to the selection, press the right mouse button and choose Bullets And Numbering from the shortcut menu. The Bullets And Numbering dialog box appears. Standard bullet symbols are shown.

3 If one of these symbols is right for your slide, double-click it to use it as the bullet symbol for your selected text. Otherwise, click the Character button. The Bullet dialog box appears.

4 Select a font from this list.

5 Click any character. It will be magnified for easier viewing.

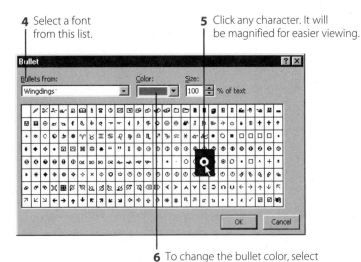

6 To change the bullet color, select a color from this drop-down list.

To change the bullet size, type a new size in the Size edit box, or click the up or down arrows on the edit box to increase or decrease the size of the bullet as a percentage of the text size. You can also change the size and color of a bullet character in the Bullets And Numbering dialog box.

Figure 5-11 shows a slide with bullet characters that are more interesting and appropriate to the topic than the default bullets.

FIGURE 5-11.

Interesting characters used as bullets.

II

The Basic Presentation

Select a Picture to Use as a Character

As an alternative to selecting a font symbol as a bullet character, you can select a picture bullet. In the Bullets And Numbering dialog box, click Picture. The Picture Bullet dialog box appears, as shown in Figure 5-12, presenting a gallery of pictures that can be used as bullets.

FIGURE 5-12.

Picture Bullet dialog box.

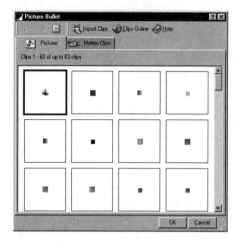

Creating Numbered Lists

PowerPoint can also automatically number paragraphs in a text object. Just select the bulleted list or paragraphs, and then on the Formatting toolbar, choose the Numbering button.

You can change the number style, size, color, and starting number. From the Format menu, choose Bullets And Numbering. Or, point to the selection, press the right mouse button and choose Bullets And Numbering from the shortcut menu. The Bullets And Numbering dialog box appears, with the Numbered tab active. Select the options you want, and then click OK.

Setting and Removing Tab Stops

You have two choices when you need to place text in columns on a slide. You can create a table in PowerPoint so easily that you'll want to use one whenever you need to place text in columns. But you can

? SEE ALSO

For more information about creating tables, see Chapter 9, "Adding Tables to Your Presentation," page 233.

also place tab stops in a text object to space text horizontally across a slide. As described in Table 5-3, PowerPoint provides four different types of tab stops. All of these are available on the ruler.

TABLE 5-3.   Tab Stops

Tab Button	Tab Stop	Description
∟	Left-aligned tab stop	Aligns the left edge of text with the tab stop
⊥	Centered tab stop	Aligns the center of text with the tab stop
⌐	Right-aligned tab stop	Aligns the right edge of text with the tab stop
⊥.	Decimal tab stop	Aligns the decimal points of numbers with the tab stop

There are preset left-aligned tab stops every half-inch along the ruler. When you enter your own tab stops, any preset tab stops to the left are automatically removed. To enter tab stops, follow these steps:

1   Click anywhere within the text object. (All text in the object will be formatted with the same tab stops.)

2 Click the Tab Alignment button until the type of tab you want appears.

3 On the ruler, click the position for the tab stop.

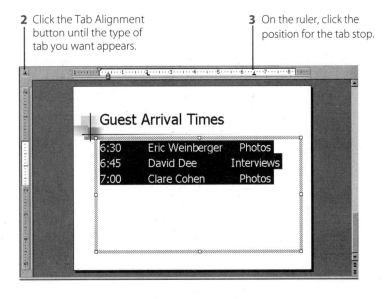

4   Continue clicking different positions in the ruler to add tab stops of the same type, or select a different tab type and then click the ruler.

II

The Basic Presentation

To move a tab stop you have set, simply drag it to its new position. To remove a tab stop you have set, drag the tab stop down and off the ruler.

Changing the Case of Text

You can automatically change the capitalization of text on a slide, without having to retype it. Select the text you want to modify, and then, from the Format menu, choose Change Case. Figure 5-13 shows the Change Case dialog box, which offers case options for text. Try each option to see its effect. Simply select an option, and then click OK. You can also cycle between uppercase, lowercase, and title case for the selected text by pressing Shift+F3.

FIGURE 5-13.

The Change Case dialog box.

Transferring Text Styles

After you format one selection of text, you can transfer the same formatting, called the *text style*, to another selection of text. By transferring a text style, you save time because you don't have to repeatedly reopen menus or reselect options to format the text in your slides in a consistent way.

To transfer the formatting of one text selection to another text selection, follow these steps:

1 Select the text whose formatting you want to transfer, as shown below.

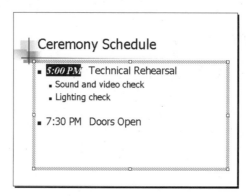

The Format
Painter button

2 On the Standard toolbar, click the Format Painter button.

3 Click and drag across the text that you want to transfer the formatting to.

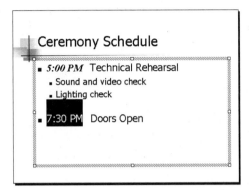

As soon as you release the mouse button, the formatting of the original text selection is transferred to the other text selection.

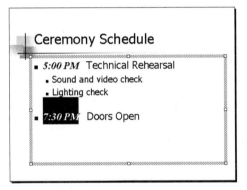

 TIP

Transfer a Format to Several Items At Once

To transfer the formatting of an object to multiple objects, select the object and *double-click* the Format Painter button. The format of the object will be transferred to each new object you select until you click the Format Painter button again to turn it off.

The Basic Presentation

II

Moving and Resizing Text Objects

The text you enter in a placeholder appears at the position of the placeholder text. But after you enter all the text you need, you may want to move the text object or change its size, perhaps to make room on the slide for a chart or graphic, or to make the slide more interesting graphically.

To move or resize a text object you have been editing, first select the entire object with one of these procedures:

- Press F2 so that the object border selection changes to the fine dots rather than the diagonal stripes.

- Click the gray object border until the object border changes to the fine dots, as shown in Figure 5-14.

FIGURE 5-14.

Border and handles of a selected object.

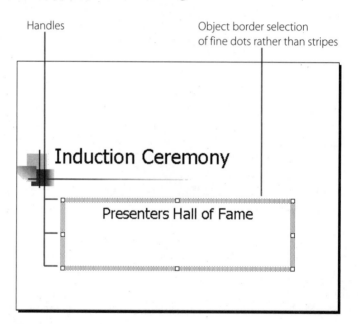

Handles

Object border selection of fine dots rather than stripes

Induction Ceremony

Presenters Hall of Fame

After you select the text object, you can move or resize it as follows:

- To move the object, position the mouse pointer on the object's border (but not on a handle) until the pointer changes to cross hairs, hold down the left mouse button, and drag the object to the new position.

- To move, or nudge, the object incrementally, press one of the arrow keys.

- To resize the object, position the mouse pointer on one of the object border handles until the pointer changes to a double arrow. Hold down the left mouse button, and drag the handle until the object is the size you want.

- To resize the object proportionally, hold down the Shift key and drag one of the corner handles. This changes the object's scale; that is, both the object's width and height are resized proportionally.

- To resize the object while leaving it centered at its current position, hold down the Ctrl key and drag one of the corner handles.

Turning Word Wrap On or Off

When you resize an object, the text inside wraps to fit the new size, as shown in Figure 5-15. Words in a paragraph that can no longer fit on a line within the object move down to the following line. Likewise, words that can fit on the previous line move up to the previous line. Because this is usually the effect you want when you resize text objects, the word wrapping option is a default setting. However, if you want more precise control over the length of the lines in your slides, you can turn this option off.

FIGURE 5-15.

Word wrapping allows words to move to the next or previous line to fit the boundaries of a text object.

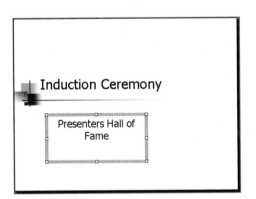

Induction Ceremony

Presenters Hall of Fame

You can turn word wrap off, as well as change internal margins, resize the object to fit the text, or rotate text with the Text Box tab in the Format AutoShape dialog box. To turn word wrap off, follow these steps:

1 Click anywhere in the text object.

2 From the Format menu, choose Placeholder. The Format AutoShape dialog box appears.

3 Click the Text Box tab. The Word Wrap Text In AutoShape check box controls word wrapping.

4 Select or clear the check box to turn word wrapping on or off.

When word wrapping is turned off, any text you add to a paragraph continues across the slide, beyond the borders of the text object, and even beyond the edge of the slide if necessary. You can press Enter or Ctrl+Enter to create line breaks exactly where you want them to be.

Changing the Text Box Margins

For more information about adding graphic boxes to object borders, see "Special Text Object Formatting," page 116.

Also on the Text Box tab in the Format AutoShape dialog box are the four Internal Margin settings. You can use these settings to adjust the space between the text and borders of a text object. Increasing the margins is helpful when you add an actual graphic box to the borders of a text object. As shown in Figure 5-16, larger margins pad the interior of the box so that the text does not appear cramped.

FIGURE 5-16.

The text object on the bottom has larger internal margins.

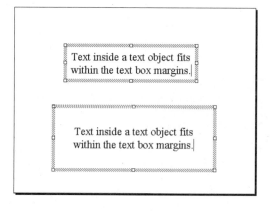

Fitting Text Objects to the Text

Sometimes the text you enter in a placeholder does not completely fill the placeholder. For example, the bottom border of the text object shown on the left in Figure 5-17 is some distance from the text. To automatically shrink the text object to fit the text you've entered, select the text, and then select the Resize AutoShape To Fit Text check box in the Format AutoShape dialog box. The text object immediately shrinks to fit the text inside, as shown on the right in Figure 5-17. If you enter additional text, the text object will grow vertically to accommodate the new text.

FIGURE 5-17.

The size of the text object on the left is not automatically adjusted to fit the text. The text object on the right shrank vertically to accommodate the existing text.

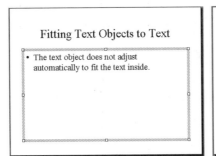
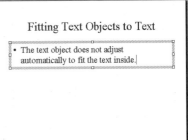

When the Resize AutoShape To Fit Text option is turned on, you can stretch the sides of a text object horizontally, but the bottom border always snaps to fit the last line of the text. When Resize AutoShape To Fit Text is turned off, newly typed text overruns the bottom border of the text object, and you can resize the object manually.

Decreasing the margins while the Resize AutoShape To Fit Text option is turned on brings the borders of the text object closer to the text.

Rotating Text

You can rotate text in a text object three ways:

- Rotate text by a standard 90-degree angle clockwise. Select the text object, and then from the Format menu, choose Placeholder, and then click the Text Box tab. Select the Rotate Text Within AutoShape By 90° check box.

- Enter a specific rotation angle. Select the text object, and then from the Format menu, choose Placeholder, and then click the Size tab. Specify the angle you want in the Rotation box.

The Basic Presentation

The Free Rotate
button

■ Drag a rotation handle to the angle you want. On the Drawing toolbar, click the Free Rotate button. Green rotation handles appear around the object. Drag one of these handles to the rotation angle you want. When finished, click the Free Rotate button again. Figure 5-18 shows the result of a rotated text object.

FIGURE 5-18.
Rotating text.

Drag a handle to rotate the text.

⭐ TIP

Get More Precision While Rotating
To obtain a bit more precision while freely rotating a text block, try this: click the Free Rotate button and then click a green rotation handle. Drag away from the text object and then start dragging the mouse pointer around the text block in a larger circle.

Special Text Object Formatting

You can surround a text object with a line, add a shadow to it, fill it with color, rotate it, resize it, and scale it. In fact, you can use any of the commands you use to change the appearance of drawing objects. You will learn about formatting drawing objects in Chapter 12, "Drawing in PowerPoint."

You can also change the size and position of a text object in sophisticated ways. After selecting a text object, you can change its size by selecting options on the Size tab in the Format AutoShapes dialog box. Under Size And Rotate, you can use the Height and Width settings to resize an object by an absolute measurement, that is, by inches. Under Scale, you can use the Height and Width settings to reduce a text object to 90 percent of its former size, for example, to make room for an added graphic. Selecting the Lock Aspect Ratio check box on this tab ensures that the object will never change shape if you change the size.

You can position a text object at a precise point that you specify. Use the settings on the Position tab in the Format AutoShapes dialog box, to pin an object to the same spot in a sequence of slides, for example.

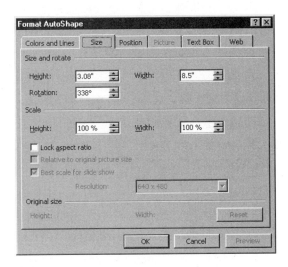

If the presentation you are creating is strictly text, as many presentations are, then you have now done everything required to create the presentation, and you can skip ahead to Chapter 10, "Reorganizing the Presentation." But if you want to add charts, organization charts, and tables to your presentation, go on to the next four chapters.

Microsoft WordArt

When your presentation title needs a little more pizzazz, you can use Microsoft WordArt to create more spirited titles. Use WordArt to create shadowed, stretched, rotated, and skewed text of any size. You can also use WordArt to create text that has been contoured to fit a number of predefined shapes.

To add WordArt text to a slide, click the Insert WordArt button 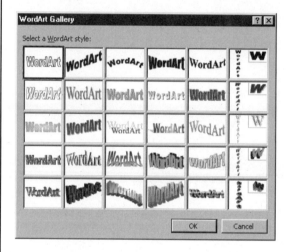 on the Drawing toolbar. (Before you click the WordArt button, you can delete the *Click To Add Title* placeholder on a title slide so that it doesn't get in your way.) When WordArt's visual menu of styles appears on the screen, choose a style, and click OK. On the Edit WordArt Text dialog box, type your text in the Text box. If you want, you can change the font, size, and style of text. Click OK to place the WordArt on the slide. To edit WordArt, double-click any WordArt text.

The WordArt toolbar appears so you can change WordArt options or make still more formatting choices such as rotating the WordArt object or making the height of all characters within the WordArt object the same.

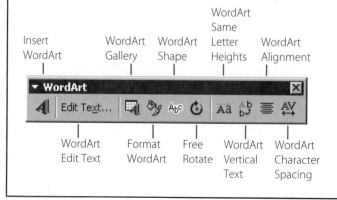

CHAPTER 6

Adding Basic Charts

You can reel off numbers until you're blue in the face, but nothing gets your message across like a chart. Microsoft Graph, included with Microsoft PowerPoint, offers 14 standard and 20 custom chart types (plus many more variations) with all the pizzazz you could want. Graph makes the process of creating charts simple and automatic. In this chapter, you'll learn how to use Graph to add the charts to slides. You'll also learn how to enter and edit the data that supports your charts, and you'll discover ways to incorporate data and charts from sources outside PowerPoint into your chart slides.

A chart can communicate any information that can be quantified, so don't hesitate to pull out and use a chart whenever your message is numeric—even if your numbers aren't precise.

Because a chart is a visual representation of data, it can have a much greater impact than words alone. For example, the statement *We out-produced any of our competitors by 2 to 1* is impressive, but not as impressive as this chart:

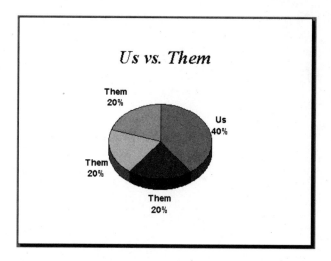

Charts are your best bet for illuminating trends, deviations, and other measurements that don't require a great deal of explanation. If an explanation is needed, you can simply add text to the chart or include a text slide. By the time you finish this chapter, you'll probably be thinking up new ways that you can use charts to enhance your PowerPoint presentations.

What Is Microsoft Graph?

Microsoft Graph is a program shared by all the Microsoft Office products. Graph creates charts for use in Microsoft Office applications such as Microsoft Word, Microsoft Excel, and, of course, PowerPoint. If you're already familiar with graphing in Excel, you'll find it an easy jump to graphing in PowerPoint; both use the same Graph program. If you're not familiar with graphing in Excel, don't worry. At every step of the way, Graph guides you through the process of converting raw numbers into professional, colorful, and illuminating charts.

When you create or modify a chart, Graph's menus and Standard toolbar replace PowerPoint's menus and toolbars, as shown in Figure 6-1, so only the commands and controls you need are on the screen.

FIGURE 6-1.

Graph's menus and Standard toolbar take over the screen when you create a chart.

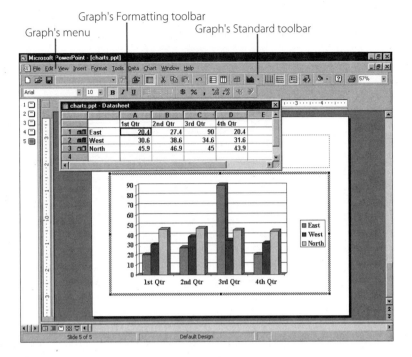

Graph's Formatting toolbar

Graph's menu

Graph's Standard toolbar

The chart you are creating in Graph appears on the current slide. When you are entering or editing chart data, a *datasheet* containing the numbers overlays the chart. Any change you make to the numbers in the datasheet is reflected immediately in the chart.

Understanding Chart Basics

You can create a special chart slide devoted to an entire chart, or you can add a chart to an existing slide to enhance a text message. Then you can select from an array of 14 standard and 20 custom chart types to ensure that the chart presents your data effectively.

Creating a Chart Slide

To create a chart slide in an existing presentation, follow these steps:

1 In Normal view or Slide view, display the slide that the new slide should follow.

2 Click the New Slide button on the Standard toolbar. The New Slide dialog box appears, as shown on the next page.

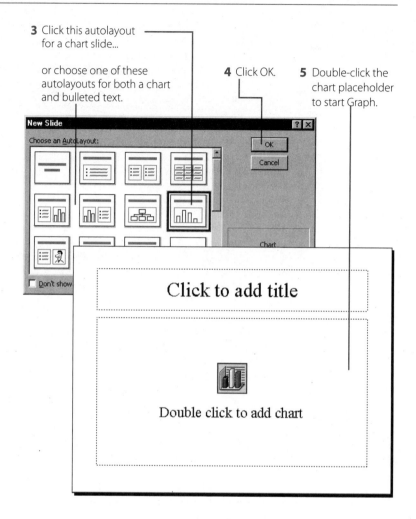

3 Click this autolayout for a chart slide...

or choose one of these autolayouts for both a chart and bulleted text.

4 Click OK.

5 Double-click the chart placeholder to start Graph.

Click to add title

Double click to add chart

A sample chart appears within the placeholder, and the data-sheet window containing the sample data for the chart overlays the chart as shown in Figure 6-1.

Adding a Chart to an Existing Slide

The Insert Chart button

To add a chart to an existing slide, on PowerPoint's Standard toolbar, click the Insert Chart button. Or, from the Insert menu, choose Chart. Either way, Microsoft Graph loads and displays a sample chart and datasheet. Don't worry about the positioning or size of the chart at this point. After you enter your data, you can move and size the chart as needed.

Selecting a Chart Type

After you create a chart slide or add a chart to an existing slide, you can select a chart type from PowerPoint's many standard or custom chart types. Selecting a chart type before you begin entering data is a good first step because you are compelled from the start to consider the message your data conveys. It also modifies the appearance of the datasheet window to show how the data will be represented. Of course, with PowerPoint, you can always change your mind at any time, so you can begin with one chart type and change to other types later.

Keep in mind that PowerPoint produces variants, called *subtypes*, of all of the standard chart types, providing even more choices for precision and creativity in presenting your data. You can go beyond these subtypes and modify any chart to a virtually unlimited degree. You can even mix chart types within the same chart, showing some data with lines and some with bars, for example.

To select a chart type, follow these steps:

1   Double-click the chart, if necessary, to activate Microsoft Graph.

The Chart Type button

2 On Graph's Standard toolbar, click the drop-down arrow by the Chart Type button.

3 Click the chart type you want.

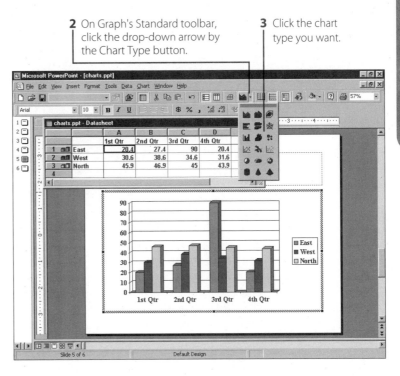

The Basic Presentation

The 18 most commonly used chart types and subtypes are shown in this list. When you click the chart type you want, your chart immediately changes to that type.

For the full selection of all standard chart types, subtypes, and custom chart types, choose Chart Type from the Chart menu or shortcut menu. When you choose this command, Graph displays the Chart Type dialog box shown in Figure 6-2. To see the custom chart types, click the Custom Types tab. Samples of the various chart types and their subtypes appear in large preview panes.

FIGURE 6-2.
The Chart Type dialog box.

To further refine your chart selection, choose a chart subtype from the right side of the dialog box. For example, Figure 6-3 shows the Chart Type dialog box that appears when you select the pie chart type. You can select a subtype and then preview your data plotted using the selected subtype by clicking the Click And Hold To View Sample button. Either click OK to implement the selected chart subtype, or click another subtype and click OK. If you want to use a particular chart type and subtype frequently in all your presentations, select them and click the Set As Default Chart button. All future chart slides you create will start out as this chart type.

FIGURE 6-3.

You can use the Chart Type dialog box to select a chart subtype.

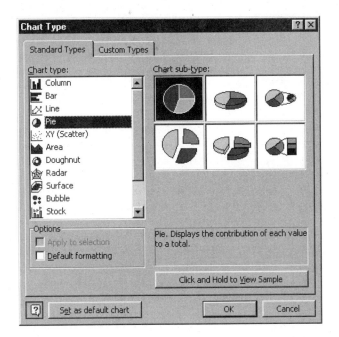

The following sections discuss PowerPoint's standard chart types and explain how each chart type presents information in its own way. Figure 6-4, on the next page, shows an example of each chart type.

🌟 **TIP**

Keep the Chart Type Palette Handy

You can "tear off" the palette of chart types and "tack it" onto an unused part of the screen for easy access later. Simply click the down arrow by the Chart Type button to see the palette. Next, position the mouse pointer on the palette's title bar, hold down the left mouse button, and drag the palette away from Graph's Standard toolbar and to the location on the screen you want. You can close the Chart Type palette by clicking its Close button.

FIGURE 6-4.

PowerPoint's 14 standard chart types.

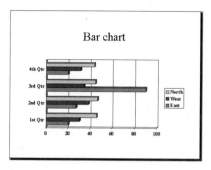

Bar Charts

Bar charts compare measurements at intervals. They emphasize measurements at discrete times rather than the changes over time. Their bars run horizontally. The stacked bar subtype shows the contributions of each measurement to a whole. The 100% stacked bar subtype shows the percentage contribution of each measurement to the whole without identifying specific numeric contributions.

Column Charts

Column charts are much like bar charts except their bars run vertically rather than horizontally. Like bar charts, they compare measurements at intervals and provide snapshot views of data taken at specific moments rather than a depiction of the change of data over time. Column charts also have stacked and 100% stacked subtypes.

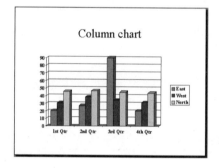

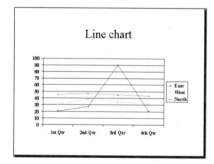

Line Charts

Line charts show changes in data or trends over time. You can show the same data using bars or columns, but lines emphasize change rather than comparisons at intervals.

Pie Charts

Pie charts show the breakdown of a total. You can separate slices of the pie to emphasize certain values. The values depicted by slices are contained in a single series on the Graph datasheet.

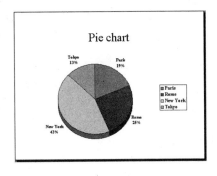

XY (Scatter) Charts

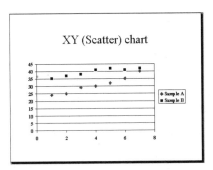

XY (scatter) charts show the degree of correspondence between two series of numbers. Generally used for scientific data, XY charts also let you depict two sets of numbers as one set of *xy*-coordinates.

Area Charts

Area charts show the amount of change in a set of values during an interval of time. Line charts are similar, but they emphasize the *rate* of change rather than the *amount* of change.

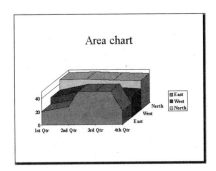

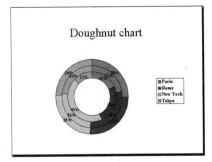

Doughnut Charts

Like pie charts, doughnut charts show breakdowns of totals, but they let you depict several series of data in successive rings around a doughnut hole.

(continued)

The Basic Presentation

FIGURE 6-4. *continued* ## Radar Charts

Radar charts compare change in
values of a several series. Each
value is plotted on axes that radi-
ate from the center of the chart.
Series of values are connected by
a line that runs from axis to axis
and circles the center of the chart.

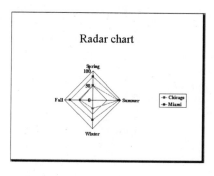

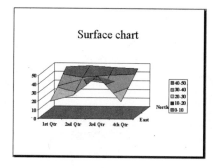

Surface Charts

Surface charts depict the best and
worst combinations of numbers.
Colors or patterns designate areas
with the same value. The four
Surface chart subtypes show a 3-D
surface, a wireframe 3-D surface,
a contour surface chart viewed
from above, and a wireframe
contour surface without color.

Bubble Charts

A bubble chart is like an xy
(Scatter) chart with the addition
of different-sized bubbles at the
data points to indicate the value
of a third number.

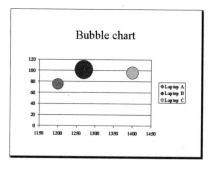

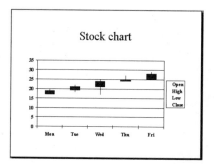

Stock Charts

Stock charts (also called high-low-
close charts) show the values of
stocks or other financial instru-
ments. They can also depict
scientific data, such as daily variations in temperature or humidity.
Stock charts can depict volume of
sales. The different stock chart
subtypes depict three or more of
these five variables: volume,
open, high, low, and close.

Cylinder, Cone, and Pyramid Charts

Cylinder, cone, and pyramid charts are just like 3-D column or 3-D bar charts, except they use more interesting and dramatic shapes to display values.

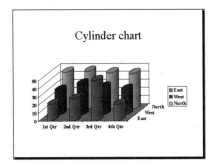

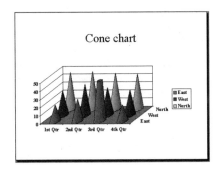

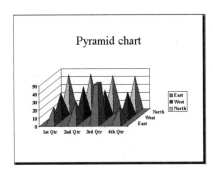

Entering the Data

The generic entries in the datasheet (*1st Qtr, 2nd Qtr*, etc.) when you start a new chart provide an example of how text and numbers should be arranged in a datasheet. The chart peeking out from behind the datasheet window displays the text and numbers in the datasheet graphically, and it is updated immediately as you enter and edit data in the datasheet. Figure 6-5, on the next page, shows the datasheet.

FIGURE 6-5.

The datasheet.

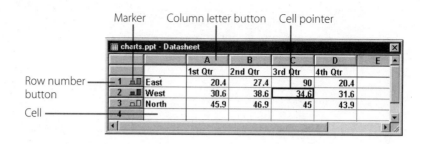

Marker   Column letter button   Cell pointer

Row number button

Cell

The datasheet is made up of *cells*, which are the rectangular intersections of the rows and columns. In Figure 6-5, text labels appear in the left-most and topmost cells of the datasheet. The actual numbers to be graphed occupy the cells below and to the right of these text labels. Each cell in this section has an *address* that consists of a column letter and row number. For example, the address of the cell at the intersection of column A and row 1 is A1.

To create a proper chart, PowerPoint must know whether the *series* (the sets of related numbers) are entered in rows or columns. By default, PowerPoint assumes that the series are arranged in rows. PowerPoint places small pictures of the *markers* that will be used in the chart (the bars, columns, lines, or other graphic shapes) on either the row number or column letter buttons in the datasheet. If the markers are on the row number buttons, the data is organized in the chart by row. If the markers are on the column letter buttons, the data is organized by column.

 TIP

Plot Your Series in Columns

If you want to place your series in columns instead of rows, from the Data menu, choose Series In Columns. *For more information about arranging data in the datasheet, see "Data Arrangements for Special Chart Types," page 141.*

Entering the Labels

Your first step in entering the data for a chart is to replace the text labels in the first row and first column of cells. To replace a label, use the mouse or the arrow keys to move the *cell pointer*—the highlight surrounding a single cell—to the cell containing the label, and then type over the existing entry. You can also double-click or press F2 to place an insertion point in a selected cell and then edit its contents. Use the same text editing techniques that you use elsewhere in PowerPoint to edit the contents of a cell in the datasheet.

Because PowerPoint's default setting arranges chart data by row, each label entered in the leftmost cell of a row appears in the chart's legend. The labels entered in the topmost cells of columns often have time or date designations, such as a specific year or month, but they can be any other text that distinguishes the individual data points in a series of numbers. Remember, if you want the column labels to appear in the chart's legend rather than in the row labels, choose Series In Columns from the Data menu.

To try your hand at entering labels, start by creating a new chart:

1 On the Formatting toolbar, click Common Tasks, and then click New Slide. Or, from the Insert menu, click New Slide.

2 In the New Slide dialog box, double-click an autolayout that includes a chart placeholder.

3 In Normal view or Slide view, double-click the *Double-click To Add Chart* placeholder to start Microsoft Graph.

Stick with the default chart type when the chart and datasheet appear, and then follow these steps, using either the suggested labels or your own.

1 Select the first cell in row 1 (the cell containing the label *East*).

2 Type *Regular mail* and press Enter. Don't worry that the label is too long to fit in the cell. The length of the label won't affect the resulting chart, and you can widen the entire column to accommodate the label at any time. (See the sidebar titled "Changing the Widths of Columns," page 132.)

3 Now replace *West* with *Overnight* and press Enter.

4 Replace *North* with *Courier*.

5 Select the first cell in column A, replace *1st Qtr* with *Package*, and then press Tab to move to the cell to the right.

6 Replace *2nd Qtr* in column B with *Box*, and press Tab.

7 Replace *3rd Qtr* in column C with *Letter*.

8 Click the column letter button for Column D. From the Edit menu, choose Delete. The datasheet looks like the illustration at the top of the following page.

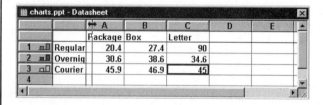

charts.ppt - Datasheet		A	B	C	D	E
		Package	Box	Letter		
1	Regular m	20.4	27.4	90		
2	Overnight	30.6	38.6	34.6		
3	Courier	45.9	46.9	45		
4						

Changing the Widths of Columns

When the label you enter in a cell exceeds the width of the cell, the label is cut off in the datasheet (but not in the chart). To widen the entire column, place the mouse pointer on the line to the right of the current column letter button until the pointer changes to a double arrow. Then hold down the left mouse button, and drag to the right. In the datasheet shown below, the first column is widened to accommodate the longest label.

charts.ppt - Datasheet		A	B	C	D	E
		Package	Box	Letter		
1	Regular	20.4	27.4	90		
2	Overniq	30.6	38.6	34.6		
3	Courier	45.9	46.9	45		
4						

To change the width of more than one column, click the column letter button for the first column, hold down the mouse button, and drag across the other column letter buttons. Then, when you widen the one column using the technique described above, the other selected columns are also widened the same amount.

You can also double-click the line between two column letter buttons to automatically adjust the width of the first column to accommodate the column's longest entry. Select several columns and double-click between any two to fit them all to their longest entry.

Entering the Numbers

After you enter the labels to create a framework for the data, you must replace the sample numbers with your own. You can select any single cell, type over the cell's contents, and then move to the next cell. However, the best way to quickly enter all the numbers is to select the range of cells that will contain the numbers, and then begin typing columns of replacement numbers. To select a range of cells, place the mouse pointer on the first cell, hold down the mouse button, and then drag across to the cell at the opposite corner of the range. You can also move the cell pointer to the first cell, hold down the Shift key, and then use the arrow keys to move to the cell at the opposite corner.

With the range of cells selected this way, when you type a number and press Enter, the cell pointer moves to the cell below. When you type a number in the last cell of a column and press Enter, the cell pointer goes to the first cell in the next column of the selected range. When you type a number in the last cell of a selected range of cells and press Enter, the cell pointer returns to the first cell in the range.

To enter the data for the chart you've created, follow these steps. (Again, you can use the suggested data or supply your own.)

1   Place the mouse pointer on cell A1, which is located at the intersection of column A and row 1.

2   Hold down the left mouse button, and drag the pointer to cell C3.

3   Release the mouse button. The rectangular range of cells from A1 to C3 is selected, as shown here:

		A	B	C	D
		Package	Box	Letter	
1	Regular mail	20.4	27.4	90	
2	Overnight	30.6	38.6	34.6	
3	Courier	45.9	46.9	45	
4					

charts.ppt - Datasheet

4   Type the numbers shown below, pressing Enter after each number. Be sure to enter the numbers by column, not by row.

8.6	10.75	.32
17.9	22	9.95
48	56	17.5

The datasheet now looks like this:

		A	B	C	D
		Package	Box	Letter	
1	Regular mail	8.6	10.75	0.32	
2	Overnight	17.9	22	9.95	
3	Courier	48	56	17.5	
4					

charts.ppt - Datasheet

II

The Basic Presentation

When using this quick data-entry technique, enter the numbers in columns, even if you're charting the data by rows.

Control the Cell Pointer

Whenever you use the quick data-entry technique of selecting the cell range and then entering numbers, pressing Enter always moves the cell pointer to the next cell in the selected range. However, when you do not have a cell range selected, you can control whether the cell pointer moves to the next cell or remains on the selected cell when you press Enter. From Graph's Tools menu, choose Options and select or clear the Move Selection After Enter check box.

Formatting the Labels and Numbers

You can use Graph's Formatting toolbar (shown in Figure 6-6) to select a different character font and number format for a datasheet. The changes you make to the font are displayed only in the datasheet, whereas the changes you make to the number formatting appear in both the datasheet and the chart. In addition, font formatting applies to the entire datasheet, regardless of what you have selected. Number formatting applies only to the cells you have selected.

FIGURE 6-6.

The Formatting toolbar in Graph.

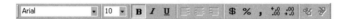

From Graph's Formatting toolbar, you can select a font, a point size, and character formatting attributes such as bold, italic, and underline for all the text and numbers in your datasheet. Although the paragraph alignment buttons are inactive in the datasheet, keep in mind that text is always left-aligned in the datasheet and numbers are always right-aligned.

If Graph's Formatting toolbar is not showing, from the View menu, point to Toolbars, and then click Formatting.

For more information about changing fonts in the chart, see "Basic Chart Formatting," page 159.

In addition to using Graph's Formatting toolbar, you can choose Font from Graph's Format menu or shortcut menu to open the Font dialog box and change the formatting of the data in the datasheet. Keep in mind that these font formatting changes are only seen by you. These changes don't affect the chart itself, which is what your audience will see in your presentation.

To change the character fonts in your datasheet, follow these steps:

1 Click anywhere in the datasheet. Any font changes you make will apply to the entire datasheet.

2 Click the Italic button. Everything is italicized, as shown here:

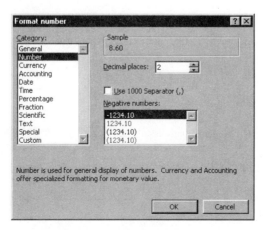

To change the formatting of numbers in a datasheet and the associated chart, first select the numbers, and then either use the number formatting buttons on Graph's Formatting toolbar or choose Number from Graph's Format menu or shortcut menu. Because number formatting applies only to the numbers in the selected cells, rather than the entire datasheet, you can select one set of numbers and format them as decimals and then select another set and format them as percentages.

Five number formatting buttons are included on Graph's Formatting toolbar. Use the first three buttons—Currency Style, Percent Style, and Comma Style—to add dollar signs, percent signs, or commas to your selected numbers. Use the last two buttons—Increase Decimal and Decrease Decimal—to increase or decrease the number of decimal places.

For additional number formatting options, choose Number from Graph's Format menu or shortcut menu. In the Format Number dialog box, shown in Figure 6-7, select a formatting category from the list at the left, and make any other number formatting choices you want.

FIGURE 6-7.

The Format Number dialog box.

To format the numbers in your sample datasheet and chart, follow these steps:

1 Select the rectangular range of numbers from cell A1 to cell C3.

The Currency
Style button

2 Click the Currency Style button on Graph's Formatting toolbar. The numbers should look like this:

charts.ppt - Datasheet					
		A	B	C	D
		Package	Box	Letter	
1	Regular mail	$8.60	$10.75	$0.32	
2	Overnight	$17.90	$22.00	$9.95	
3	Courier	$48.00	$56.00	$17.50	
4					

The numbers on the vertical axis of the chart itself also change to the currency style.

> If you enter or make a formatting change to numbers that causes a number in your datasheet to become longer than the column width, the number is replaced by a series of hash marks (###). This prevents the misunderstanding of a cut-off number. Just widen the column by dragging or double-clicking the line to the right of the column letter button, and the number appears again.

To remove number formatting from the data, select the data, and then from Graph's Edit menu, point to Clear, and then choose Formats.

> Choosing Contents from the Clear submenu removes the data from selected cells without deleting and shifting the cells. (You can also remove the data from selected cells by choosing Clear Contents from Graph's shortcut menu.) *For more information about removing data, see "Inserting and Deleting Data," page 139.*

Viewing the Chart

The View
Datasheet
button

As you revise data in the datasheet, the chart adjusts to reflect the changes. If you're done working with the datasheet and you want to examine and work in the chart, close the datasheet window. On Graph's Standard toolbar, click the View Datasheet button, or click the Close button in the datasheet window. Figure 6-8 shows the chart created from the sample datasheet.

FIGURE 6-8.

Chart created from the sample datasheet.

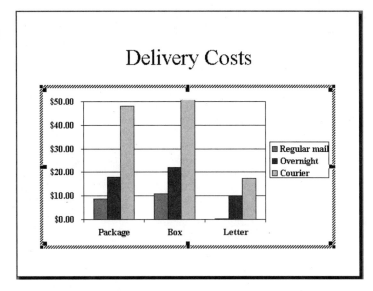

To work in the datasheet again, on Graph's Standard toolbar, click the View Datasheet button. Or, from Graph's View menu, choose Datasheet.

(?) SEE ALSO

For more information about formatting charts, see "Basic Chart Formatting," page 159.

The numbers along the vertical axis of the chart in Figure 6-8 are formatted with the currency style you specified earlier in the datasheet window. Other aspects of the graph's appearance are controlled by the template that formats the current presentation and by the chart type you selected. The template gives the chart its color scheme and font selections. The chart type gives the chart its overall design and special option settings. If necessary, you can now start revising the content of the chart and adjusting the appearance of the chart.

Editing the Data

PowerPoint offers a variety of ways to edit the data displayed by the chart, including moving, copying, inserting, and deleting. Before you can put any of these techniques to work, however, first activate the datasheet. On Graph's Standard toolbar, click the View Datasheet button. Or, from Graph's View menu, choose Datasheet.

The Basic Presentation

> **Change Numbers by Dragging the Bar, Pie Slice, or Line**
> If you are working in a 2-D chart, you can use the mouse to change the number represented by the marker. Just click the bar, column, pie slice, or line, and then click it again (but don't double-click). Handles appear around the marker. Drag the handle to change the value of that marker. The number changes in the datasheet as you drag.

Moving and Copying Data

You might want to move data in your datasheet to make room for new data. Or you might want to rearrange the data so that the chart becomes more meaningful. For example, by ordering the data in your datasheet from largest to smallest or vice versa, you can enhance the impression the chart makes. You can move or copy data in the datasheet by selecting it and then using the Cut, Copy, and Paste buttons on Graph's Standard toolbar; Cut, Copy, and Paste from Graph's Edit menu or shortcut menu; or the shortcut key combinations. You can also use the drag-and-drop method to drag the data to a new location.

To move data by dragging, select the rectangular region of cells you want to move, place the pointer on the border of the selected cells (the pointer changes to an arrow), hold down the mouse button, and then drag the cells to a new location. Release the mouse button when the cells are in the correct position in the datasheet.

You can copy (instead of move) the selected cells by holding down the Ctrl key as you drag. A small plus sign appears next to the pointer when you hold down the Ctrl key.

Now try using a drag-and-drop operation to rearrange the data in your chart.

1 Select the three columns of data you've entered by dragging across the column letter buttons A, B, and C.

2 Place the pointer on the border of the selected range, hold down the mouse button, and drag the data to columns E, F, and G.

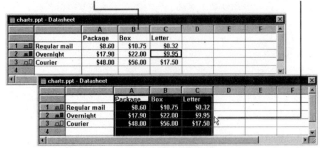

3   Release the mouse button to drop the data into place.

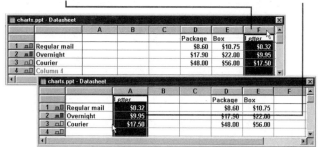

4 Click the column F button to select the contents of that column.

5 Drag the contents of column F to the left until it's over column A, then release the mouse button.

6   Finally, select columns D and E, and drag them to columns B and C. Now the data is arranged sequentially from least expensive to most expensive.

> **NOTE**
>
> Graph displays a warning if you try to drop data on a cell that already contains data. If that's what you want, click OK. If you want to drop the data elsewhere, click Cancel and try again.

Inserting and Deleting Data

To insert a row or column of cells in the datasheet, click a row number or column letter button, and then from Graph's Insert menu, choose Cells. Or, from the shortcut menu, choose Insert. A new row is inserted above the selection. A new column is inserted to the left of the selection.

To remove a row or column from the datasheet, click the row number or column letter button, and then choose Delete from Graph's Edit menu or shortcut menu.

To add or remove more than one row or column at a time, drag across the row number or column letter buttons for as many rows or columns as you want to add or remove before you choose the Cells command or the Delete command. For example, to add three columns, drag across three column letter buttons, and then from Graph's Insert menu, choose Cells.

When you select only some of the cells in a row or column and then choose Cells from Graph's Insert menu, the Insert dialog box appears, shown in Figure 6-9. Here you can specify whether you want to push aside (shift) the other cells in the row or column or insert an entire row or column. If you want to push the cells aside, select Shift Cells Right or Shift Cells Down. If you want to insert an entire row or column, select Entire Row or Entire Column.

FIGURE 6-9.

The Insert dialog box.

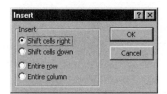

In the same way, if you select only some of the cells in a row or column and then choose Delete from Graph's Insert menu or the shortcut menu, the Delete dialog box appears. Specify whether you want to shift the other cells in the row or column to fill the space left by the deleted cells, or delete the entire row or column.

If you simply want to delete data from cells without shifting cells, select the cells you want to clear. On Graph's Edit menu, point to Clear, and then choose Contents. Or, from the shortcut menu, choose Clear Contents. Yet another method is to simply press the Delete key.

Excluding Data

You can temporarily exclude data from a chart without deleting the data from the datasheet. Excluding data can be helpful when you want to use the same set of data to create several charts. In one chart, you can compare only certain sets of data, and then in another chart, you can compare different sets of data from the same data pool.

To exclude a row or column of data, double-click the corresponding row number or column letter button. The selected data in the row or column appears dimmed, and the chart adjusts immediately. To include the selected data once again, double-click the same row number or column letter button.

You can also exclude multiple adjacent rows or columns of data by first selecting one or more cells in the rows or columns you want to exclude. Then, from Graph's Data menu, choose Exclude Row/Col. If the Exclude Row/Col dialog box appears, as shown in Figure 6-10, select whether you want to exclude the row or column.

FIGURE 6-10.
The Exclude Row/Col dialog box.

To return excluded data to a chart, select the excluded row or column, and then from the Data menu, choose Include Row/Col.

Data Arrangements for Special Chart Types

When creating a chart, Graph follows very specific rules in interpreting the data arrangement in your datasheet. You need to know these rules to make sure your data is set up the way you need to present the information correctly in the chart type you have chosen. The following sections explain these guidelines for the different chart types.

Pie Charts and Doughnut Charts

A pie chart can plot only one series, with each number in the series represented by a pie slice. To plot more than one series, use a doughnut chart, which plots multiple series in two dimensions as concentric rings in the chart. To show multiple breakdowns in three dimensions, consider using the stacked or 100% stacked subtype of a bar or column chart. Each bar or column can show the breakdown of a different series.

If you've entered more than one series in the datasheet for a pie chart, the chart plots the first series only. To plot a different series, exclude the earlier series. For example, to plot the third series in a datasheet, exclude the first and second series. Figure 6-11, on the next page, shows a pie chart that plots the data in row 1 of the datasheet. Notice that rows 2 and 3 have been excluded and that a pie chart marker appears on the row 1 button.

The Basic Presentation

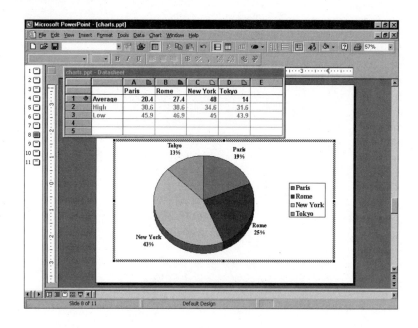

Area, Bar, Column, Line, Surface, Cylinder, Cone, and Pyramid Charts

Charts with areas, bars, columns, lines, or a surface as their markers all require the same arrangement of data in the datasheet. You enter each series of numbers in a row or a column, and then allow Graph to create the chart. By default, Graph interprets each row of numbers as a series. If you want Graph to interpret each column of numbers as a series, from Graph's Data menu choose Series In Columns.

Choosing Series In Columns after you've entered numbers in rows can give you an equally legitimate view of the data, whether you create a bar chart or column chart. In fact, you can try both options to see which presents your case more clearly. For example, Figure 6-12 shows a chart plotted by row. Figure 6-13 shows the same chart plotted by column. The chart in Figure 6-12 emphasizes the comparison of delivery methods, whereas the one in Figure 6-13 emphasizes the comparison of package types.

FIGURE 6-12.
A chart plotted by row.

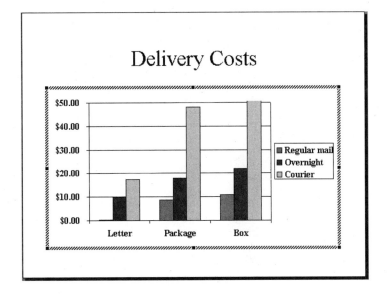

FIGURE 6-13.
The same chart plotted by column.

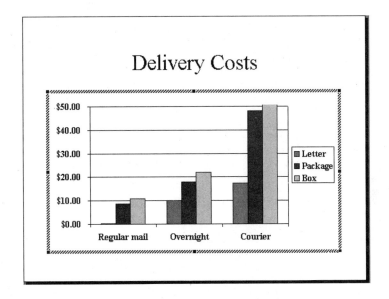

XY (Scatter) and Bubble Charts

To create an XY (scatter) chart, enter the x values in one column and the y values in adjacent columns. To create a bubble chart, enter the x values, y values, and bubble sizes in adjacent columns. On the next page, Figure 6-14 shows an XY (scatter) chart and its data and Figure 6-15 shows a bubble chart and its data.

FIGURE 6-14.
An XY (scatter) chart
and its datasheet.

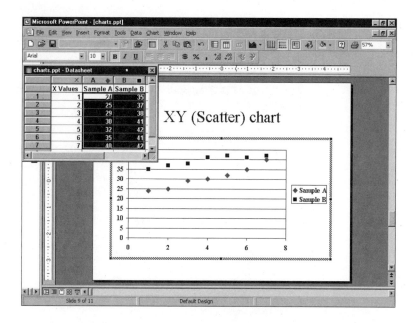

FIGURE 6-15.
A bubble chart
and its datasheet.

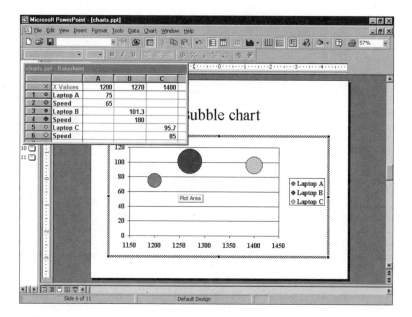

Radar Charts

The numbers in a series are represented as data markers on different
radial axes of a radar chart. All the data markers in the same series are
connected by a line that forms a ring around the chart.

When you enter series in rows, each column is represented by a different radial axis (the labels at the top of the columns identify the axes). Figure 6-16 shows a radar chart and its datasheet.

FIGURE 6-16.

A radar chart
and its datasheet.

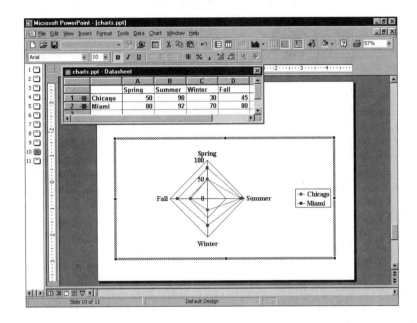

Stock Charts

To create a stock chart, you must enter all the high numbers in one series, all the low numbers in another series, and so forth. The order in which you enter the numbers is important. If the chart depicts data series in rows, follow one of the patterns listed in Table 6-1:

TABLE 6-1.   Stock Chart Values

Row	High-Low-Close Chart	Open-High-Low-Close Chart	Volume-High-Low-Close Chart	Volume-Open-High-Low-Close Chart
1	High value	Opening value	Volume value	Volume value
2	Low value	High value	High value	Opening value
3	Closing value	Low value	Low value	High value
4		Closing value	Closing value	Low value
5				Closing value

II

The Basic Presentation

Figure 6-17 shows an open-high-low-close chart and the datasheet that supports it.

FIGURE 6-17.
An Open-high-low-close chart and its datasheet.

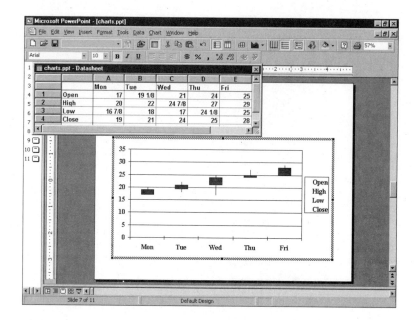

To add volume numbers to a chart, enter the volume values as the first series and choose Stock as the chart type and choose Volume-Open-High-Low-Close as the subtype. Volume values will be plotted as a secondary value axis at the right side of the chart. You can format this axis separately from the primary value axis.

Using Data from Microsoft Excel

If you've already typed the numbers for a chart in a Microsoft Excel worksheet, the last thing you want to do is retype the numbers in PowerPoint. Fortunately, there's an easy way to transfer your Excel data to PowerPoint. In fact, if you want, you can even set up a link between the original numbers in Excel and the copies in PowerPoint. Then, if you change the numbers in Excel, the numbers in PowerPoint are updated automatically. You can also import an existing Excel chart into PowerPoint by dragging it from an Excel window directly onto a PowerPoint slide.

Importing Excel Data into Graph

To transfer data from an Excel worksheet to Graph, you can use Import File from Graph's Edit menu. You can then specify the Excel file and the range that contains the data you want to import.

To import data from an Excel worksheet like the one shown here, follow the steps below.

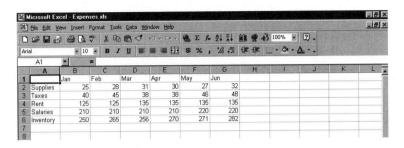

1 Make sure the Graph datasheet is open. If it's not showing, click the View Datasheet button on Graph's Standard toolbar or choose Datasheet from Graph's View menu.

2 In the datasheet, click the cell located in the upper-left corner of the area into which you want to import the data.

3 From Graph's Edit menu, choose Import File. The Import File dialog box appears, as shown here:

4 Use the Look In drop-down list, the Up One Level button, and File Name list as necessary to navigate to the Excel file containing the data.

5 Double-click the file name.

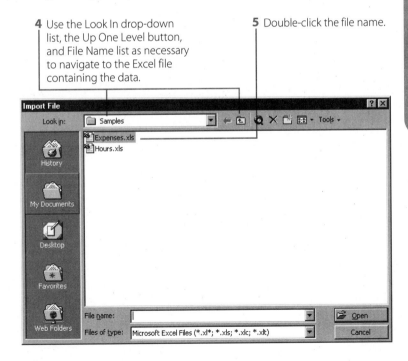

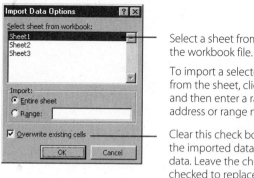

Select a sheet from the workbook file.

To import a selected range from the sheet, click Range and then enter a range address or range name.

Clear this check box to append the imported data to existing data. Leave the check box checked to replace existing data.

8 Click OK to import the data. When the data is imported, it appears in the Graph datasheet like this:

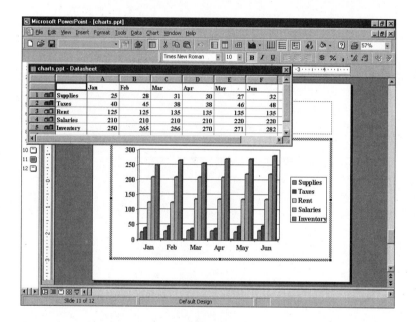

⭐ **TIP**

Consolidate Data from Several Excel Worksheets

You can use the Import Data command to consolidate data from several Excel worksheets into a single Graph datasheet. After you import data from the first worksheet, select another location in the datasheet, import data from the second worksheet, and so on. Be sure to select the cell in which you want succeeding data to start, and clear the Overwrite Existing Cells check box in the Import Data Options dialog box so that the data appends rather than replaces the existing data.

NOTE

> Use the Import File command when you want to simply copy data from an Excel worksheet. However, to establish a link between the Excel data and the PowerPoint chart, you must use a different procedure, which is described in the next section.

Creating a Link Between Excel and Graph

Establishing a link between data in an Excel worksheet and the same data in a Graph datasheet allows you to update the numbers in Excel and then see the changes automatically reflected in PowerPoint.

Simply by copying the data to the Windows Clipboard in Excel and then using Paste Link from Graph's Edit menu to paste the data from the Clipboard to the datasheet, you automatically establish a link.

To create a link, follow these steps:

1 In Excel, select the range of data you want to link to PowerPoint, as shown here:

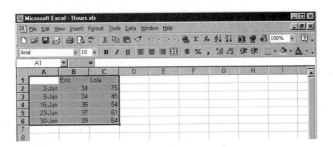

2 From Excel's Edit menu, choose Copy. The data is copied to the Windows Clipboard.

3 Switch to the datasheet in PowerPoint, and then select the cell in the upper left corner of the area into which you want to paste the data.

4 From Graph's Edit menu, choose Paste Link. If Graph displays a message box cautioning you about overwriting existing data, click OK to continue or click Cancel and try again in another location. The data appears in the Graph datasheet.

II

The Basic Presentation

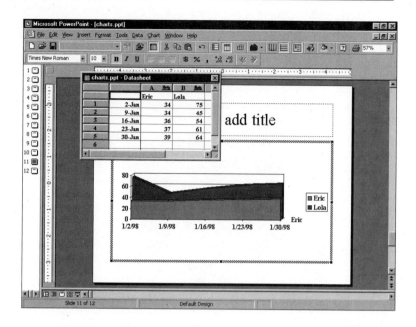

Updating the Link

After you create a link between Excel and PowerPoint, the link will be updated automatically unless you change it to a manual update link. Just for interest's sake, you can arrange the Excel and PowerPoint windows side by side to see the link in action; when you change a number in Excel, you can immediately see the number updated in PowerPoint.

Although you can edit information in PowerPoint's Graph datasheet, as soon as the link is updated from Excel, those changes revert to the Excel information. This is because it's a one-way link; that is, changes made in Excel are updated in PowerPoint, but changes made in PowerPoint do not update the original Excel worksheet.

To change the characteristics of the link, from the Graph Edit menu, choose Links. The Links dialog box appears, as shown in Figure 6-18. To change the link so that it updates only when you click the Update Now button, select the Manual option at the bottom of the Link dialog box. Other options in this dialog box allow you to open the original data in Excel for editing; select a different data source—perhaps a different range in the Excel worksheet; or break the link between Excel and PowerPoint. If you break the link, the data remains in the Graph datasheet, but it is no longer updated when you make changes in the Excel worksheet.

FIGURE 6-18.

The Link dialog box.

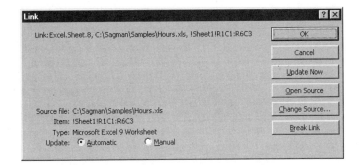

Using Text and Data from Data Files

When the data you need for a chart is stored in an *ASCII text file*; that is, a plain text file without any formatting, you can import the file into Graph using the Import File command. The columns of data in the file should be separated by tabs, semicolons, commas, or spaces.

To import an ASCII text file into Graph, follow these steps:

1 In the Graph datasheet, click the cell in the upper left corner of the area into which you want to paste the data.

2 From Graph's Edit menu, choose Import File. The Import File dialog box appears. In the Files Of Type drop-down list, select Text Files.

3 Use the Look In drop-down list, the Up One Level button, and File Name list as necessary to navigate to the file you want to import, and then double-click the file name. The Text Import Wizard opens, as shown below:

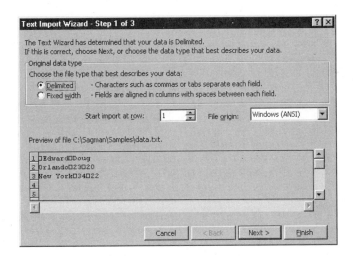

If the columns of data are separated by tabs, semicolons, or commas, the file is *delimited*, and by default the Delimited option is selected as the file type. If the columns of data are separated by spaces, the Fixed Width option is selected. A preview at the bottom of the first Text Import Wizard dialog box shows the data to be imported.

4 Click the Next button to move on to step 2.

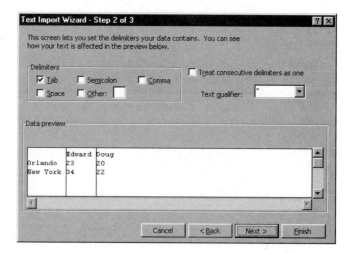

5 If the Text Import Wizard has not properly identified the delimiter used in the file (tabs or commas, for example), select the correct delimiter in the Step 2 dialog box. Vertical lines should properly separate the columns of data in the Data Preview box.

6 Click the Next button to go on to step 3, shown below:

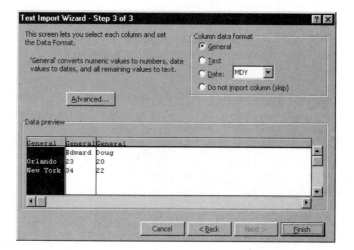

7   Select each column of data in the Data Preview box by clicking anywhere in the column. Then check the Column Data Format section in the upper right corner. If the Text Import Wizard has selected an incorrect data format, select the correct format now.

8   Click the Finish button to complete the import procedure. The data appears in the Graph datasheet, and you can then format the resulting chart to suit your needs.

That completes your introduction to creating charts and chart slides. If you're done with charts for now and need to add an organization chart or table to your presentation, skip to Chapter 8, "Adding Organization Charts," or Chapter 9, "Adding Tables to Your Presentation." But if you want to continue working with charts, go on to the next chapter in which you'll learn how to create custom charts you can tailor to meet the most demanding requirements.

II

The Basic Presentation

CHAPTER 7

Customizing Charts

When all you need is a standard-issue chart to get your message across, the basic steps of entering data and selecting a chart type or autoformat—covered in Chapter 6—are as far as you need to go. Microsoft Graph, the graphing module used by Microsoft PowerPoint, creates a professional-quality chart that vividly portrays your data and harmonizes with the design of your presentation.

But sometimes you want the chart to *communicate* in a special way—to accentuate a trend, de-emphasize an outcome, or call attention to a result. At times like these, creating the basic chart is only the first step. Formatting the chart to make it truly expressive is an equally important part of the process.

In this chapter, you'll learn how to emphasize patterns or trends in your charts in a variety of ways, including getting down to the nitty gritty of changing the appearance of the markers that represent numbers, and changing the structure and design of the chart axes. You'll also learn how to format the titles, legend, gridlines, and other parts of the chart to communicate your data more effectively.

Activating a Chart for Formatting

After you create a basic chart by following the steps in Chapter 6, the chart appears on a slide with the default formatting prescribed by its particular chart type. For example, a new pie chart has the default formatting for pie charts.

To activate the chart so that you can modify any aspect of its formatting, use one of these methods:

- Double-click the chart.

- Click the chart and press Enter.

- Click the chart, and then from PowerPoint's Edit menu, point to Chart Object and choose Edit.

 **TIP**

> You can select each object on a slide in succession by pressing the Tab key.

When you activate a chart, Graph's menus and toolbars replace those of PowerPoint. The chart appears on a slide within a frame surrounded by handles, as shown in Figure 7-1. You haven't left PowerPoint, but you can now use any of Graph's menus and toolbar buttons to work with the chart. In Chapter 6, you used Graph's Formatting toolbar to make changes to the datasheet. You can also use Graph's Standard toolbar, as shown in Figure 7-2, to make changes to the entire chart.

FIGURE 7-1.

An active chart on a slide.

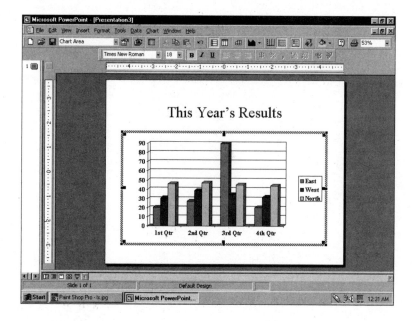

FIGURE 7-2.

Graph's Standard toolbar.

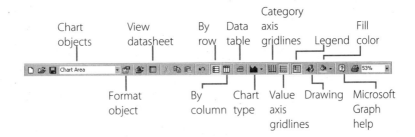

After you finish formatting the chart, click outside the gray frame to exit Graph and to redisplay PowerPoint's menus and toolbars.

Open Microsoft Graph in a Separate Window

If you want, you can open Microsoft Graph so that its menus and its toolbar appear within a separate Graph window that overlays PowerPoint. First click the chart, and then from PowerPoint's Edit menu, point to Chart Object and choose Open. When you finish editing in Graph, from Graph's File menu, choose Update. Then, also from Graph's File menu, choose Exit & Return To *<Presentation name>*.

Zoom the Chart

You can zoom in or out on the chart in either Graph or PowerPoint. If you zoom in Graph, you can make changes to the magnified chart. If you zoom in PowerPoint, you can view the magnified chart, but not make any changes.

To zoom in Graph, in the PowerPoint window, double-click the chart to start Graph. Use the Zoom drop-down list on Graph's Standard toolbar, or the Zoom command on Graph's View menu.

To zoom in PowerPoint, use the Zoom drop-down list on PowerPoint's Standard toolbar. Or, from PowerPoint's View menu, choose the Zoom command.

Selecting a Chart Object for Formatting

In addition to changing the entire chart in Graph, you can change individual components, called *chart objects*. To understand which chart objects you can change, you need to know a little about the anatomy of a chart. Figure 7-3 on the next page shows a typical chart and its chart objects. You'll have plenty of opportunities to become familiar with these names as you work through the sections of this chapter, which cover each chart object in depth.

To check the name of any chart object, make sure that the chart is activated in Graph. Rest the mouse pointer on the chart object without clicking. The name of the chart object appears in a *ScreenTip*.

FIGURE 7-3.

A typical chart and its chart objects.

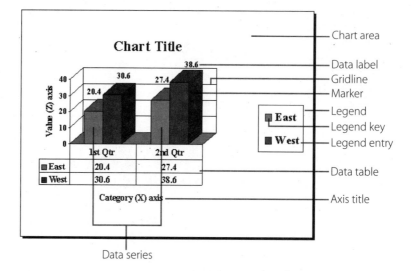

Data series

In some cases, chart objects can be selected and then formatted as a group or individually. For example, a bar on a bar chart can represent the data series, or the individual data point. Also, within a legend are the individual legend entries and the individual legend keys. To select individual items within such a group, in Graph, click the object once, and then click it again. The individual object is selected.

You can also use the keyboard to select a chart object. First press the Up or Down arrow key to move from one group of chart objects to the next in succession. Then, to select an individual chart object from the group, such as one of the columns of a column series or one of the legend entries of the legend, press the Right or Left arrow key.

To change a selected chart object in Graph, simply double-click the object. The format dialog box specific to the selected object appears. You can double-click and format the bars in a bar chart, for example, and then double-click and format the legend.

There are other ways to open the format dialog box for the selected chart object. You can:

The Format Object button

- Click the Format Object button on Graph's Standard toolbar. The name of the command depends on which chart object is selected. If you select an axis, for example, the command is Format Axis. If you select a legend, the command is Format Legend, and so on.

- Click the first command on Graph's Format menu. This command reflects the selected chart object.

- Press Ctrl+1.

- Click the right mouse button on the selected chart object to open the shortcut menu. Select the format command at the top of the menu.

Save a Chart Type for Future Use

When you have formatted chart objects to create a chart with the look you want, you can save the combination of formatted chart objects as a custom chart type. Then you can select the custom chart type to quickly apply its settings to all the chart objects in any new chart. *For more information about saving a formatted chart as a custom chart type, see "Saving Chart Formatting as a Custom Chart Type," page 205.*

The Basic Presentation

Basic Chart Formatting

Each chart object has its own special formatting options. This section, which covers basic formatting options for charts, assumes that you have already activated the chart in Graph and are ready to select a chart object for formatting.

Changing the Color of a Data Series

In a chart, a *data series* is represented by one or more *markers*: an area, a group of bars or columns, a line, the slices of a pie, the rings of a doughnut chart, the lines of a radar chart, or the groups of points in an XY (scatter) chart. The color of a data series is the color displayed by the markers of that series. These markers can also contain a gradient, texture, pattern, or picture.

To easily change the color of a data series, follow these steps:

1 Click the series, that is, the bar, column, line, or whatever shape is representing the data series.

2 On Graph's Standard toolbar, click the drop-down arrow next to Fill Color button.

The Fill Color button

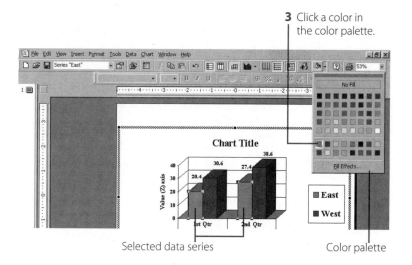

3 Click a color in the color palette.

Selected data series

Color palette

To select a gradient, texture, pattern, or picture, on Graph's Standard toolbar, click the down arrow next to the Fill Color button, and then click Fill Effects. Click one of the four tabs in the Fill Effects dialog box (Gradient, Texture, Pattern, or Picture), and then specify the settings you want.

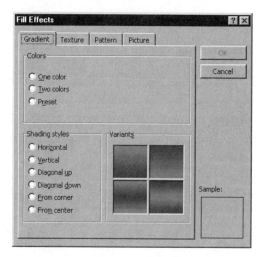

To select a border color for the markers at the same time you're specifying the color or pattern for the data series markers themselves, use the Format Data Series dialog box instead. Follow these steps:

1   Double-click any of the markers in a data series to open the Format Data Series dialog box shown at the top of the facing page.

2 On the Patterns tab, modify the border with these Border controls, or choose Automatic for a default border.

3 Modify the marker appearance with these Area controls.

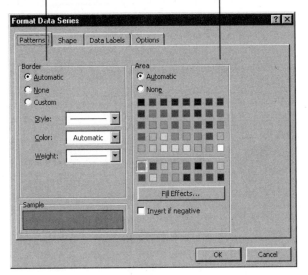

The Format Data Series dialog box contains at least two tabs. The Patterns tab includes options that change the patterns and colors of the data series. You can use the Data Labels tab to specify the numeric values of the data points. Depending on the type of chart you're working with, other tabs might also be available. The advanced formatting options for specific chart types are covered later in this chapter.

> **NOTE**
>
> If the series is represented by a line, the options in the Border section control the appearance of the line.

If, for example, you want to surround an area marker in an area chart with a white line and fill the area marker with dark blue, first double-click the marker. Then, in the Format Data Series dialog box, under Border, click white in the Color drop-down list. Under Area, select dark blue. A preview of the marker appears in the Sample box.

The Basic Presentation

 **TIP**

> **Select Contrasting Data Series Colors**
> When you change the color of a data series, be sure to select a color that contrasts effectively with the background of the chart and with the colors of the other data series.

Adding and Formatting Titles

After you enter your data, the basic chart that PowerPoint draws displays no text other than the labels that mark increments along the axes and the text in the legend. Figure 7-4 shows a chart at this early stage. You may want to enter a title for each of the chart axes to identify what they measure. You may also want to add a title above the chart to describe the chart's purpose, especially if you've used the slide title to describe the slide in general rather than the specific chart.

FIGURE 7-4.

A basic chart without titles.

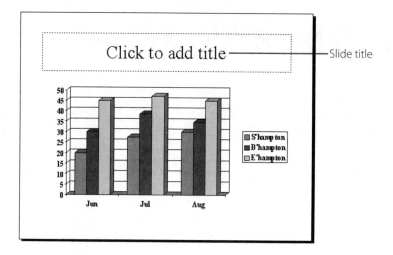

Adding the Titles

To add titles for the chart and its axes, follow these steps:

1 Be sure that the chart is activated in Graph.

2 Choose Chart Options from Graph's Chart menu or the shortcut menu. Graph displays the Chart Options dialog box with the Titles tab, shown on the facing page:

3 Enter the titles here.

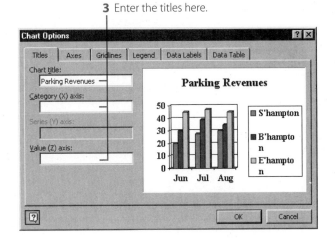

A preview of your chart with the new titles appears in the sample area.

After you add a title, you can reposition it on the chart by following these steps:

1 Click the title. The title's text box appears.

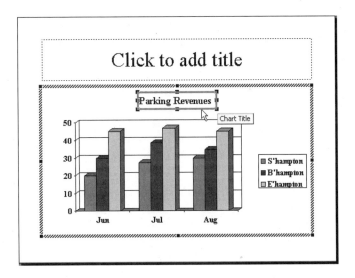

2 Place the pointer on the text box border or on one of the handles, and drag to move the box to the place you want.

II

The Basic Presentation

NOTE

> Dragging the handles does not stretch the text box. Instead, the entire text box moves.

Editing or Removing the Titles

Once you have added a title, you can edit, replace, or remove it.

 SEE ALSO

For more information about editing text, see "Editing Text in Outline View," page 63.

■ To edit a title, click the title once, and then click to position the insertion point where you want to start editing. Edit the text as you would edit any text in PowerPoint. Press Esc or click elsewhere on the chart when you finish editing. If you're editing a vertical axis title, the title is temporarily positioned horizontally. Once you click elsewhere, the title returns to its vertical orientation.

■ To replace a title, click the title so that the text box appears. Type the replacement text.

■ To remove a title, click the title so that the text box appears. Press Delete. Or, click the right mouse button, and from the shortcut menu choose Clear.

Formatting the Titles

The default formatting of the chart determines the formatting of its chart and axis titles. However, you can select and format each title separately—making the chart title larger and the axis titles smaller, for example. In fact, you must select and format each title separately. With titles, you can format:

■ The text of the title

■ The text box border

■ The area within the text box

To format both a title and its text box, double-click the title's text box border. Or, click the text box border once and then on Graph's Standard toolbar, click the Format Title button. The Format Chart Title or Format Axis Title dialog box appears, as shown in Figure 7-5.

 NOTE

> If the title is already selected, be sure to double-click the text box border, or you will select the title text instead.

FIGURE 7-5.

The Format Chart Title dialog box appears when you double-click the chart title.

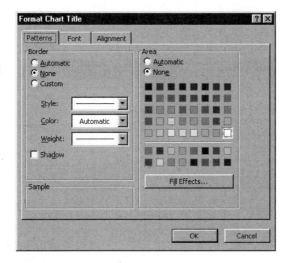

There are three other ways to display the Format Title dialog box. Click the title and then:

- From Graph's Format menu, choose Format Chart Title or Format Axis Title.

- Press Ctrl+1.

- Click the right mouse button on the title and then choose the Format command from the shortcut menu.

To format the color and pattern of the title's text box border and background, use the Patterns tab in the Format Title dialog box. The Border options control the appearance of the text box border. The Area options control the color and pattern of the interior of the text box. The sample in the lower left corner shows a preview of your border and area settings. You can select the None option if you want the text box to have no border or a clear interior. To restore the defaults for the Border or Area options, select the Automatic option.

Select Contrasting Area Colors

When selecting a text box area color, be sure to select a color that contrasts well with the colors of the chart plot area and the title's font color. You may want to change the text color to contrast with the text box area color, which is described in the text that follows.

To add a border to a title, under Border, click Custom, and then select a Style, Color, and Weight option from the drop-down lists. To add a

The Basic Presentation

shadow to the border, select the Shadow check box. The color of the shadow is determined by the Shadow color of the presentation template's color scheme.

To change the appearance of the title's text, follow these steps:

1 Select the title, and open the Format Title dialog box.

2 Click the Font tab.

3 Use the Font, Font Style, Size, Underline, and Color options to change the look of the text.

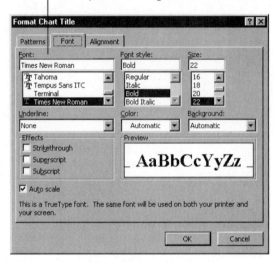

Leaving the Color option set to Automatic applies the text color specified by the presentation template's color scheme. Selecting the Auto Scale check box resizes the text to fit changes you make to the chart's size.

Another way to format just the text of a title, or even just part of the title text, is to click the title and then select only the text you want to format. Use the text formatting buttons on Graph's Formatting toolbar.

The Background option on the Font tab is a fine-tuning control. When set to Automatic, Graph selects a background that contrasts properly with the foreground text color. If the text and text box are the same color, the Automatic setting fills the area behind the letters of the text with a contrasting color to ensure that the text is readable. You can select Transparent to make the area behind the letters transparent so that the text box color shows through, or you can select Opaque to make this area a solid color. When you select Opaque, any pattern is removed from the area behind the text.

Under Effects are check boxes you can use to specify a Strikethrough (a horizontal line through the text), Superscript, or Subscript effect for selected text. Figure 7-6 shows an axis title with a subscript character.

FIGURE 7-6.

An axis title with a subscript character.

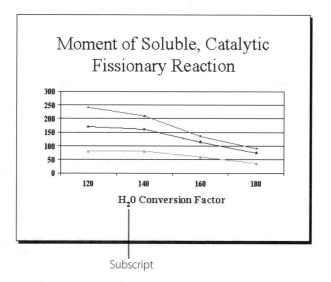

Subscript

To change the alignment of the text within the title's text box, click the Alignment tab of the Format dialog box (see Figure 7-7.) You can then position the text within the text box by selecting options in the Text Alignment section. For example, selecting Left for Horizontal and Center for Vertical aligns the text against the center-left interior edge of the text box.

FIGURE 7-7.

The Alignment tab of the Format Axis Title dialog box.

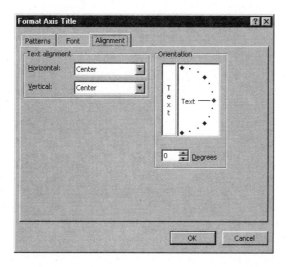

The Basic Presentation

The Orientation option is especially useful for rotating the title vertically next to the *value axis*, or *Z axis*, as shown in Figure 7-8. (In a 3-D chart, the vertical value axis is called the Z axis.)

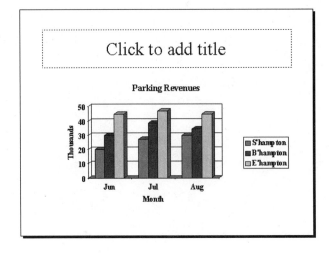

Formatting All the Chart Text

You can change the color and font of all text in the chart at once. Instead of double-clicking the individual titles, double-click the chart area. The Format Chart Area dialog box appears, with the Patterns and Font tabs available.

Adding and Formatting a Legend

The Legend button

If the chart you've created does not already have a legend, you can add one by clicking the Legend button on Graph's Standard toolbar. Or, from Graph's Chart menu, choose Chart Options. On the Legend tab, click the Show Legend check box. The plot area of the chart shrinks, moving in from the right to allow space for the legend.

If you change your mind, you can quickly remove the legend by clicking the Legend button again or by clicking the legend and pressing Delete.

Repositioning the Legend

If you want the legend to appear above, below, or to the left of the chart instead of to the right, you can select a preset legend location by choosing a menu command, or you can drag the legend into position. If you use the menu command, Graph adjusts the plot area to make room for the legend and adjusts the shape of the legend to fit its new location. If you drag the legend, you can place it anywhere you want—even within the chart—as long as it doesn't obscure data. Placing the legend within the chart allows you to recover the space formerly taken up by the legend. You can then stretch the plot area of the chart to make the chart larger and easier to read.

To reposition a legend using a menu command, follow these steps:

1 Click the legend, and then from Graph's Format menu, choose Selected Legend. Or, on Graph's Standard toolbar, click the Format Legend button.

2 Click the Placement tab.

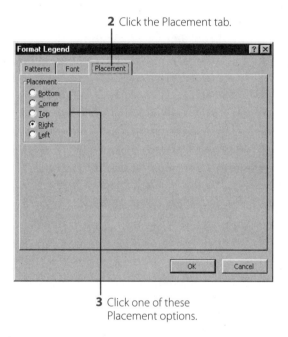

3 Click one of these Placement options.

You can directly drag a legend above, below, or to the left of the chart by clicking it and dragging it to the place you want. When you drag a legend, however, the plot area of the chart does not adjust to make space. Also, the legend does not automatically change shape to fit its new location. You can size and reshape the legend yourself by selecting it and dragging any of its handles. As the boundaries of the legend move, dotted boxes in the legend show the new arrangement of the legend entries, as shown in Figure 7-9 on the next page.

The Basic Presentation

FIGURE 7-9.
Stretching a vertical legend horizontally.

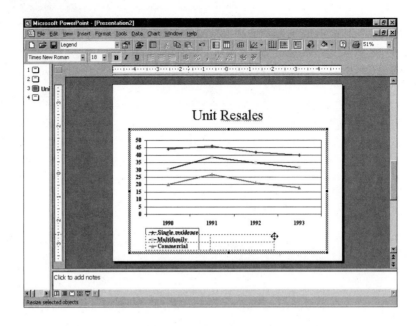

Use the same technique to resize or reshape the plot area of the chart to accommodate the new position of the legend.

⭐ **TIP**

Emphasize Positive Change

When you move a legend from the right or left of the chart to the top or bottom, you can widen the chart to reclaim the legend's space. But when you widen an area, bar, column, or line chart, you decrease the impression of change over time. The lines of a line chart, for example, do not appear to climb or fall as rapidly. You can use this fact to your advantage. To emphasize positive change, place the legend on the left or right side of the chart; to de-emphasize negative change, place the legend above or below the chart.

Formatting the Legend Entries

With a legend, you can format:

- The legend box

- The text within the legend

- An individual legend text entry

- A legend *key*, that is, the small box within the legend that shows the identifying color or pattern

To format the legend box and all the text within it, double-click the legend to display the Format Legend dialog box. To format a legend entry or legend key, double-click the legend entry or legend key to display the Format Legend Entry dialog box or the Format Legend Key dialog box, respectively.

> **NOTE**

When you change the color or pattern of a legend key, the color or pattern of the corresponding data series changes as well.

> **SEE ALSO**
For more information about the Patterns and Font tabs, see "Formatting the Titles," page 164.

In the Format Legend dialog box, use the options on the Patterns tab to format the legend box and legend key, and use the options on the Font tab to format the legend text. These tabs work the same way with legends as they do with chart titles.

Formatting the Axes and Tick Marks

The *axes* of an area, bar, column, line, XY (scatter), bubble, or radar chart are the scales against which the values of the markers in the chart are measured. Pie and doughnut charts do not have axes. By *scaling* the axes, that is, changing the minimum or maximum values, you can emphasize or de-emphasize the chart's data. By adding, removing, and formatting tick marks and tick mark labels, you can make the chart easier to interpret—or harder, if that's your goal.

Showing or Hiding the Axes

By default, axes are displayed on the basic chart that Graph creates, but you can remove one or both axes if you want to display only the markers of the chart. For example, you may not need to give your audience a scale against which to measure the actual values in the chart. Or you may prefer to omit the axes and instead display data point labels, which specify the exact value of each data point.

To include or remove an axis, follow these steps:

1 From Graph's Chart menu, choose Chart Options.

2 In the Chart Options dialog box, click the Axes tab.

3 Select the Category (X) Axis and Value (Y) Axis check boxes to include X and Y axes. Clear the following check boxes to remove axes.

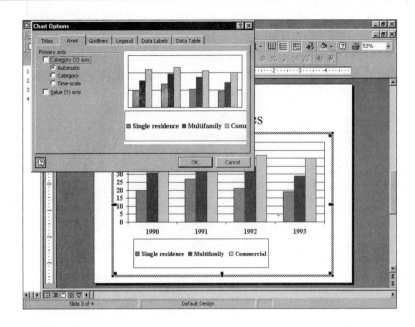

? **SEE ALSO**

For more information about adding data point labels, see "Adding and Formatting Data Labels," page 182.

For example, clearing the Value (Y) Axis check box and adding data point labels produces the chart below.

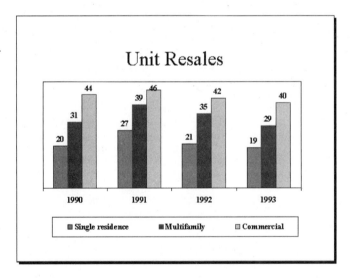

A quick way to remove an axis is to click the axis, and then press Delete or choose Clear from the shortcut menu. This has the same effect as clearing the check boxes on the Axes tab.

Formatting the Axes

To change the color or line style of an axis, double-click the axis. Or, click the axis and then on Graph's Standard toolbar, click the Format Axis button. When the Format Axis dialog box appears, click the Patterns tab, shown in Figure 7-10.

FIGURE 7-10.

The Patterns tab of the Format Axis dialog box.

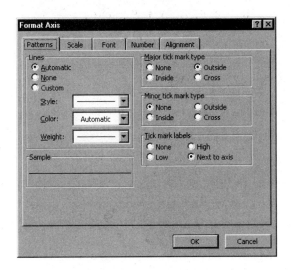

TIP

Easily Select an Axis

If you have trouble double-clicking the axis, try double-clicking any of the labels along the axis. This also opens the Format Axis dialog box.

Under Lines, click the Custom option, and then select a line style, line color, or line weight from the drop-down lists. The Sample box shows a preview of your changes. Click OK to apply your changes and return to the chart. Or, click a different tab to make other formatting changes to the axis.

Scaling the Axes

Graph automatically determines appropriate axis scaling for the numbers you entered in the datasheet. The maximum value of the value axis is set to the next major interval above the largest value in the data. However, you can change the automatic settings to achieve specific effects. To accentuate change in a line chart, for example, you can reduce the maximum value and increase the minimum value.

To change the scale of an axis, use the Scale tab in the Format Axis dialog box. Figure 7-11 on the next page shows the Scale tab for a value (Y) axis. Figure 7-12 shows the Scale tab for a category (X) axis. An XY (scatter) chart has two value axes.

FIGURE 7-11.

The Scale tab in the Format Axis dialog box when a value (Y) axis is selected.

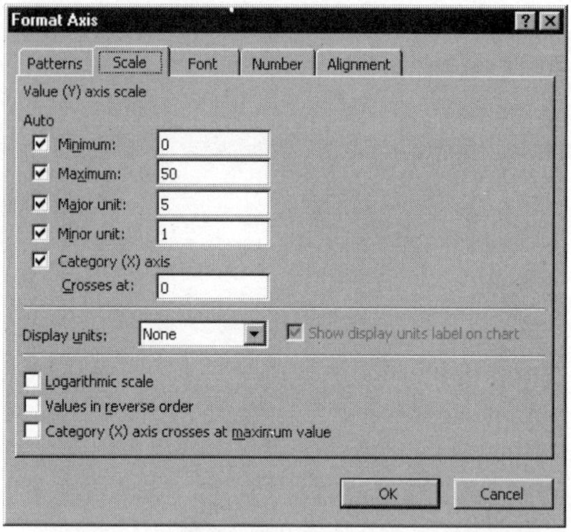

FIGURE 7-12.

The Scale tab in the Format Axis dialog box when a category (X) axis is selected.

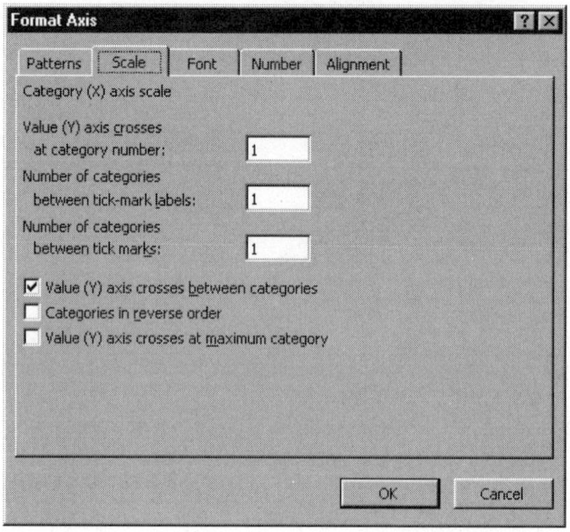

If you've selected a value axis, the Scale tab shows the current axis settings, which are described in Table 7-1. The check boxes under Auto are selected or cleared to show the standard setting that Graph has automatically supplied. When you change a setting, Graph clears the corresponding check box.

TABLE 7-1. The Value (Y) Axis Scale Options

Option	Description
Minimum	The minimum value along the axis.
Maximum	The maximum value along the axis.
Major Unit	The distance between tick marks.
Minor Unit	The distance between the minor units that appear between the major units along the axis.
Category (X) Axis Crosses At	The point on the value axis at which the category axis intersects. This setting might be less than 0 if your data includes negative values.

NOTE

The minimum value of a bar or column chart must always be 0. Anything other than 0 hides the full lengths of the bars or columns. If your audience can't see the full bars or columns, they can't gauge their relative lengths, making the chart misleading.

To use a logarithmic scale along the value axis (appropriate when your data has vast variations), select the Logarithmic Scale check box. Then each successive interval along the axis is 10 times the previous interval. To invert an entire chart, select the Values In Reverse Order check box. Figure 7-13 shows an inverted chart.

FIGURE 7-13.

An inverted chart created by selecting the Values In Reverse Order check box on the Scale tab of the Format Axis dialog box.

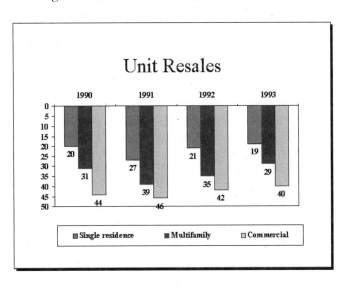

The Basic Presentation

To invert a chart without inverting the value axis, select the Category (X) Axis Crosses At Maximum Value check box. You can use such a chart to show the amount of progress still needed to reach a goal. To do this, set the Maximum option to the value of the goal and enter the progress so far on the datasheet. Figure 7-14 shows such a chart.

FIGURE 7-14.

An inverted chart created by selecting the Category (X) Axis Crosses At Maximum Value check box on the Scale tab of the Format Axis dialog box.

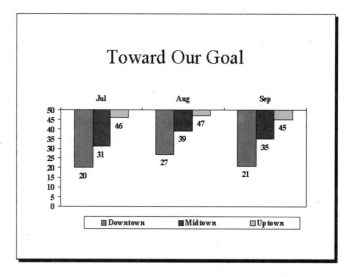

If you've selected a category axis, the Scale tab shows the three edit boxes described in Table 7-2.

Table 7-2. The Category (X) Axis Scale Options

Option	Description
Value (Y) Axis Crosses At Category Number	Moves the value axis to the right along the category axis to the category number in the edit box.
Number Of Categories Between Tick-Mark Labels	Determines the number of labels along the category axis. Enter 2, for example, to show every other label.
Number Of Categories Between Tick Marks	Determines the number of tick marks along the category axis. Enter 2, for example, to show every other tick mark.

The Scale tab for a category axis also has three check boxes.

■ Clearing the Value (Y) Axis Crosses Between Categories check box draws the value axis in the middle of a category rather than between categories.

- Selecting the Categories In Reverse Order check box reverses the order of the categories along the category axis. For example, if the categories are chronological, they appear in reverse chronological order.

- Selecting the Value (Y) Axis Crosses At Maximum Category option moves the value axis to the right side of the chart (or to the left side if the categories are reversed).

Formatting the Tick Marks Along the Axes

Major and minor *tick marks* are the notches that appear along the value axis of a chart to indicate the major and minor units specified on the Scale tab of the Format Axis dialog box. Tick marks also appear between categories on the category axis.

An axis can have major and minor tick marks inside, outside, or crossing the line of the axis. These tick marks automatically have the same color and pattern as the axis to which they are attached. Figure 7-15 shows a chart with major tick marks that appear outside the value axis and minor tick marks that appear inside the axis.

FIGURE 7-15.

An axis with major tick marks outside and minor tick marks inside.

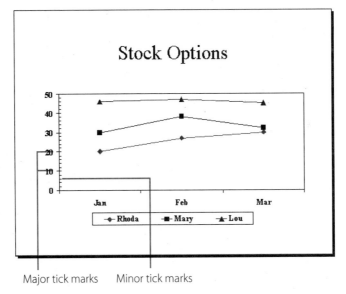

Major tick marks   Minor tick marks

To change the position of the tick marks, follow these steps:

1   Double-click the value or category axis to open the Format Axis dialog box for that axis.

2   Click the Patterns tab.

The Basic Presentation

3 Under Major Tick Mark Type, click the option you want.

4 Under Minor Tick Mark Type, click the option you want.

Formatting the Labels Along the Axes

Tick mark labels appear at the major tick marks of the value axis and between tick marks on the category axis. You control the formatting of these labels by using options on different tabs of the Format Axis dialog box.

To change the location of the tick mark labels, follow these steps:

1 Double-click the value or category axis to open the Format Axis dialog box for that axis.

2 Click the Patterns tab.

3 Under Tick Mark Labels, click the position you want for the labels in relation to the axis.

The default setting, Next To Axis, places the labels near their own axis. To place them near the maximum or minimum values of the other axis, select High or Low, respectively. For example, selecting High moves the tick mark labels to the opposite side of the chart, adjacent to the maximum value on the other axis, as shown in Figure 7-16.

> **NOTE**
>
> The Font tab options for formatting the text of tick mark labels work just like the Font tab options for formatting titles. *For more information about the Font tab options, see "Formatting the Titles," page 164.*

FIGURE 7-16.

A chart for which the Tick Mark Labels option is set to High.

Tick marks

Tick mark labels

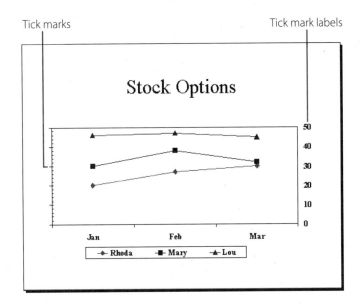

To remove tick mark labels, click None. However, unless you want to show only relative values in a chart, be sure to use data point labels to specify the absolute values.

Use the options on the Number tab, shown in Figure 7-17, to modify the formatting of the numbers along a numeric axis. If the Linked To Source check box is selected, these numbers have the same formatting as the numbers in the datasheet. To change the formatting, click a category from the Category list, and then select any other options as presented for that category. The Sample number in the dialog box reflects the selected number formatting.

FIGURE 7-17.

The Number tab of the Format Axis dialog box.

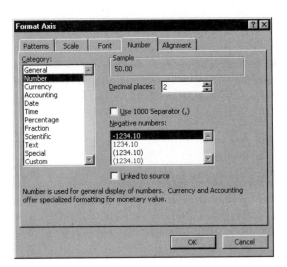

Use the options on the Alignment tab to change the orientation of the tick mark labels. The Automatic setting (horizontal) usually works best for the value tick mark labels, but you may want to select a vertical orientation for the category tick mark labels if the labels are long. Figure 7-18 shows a chart with –90-degree tick mark labels along the category axis.

FIGURE 7-18.

A chart with –90-degree tick mark labels along the category axis.

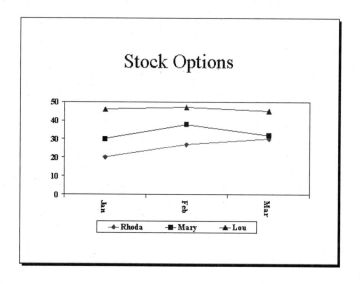

> **NOTE**
>
> Setting the tick mark label orientation to vertical leaves less vertical space for the chart, so the chart becomes shorter without a corresponding change in its width. Changing a chart only vertically or only horizontally can increase or decrease the impression of change.

Showing or Hiding Gridlines

The Category Axis Gridlines button

The Value Axis Gridlines button

Gridlines extend from major unit tick marks and help you gauge the heights of areas and lines, the lengths of bars and columns, and the position of data points. The easiest way to turn gridlines on or off is to click the Axis Gridlines buttons on Graph's Standard toolbar. Click once to turn on gridlines, and click again to turn them off. Or, from Graph's Chart menu, choose Chart Options, and then specify which gridlines are showing or hiding on the Gridlines tab.

Formatting the Gridlines

When gridlines are showing, you can format them by double-clicking them to display the Format Gridlines dialog box. On the Patterns tab, use the Custom options to set the style, color, and weight of the gridlines. Click the Automatic option to return gridlines to their default settings.

NOTE

Use the options on the Scale tab in the Format Gridlines dialog box to set the scaling of the axis from which the gridlines emanate. These are the same options provided on the Scale tab in the Format Axis dialog box. *For more information about scaling, see "Scaling the Axes," page 173.*

Modifying the Chart Background

A chart has two background areas you can format: the *plot area* immediately behind the markers, axes, and axis tick mark labels; and the *chart area* within the heavy border surrounding the chart, including the area occupied by the legend and the chart title. To identify each area of the chart, point to the area and view the ScreenTip.

Formatting the Plot Area

To format the plot area, first double-click within the chart but away from the axes or markers. If the chart is three-dimensional, double-click just outside the chart, but away from the axes or axis labels. You can also click once to select the plot area and, when you see a border appear around the plot area, choose Selected Plot Area from Graph's Format menu. In the Format Plot Area dialog box, use the options under the Border and Area to change the look of the plot area. Figure 7-19 shows the plot area of a chart filled with a texture.

FIGURE 7-19.

The plot area of a chart filled with a texture.

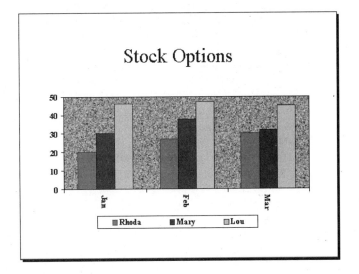

II

The Basic Presentation

Formatting the Chart Area

To format the chart area, double-click within the heavy border of the chart but outside the plot area. Or, click once to select the chart area, and then from Graph's Format menu, choose Selected Chart Area. The Format Chart Area dialog box appears.

On the Patterns tab, use the options under Border and Area to change the look of the border and the interior of the chart area. You can select a border style, color, and weight, and you can fill the chart area with a background color and pattern. On the Font tab, use the options to change the look of all the text in the chart. Figure 7-20 shows a line chart with contrasting formatting in the plot and chart areas.

FIGURE 7-20.

A line chart with contrasting chart and plot area formatting.

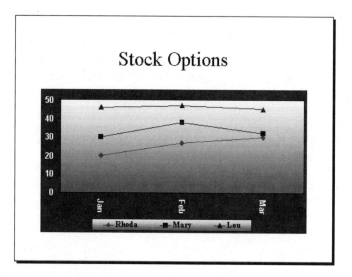

NOTE

The Replace Fonts command on PowerPoint's Tools menu, which changes the fonts used throughout a presentation, does not affect the fonts used by chart text. After changing the presentation font, you can quickly change a chart's font to match by using the options on the Font tab of the Format Chart Area dialog box. This way, you don't have to select and format each chart text object individually.

Adding and Formatting Data Labels

The markers of a data series provide only an approximate representation of the numbers in the datasheet. To show the actual numbers, you can either provide a table of numbers or place the numbers directly on the markers as data labels.

To add data labels to a data series, follow these steps:

1 Double-click the data series to which you want to add data labels.

2 In the Format Data Series dialog box, click the Data Labels tab.

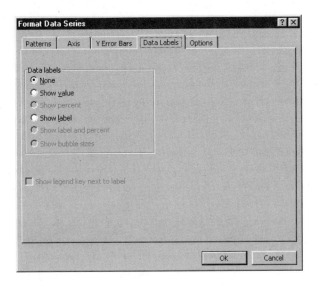

With the Data Labels tab, you can:

- Click Show Value to display the numeric value of each data point in the series.

- Click Show Label to display the category assigned to the data point.

Depending on the type of chart you're creating, you might have other options on this tab as well:

- Click Show Label And Percent to display both the category or series names and the percentages.

- Click Show Percent if the chart is a stacked bar, stacked column, pie, or doughnut chart and you want to show the percentages represented by the segments or slices.

- Click Show Label to display the series names in an area chart.

- Click Show Bubble Sizes to display the size of the bubbles in a bubble chart.

If the Show Legend Key Next To Label check box is available, you can check it to place the legend key next to the data label.

TIP

> ### Add a Data Label to a Single Marker
> You can add a data label to a single marker—an outstanding result, for example—by clicking the marker first to select the data series and then clicking it again to select the individual data point. Double-click the data point marker to open the Format Data Point dialog box. This dialog box contains the same Data Labels and Patterns tabs as the Format Data Series dialog box but changes only the selected data point.

 TIP

> ### Add Data Labels to All Markers
> To add data labels to all the markers in the chart, click the chart area and then from the Graph's Chart menu, choose Chart Options. The Data Labels tab in the Chart Options dialog box shows the same options as the Data Labels tab of the Format Data Series dialog box. The changes you make here apply to all markers in the chart.

To format the data labels on a chart, double-click any data label in a series. The Format Data Labels dialog box appears. The options on the four tabs of the dialog box (Patterns, Font, Number, and Alignment) work just as they do when you format other text in a chart. For example, you can use the options on the Patterns tab to create a filled box around each data label and the options on the Number tab to change the number of decimal places shown in the data labels.

To format a single data label, click the data label once to select the series, and then click the data label a second time to select the individual label. Double-click the border of that data label, and use the options in the Format Data Labels dialog box as usual. You can also select a single data label, click to position the insertion point, and then edit or add text. For example, you might want to add text to a data label, as shown in Figure 7-21.

 TIP

> ### An Alternative to Crowding Charts
> Don't try to crowd too many data labels on a chart. Just include data labels for the most significant numbers. Or, add a table to the slide or to the following slide showing the numbers.

FIGURE 7-21.

Text added to a data label.

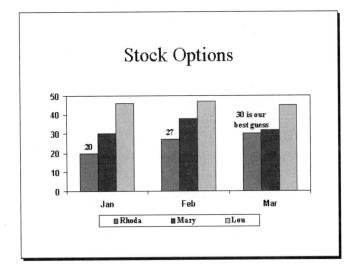

Moving and Resizing Chart Objects

You've already seen that you can move a chart's title or legend by dragging its border. You can also drag the border of the entire chart to move it on the slide, and drag the plot area to move or resize the area of the chart bounded by the axes and axis labels. (Enlarging the plot area of a chart can make interpreting the markers easier, but changing the shape of the plot area alters the impression of change in the chart.) You can even drag each data label to reposition it relative to its data point or marker.

To move or resize a chart object, click the object and then drag the object's border. To drag a data label, for example, first click the data label to select it, and then drag the border surrounding the data label.

After you finish formatting the chart, click outside the chart's border to redisplay PowerPoint's menus and toolbars. Later, if you want to make additional changes to the chart, you can reopen Graph by simply double-clicking the chart.

3-D Chart Formatting

PowerPoint's 3-D chart types are often worthy alternatives for their 2-D equivalents. They add a touch of depth and, if you want, perspective. All the techniques that format 2-D charts apply to 3-D charts. You can also apply additional formatting options to 3-D charts. These options are discussed in this section.

II

The Basic Presentation

Adjusting the 3-D View

PowerPoint offers 3-D versions of area, bar, column, line, and pie charts as subtypes when you choose a new chart type. You can slant, rotate, and change the height of 3-D charts by changing their 3-D view. For all types other than 3-D bar and 3-D pie charts, you can also increase the illusion of depth by adding perspective.

To change both the *elevation* (the forward slant) and the *rotation* (the horizontal angle) of a 3-D chart, you don't even have to use a dialog box. You can simply drag the corners of the chart by following these steps:

1 Click the walls or the floor of the chart. A handle, labeled as "corners" in the ScreenTip, appears at every corner of an imaginary 3-D box that encloses the chart. (If you see handles only at the corners of the back wall, try clicking the corner again or clicking a different corner.)

2 Place the mouse pointer on one of the corner handles, hold down the mouse button, and drag the mouse slightly. The outlines of the imaginary box appear. If you hold down the Ctrl key as you drag, you see outlines of the markers, too, as shown:

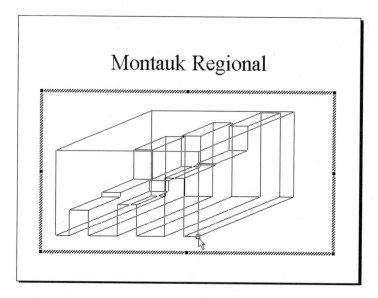

3 Still holding down the mouse button, drag the corner up or down to change the elevation, or drag the corner left or right to rotate the chart.

4 Release the mouse button. The chart is redrawn with the new elevation or rotation.

You can also change the elevation and rotation of a 3-D chart using options in the 3-D View dialog box. Click the chart and then from Graph's Chart menu, choose 3-D View to open the dialog box shown in Figure 7-22. As you can see, you can use additional options to change the height of 3-D charts and, in some charts, add perspective.

FIGURE 7-22.

The 3-D View dialog box.

Increase elevation   Decrease elevation   Decrease perspective   Increase perspective

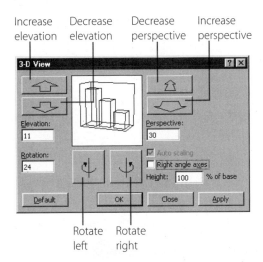

Rotate left   Rotate right

In the 3-D View dialog box, a model of the 3-D chart shows the current option settings. By viewing the model as you change the options, you can determine how the actual chart will look when you click OK.

■ To change the elevation of the chart, enter a number in the Elevation edit box. Or, click the up or down arrow button to the left of the model to increase or decrease the elevation. Each click changes the elevation by 5 degrees. Valid elevation numbers are between –90 and 90 degrees.

■ To change the rotation, enter a number in the Rotation edit box. Or, click the rotate left or rotate right button below the model. Each click changes the rotation by 10 degrees. Valid rotation values are between 0 and 360 degrees.

■ To change the height of the chart, first select the Right Angle Axes check box (so the chart has no perspective), clear the Auto Scaling check box, and then edit the number in the Height edit box. The height of the chart is specified as a percentage (0 to 100 percent) of the length of the base. Click Apply to see the result in your chart. To let PowerPoint select a height that is appropriate for the chart, select the Auto Scaling check box.

II

The Basic Presentation

NOTE

> You cannot change the height of a 3-D pie chart.

- To add perspective, clear the Right Angle Axes check box. Then edit the number in the Perspective edit box or click the up or down arrow button to the right of the model to decrease or increase perspective. Each click changes the perspective by 5 units. Valid perspective values are 0 to 100. The default perspective setting of 30 is just enough to give the chart a true sense of depth without the kind of distortion shown in Figure 7-23.

FIGURE 7-23.

A rotated 3-D column chart distorted by a Perspective setting of 55.

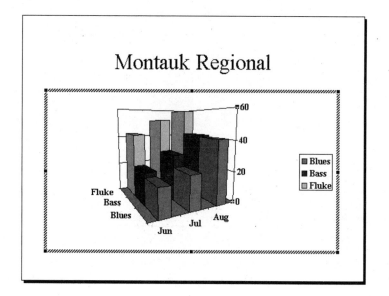

 NOTE

> The Right Angle Axes check box cannot be cleared for 3-D bar charts or 3-D pie charts because these charts cannot have perspective.

After you change the options in the 3-D View dialog box, click Apply to apply the new settings without closing the dialog box. Or, click OK to return to the chart. If you click Apply, drag the dialog box aside to see the revised chart. If you want to return the chart to its original default 3-D view settings, click Default.

To change the depth of a 3-D chart, click a series in the chart and then from Graph's Format menu, choose Selected Data Series. In the Format Data Series dialog box, click the Options tab. Figure 7-24 shows the Options tab of the dialog box. Then change the value in the Chart Depth edit box. Valid chart depth values range from 20 to 2000.

FIGURE 7-24.

The Options tab of the Format Data Series dialog box.

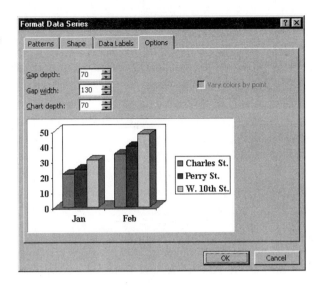

Formatting 3-D Chart Objects

3-D charts have unique chart objects that 2-D charts do not have. Figure 7-25 identifies the chart objects that are unique to 3-D charts.

FIGURE 7-25.

The unique chart objects of a 3-D column chart.

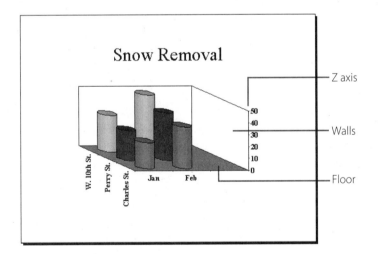

Formatting the Axes

When the series in a 3-D chart appears behind one another at various depths in the chart, a third axis—the series axis—extends along the floor of the chart from front to back. This is the Y axis. The category axis remains the X axis, but the value axis is the Z axis, and rises from the floor. The chart shown in Figure 7-25 shows all three axes.

II

The Basic Presentation

Formatting the value axis of a 3-D chart is just like formatting the value axis of a 2-D chart. Double-click the value axis to display the Format Axis dialog box. The options on the various tabs of this dialog box are the same as those for 2-D charts. However, the Scale tab includes an additional option, Floor (XY Plane) Crosses At, which you can use to change the position of the floor within a 3-D area, bar, column, line, or surface chart.

When you change the vertical position of the floor, markers in 3-D area and column charts extend either above the floor or below the floor, but they do not cross the floor to reach their proper length along the value axis. Figure 7-26 shows a chart with the floor set at 35. Such a chart can show an excess above or deficiency below a budget or target value. In 3-D bar charts, the floor runs vertically, so markers extend to the left or right of the floor. In 3-D line and 3-D surface charts, the floor appears as a transparent panel within the chart and has no effect on the display of the lines or surface; values extend above or below the floor.

FIGURE 7-26.

A chart in which the floor (XY plane) crosses at 35.

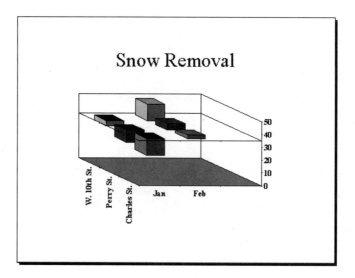

You can select the Floor (XY Plane) Crosses At Minimum Value check box to return the floor to the automatic minimum value of the value axis.

Formatting the Walls and Floor

Except for 3-D pie charts, all 3-D chart types have walls and a floor. The walls are behind and to the side of the markers, and the markers rest on the floor.

By double-clicking the walls of a 3-D chart, you can open the Format Walls dialog box. Use the options under Border and Area to change the border and surface color, pattern, or texture of the walls. Figure 7-27 shows a 3-D chart with textured walls. You format the floor separately from the walls. Double-click the floor to open the Format Floor dialog box, and again, use the options under Border and Area to change the color, pattern, or texture of the floor.

FIGURE 7-27.

Textured walls in a 3-D chart

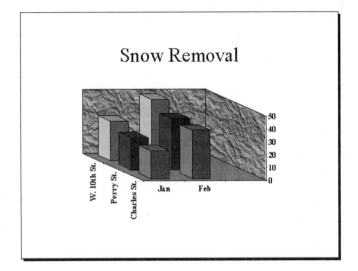

Formatting the Gridlines

When a chart has three axes, you can add major and minor gridlines to all three axes. From Graph's Chart menu, choose Chart Options, and then click the Gridlines tab (shown in Figure 7-28). Use this tab to turn on major and minor gridlines for the category, series, and value axes.

FIGURE 7-28.

The Gridlines options for a 3-D chart.

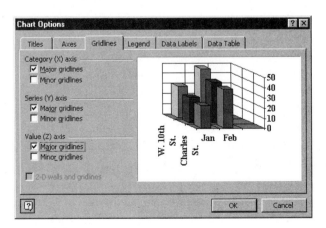

The Basic Presentation

When 3-D charts contain markers that look three-dimensional but are not at planes of different depths, you can display 2-D walls and gridlines by selecting the 2-D Walls And Gridlines check box at the bottom of the Gridlines tab in the Chart Options dialog box.

Formatting Area, Bar, Column, and Line Charts

In Chapter 6, while creating basic charts, you learned about selecting a chart type and subtype. Each subtype has a unique style and arrangement of markers that convey a different message. Changing the subtype is the quickest way to dramatically change the look of a chart.

To change the subtype of a chart, select the chart, and then from Graph's Chart menu, choose Chart Type. Select the chart subtype you want.

If you select the 2-D stacked bar or 2-D stacked column subtype, you can connect the series in the columns with lines. In the Format Data Series dialog box, click the Options tab, and then select the Series Lines check box.

Creating Combination Charts

You can't mix chart types in a 3-D chart.

In PowerPoint, you can mix different 2-D chart types, selecting the best chart type for each series or group of series in the chart. You might use a line for one series and columns for another to compare the fluctuating change of a series (for example, sales volume) in response to incremental adjustments in another series (for example, price). Figure 7-29 shows such a chart.

To change the chart type of one or more series, select the series, and then from Graph's Chart menu, choose Chart Type. Then select a different 2-D chart type from the palette of chart types. In the Chart Type dialog box, be sure to select the Apply To Selection check box. To return all series to one type, click the chart area and then select a chart type.

When a chart has two or more series with different chart types, you can add a secondary category or value axis against which you can plot one or more of the chart type groups. A secondary axis appears on the opposite side of the chart and is scaled according to the series assigned to it. As a result, the same chart can show two chart types that have very different ranges of values. For example, you might plot the price of a product over time against the primary axis, which ranges from $1.40 to $1.80, and plot the units sold against the secondary axis, which ranges from 190 to 210.

FIGURE 7-29.

A chart that compares price (shown as a line) and volume (shown as columns).

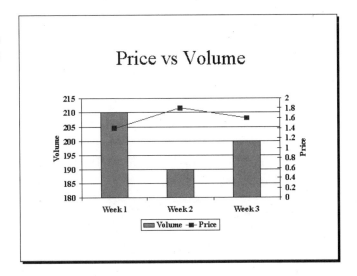

To add a secondary axis, from Graph's Chart menu, choose Chart Options. In the Chart Options dialog box, click the Axes tab. Under Secondary Axis, select the Category (X) Axis check box or the Value (Y) Axis check box. Select one or both check boxes to add one or two axes to the chart.

To assign a series to a secondary axis, click the series and then from Graph's Chart menu, choose Chart Options. Click the Axes tab. Select either the Primary Axis or Secondary Axis check box, as shown in Figure 7-30.

FIGURE 7-30.

The Axes tab of the Chart Options dialog box.

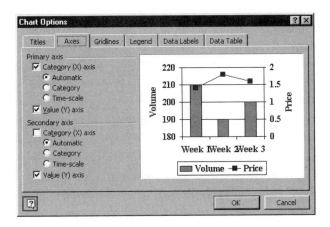

Adjusting the Spacing
of Areas, Bars, Columns, and Lines

You can modify the spacing, or the *gap width*, between 2-D and 3-D areas, bars, and columns, and between 3-D lines. For 3-D charts, you can also set the *gap depth*. For 2-D bar and column charts, you can also use the Overlap option. To do this, follow these steps:

1 Double-click the data series. The Format Data Series dialog box appears.

2 Click the Options tab.

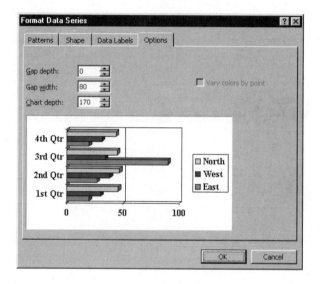

Depending on the type of chart you're creating, you'll have the Gap Width, Gap Depth, or Overlap edit boxes available.

The bars or columns of a default chart are arranged in clusters along the category axis. To change the spacing between clusters, change the Gap Width setting, which can range from 0 to 500 percent of the width of a single bar or column. A setting of 0 percent creates a step chart or histogram. The default setting of 150 percent leaves 1.5 times the width of a bar or column between each cluster. As you increase the gap width, the width of the bars or columns decreases.

To separate the areas, bars, columns, or lines along the Y axis of a 3-D chart, change the Gap Depth setting on the Options tab. The gap depth, like the gap width, is calculated as a percentage of the depth of a single marker.

To change the spacing of 2-D bars or columns within a cluster, rather than between clusters, change the Overlap setting. At 0 percent, the bars or columns are side by side without overlapping. At 100 percent, they overlap completely. Figure 7-31 shows a column chart with a 50-percent overlap and a 100-percent gap width.

FIGURE 7-31.

A column chart with a 50-percent overlap and a 100-percent gap width.

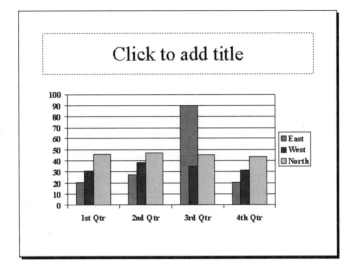

TIP

Separating Markers within a Cluster

To separate the bars or columns within a cluster, you can enter a negative overlap percentage. An overlap setting of –50 percent, for example, separates the columns within a cluster by half the width of a single column.

Adding Drop Lines to Area and Line Charts

Drop lines are vertical lines that help identify the data points of 2-D and 3-D area and line charts. They run from the data points of the areas or lines to the category axis of the chart. Figure 7-32 on the next page shows a 3-D line chart with drop lines.

To turn on drop lines, double-click the data series. In the Format Data Series dialog box, click the Options tab. Select the Drop Lines check box.

The Basic Presentation

FIGURE 7-32.

A 3-D line chart with drop lines.

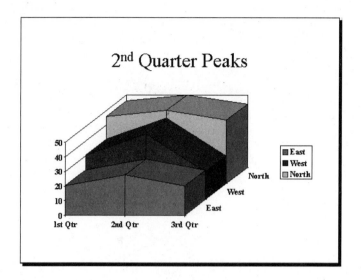

Adding High-Low Lines to Line Charts

If you want to depict the range over which a measurement varies, such as the high and low temperature of the day or the high and low test scores of different groups of people, you can add high-low lines to individual lines or to all lines in a 2-D line chart. Figure 7-33 shows high-low lines added to all the data series in a temperature fluctuation chart.

FIGURE 7-33.

High-low lines added to a temperature fluctuation chart.

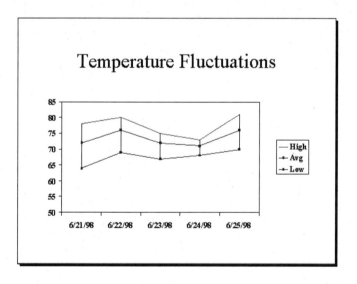

You can create a chart that shows discrete ranges of measurements instead of connected series. To do this, follow these steps:

1 Double-click the data series to open the Format Data Series dialog box.

2 Click the Options tab.

3 Select the High-Low Lines check box.

4 Click the Patterns tab.

5 Under Line, click the None options.

Figure 7-34 shows the resulting temperature fluctuations chart.

FIGURE 7-34.

A 2-D line chart with high-low lines and individual markers instead of connected lines.

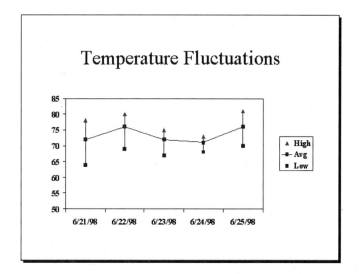

To change the style, color, and weight of drop lines and high-low lines, first double-click a line. On the Patterns tab, make the changes you want under Line.

Showing and Predicting Trends with Trendlines

When working with area, bar, column, line, and XY (scatter) charts, you can add an automatic regression line that depicts the general trend of the numbers in a data series and predicts approximate future data points based on the existing data. The regression line, called a *trendline*, overlays the series markers.

The default trendline is a linear regression that depicts a "best fit" straight line passing nearest to all the data points. You can select one of five other regression types, each based on a different mathematical regression formula. You can also format the trendline to:

■ Set the intercept.

■ Change the number of forecast periods.

■ Display the trendline name, the R-squared value, or the regression equation on the chart.

 **NOTE**

> If terms like "intercept" and "R-squared value" puzzle you, you might want to stick with a simple linear regression trendline and leave the higher math to the statisticians.

Figure 7-35 shows standard linear regression lines in a chart.

FIGURE 7-35.

Linear regression lines
on a column chart.

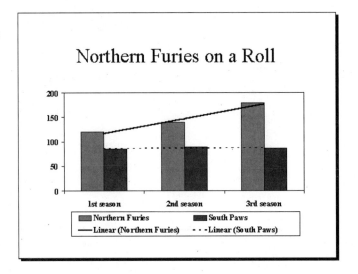

To add a trendline to a chart, from Graph's Chart menu, choose Add Trendline. On the Type tab, shown in Figure 7-36, select a Trend/Regression Type, and under Based On Series, click the series upon which the trend line will be based.

To delete a trendline quickly, select the line and then press Delete. Or, choose Clear from the shortcut menu.

To format a trendline, double-click it. In the Format Trendline dialog box, click the Options tab. You can enter a custom trendline name that will replace the default name in the legend. Use the options under Forecast to extend the trendline beyond the actual data by adding a number of forecast periods forward and backward. If regressions are the stuff of your daily life, you will want to vary the intercept by entering values in the Set Intercept edit box and display the math behind the trendline by selecting the Display Equation On Chart and Display R-Squared Value On Chart check boxes.

FIGURE 7-36.

The Type tab of the Add Trendline dialog box.

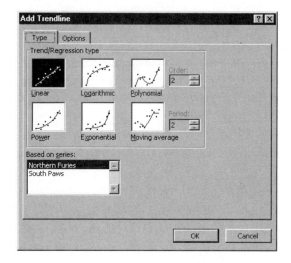

To change the line style, color, and weight of the regression line, in the Format Trendline dialog box, use the options on the Patterns tab.

Allowing for Error with Error Bars

Error bars in a chart allow you to depict the minor deviations that you expect in your data. You can enter this "margin of error" as:

- A fixed number.

- A percentage.

- The number of standard deviations from the mean of plotted values.

- The standard error.

You can also add a custom plus and minus error value. 2-D area, bar, column, and line charts have Y error bars that apply to the Y axis only. XY (scatter) charts can have both X error bars and Y error bars. Figure 7-37 on the next page shows a column chart with Y error bars.

To add error bars that extend from each data point in a series, double-click each series in turn. In the Format Data Series dialog box, click the Y Error Bars tab, shown in Figure 7-38 on the next page.

II

The Basic Presentation

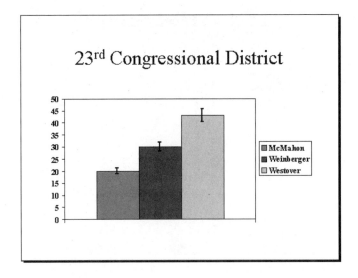

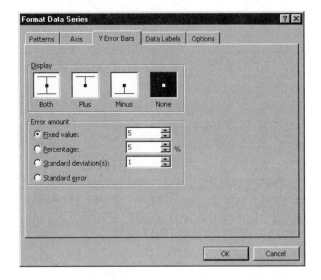

On the Y Error Bars tab, select a display type by clicking Both, Plus, Minus, or None under Display section. Under Error Amount, select an error type and amount. If the chart is an XY chart, the Format Data Series dialog box also includes the X Error Bars tab, including the same options.

To format the error bars, double-click one of the error bars, and then in the Format Error Bars dialog box, click the Patterns tab. Select the style, color, and weight of the bars. You can also select one of two marker styles: a T or a straight line extending from the data point.

Varying the Colors of a Single Series Chart

When a chart displays only one series, you can have each marker in the series display a different color rather than all one color. Double-click the series, and in the Format Data Series dialog box, click the Options tab, and then select the Vary Colors By Point check box. The Vary Colors By Point check box is not available for 2-D area, 3-D area, or 3-D surface charts.

 **NOTE**

A related option, Vary Colors By Slice, applies a different color to each slice in a pie or ring in a doughnut chart. This check box is selected by default.

Formatting Pie and Doughnut Charts

Pie and doughnut charts offer special formatting options that are unique to their chart types. You can select and format the entire pie or doughnut group, or you can select and format a pie slice, a doughnut ring, or a segment of a doughnut ring.

Separating Slices

To call attention to certain pie slices, you can separate them from the rest of the pie by dragging them away from the center one by one. You can also separate segments of the outermost doughnut ring by dragging them.

Labeling Slices

The easiest way to label the slices of a pie is to select Chart Options from Graph's Chart menu, and then click the Data Labels tab. Select the Data Label option you want.

- Selecting Show Value places the value of each slice next to the slice.

- Selecting Show Percent shows the calculated percentage of each slice.

- Selecting Show Label shows the name of the slice. You may prefer to show slice names rather than a legend so that the viewer can see what each slice represents without having to match the legend key to the slice colors.

- Selecting Show Label And Percent shows both the name and percentage next to each slice, as shown in Figure 7-39 on the next page.

The Basic Presentation

FIGURE 7-39.
A pie chart with
label and percent
data labels.

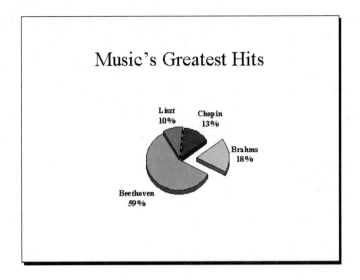

If you want to label just a single slice, first click that slice, and then from Graph's Chart menu, choose Chart Options. Click the Data Labels tab and select the data label option you want.

> **What You Can't Do with Pie Slice Labels**
>
> You can drag the values, percentages, or labels onto their corresponding pie slices. But if you have turned on the Show Label And Percent option, you cannot drag the percentages onto the slices and leave the labels off to the side unless you convert the pie to graphic objects. *For more information, see "Converting a Chart to Graphic Objects," page 206.*

Varying Colors by Slice

By default, the Vary Colors By Slice check box on the Options tab of the Format Data Series dialog box is selected. If you clear this check box, all slices become the same color, and the legend is no longer helpful unless the slices are filled with different patterns.

Changing the Angle of the First Slice

On the Options tab of the Format Data Series dialog box or the Format Doughnut Group dialog box, you can set the Angle Of First Slice edit box to rotate the entire pie or doughnut. Slices or segments start in the location specified by the Angle Of First Slice edit box and are plotted clockwise within the pie. The default setting is 0 degrees. To rotate the pie 90 degrees to the right, for example, change the Angle Of First Slice setting to 90 degrees.

NOTE

You can also rotate a 3-D pie chart by changing the Rotation setting in the Format 3-D View dialog box. *For more information about rotating a 3-D chart, see "Adjusting the 3-D View," page 186.*

Changing the Hole Size of a Doughnut Chart

Reducing the hole size of a doughnut chart enlarges the segments so that they are easier to see. The default hole size, specified as a percentage of the width of the chart, is 50 percent. To change the hole size, in the Format Data Series dialog box, click the Options tab, and then simply modify the Doughnut Hole Size percentage edit box.

Formatting Radar and 3-D Surface Charts

The size of the ring of each data series in a radar chart shows the aggregate of the values in the series. Where the ring bulges from the center, the series shows the greatest measurements. For example, Figure 7-40 shows a radar chart in which each ring represents the yearly sales, by month, of a store in a three-store chain. As you can see, the sales of all three stores swelled during the months before Christmas. The store with the largest ring, Fifth Ave., had the greatest overall sales.

FIGURE 7-40.

A radar chart showing the monthly sales of three stores.

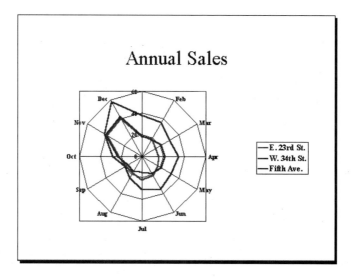

In a radar chart, value (Y) axes extend from the center of the chart, evenly spaced, in different directions. Each data point in the series has

The Basic Presentation

its own value axis. Double-clicking any axis and changing a setting in the Format Axis dialog box formats all the axes at once. Tick mark labels appear only on the axis that rises vertically from the center of the chart.

To format a radar chart, double-click a series in the chart and then change the settings in the Format Data Series dialog box. To label the axes of the radar chart, on the Options tab, select the Category Labels check box. To display markers at each data point, from Graph's Chart menu, choose Chart Type, and then select the second radar chart subtype. To display each series as a filled ring, select the third subtype.

Formatting Surface Chart Intervals

In a surface chart, each height interval along the vertical (Z) axis—the 3-D axis—has its own color, as shown in the chart's legend. The color of a 3-D surface chart region indicates the height interval along the Z axis that the region has reached. If you want to change the colors of the Z axis intervals, double-click the legend keys. In the Format Legend dialog box, click the Patterns tab, and then under Area, change the Color or Fill Effects options.

Creating Picture Charts

By filling the markers of a chart with pictures, you can create a picture chart. The pictures can identify the series and communicate more information at a glance, as shown in Figure 7-41.

FIGURE 7-41.

A picture chart.

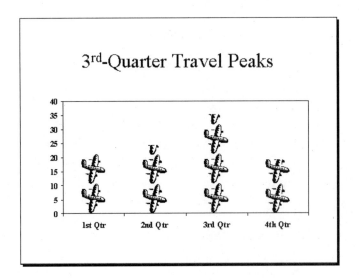

To turn a regular chart into a picture chart, follow these steps:

1 With the chart activated in Graph, double-click one of the series of markers you want to replace with pictures. The Format Data Series dialog box appears.

2 Click the Patterns tab, and then under Area, click the Fill Effects button.

3 In the Fill Effects dialog box, click the Picture tab.

4 Click the Select Picture button to choose a picture file. The Select Picture dialog box appears.

5 Use the Look In box, the Up One Level button, and the list of folders and files to browse and find the picture file you want.

6 Click the Insert button. The picture appears in the Fill Effects dialog box.

7 Under Format, you can select the Stretch option to stretch the image to fill the markers. Or, select the Stack option to stack the pictures instead, using as many copies of the picture at its original size as necessary to fill the marker. You can also stack the pictures at a size you specify with the Stack And Scale To option.

 NOTE

When you fill the markers of a line, XY, or radar chart with pictures, the pictures always appear at their original size. They cannot be stretched, stacked, or scaled.

Saving Chart Formatting as a Custom Chart Type

After creating a special combination of chart formatting that you like, you can save the combination as a custom chart type that you can then quickly apply to other charts. To create a new custom chart type, follow these steps:

1 Activate a completed chart, and then from Graph's Chart menu, choose Chart Type. The Chart Type dialog box appears.

2 Click the Custom Types tab.

3 Under Select From, click the User-Defined option.

4 Click the Add button. The Add Custom Chart Type dialog box appears.

The Basic Presentation

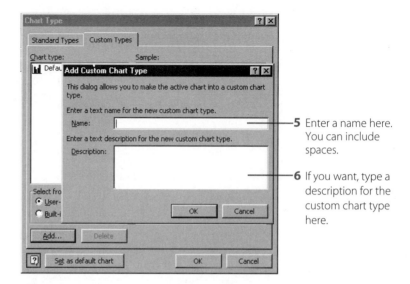

5 Enter a name here. You can include spaces.

6 If you want, type a description for the custom chart type here.

7 Click OK. The name of your new chart type appears in the Chart Type list, and a picture of the chart type as you created it appears in the Sample dialog box.

To delete a custom chart type, follow steps 1 through 3 above. Then, click the name of the custom chart type you want to delete and click the Delete button.

Converting a Chart to Graphic Objects

PowerPoint offers a wealth of choices that allow you to change the appearance of a chart. But for the ultimate in flexibility, you can convert the chart to a collection of graphic objects, each of which can be modified individually. You can convert the columns of a column chart to a collection of rectangles, for example, and then revise them with PowerPoint's comprehensive drawing and editing commands.

(?) SEE ALSO

For more information about editing graphic objects, see "Editing Objects," page 313.

When you convert a chart to a set of graphic objects, it loses its identification as a chart object that represents an underlying set of data. You can no longer use Graph's commands and controls, and the datasheet is no longer available. The result of the conversion is a picture of what was once a chart. And the conversion process is a one-way street; you cannot convert the collection of graphic objects back to a chart.

Before you convert a chart to a set of graphic objects, you might want to copy the chart to another presentation slide. Then you can convert the copy of the chart to graphic objects, knowing that you can always return to the original, unchanged chart. You can even hide the slide containing the original chart so that you can access it even though it does not appear when you display the presentation.

To convert a chart to a collection of graphic objects, follow these steps:

1 Click the chart once to select it without activating it in Graph.

2 On PowerPoint's Drawing toolbar, click the drop-down arrow next to the Draw list, and then choose Ungroup from the drop-down list. PowerPoint warns you that proceeding will permanently discard any embedded data, and asks whether you want to convert the chart to drawing objects.

3 Click Yes to convert the chart. After a moment, the chart reappears as a collection of graphic objects, each of which is selected.

4 Click outside the chart to deselect the objects.

Now you can select the objects one by one and make any necessary modifications.

In this chapter, you learned how to modify the appearance of the charts in your presentation. In the next chapter, you'll learn how to add organization charts to your presentation.

Adding Organization Charts

An organization chart, or *org chart*, shows the hierarchy of an organization using a series of boxes and connecting lines. A classic hierarchy is the military's chain of command—officers and enlisted men and women. But an org chart can also depict the structure of a company, a division within a company or a department of the government, or even groups of organizations that are affiliated in a "top-down" arrangement. It might even be used to represent information other than an organization of people, such as types of books by different authors or categories of events at a sporting competition.

This chapter introduces you to PowerPoint's built-in organization chart tool. You'll learn how to create an org chart slide from scratch, how to add an org chart to an existing slide, and how to incorporate an existing org chart in a presentation. In addition, you'll learn how to create and modify the org chart's structure and how to format its text, boxes, and connecting lines.

Understanding Org Chart Basics

The procedure you use to add an organization chart to your presentation depends on where you want the chart to appear. If you want the org chart to be on a new slide that is dedicated to the chart, you can create a new slide and then select a layout that includes an org chart placeholder. If you want the chart to be on an existing slide or if you want to use an existing org chart, you can add an org chart object to a slide.

Creating an Org Chart Slide

PowerPoint's autolayouts make it easy to create an org chart slide for a presentation. When you start a new slide and select the Organization Chart autolayout, PowerPoint creates a new slide with an org chart placeholder.

To create an org chart slide, follow these steps:

1 In Normal view or Slide view, display the slide that you want the org chart slide to *follow*.

2 On the Formatting toolbar, click Common Tasks, and then click New Slide. The New Slide dialog box appears.

NOTE

> If you have installed PowerPoint using the Typical installation, and if this is the first time you're trying to create an organization chart, the Organization Chart software is not yet set up on your computer. Follow the instructions on your screen to set up Microsoft Organization Chart.

3 Double-click the Organization Chart autolayout.

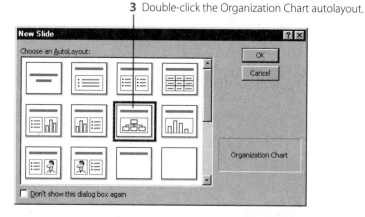

4 Double-click the org chart
placeholder to start a new org chart.

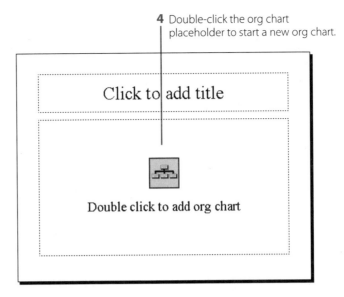

The Microsoft Organization Chart window opens.

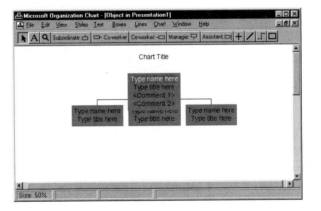

As you can see, the org chart contains a number of placeholders to simplify the task of entering information in the chart. And Microsoft Organization Chart comes equipped with its own menu bar and toolbar so you can easily edit and format the org chart.

Adding an Organization Chart to an Existing Slide

To include an org chart along with another object on a single slide, such as bulleted text or a graph, you can add an org chart to an existing slide. The bulleted text items can help explain the org chart, for example. Or, a graph can depict a numeric achievement that resulted from a change in the organization's structure.

To add an org chart to an existing slide, display the slide in Normal view or Slide view, from the Insert menu point to Picture, and then choose Organization Chart.

Add an Org Chart Button to the Toolbar

If you'll be creating org charts frequently, you can add an Insert Organization chart button to the Standard toolbar using the procedure described in "Customizing Toolbars," on page 510.

Here's another method for adding a new org chart to an existing slide:

1 Display the slide that will contain the org chart.

2 From the Insert menu, choose Object. The Insert Object dialog box appears, as shown below:

3 Make sure the Create New   **4** Scroll down and then double-
   option is selected.   click MS Organization Chart 2.0.

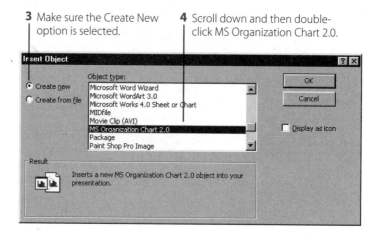

Microsoft Organization Chart opens in a separate window in which you can create the org chart. When you update and return to the presentation, the organization chart will be drawn along with the bullets, graph, or other information on the slide. If you want, you can then drag within the chart object to move the org chart to the position you want on the slide. You can also drag the chart's resize handles to change the height or width of the entire org chart so your audience can read all your information clearly.

Using an Existing Org Chart

If you've already created and saved an org chart, you can pull it into a presentation by inserting the chart as an object. You can then double-click the chart to edit it from within PowerPoint. To do this, follow these steps:

1 Display the slide to which you want to add the org chart.

2 From the Insert menu, choose Object.

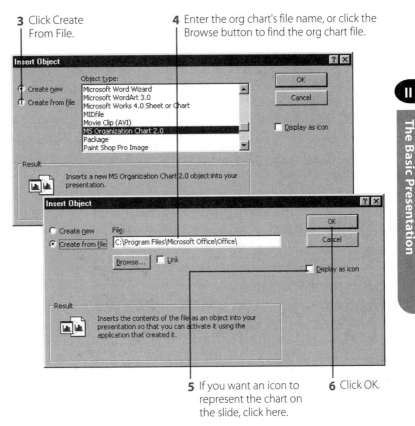

3 Click Create From File.

4 Enter the org chart's file name, or click the Browse button to find the org chart file.

5 If you want an icon to represent the chart on the slide, click here.

6 Click OK.

If you choose to place an icon for the chart on a slide, you can then "drill down" to the organization chart by double-clicking the icon. The org chart opens in the Organization Chart window so you can view or modify it right in front of your audience.

7 If necessary, resize or move the organization chart (or icon) where you want on the slide.

II

The Basic Presentation

If you want to establish a link between the original org chart file and the picture of the org chart that will be displayed in PowerPoint, select the Link check box in the Insert Object dialog box. Linking allows the chart in the presentation to reflect any subsequent changes that are made in the original org chart file. But be careful: If you select Link and then move the presentation to another computer, the chart will not come along for the ride. That's because the data for the chart is stored in the external org chart file rather than in PowerPoint. To store the data for the org chart in PowerPoint, leave the Link check box clear in the Insert Object dialog box.

Creating the Org Chart Structure

When the Microsoft Organization Chart window opens, the beginning of a hierarchy (one manager and three subordinates) is displayed in four boxes.

If you see only one box in the Organization Chart window, from the Organization Chart Edit menu, choose Options. Select the Use Standard 4-Box Template For New Charts option and click OK. Close the Organization Chart window and click No when the program asks whether to update the presentation. Now when you start a new org chart, it will be created with four boxes.

Before you begin entering text in the org chart's boxes, you may want to give the chart a title. Select the text *Chart Title* at the top of the chart and type a new title, such as *Our Division*. You can press Enter at the end of the title line to add a line for a subtitle. In fact, you can create a series of subtitles, but be sure to leave room for the chart!

Depicting Complicated Organizations
You may want to diagram each division of a complicated organizational structure in a separate chart to avoid overcrowding. You can create a preliminary organization chart that depicts the broad picture (the branches of the organization without any of the "leaves"), and then show each division in detail in a separate chart.

Filling in the Boxes

To start entering names in the org chart's boxes, follow these steps:

1 Click to select the first box.

2 Type a name in the first box and press Enter. You can also press the Tab key or the Down arrow.

3 Type the title here and press Enter.   **4** Enter up to two comments if you want, pressing Enter after each one.

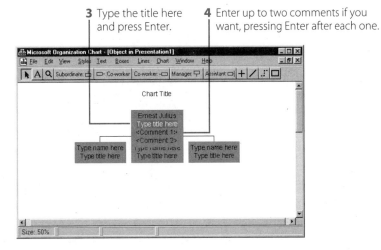

5 Press Ctrl+Down arrow to move to the first subordinate box.

6 Enter a name, title, and comments.

7 To move to the box to the right, press Ctrl+Right arrow. You can also press Ctrl+Left arrow to move to the box to the left or Ctrl+Up arrow to move to the top box.

Editing the Text

You can edit the text in an org chart box. Click the box once to select it, and then click in the text to position the insertion point where you want to edit. You can use all the same text selection and editing techniques you use elsewhere in PowerPoint.

The Enter Text button

You can also edit the text in an org chart by clicking the Enter Text button on the Organization Chart toolbar and then clicking any of the text in the chart. As you'll learn later, the Enter Text button is useful for typing text directly on the chart background as well.

The Basic Presentation

Adding and Deleting Boxes

Chances are your organization has more than three members, so you need to know how to add more boxes to the org chart. Fortunately, adding boxes is easy. On the Organization Chart toolbar, you click the button for the type of box you want to add and then click the box to which you want to connect the new box. To add more than one box at a time, click the appropriate toolbar button as many times as boxes you need, and then click an existing box.

The types of boxes you can add to an org chart are shown in Table 8-1, along with their corresponding buttons and a description of each button's function.

To add a subordinate to one of the three subordinates already in the chart, follow these steps:

The Subordinate button

1   Click the Subordinate button on the Organization Chart toolbar.

2   Click the box in the second row of the chart that you want to attach a subordinate to. A new box appears, ready for you to type in a name, title, and comment.

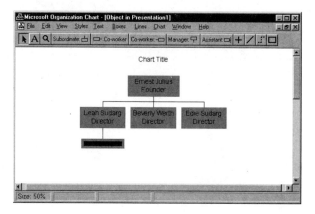

Deleting an org chart box is as easy as adding one. Simply click the box and then press Delete. Or, from the Organization Chart Edit menu, choose

Quickly Delete Adjacent Boxes

If the org chart boxes you want to delete are adjacent to one another, you can click the Select button (the arrow) on the Organization Chart toolbar, drag a selection box around the boxes, and then press Delete.

Clear. To delete two or more boxes, first click one box, and then hold down Shift and click the other boxes. Press Delete to delete all the selected boxes.

TABLE 8-1. The Org Chart Boxes and Toolbar Buttons

Button	Name	Function
Subordinate:	Subordinate	Adds a box at the level below the selected box
Co-worker	Left Co-worker	Adds a box to the left of the selected box at the same level
Co-worker:	Right Co-worker	Adds a box to the right of the selected box at the same level
Manager:	Manager	Adds a box at the level of the selected box and moves the selected box down one level. The selected box is attached to the new box as a subordinate.
Assistant:	Assistant	Adds a box below the selected box. The new box is attached to the line of command but is not a part of it (a staff position).

A Sample Org Chart

To try your hand at creating an org chart with an assortment of boxes, follow this example: Imagine that you need to diagram the structure of a nonprofit organization and its regional affiliates. If you've been following along by creating an actual chart, choose Close And Return To <*Presentation*> from the Organization Chart File menu, and then click No when asked if you want to update the chart. When you return to PowerPoint, start a new org chart by double-clicking the org chart placeholder and then follow these steps:

1 After the Organization Chart window opens, select the text *Chart Title* at the top of the new chart and type *League of Lefties*.

2 Click the topmost box once, type *Renee A. Gauche* as the name, press Enter, and type *National Director* as the title.

3 For the first comment, type *Wash., D.C.* You won't enter a second comment, so press Ctrl+Down arrow to move to the first subordinate box.

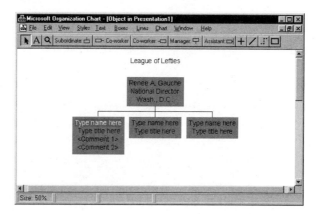

4 In the first subordinate box, type *Greta Links*, press Enter, and type *Director* as the title and *California* as the first comment. Then press Ctrl+Right arrow to move to the second subordinate box.

5 In the second subordinate box, type *Leanora Izquierda*, press Enter, and type *Director* as the title and *New York* as the first comment.

6 The League of Lefties does not have a third individual at the Director level, so click the third subordinate box and press Delete. The chart now looks like this:

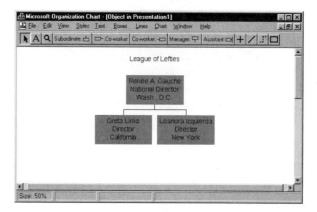

7 Greta Links has two subordinates, so click the Subordinate button on the toolbar twice and then click Greta's box. Two subordinates appear.

8 Leanora Izquierda has three subordinates, so click the Subordinate button three times and then click Leanora's box.

9 Renee A. Gauche has an assistant, so click the Assistant button and then click Renee's box. Type *Sylvia Southpaw* as the name, type *Assistant* as the title, and then click anywhere outside the org chart.

10 Enter the names of the subordinates under both Greta and Leanora. Click the first subordinate box under Greta, type *Tiffany*, press Ctrl+Right arrow, and then type *Bijou*. Type *Sal*, *Howie*, and *Clarice* as the subordinates under Leanora.

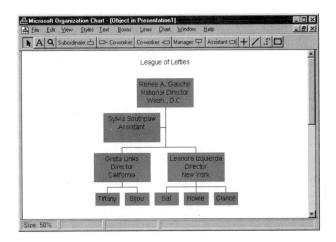

Later in this chapter, you'll modify the structure and change the formatting of the org chart you've just created. For now, return with the chart to PowerPoint. From the Organization Chart File menu, choose Update <*Presentation*>, and then also from the File menu, choose Close And Return To <*Presentation*>. In a moment, the chart appears on the current PowerPoint slide. Save the PowerPoint presentation with a name of your choosing so that you can retrieve it later.

Moving Boxes

The ease with which you can modify the structure of an org chart suits today's dynamic organizations. But fortunately or unfortunately (depending on your place in the organization), restructuring an actual org chart in PowerPoint is far easier than restructuring an actual organization.

Restructuring an organization in real life often results in moving people from one manager to another. The counterpart in PowerPoint is dragging a box from one place in the org chart to another. You can drag boxes to other positions at the same level in the chart, or move them up or down within the organization's structure.

To move a box in an org chart, follow these steps:

1 Open the org chart in the Organization Chart window.

2 Place the mouse pointer on the border of the box you want to move. The mouse pointer changes to the white arrow.

3 Hold down the left mouse button and drag the box's frame.

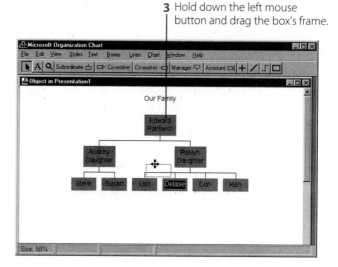

4 When the border is in position, release the mouse button.

When you drag a box's border near the left or right inside edge of another box and release the mouse button, the moved box appears to the left or right of the other box, at the same level. When you drag the border near the bottom inside edge of another box, the moved box appears below the other box, as a subordinate.

When you drag the border on top of another box, an arrow indicator appears inside the border. The indicator is a left arrow when the moved box will appear at the left side of the existing box, as shown in Figure 8-1. The indicator is a right arrow when the moved box will appear at the right side of the existing box. The indicator is a subordinate box icon when the moved box will appear below the existing box as a subordinate.

Try moving a box in the org chart you created earlier. If necessary, open the presentation file, double-click the org chart to open the Organization Chart window, and then place the mouse pointer on Sal's box. Next, hold down the left mouse button and drag Sal's box onto Greta's box without releasing the mouse button. Then move Sal's box toward the bottom of Greta's box, and when the subordinate indicator appears,

FIGURE 8-1.

The left arrow indicates that the moved box will appear to the left of the existing box.

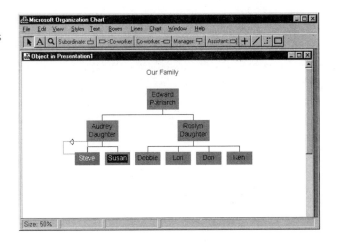

release the mouse button to drop Sal's box into place. (Sal now appears to the right of Bijou.) Next, move Sal between Tiffany and Bijou by clicking anywhere outside the chart, to deselect Sal's box, and then dragging Sal's box onto Bijou's box. Notice the left arrow inside Bijou's box when you drag it onto Bijou's box. The arrow indicates that Sal's box will drop to the left of Bijou's box, just as you want. Release the mouse button. Your chart should look similar to the one shown in Figure 8-2.

FIGURE 8-2.

The revised org chart.

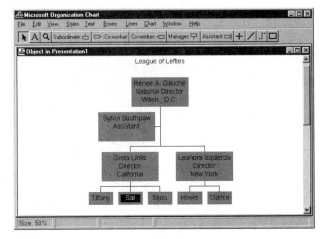

Return to the presentation. From the Organization Chart File menu, choose Update *<Presentation>* and then choose Close And Return To *<Presentation>* from the same menu. To save your changes, on the Standard toolbar, click the Save button, choose Save from the File menu, or press Ctrl+S.

Changing the Style of Groups and Branches

The subordinates under a manager are called a *group*. By default, PowerPoint displays a group in boxes that are side by side. But, from the Organization Chart Styles menu, you can choose several other ways to display a group. For example, the members of a group can be shown as a vertical list, or they can be depicted as leaves that emanate from a central branch.

Before you can change the style of an org chart group, you must select the group. There are several ways to select all members of a group:

- Double-click any member of the group.

- Click a member and then press Ctrl+G (*G* for *Group*).

- Select one member of the group and then, from the Organization Chart Edit menu, point to Select and then choose Group.

Figure 8-3 shows the members of a group after they have been selected. Note that the group members all report to the same manager.

FIGURE 8-3.

The members of a selected group.

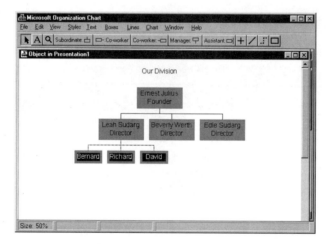

After you select a group, from the Organization Chart Styles menu, choose one of the six group style buttons at the top of the menu, as shown in Figure 8-4. For a group at the lowest level of a chart, a useful style is the one shown on the second button in the second row of styles. Arranging a group in this style can reduce the horizontal space needed by a chart when the organizational structure is wide rather than deep.

Just as you can change the style of an org chart group, you can also change the style of an org chart *branch*. A branch consists of a manager and all the manager's subordinates. To select a branch, select the

FIGURE 8-4.

The Organization
Chart Styles menu.

manager at the top of the branch, and then press Ctrl+B (*B* for *Branch*).
Or, from the Organization Chart Edit menu, point to Select and then
choose Branch. After you select a branch, you can choose one of the
styles from the Styles menu.

 TIP

Select a Chart Group or Branch
You can also select an org chart group or branch by clicking the Select button
on the Organization Chart toolbar and dragging a selection box around the
group or branch.

You can use two special styles at the bottom of the Styles menu to change
the rank of members of a group. The Assistant style changes selected
members of a group to assistants. For example, Figure 8-5 displays two
org charts on a slide. The left chart shows three subordinates under a
manager. The right chart shows the result after two of the subordinates
are converted to assistants with the Assistant style.

FIGURE 8-5.

Subordinates
converted to
assistants with the
Assistant style.

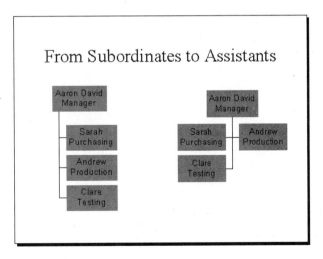

You can use the Co-manager style, also on the Styles menu, to indicate
two or more members of the organization who report to the same

manager and share power. After you select the members you want to make co-managers, on the Styles menu, click the Co-manager style. Figure 8-6 shows two subordinates who have become co-managers.

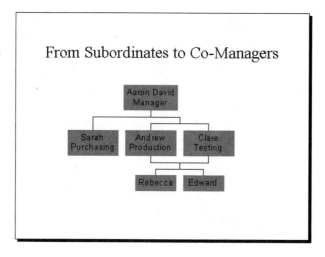

Try changing the style of the groups in the sample org chart you created earlier. If necessary, open the presentation file, and then double-click the org chart to open the Organization Chart window. Next, click one of the subordinates under Greta and press Ctrl+G to select the entire group of subordinates who report to Greta. From the Organization Chart Styles menu, choose the second style in the second row. The three side-by-side boxes of the group change to a small ladder that lists the three subordinates. You can try other styles or choose the same style for Leanora's group of subordinates. Figure 8-7 shows Greta's group with its new style.

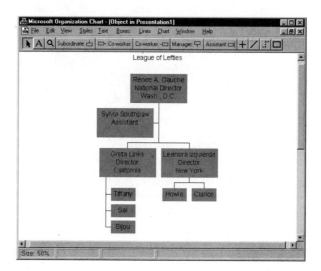

Formatting the Org Chart

An organization chart inherits the design characteristics of the template attached to the current presentation. That is, the template determines the font of the text and the color of the boxes in the org chart. However, as you'll learn in this section, after you complete an organizational structure, you can still make changes to the appearance of the chart. For instance, you can emphasize the titles of the organization members with a special color or change the box borders.

Zooming In and Out

Before you start formatting an org chart, get acquainted with the Organization Chart zoom feature. This way, you can see exactly what you're doing when you make changes to a chart.

The Zoom In button

The Zoom Out button

To zoom in on an org chart, on the Organization Chart toolbar, click the Zoom button, and then click the area of the org chart you want to magnify. To zoom out, click the Zoom button again (the Zoom button now displays a miniature org chart instead of a magnifying glass), and then click the org chart. You can also use the following commands to change the zoom percentage of the chart:

- To fit the entire chart within the Organization Chart window, from the Organization Chart View menu, choose Size To Window menu. Or, simply press F9.

- To reduce the chart to 50 percent of actual size (which, in turn, is about 50 percent of its printed size), from the View menu, choose 50% Of Actual. Or, simply press F10.

- To view the chart at actual size, from the View menu, choose Actual. Or, simply press F11.

- To enlarge the chart so you can focus on chart detail, from the View menu, choose 200% Of Actual. Or, simply press F12.

Formatting the Text

The procedures for formatting the text in an org chart are similar to the procedures for formatting text elsewhere in PowerPoint. The difference is that instead of using the Format menu commands, you use commands on the Organization Chart Text menu. You can use this menu to change the font, color, and alignment of text in organization chart boxes.

Of course, before you can use the commands on the Organization Chart Text menu, you must select the text you want to format.

- To select all the text in a box, click the box.

- To select all the text in several boxes, hold down Shift as you click each box.

- To select specific boxes, use the Select commands on the Organization Chart Edit menu. Table 8-2 describes each of the Select commands.

- To select several adjacent boxes, click the Select button on the Organization Chart toolbar and drag a selection box around the boxes you want.

TABLE 8-2.   The Select Commands

Command	Function
All	Selects all boxes in the org chart
All Assistants	Selects all assistants
All Co-Managers	Selects all members who have been made co-managers with the Co-manager style
All Managers	Selects only members who have subordinates
All Non-Managers	Selects only members who do not have subordinates
Group	Selects the other members of a group. You must have one group member selected first
Branch	Selects the other members of a branch. You must have one branch member selected first
Lowest Level	Selects only the boxes at the lowest level of the org chart
Connecting Lines	Selects only the connecting lines between boxes
Background Objects	Selects only the boxes and lines drawn with the drawing tools

To format specific text within a box, such as the title only, click the box, and then click to position the insertion point in the text you want to format. Next, use any of the standard text selection techniques to select the text in the box. For example, drag across the text with the mouse, double-click a word, or hold down Shift as you press the Left or Right arrow key. By selecting only specific text within a box, you can change the appearance of as little or as much text as you want. You can even format a single character with a special font or color.

Unfortunately, PowerPoint offers no easy method for selecting all names or all titles in an org chart. You must move from box to box, selecting the name or the title, if you want to apply special formatting or editing to only those elements.

Formatting the Boxes

By selecting an org chart box and then using the commands from the Organization Chart Boxes menu, you can change the box's color, add a shadow, or modify the box's borders. Before you can make any of these changes, however, you must select the box or boxes you want to format using the techniques described in the previous section. Then simply choose the commands you want from the Boxes menu. For example, suppose you want to format a box with the color red and an extra-thick border. First click the box to select it, and then from the Boxes menu, choose Color. Click the red color option in the Color dialog box and then click OK. Next, also from the Boxes menu, point to Border Style, and then in the submenu, choose the second border option in the second column.

You can use the Color command to apply any of the colors in the current color palette to the interior of the selected box or boxes. (After you finish creating the org chart, you'll see it on the slide, against the slide background, and you'll be able to determine whether the box interior color clashes with the slide background color.)

The Shadow command allows you to apply a shadow that extends in one or more directions behind the selected box or boxes. Shadows give boxes a three-dimensional look. Figure 8-8 shows shadows added to the boxes in the sample org chart.

FIGURE 8-8.

The sample org chart with shadows added.

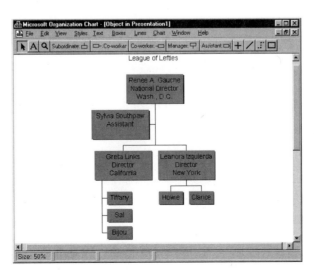

To change the style, color, and line style of a selected box's border, use the three border commands on the Boxes menu. Figure 8-9 shows the sample org chart formatted with double borders.

FIGURE 8-9.

The sample org chart formatted with double borders.

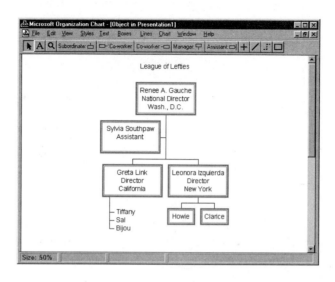

While you can't resize individual boxes in an org chart, you can resize the shape and proportion of the entire org chart. From the Organization Chart File menu, choose Update *<Presentation>*, and then also from the File menu, choose Close And Return To *<Presentation>*. In PowerPoint, drag one of the resize handles surrounding the org chart to change the size or shape of all the boxes and lines in the chart.

Formatting the Lines

You can change the thickness, style, and color of the lines that connect org chart boxes just as easily as you change the formatting of the boxes themselves. As always, before you can change the formatting of a line, you must select the line by clicking it. A selected line is temporarily highlighted with a dashed light gray style. You can select multiple lines by holding down Shift as you click each line. Or you can select all the lines at once. From the Organization Chart Edit menu, point to Select and then choose Connecting Lines.

Select Multiple Lines

You can also select multiple lines by clicking the Select button on the toolbar and dragging a selection box around the lines.

After you select the line or lines you want to format, from the Organization Chart Lines menu, choose Thickness, Style, or Color. Figure 8-10 shows the sample org chart formatted with thicker connecting lines. Figure 8-11 shows the chart's connecting lines with the dotted line style.

FIGURE 8-10.

The sample org chart formatted with shadowed boxes and thicker connecting lines.

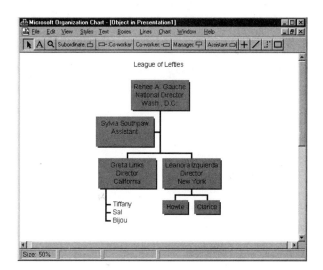

FIGURE 8-11.

The sample org chart formatted with shadowed boxes and dotted connecting lines.

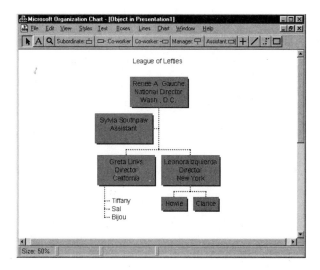

II

The Basic Presentation

Drawing Boxes and Lines with the Drawing Tools

Sometimes the built-in box arrangements (subordinates under managers, assistants below managers, and co-managers sharing power) simply cannot describe the complicated, spaghetti-like reporting structures in an organization. Fortunately, you can add new boxes and lines easily with the Microsoft Organization Chart drawing tools, shown below.

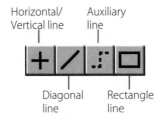

Horizontal/ Vertical line   Auxiliary line

Diagonal line   Rectangle line

 NOTE

> If you don't see four drawing tools to the right of the Assistant button on the toolbar, from the View menu, choose Show Draw Tools. Or, press Ctrl+D.

The Horizontal/Vertical Line button

To draw a horizontal, vertical, or diagonal line on the chart, click the Horizontal/Vertical Line or Diagonal Line button, place the crosshair pointer at the starting point for the line, hold down the left mouse button, and then drag to draw the line. After you add a line, you can select the line by clicking it with the mouse. You can then:

The Diagonal Line button

- Format the line with the commands from the Organization Chart Lines menu.

- Change the line's length by dragging the handle at either end.

- Move the line by dragging it with the mouse.

- Delete the line by pressing Delete.

The Auxiliary Line button

To connect two boxes with a line, click the Auxiliary Line button, place the pointer at the edge of the first box, and then drag to the edge of the second box, as shown in Figure 8-12. As you drag, you'll see the connecting line appear. If the connecting line has three segments (like the one in Figure 8-12), you can drag the middle segment to change the size or shape of the line. You may have to move the middle segment if the connecting line overlaps an existing line or box.

FIGURE 8-12.

A new connecting line has been added to the sample org chart.

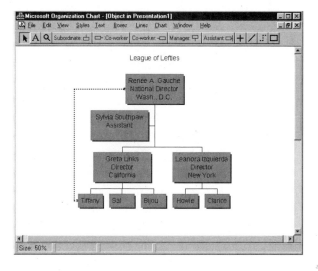

The Rectangle button

To draw a new box, as shown in Figure 8-13, click the Rectangle button, place the crosshair pointer where you want the box to appear, and then drag to create the new box. To adjust the size or shape of the new box, drag one of the handles around the box. To move the box, place the mouse pointer anywhere in the box and drag it where you want.

FIGURE 8-13.

A new box added to the sample org chart.

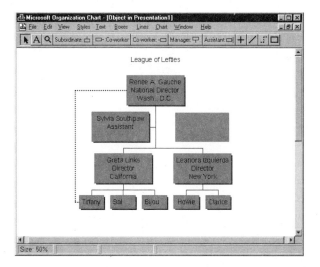

You cannot use the Auxiliary Line button to connect new boxes with existing chart boxes or with other new boxes. To connect new boxes, you must draw lines with the Horizontal/Vertical Line tool or the Diagonal Line tool.

NOTE

To save an org chart in a separate file, from the File menu of the Organization Chart module, choose Save Copy As. The chart will be saved as an OPX file, which can be opened in Microsoft Organization Chart and used in other PowerPoint presentations.

Returning to PowerPoint

When the org chart is complete, from the Organization Chart File menu, choose Update *<Presentation>*, and then also from the File menu, choose Close And Return To *<Presentation>*. If you exit without choosing Update *<Presentation>* first, PowerPoint displays a dialog box asking whether you want to update the chart. Click Yes to proceed.

The new org chart appears on the current PowerPoint slide. You can move the entire chart or drag a corner handle to resize the chart, but the chart always remains the same shape. To edit the chart, double-click it. The Organization Chart window reopens with the chart inside.

In this chapter, you've learned to place organization charts on slides. In the next chapter, you'll continue the survey of special object types by learning about table slides.

CHAPTER 9

Adding Tables to Your Presentation

When you want to display text paragraphs side by side—to lay out the pros and cons of an issue, for example—you can use the row-and-column format of a table. PowerPoint's table slides are quick to make and easy to modify, especially when compared to the alternative, which is to align text in columns with tab stops.

Table slides often hold only text, but they can contain numbers just as easily. When you don't need the power of a graph to illustrate a result, a table can do quite nicely. Tables are also useful as a backup to a graph, when the audience needs to see the raw data.

Previous versions of PowerPoint used the table-making features of Microsoft Word to create tables. When you started a Power-Point table, Word opened and offered its table features. Now PowerPoint has its own built-in table feature so that you can still easily create and edit tables in PowerPoint even if Word is not installed.

This chapter focuses on how to create a slide devoted entirely to a table and how to add a table to an existing slide.

233

Understanding Table Basics

When you need to include a table in a presentation, you can create a new slide with the Table AutoLayout. Or you can add the table to an existing slide that already contains other objects, such as a group of bulleted items.

Creating a Table Slide

To create a table slide for a presentation, just follow these steps:

1 In Normal view or Slide view, display the slide that you want the table slide to follow.

2 On the Standard toolbar, click the New Slide button.

3 In the New Slide dialog box, double-click the Table AutoLayout.

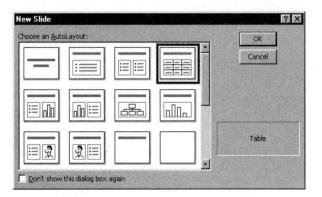

As you can see, the new slide contains two placeholders, one for the slide title and one for the table.

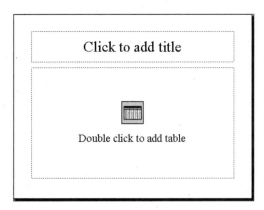

4 Double-click the table placeholder to display the Insert Table dialog box:

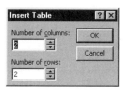

5 In the Number Of Columns and Number Of Rows boxes, type the number of columns and rows you want to include in the table. Or click the up or down arrows next to the edit boxes to select the numbers you want. Then click OK to create the table. The table, made up of the number of columns and rows you specified, appears on the slide, along with the Tables And Borders floating toolbar.

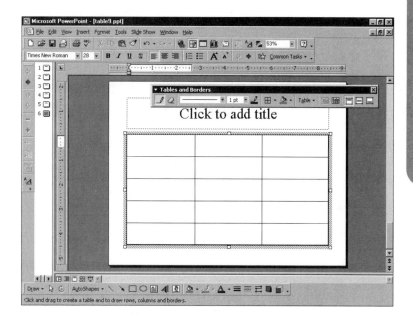

Using a Microsoft Excel Table

If the data for a table comes from Microsoft Excel, you might want to include a slide to display the Excel spreadsheet. (This way, if someone asks for clarification of the table's data, you can produce the original Excel table.) When you embed an Excel table in a PowerPoint slide, the table appears just as it does in Excel, and you gain all the advantages of Excel's data calculation powers while in PowerPoint. For example, Excel tables (actually small worksheets embedded in PowerPoint slides) can include formulas that carry out complicated calculations, and the formula results are updated automatically when any of the numbers change. *For information about embedding an Excel table, see "Using PowerPoint with Microsoft Excel," page 490.*

Adding a Table to an Existing Slide

There are two methods for adding a table to an existing slide. To use the button method, follow these steps:

The Insert Table button

1 On the Standard toolbar, click the Insert Table button. A grid of table cells drops down.

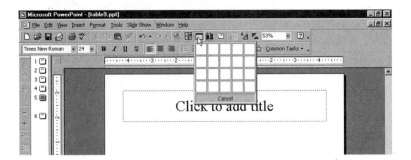

2 Position the mouse pointer on the lower right cell in the grid that represents the furthest extent of the table size you want—that is, the number of columns and rows you want. As you move the mouse pointer, the cells in the grid are highlighted to show the columns and rows selected. For example, the result of the grid selected below is a table with three rows and three columns.

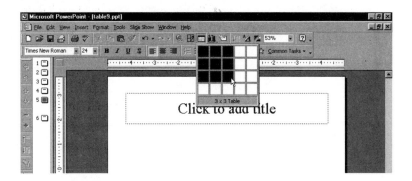

3 Click the mouse button. The table is added to the current slide with the specified table size.

You can also add a table to an existing slide using menu commands. To use the command method, follow these steps:

1 From the Insert menu, choose the Table command.

2 In the Insert Table dialog box, enter the number of columns and rows you want.

After you add a table to an existing slide, you can move or resize it. To move the selected table, position the pointer on the table's gray object border until the pointer changes to a crosshair. Drag the table to the location on the slide you want. To resize the selected table, position the pointer on one of the white handles on the table's gray object border until the pointer changes to a double arrow. Drag to resize the table to the dimensions you want.

Insert a Microsoft Word Table into PowerPoint

If you'd prefer to use all the text-editing features of Microsoft Word when you create a table, you can also create the table using the Microsoft Word table features. From the Insert menu, point to Picture and then choose the Microsoft Word Table command. Enter the number of columns and rows you want, and then click OK. The Word table is created within PowerPoint, and the PowerPoint menus and toolbars change to those of Word until you click outside the table.

If you've already created a table in Word, you can drag the table onto a PowerPoint slide. *For more information, see "Using PowerPoint with Microsoft Word," page 472.*

II

The Basic Presentation

Entering Text in a Table

When you create a new table on a new or existing slide, an empty table appears within a gray object border on the slide. The floating Tables And Borders toolbar appears, as shown in Figure 9-1, providing tools for formatting the table.

FIGURE 9-1.

The Tables And Borders toolbar.

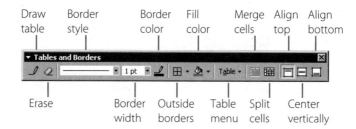

The Tables And Borders toolbar appears whenever you click a table on a slide. You can hide the toolbar by clicking its Close button. To show it again, click the Tables And Borders button on the Standard toolbar. Or, from the View menu, point to Toolbars, and then click the Tables And Borders command.

The Tables And Borders button

When you enter text in a table, the first thing you should consider is the structure of the table. You'll probably want to use the cells at the tops of columns or beginnings of rows for table headings. Then you can enter the data accordingly. As you'll learn later in the chapter, it's not necessary to know exactly how many columns and rows you need from the start, because you can easily add columns and rows at any time.

② SEE ALSO

For more information about manually changing the height of rows and the width of columns, see "Changing Column Width and Row Height," page 249.

When you start a table, the insertion point flashes in the upper left cell in the table. As always, whatever you type is entered at the location of the insertion point. To move the insertion point to the next cell, press the Tab key. To move the insertion point to a previous cell, press Shift+Tab. Or simply click the cell in which you want to type.

As you type, the text wraps within the current width of the cell. In other words, when you've typed all the way across a cell, the next word you type moves to a second line within the cell, as shown in Figure 9-2.

FIGURE 9-2.
The text in four cells of this table has wrapped to the second line.

Name	Region	Division	Description
Audrey Marr	Northeast	Circulation	Director of Circulation
Eric Weinberger	Northeast	Sales	Sales Manager

In fact, as shown in Figure 9-3, the entire table row grows vertically rather than horizontally to accommodate its longest text entry.

FIGURE 9-3.
A table row grows vertically to accommodate its longest text entry.

Name	Region	Division	Description
Audrey Marr	Northeast	Circulation	Director of Circulation and Advertising
Eric Weinberger	Northeast	Sales	Sales Manager

⭐ **TIP**

Use Short Text Entries for Clarity
Although a cell can accommodate lengthy text entries, try to use short text entries to avoid overwhelming the slide with too many words. Type a word or two rather than a sentence. Remember that in tables, as in charts, less is more.

▶ **NOTE**

When you press Tab to move to a cell that contains text, all the text is highlighted. You can then replace the highlighted text simply by typing new text. (Remember, any selected text is instantly replaced when you type.)

As you enter text in a cell, you can end a paragraph and start a new paragraph by pressing Enter. When you get to the end of the last cell in the last row, you can add a new row at the bottom of the table by pressing the Tab key.

A Sample Table

Now try your hand at creating a sample table. Imagine that you need to compare two vendors who want to supply coffee for your office kitchen. You can start by creating a new presentation, or you can use an existing presentation. Then follow the steps below.

1 On the Standard toolbar, click the New Slide button to start a new slide. In the New Slide dialog box, double-click the Table AutoLayout.

2 On the new slide, double-click the table placeholder to start the table. In the Insert Table dialog box, click in the Number Of Rows edit box, and then enter *3* to specify 3 rows. Click OK. A new table of 3 rows by 2 columns is created.

3 With the insertion point in the first cell of the table, type *The Coffee Pot*, press Tab to move to the next cell, and then type *Roast and Brew*. Now you can begin typing the benefits provided by each service in the cells below.

4 Press Tab to move to the second cell in the first column, and type *Freshly ground beans each week*. Then press Tab to move to the second cell in the second column, and type *Free donuts on Fridays*.

5 Press Tab again to move to the third cell in the first column, and type *Daily 7 AM service*. Then press Tab one more time, and type *Jelly donuts, too*. Your table should now look similar to the table shown below:

The Coffee Pot	Roast and Brew
Freshly ground beans each week	Free donuts on Fridays
Daily 7 AM service	Jelly donuts, too

As you can see, this table could use a little formatting. The rows are too tall, and the column headings are not distinguished in any way. Later in this chapter, you'll learn how to make these and other improvements. But first, you'll learn how to make basic modifications to the table structure, such as inserting a new column when a third vendor submits a bid.

Modifying the Table

After you've created a table, you can easily modify its structure by adding, deleting, moving, and copying cells, columns, and rows. You can also change the widths of columns, the heights of rows, and merge and split cells to accommodate the contents of your table.

Selecting Cells, Columns, and Rows

You know that if you want to modify anything in PowerPoint, you must select it first. Typically, all you need to do is click the item to select it. With table elements, however, you need to do a little more to select exactly the item you want. The following lists the various ways you can select table cells, columns, and rows.

- To place the insertion point inside the cell, simply click in the cell where you want the insertion point to be located. This also selects the cell itself.

- To select adjacent cells in the same row, click anywhere in the first cell, and drag across the row. Figure 9-4 shows a table with all the cells in one row selected.

FIGURE 9-4.

All the cells in the second row have been selected.

Name	Region	Division	Description
Audrey Marr	Northeast	Circulation	Director of Circulation and Advertising
Eric Weinberger	Northeast	Sales	Sales Manager

- To select adjacent cells in the same row, or even across adjoining rows, click the first cell, hold down Shift, and then click the last cell in the group. Or use the mouse or keyboard to place the insertion point in the first cell you want to select, hold down Shift, and then press the arrow keys to select adjacent cells.

- To select adjacent cells in the same column, click anywhere in the first cell, and drag down the column.

■ To select all cells in a column, position the mouse pointer on the top border of the column until the pointer changes to a down arrow. Click the left mouse button. The column is selected, as shown in Figure 9-5.

FIGURE 9-5.

The third column in this table has been selected.

Name	Region	Division	Description
Audrey Marr	Northeast	Circulation	Director of Circulation and Advertising
Eric Weinberger	Northeast	Sales	Sales Manager

⭐ **TIP**

Select Rows and Columns with Menu Commands

If you have trouble selecting rows and columns with the mouse, you can use Table menu commands instead. First use the arrow keys and the Tab key to move the insertion point to a cell in the row or column you want to select. Then, on the Tables And Borders toolbar, click Table, and choose Select Column or Select Row, as shown in Figure 9-6.

FIGURE 9-6.

The Table menu is available from the Tables And Borders toolbar.

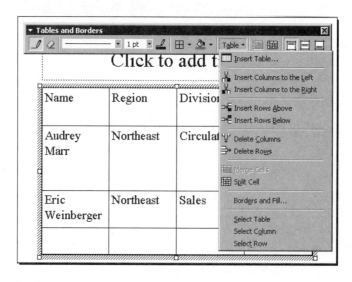

Adding and Deleting Columns and Rows

If you find you need more columns and rows than you have originally planned, you can easily insert new ones. Likewise, if you have created a table with more columns or rows than you ended up needing, you can delete the extras.

NOTE

You cannot insert or delete individual cells, only columns and rows. However, you can insert and delete text within the individual cells using normal Power-Point text editing techniques. *For more information about inserting and deleting text, see "Editing Text in Outline View," page 63.*

Inserting Columns and Rows

To insert a new column, follow these steps:

1 Click anywhere in the column next to where you want the new column to appear.

2 On the Tables And Borders toolbar, click Table, and then choose Insert Columns To The Left or Insert Columns To The Right. A column is inserted to the left or right of the selected column.

TIP

Insert a New Column using the Shortcut Menu

Select the entire column to the left of which you want the new column to be inserted. Remember, to select a column, position the mouse pointer on the top border of the column until the pointer changes to a down arrow, and then click the left mouse button. Use the right mouse button to click somewhere in the selected column. From the shortcut menu, choose Insert Columns.

To insert a new row, follow these steps:

1 Click anywhere in the row next to where you want the new row to appear.

2 On the Tables And Borders toolbar, click Table, and then choose Insert Rows Above or Insert Rows Below. A row is inserted above or below the selected row.

TIP

Insert a New Row using the Shortcut Menu

Click somewhere in the row above which you want the new row to be inserted. Use the right mouse button to click somewhere in the selected row. On the shortcut menu, click Insert Rows.

If you want to add a new row to the end of a table, click the last cell in the table, and then press the Tab key.

> When you insert a new column, it adopts the same width as the column to its right. When you insert a new row, it adopts the same height as the row below it. *For more information about column and row sizes, see "Changing Column Width and Row Height," page 249.*

To insert more than one column or row at a time, first drag to select the number of columns or rows that you want to insert, and then choose the insert command you want. For example, if you want to insert three new rows, first drag to select three existing rows, and then from the Table menu, choose Insert Rows Above or Insert Rows Below. As shown in Figure 9-7, three new rows are inserted above or below the three existing rows you selected.

FIGURE 9-7.

Three rows are selected to enable three new rows to be inserted.

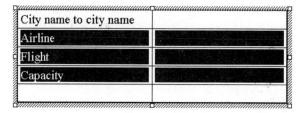

Deleting Columns and Rows

To delete a column, click somewhere in the column you want to delete. On the Tables And Borders toolbar, click Table, and then choose Delete Columns. Or select the entire column, and then from the shortcut menu, choose Delete Columns. To delete a row, click somewhere in the row you want to delete. On the Tables And Borders toolbar, click Table, and then choose Delete Rows. Or, from the shortcut menu, choose Delete Rows.

Moving and Copying Cells

You can move or copy the selected contents of a cell to another cell using the drag-and-drop editing techniques. As an alternative, you can also use the Cut, Copy, and Paste buttons on the Standard toolbar or the commands on the Edit menu or shortcut menu.

To move a cell's contents using drag-and-drop editing, follow these steps:

1 Select the information you want to move.

Feature		Benefit
Hub Lock 23	Quick-locking hub	Easy tire removal
Spoke 17	Aluminum and titanium spoke	Lightweight, flexible, high lateral strength

2 Position the pointer over the selected information until the pointer becomes an arrow.

SEE ALSO
For more information about selecting text, see "Selecting Text for Editing," page 64.

3 Hold down the left mouse button and drag to the location you want in the destination cell.

	Feature	Benefit
Hub Lock 23	Quick-locking hub	Easy tire removal
Spoke 17	Aluminum and titanium spoke	Lightweight, flexible, high lateral strength

The Basic Presentation

The information is dragged into place and moved from the other cell.

To copy rather than move the contents of a cell while dragging, hold down Ctrl while dragging the cell contents. A plus sign appears next to the pointer to indicate that you're copying instead of moving.

To move or copy a cell's contents using menu commands, follow these steps:

1 Select the information you want to move.

2 From the Edit menu or the shortcut menu, choose Cut (to move) or Copy. Or, on the Standard toolbar, click the Cut or Copy button.

3 Click in the table to position the insertion point where you want to insert the cut or copied information.

4 From the Edit menu or the shortcut menu, choose Paste. Or, on the Standard toolbar, click the Paste button. The cut or copied information is moved or copied at the insertion point.

Moving and Copying Columns and Rows

Suppose you have the contents you want in your columns and rows, but you want to do some rearranging. You can move or copy entire columns and rows in your table. You can drag columns and rows. You can also use the Cut, Copy, and Paste commands or toolbar buttons.

Using the drag-and-drop technique to move or copy columns and rows replaces the contents of the destination column or row, rather than inserting the column or row between existing ones. Unless this is what you want, first insert a new column or row, and then drag the column or row into the new blank one. You might then want to delete the old blank column or row.

To move a column or row using drag-and-drop editing, follow the steps on the opposite page.

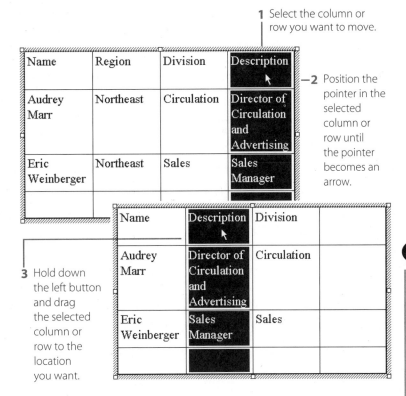

1 Select the column or row you want to move.

—2 Position the pointer in the selected column or row until the pointer becomes an arrow.

3 Hold down the left button and drag the selected column or row to the location you want.

4 The information dragged is dropped into place, moved from the original column or row, replacing any existing information in the destination column row.

To copy rather than move a column or row while dragging, follow the same steps as above, but hold down Ctrl while dragging. A plus sign appears next to the pointer to indicate that you're copying instead of moving.

You can move or copy multiple columns or rows by selecting all the columns or rows that you want to move or copy before you drag.

When you use menu commands or toolbar buttons to move or copy columns and rows, they are inserted between existing ones, and no information is overwritten. Columns are inserted to the left of the selected one, and rows are inserted above the selected one. The new columns and rows adopt the size of the selected ones.

To move or copy a column or row using menu commands, follow the steps on the next page.

The Basic Presentation

1 Select the entire column or row you want to move or copy.

City name to city name	
Flight	
Capacity	
Airline	
Flight	
Capacity	

2 From the Edit menu or the shortcut menu, choose Cut (to move) or Copy. Or, on the Standard toolbar, click the Cut or Copy button.

3 Click the column to the left of which you want the moved or copied column to be inserted. Click the row above which you want the moved or copied row to be inserted.

City name to city name	
Flight	
Capacity	
Airline	
Flight	
Capacity	

4 From the Edit menu or the shortcut menu, choose Paste. Or, on the Standard toolbar, click the Paste button. The cut or copied column or row is inserted.

City name to city name	
Airline	
Flight	
Capacity	
Airline	
Flight	
Capacity	

Changing Column Width and Row Height

Now imagine that you are finally satisfied with the content, number of rows and columns, and the logical arrangement of your information. This is a good time to make any necessary adjustments to the column width and row height. You can even adjust the size of the overall table, making global width and height changes to the columns and rows.

Changing Column Width

To change the width of a column in a table, follow these steps:

1 Position the pointer anywhere on the column's right border until the pointer changes to a double line and arrow.

2 Drag the column border to the left or right to decrease or increase the column width. A dashed line indicates the target column width.

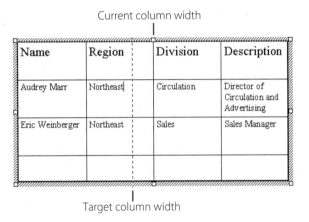

Current column width

Target column width

3 Release the mouse button. The column width is changed to the new size you specified by dragging. If you reduce the width of a column so that some of the text no longer fits within the width of the column's cells, the extra text in each cell wraps to a second line.

Name	Region	Division	Description
Audrey Marr	Northeast	Circulation	Director of Circulation and Advertising
Eric Weinberger	Northeast	Sales	Sales Manager

TIP

Automatically Fit the Column to its Widest Text

To change the column width to the widest text contained in the column, position the pointer anywhere on the column's right border until the pointer changes to a double line and arrow, and then double-click. The column width increases or decreases to the size of its widest text.

If you change the width of the far right column, the width of the overall table changes to accommodate the new size, whether it's narrower or wider.

Changing Row Height

To change the height of a row in a table, follow these steps:

1 Position the pointer anywhere on the row's bottom border until the pointer changes to a double line and arrow.

2 Drag the row border up or down to decrease or increase the row height. A dashed line indicates the target row height.

Name	Region	Division	Description
Audrey Marr	Northeast	Circulation	Director of Circulation and Advertising
Eric Weinberger	Northeast	Sales	Sales Manager

Current row height —

Target row height —

3 Release the mouse button. The row height is changed to the new size you specified by dragging. The minimum row height is that which is necessary to show all the text. In other words, you cannot reduce the height of a row to be so narrow that some of the text is cut off.

Name	Region	Division	Description
Audrey Marr	Northeast	Circulation	Director of Circulation and Advertising
Eric Weinberger	Northeast	Sales	Sales Manager

If you change the height of the bottom row, the height of the overall table changes to accommodate the new size, whether it's shorter or taller.

Changing the Table Size

When you change the width of the far right column, you are also changing the width of the table itself. Likewise, when you change the height of the bottom row, you are also changing the height of the table itself.

Also, you can only resize one column or row at a time by dragging or double-clicking the column or row border.

However, you can uniformly resize all the columns and rows in your table by changing the overall table width and height. Figure 9-8 shows the resize handles on the table object border.

FIGURE 9-8.

Resize the overall table by dragging the resize handles.

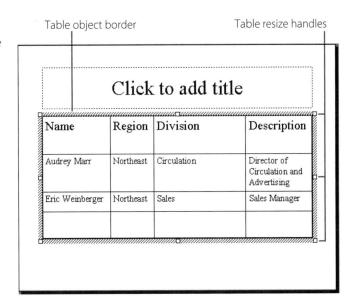

Table object border   Table resize handles

Click to add title

Name	Region	Division	Description
Audrey Marr	Northeast	Circulation	Director of Circulation and Advertising
Eric Weinberger	Northeast	Sales	Sales Manager

To change the table width, follow these steps:

1 Position the pointer on the resize handle in the middle of the right or left table object border. The pointer changes to a double arrow.

2 Drag the handle to the left or right to increase or decrease the overall table width. Dashed lines throughout the table indicate the target size of the table and all of its columns.

The Basic Presentation

Name	Region	Division	Description
Audrey Marr	Northeast	Circulation	Director of Circulation and Advertising
Eric Weinberger	Northeast	Sales	Sales Manager

3 Release the mouse button. The table width changes to the new size you specified by dragging. The column sizes also change proportionally.

Name	Region	Division	Description
Audrey Marr	Northeast	Circulation	Director of Circulation and Advertising
Eric Weinberger	Northeast	Sales	Sales Manager

To change the table height, follow these steps:

1 Position the pointer on the resize handle in the middle of the bottom table object border. The pointer changes to a double arrow.

2 Drag the handle up or down to decrease or increase the overall table height. Dashed lines throughout the table indicate the target size of the table and all of its rows.

3 Release the mouse button. The table height changes to the new size you specified by dragging. The row sizes also change proportionally.

To change both the table width and height at the same time, drag any one of the four corner resize handles.

> **NOTE**
>
> The minimum table height is that which is necessary to show all the text in the table. In other words, you cannot reduce the table height to be so narrow that some of the text is cut off. If you need to make your table smaller than is allowed, first shrink the text font size, and then resize the table.

Merging and Splitting Cells

To create one cell that spans two or more cells, you can merge adjacent cells. As shown in Figure 9-9, merging cells allows you to enter a column heading in one large cell that occupies the same width as several smaller cells below.

FIGURE 9-9.
The cells in row 1 of columns 2 and 3 and of columns 4 and 5 have been merged to accommodate the column subheadings.

	Alternative #1		Alternative #2	
	Pros	Cons	Pros	Cons
Alternative X				
Alternative Y				

To merge two or more cells, follow these steps:

1 Select the cells you want to merge.

The Merge Cells button

2 On the Tables And Borders toolbar, click the Merge Cells button. Or, from the Table or shortcut menu, choose Merge Cells.

You can split any cell (whether previously merged or not) into two cells of equal width.

To split a cell, follow these steps:

1 Select the cell that you want to split. You can only split one cell at a time.

The Split Cells button

2 On the Tables And Borders toolbar, click the Split Cell button. Or, from the Table menu, choose Split Cell. The cell is split into two cells of equal width, with any text appearing in the cell on the left.

After splitting a cell, you might want to adjust the cell width to make it look right in your current cell structure and layout.

Formatting the Table

SEE ALSO
For more information about formatting text, see "Formatting Text in Slide View," page 96.

After you make any necessary table structure and size adjustments, you can turn your attention to the overall appearance of the table. By default, PowerPoint uses the current presentation template to format elements of the table such as text font and color. You can change the formatting of table text using the same methods you use to change the formatting of text elsewhere in PowerPoint. Simply select the text, and then use the buttons on the Formatting toolbar or the commands on the Format and shortcut menus.

In addition to the text, however, there are other elements to consider when you format a table, such as borders and shading. These elements are discussed in this section.

Adding Borders and Fills

PowerPoint establishes default borders around cells and the table itself, based on the current presentation template. You can change borders separating cells, columns, and rows, or around the entire table. You can also add fills or shading to emphasize certain parts of the table.

To add or change the borders and fills in your table, you use the Tables And Borders toolbar. As you know, the Tables And Borders toolbar appears whenever you click a table on a slide. If the toolbar does not appear, click the Tables And Borders button on the Standard toolbar.

Changing Table Borders

You can specify a variety of border formatting in your table. You can choose:

- The border format (column borders only, row borders only, table border only, and so on)

- The border style (solid line, dashed line, dotted line, and so on)

- The border width (1/4 point to 6 points)

- The border color

To specify the type of border and border format you want, follow these steps:

1 Select the entire table, or the cells, columns, or rows around which you want to specify the new borders.

2 On the Tables And Borders toolbar, click the down arrow next to the Borders button. The actual name of this button changes depending on what was last selected. The borders palette drops down to show all the different border types.

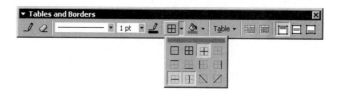

3 Click the border you want. The selected portion of your table changes to reflect the new border type.

4 If you want to change the border style, on the Tables And Borders toolbar, click the down arrow next to the Border Style tool. The Border Style palette drops down.

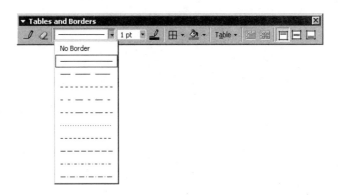

5 Click the border style you want. If the selected portion of your table does not change to the new border style right away, on the Tables And Borders toolbar, click the Borders button. The table is redrawn to reflect the new border style you selected.

6 If you want to change the border width or border color, repeat steps 4 and 5 with the Border Width tool and the Border Color button. After making a change, click the Border button if necessary to redraw the table with the new formatting.

7 When you're finished making formatting changes, on the Tables And Borders toolbar, click the Draw Table button to turn it off. This button turns on whenever you click any border formatting tool, so you can draw freehand table borders. You'll learn more about this later in this section.

Another way to change the borders in your table is to select the portion of your table (typically the entire table) to which you want the new border formatting to apply. Then, on the Tables And Borders toolbar, click Table, and choose Borders And Fill. In the Format Table dialog box, click the Borders tab, as shown in Figure 9-10 on the next page.

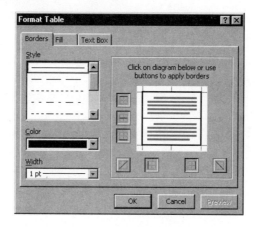

Select a border style, color, and width and then click specific borders on the diagram. To remove a specific border, simply click the border in the diagram.

Adding Fill Colors and Effects to the Table

You can specify a variety of fills to cells, columns, or rows in your table. You can choose:

- Fill colors

- Gradients

- Textures

- Patterns

- Pictures

To specify the fill you want, follow these steps:

The Fill Color button

1 Select the cells, columns, or rows in which you want to add a fill.

2 On the Tables And Borders toolbar, click the arrow next to the Fill Color button. The fill color palette drops down.

3 If you want a color that corresponds with the current presentation template, click a color from the list shown. If you want a different color, click More Fill Colors.

If you want a gradient, texture, pattern, or picture, click Fill Effects. The Fill Effects dialog box appears.

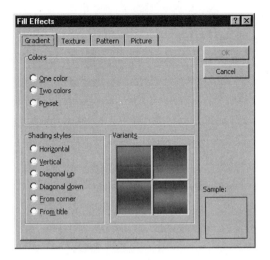

4 Specify the fill color or effect you want—it is applied to the selected portion of your table. Figure 9-11 shows a color applied to the heading row.

FIGURE 9-11.

The top row has been formatted with a color.

Employee Performance

Employee	Years of Service	Start Date	Rating
Audrey Marr	13	11/14/84	98
Eric Weinberger	11	12/1/86	92

You can also apply fill colors and effects with the Format Table dialog box. Select the portion of your table to which you want to apply a fill color or effect. On the Tables And Borders toolbar, click Table, and then choose Borders And Fill. In the Format Table dialog box, click the Fill tab, as shown in Figure 9-12 on the next page.

FIGURE 9-12.
The Fill tab of the Format Table dialog box.

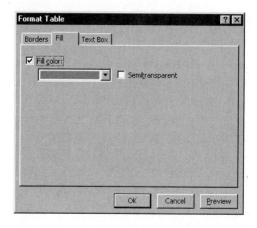

Click the down arrow next to the fill color box, and then select the color, fill effect, or background you want.

Drawing Lines in the Table

The Draw Table button

Using the Draw Table button on the Tables And Borders toolbar, you can draw new lines in your table. You can also draw over existing lines to change their appearance.

The Eraser button

You can use the Eraser button, also on the Tables And Borders toolbar, to remove existing table lines. In addition, you can use the Eraser button to remove line formatting without removing the line itself.

To draw lines in your table, follow these steps:

1 On the Tables And Borders toolbar, click the Draw Table button.

2 If you want, change the border formatting with the Border Style, Border Width, and Border Color tools.

3 Move the mouse pointer onto your table where you want to draw the line. The pointer is now a pencil icon.

4 Draw the line you want. You can draw vertical, horizontal, and diagonal lines across the cells, rows, and columns of your table. The line is drawn with the border formatting you have specified.

5 When finished drawing lines, click the Draw Table button again to turn it off.

To erase lines in your table, follow these steps:

1 On the Tables And Borders toolbar, click the Eraser button.

2 Move the mouse pointer onto your table where you want to erase the line. The pointer is now an eraser icon.

3 Click the line you want to erase. You can erase either the lines you drew with the Draw Table button, or the regular table border lines.

4 When finished erasing lines, click the Eraser button again to turn it off.

Positioning Text in a Table

In addition to the regular text formatting you can do in your table, you can position your table text in special ways.

■ You can indent text within a cell. Click the cell, and then on the ruler, drag the left indent marker where you want the text to be indented. *For more information about indenting text, see "Changing the Indents, Alignment, and Spacing," page 100.*

■ You can set and use tabs within a cell. Click the cell, and then to the left of the ruler, click the Tab Alignment button until the tab type you want is showing. Then in the ruler for the cell, click the location for the tab. When typing in the cell, to move to a tab stop, press Ctrl+Tab. *For more information about tabs, see "Setting and Removing Tab Stops," page 108.*

The Align Top button

■ You can align text horizontally and vertically within a cell. For horizontal alignment, select as many cells as you want, and then on the Formatting toolbar, click the Align Left, Center, or Align Right button. For vertical alignment, select as many cells as you want, and then on the Tables And Borders toolbar, click the Align Top, Center Vertically, or Align Bottom buttons.

The Center Vertically button

■ You can set internal cell margins. Select the cells and, on the Tables And Borders toolbar, click Table. Then choose Borders And Fill and click the Text Box tab. Under Internal Margin, enter the margins you want in the Left, Right, Top, and Bottom boxes.

The Align Bottom button

■ You can rotate text in a cell. Select the cells and, on the Tables And Borders toolbar, click Table. Then choose Borders And Fill and click the Text Box tab. Select the Rotate Text Within Cell By 90° check box.

Now that you've learned how to create table slides and add them to a presentation, you know how to work with all the basic presentation building blocks. In Part 3, you'll learn how to make overall changes to the presentation and how to add enhancements to strengthen its powers of communication.

II

The Basic Presentation

PART III

Fine-Tuning the Presentation

CHAPTER 10

Reorganizing the Presentation

S lide Sorter view, the fourth of PowerPoint's views, displays the slides of a presentation as miniatures arranged neatly on the screen to give you a working view of the presentation as a whole. But Slide Sorter view allows you to do more than just see the overall presentation. You can also do real work on the presentation.

In Slide Sorter view, you can accomplish these tasks:

- Check the presentation from start to finish for design flaws and inconsistencies, such as missing headings.

- Rearrange slides for a more logical or stronger sequence.

- Change the template, color scheme, and background of all slides or only selected slides.

- Duplicate slides.

- Move or copy slides between two presentations.

- Set up and preview the transition and build effects that will appear in Slide Show view.

All of these tasks except the last one are covered in this chapter. Creating slide shows while in Slide Sorter view is the subject of Chapter 15, "Making Lively Slide Shows."

Switching to Slide Sorter View

The Slide Sorter
view button

Switching to Slide Sorter view is easy: just click the Slide Sorter View button in the lower left corner of the presentation window. You can also choose Slide Sorter from the View menu.

Click the Slide Sorter view button.

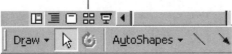

When you switch to Slide Sorter view, the current presentation is displayed as a set of miniature slides, and the Slide Sorter toolbar replaces the Formatting toolbar below the Standard toolbar. Figure 10-1 shows a presentation in Slide Sorter view.

FIGURE 10-1.

A presentation in
Slide Sorter view.

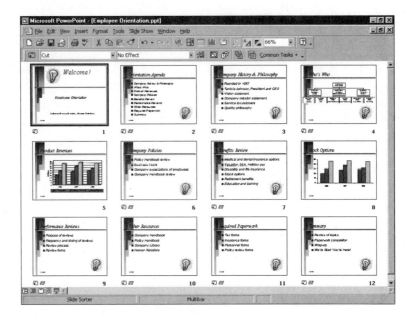

To leave Slide Sorter and look at a single slide, double-click the slide. You can also use the arrow keys to move the highlighted border to a slide, and then press Enter. The slide will be displayed in either Normal view or Slide view, depending on which view you worked in last.

Zooming In and Out

Zooming in allows you to inspect slides more closely to check for errors. Zooming out allows you to view more of the presentation as a whole so that you can check the consistency of the slides' design. To zoom in and out on the slide miniatures in Slide Sorter view, on the Standard toolbar, click the down arrow next to the Zoom tool. Or, from the View menu, choose Zoom to open the Zoom dialog box. Either way, select one of the preset zoom percentages or type a new percentage in the edit box.

Changing the Presentation in Slide Sorter View

In Slide Sorter view, as in most other views, you can change the appearance of the presentation by rearranging slides, adding and deleting slides, duplicating existing slides, applying a different template, and moving and copying slides between presentations. However, this is not the view for changing the content of individual slides. Creating and editing individual slides are tasks that you perform in Normal view, Slide view, or Outline view.

 TIP

> **Speed Your Work in Slide Sorter View**
>
> By clicking the Show Formatting button on the Standard toolbar, you can temporarily turn off formatting to display only the slide titles. This way, as you work with the slides, you don't have to wait for them to redraw. To redisplay the slide contents, click the Show Formatting button again to turn formatting back on.

Rearranging Slides

 SEE ALSO

For more information about creating and editing slides, see Chapter 4, "Writing the Text in Outline View," page 53, and Chapter 5, "Creating Slides in Slide View," page 87.

Slide Sorter view is most commonly used for moving slides to new positions in the presentation, the same way you'd sort 35-mm slides on a light table before placing them in a slide projector. The simplest way to reposition a slide is to use the good old drag-and-drop technique. However, you can also move a slide by using the Cut and Paste commands or toolbar buttons.

To rearrange the order of slides using the drag-and-drop technique, follow the steps on the next page.

III

Fine-Tuning the Presentation

1 Position the mouse pointer on the slide you want to move.

2 Hold down the left mouse button and drag the vertical marker to a position between two other slides.

3 Release the mouse button to drop the slide into place.

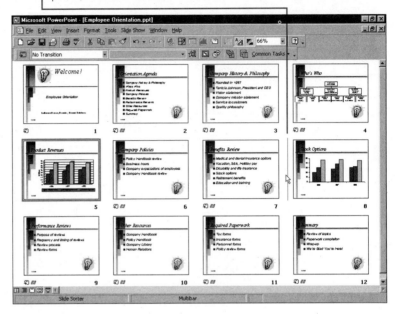

To move a slide using Cut and Paste, follow these steps:

1 Click the slide you want to move.

2 On the Standard toolbar, click the Cut button. Or, from the Edit or shortcut menu, choose Cut.

3 Click an insertion point to indicate the slide's new position (a vertical line appears), and click the Paste button. Or, from the Edit or shortcut menus, choose Paste.

Copy a Slide in Slide Sorter View

To copy a slide rather than move it, hold down the Ctrl key as you drag the slide. To copy a slide with the toolbar buttons, on the Standard toolbar, click the Copy button instead of the Cut button, click where you want the copied slide to be inserted, and then click the Paste button. To copy a slide with menu commands, from the Edit or shortcut menu, choose Copy, click where you want the copied slide to be inserted, and then choose Paste. A copy of the slide appears at the destination location, while the original is still intact.

Rearranging a group of slides is just as easy as rearranging a single slide. After you select the group, you can use the same techniques as described above for moving a single slide.

To select a group of adjacent slides, click the first slide you want in the group, hold down Shift, and then click the last slide you want in the group. As shown in Figure 10-2, all slides between the first and last in the series are selected, as indicated by the highlighted border.

FIGURE 10-2.

You can select a group of adjacent slides using the Shift key. The highlighted border indicates that the slide is selected.

First slide in the series

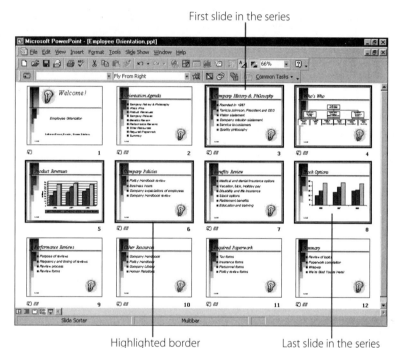

Highlighted border

Last slide in the series

To select a group of adjacent slides, you can draw a selection box across the group, like this:

1   Position the mouse pointer just outside the first slide you want to select. If you position the pointer within a selected slide, you'll end up dragging the slide to another location, rather than selecting a group of adjacent slides.

2   Hold down the left mouse button, and drag from the first to the last slide of the series you want to select. All slides in between are selected.

III

Fine-Tuning the Presentation

You can also select a group of nonadjacent slides—that is, slides located in different parts of the presentation. Click the first slide in the series, hold down Ctrl, and then click all the other slides you want in the group. As shown in Figure 10-3, all the slides you click are selected, as indicated by the highlighted border. If you want to deselect a slide, click it again.

FIGURE 10-3.

You can select a group of nonadjacent slides using the Ctrl key.

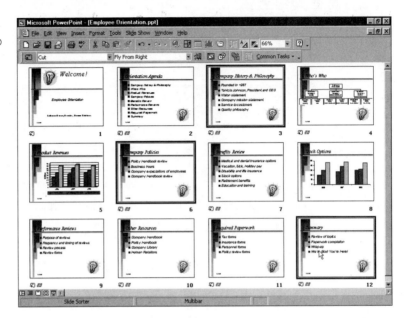

After you select the slides, place the pointer on any slide and drag the group to its new location in the presentation. As with single slides, you can also use the Cut and Paste commands.

When you move or copy a group of nonadjacent slides to a new location, the slides appear in the same consecutive order in the new location. That is, a slide from the first part of the presentation appears first, followed by a slide from the next part of the presentation, and so on.

Adding and Deleting Slides

Slide Sorter view is the perfect view for adding and deleting slides because you can quickly see the effect of such changes on the entire presentation.

To add a slide, follow these steps:

1 In the presentation, click the slide that you want the new slide to follow.

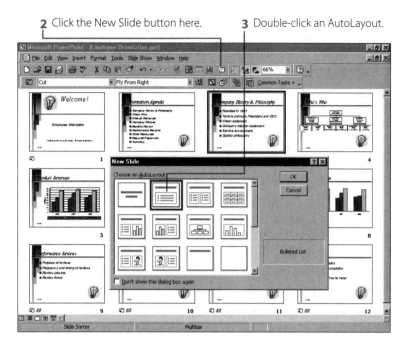

2 Click the New Slide button here.   **3** Double-click an AutoLayout.

Deleting a slide is even easier. Just click the slide you want to delete and then press Delete on the keyboard. You can also delete a group of slides by using one of the methods described earlier for selecting a group and then pressing Delete.

Duplicating Slides

You can also use Slide Sorter view to duplicate slides that have some feature you want to reproduce. Let's say you need to create the same pie graph for each salon in a chain of six beauty salons. You can create the first graph on a slide, switch to Slide Sorter view, and duplicate the slide five times. Then you can switch back to Normal view or Slide view and edit the data in each of the duplicate slides. The design of the first graph and special formatting you've applied are carried over to the other slides, as shown in Figure 10-4 on the next page.

> **NOTE**
>
> If you often need to use the same chart design, you can save the formatting of the chart as an autoformat that you can apply to a new chart. *For more information about autoformats, see "Saving Chart Formatting as a Custom Chart Type," page 205.*

III

Fine-Tuning the Presentation

FIGURE 10-4.

Duplicating a slide lets you carry special formatting throughout a presentation.

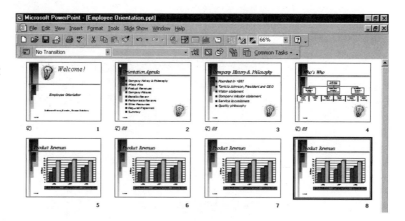

To duplicate a slide in Slide Sorter view, follow these steps:

1 Click the slide you want to duplicate.

2 From the Edit menu, choose Duplicate, or press Ctrl+D. The duplicate appears to the right of the original slide.

Duplicating is similar to copying a slide. When duplicating, you don't have to choose the Paste command; the duplicate slide is automatically inserted to the right of the original duplicated slide. On the other hand, if you want the copy to be placed elsewhere in the presentation, you might prefer to use the Copy and Paste commands.

Moving and Copying Slides Between Presentations

Just as you can move and copy slides within a presentation, you can also move and copy slides between presentations. Moving and copying slides between presentations lets you transfer an existing slide to a new presentation rather than re-create its content there.

Before you can actually move or copy slides between two presentations, first arrange the presentations side by side in Slide Sorter view. To do this, follow these steps:

1 Open two presentations. Close any other presentations you might have open.

2 In each presentation, switch to Slide Sorter view. To switch from one presentation to the other, from the Window menu, choose the presentation's file name.

3 From the Window menu, choose Arrange All. The two presentations are arranged one above the other, as shown on the facing page.

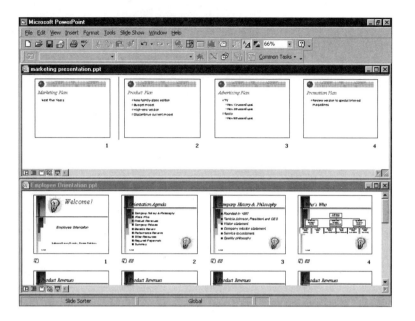

NOTE

You might want to use the same zoom percentage for both presentations. You can select a presentation by clicking it, and then change its zoom percentage independently. *For more information about changing the zoom percentage, see "Zooming In and Out," page 69.*

After the presentations are arranged side by side, you can move a slide from one presentation to another by clicking a slide in one presentation and dragging it to the other presentation. The slide that was moved takes on the design of the destination presentation's template. To copy a slide rather than move it, hold down Ctrl as you drag the slide to the destination presentation.

You can also transfer slides between presentations by first selecting a slide in one presentation and clicking the Cut or Copy button on the Standard toolbar or by choosing Cut or Copy on the Edit or shortcut menus. Then you can click an insertion point in the other presentation, and click the Paste button on the Standard toolbar or choose Paste from the Edit or shortcut menus.

NOTE

You can move or copy a group of slides between presentations by selecting the group before you use the drag-and-drop technique, the toolbar buttons, or the menu commands. *For more information about selecting a group of slides, see "Rearranging Slides," page 265.*

III

Fine-Tuning the Presentation

Changing the Design in Slide Sorter View

In Chapter 11, you will learn more about changing the template, color scheme, and background of a slide. The following sections describe how to do this in Slide Sorter view. Slide Sorter view is the ideal place to make these changes because you can easily see how the entire presentation is affected.

Changing the Template and Color Scheme of the Presentation

In Slide Sorter view, you can use the same techniques to change the template and color scheme of the presentation that you use in Normal view or Slide view.

To change the presentation template, follow these steps:

1 From the Format menu, choose Apply Design Template.

2 Select a different template in the Apply Design Template dialog box.

? SEE ALSO

For more information about changing a presentation's template and color scheme, see Chapter 11, "Changing the Look," page 275.

To change the color scheme of the entire presentation, follow these steps:

1 Select at least one of the slides in the presentation.

2 From the Format menu, choose Slide Color Scheme.

3 Click the color scheme you want.

4 Click Apply To All.

When you change the template or color scheme in Slide Sorter view, you can immediately see the effect of the redesign on all the slides at once.

Changing the Color Scheme of Selected Slides

In Slide Sorter view, you can select specific slides and change their color scheme. For example, you can select all the slides that cover a general topic and modify their color scheme. You can even give each segment of the presentation a different color scheme to differentiate it from the other segments.

? SEE ALSO

For more information about changing the color scheme, see "Changing the Color Scheme," page 272.

To modify the color scheme for specific slides, follow these steps:

1 Select the slide or slides for which you want a different color scheme.

2 From the Format menu, choose Slide Color Scheme.

3 Click the color scheme you want.

4 Click Apply. The color scheme is revised only in the selected slides.

Copying Color Schemes Among Slides

After you change the color scheme for selected slides, you can copy the color scheme to other slides in the presentation. Copying the color scheme can be a real time-saver because you don't have to repeat the process of choosing commands and selecting options. You simply select a slide that has already been formatted with the color scheme you want and copy the scheme to one or more other slides.

To copy a color scheme from one slide to another, follow these steps:

1 Select the slide with the color scheme you want to copy.

2 On the Standard toolbar, click the Format Painter button.

3 Click the slide to which you want to copy the color scheme.

Changing the Background

You can change the background color of selected slides just as easily as you can change their color scheme. The Background command on the Format menu works as it does in Normal view or Slide view: you can change only the background color, or you can apply a gradient, texture, or picture to the background without affecting the other presentation colors. To change the background color for the entire presentation, follow these steps:

1 Select at least one of the slides in the presentation.

2 From the Format menu, choose Background.

3 Click the down arrow next to the color edit box.

4 Click the color you want. You can click More Colors for a complete color selection. Or click Fill Effects to choose a gradient, texture, pattern, or picture as the background.

5 Click Apply To All.

> **NOTE**

If you have a different color scheme applied to some slides in the presentation, the background color you see might be different on those slides because your change follows the scheme color. If you select a color from the More Colors dialog box, however, the background color for all slides change to that color.

III

Fine-Tuning the Presentation

? SEE ALSO

For more information about changing the background scheme of a presentation, see "Altering the Custom Background," page 288.

To modify the background color scheme for specific slides, select the slide or slides for which you want a different background color or effect. Follow the same steps as in the above procedure, and then click Apply. The background color is revised only in the selected slides.

In the Background dialog box, you can also select the Omit Background Graphics From Master check box to turn the background design on or off for the selected slides. You might want to select slides and turn off their background graphics when you need a simple background on which to draw diagrams or create complicated foreground images. Figure 10-5 shows a presentation with three slides that have had their display of background graphics turned off so that the charts will display more clearly.

FIGURE 10-5.

The background graphics have been turned off on three slides in this presentation.

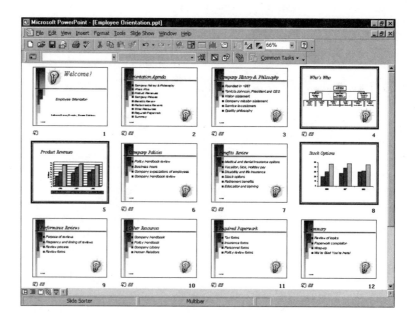

In this chapter, you've learned how useful Slide Sorter view can be when you want to rearrange slides and change a presentation's design. In Chapter 11, you'll learn more details about how to change the template, color scheme, title master, slide master, and slide background.

Changing the Look

As you've seen, PowerPoint offers a sophisticated system for creating an entire presentation's worth of slides that share a common design. This chapter focuses on the central controls behind the presentation design process: the template, the color scheme, and the title and slide masters. You can use these controls to make overall changes to your presentation, such as redesigning the background or applying a different combination of colors to all the slides. The following list describes the elements that are managed by each of the three controls:

- The template contains a color scheme, a title master and slide master, and a set of AutoLayouts that control where objects are positioned on slides.

- The color scheme contains a background color and seven other colors that are applied to particular elements in the presentation.

- The title and slide masters contain a background design and default text formatting for the slide titles and main text items. The background design can contain graphic objects or can be shaded, patterned, or textured. The default text formatting is applied to the slide titles and the bulleted text items.

What is so powerful—and potentially confusing—about these controls is the way they overlap. When you alter the title or slide master, for example, you can change the current color scheme, which can change the background color. To make things even more interesting, you can also change the background color directly, without changing the color scheme. To help you understand how these controls interact, this chapter first looks at the big picture. It begins with a discussion of the controls that have the broadest influence on a presentation, and then goes on to cover the controls that affect a single aspect of a slide.

Applying a Different Template

The easiest—and most sweeping—step you can take when you want to change the appearance of a presentation is to apply a different design template. Changing the design template makes a wholesale change to just about every aspect of the presentation's appearance. Figure 11-1 shows a basic presentation, before (top) and after (bottom) the Expedition template is applied.

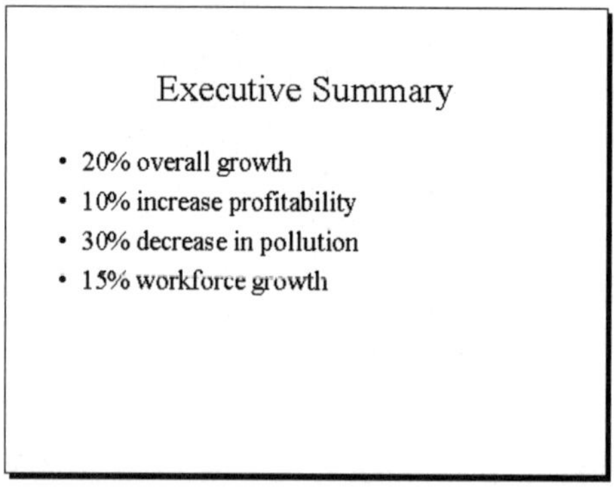

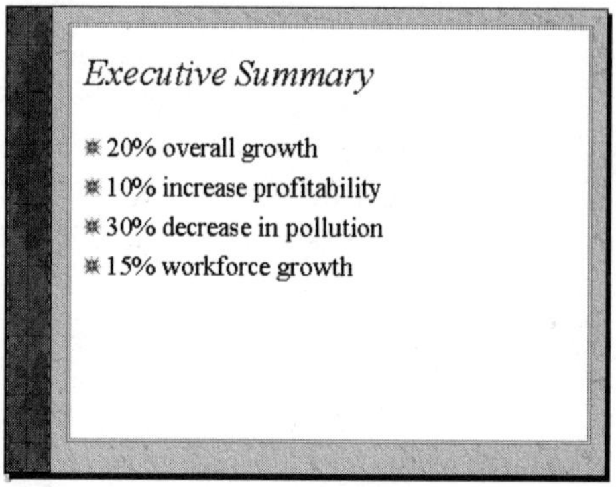

FIGURE 11-1.

A presentation slide before (top) and after (bottom) the Expedition template is applied.

Executive Summary

- 20% overall growth
- 10% increase profitability
- 30% decrease in pollution
- 15% workforce growth

Executive Summary

- 20% overall growth
- 10% increase profitability
- 30% decrease in pollution
- 15% workforce growth

The template is the most powerful and all-encompassing of the central controls. Among other things, changing the template:

- Changes the color scheme that controls the colors used in the presentation

- Changes the title master and slide master, which in turn changes the background design and default text formatting

The templates that come with PowerPoint were created by professional artists. Because of this, these templates produce polished, attractive presentations. So you might not need to make further changes to the appearance of the presentation after you apply a template.

Other Ways to Change the Design

By changing the template, you can give your presentation an entirely new look: All the slides in the presentation get the same new background and new color scheme, and even a new selection of text fonts. But you can control each of these design aspects individually without having to apply a new template. You can even make design changes on selected slides, leaving the other slides to conform to the template's design. Some of the overall changes you can make without changing the template are:

- Decorating the background with a company logo or project name

- Adding special text to the background that spells out the presentation's subject

- Modifying the presentation colors to match a client's corporate color palette

- Changing the font and text formatting used in slide titles to give the presentation a more playful or more serious character

---

If someone else has created a unique new presentation design, it might have been saved in a template that you can use. When you apply the custom template to your presentation, you get the same special presentation design. Often, the chief PowerPoint user in an organization will create a template you can use to conform to the company look. In fact, the design guru may have changed the characteristics of the default template so that each new presentation you create starts out automatically with the approved presentation design.

TIP

Check the Name of the Current Template

To find out which template is applied to the current presentation, check the status bar at the bottom of the PowerPoint window. The template name appears in the center of the status bar.

Selecting an Existing Template

When you create a new presentation using the AutoContent Wizard, a design template is attached to the presentation. To select a template by name as you start a new presentation, click the Design Templates tab of the New Presentation dialog box and then select a template.

To change the template for an existing presentation, follow these steps:

1 On the Formatting toolbar, click Common Tasks and then click Apply Design Template. Or, from the Format menu, choose Apply Design Template.

2 Click any template to preview it.   **3** Click apply.

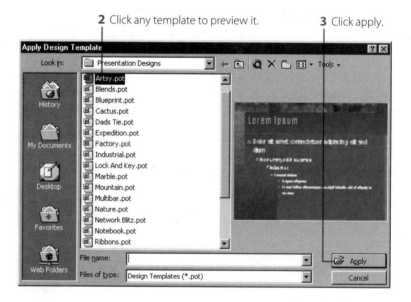

The new template reformats every slide in the presentation.

If you've never changed a template before, you can get some practice by creating a simple presentation. (You can use the AutoContent Wizard to quickly generate a multipage dummy presentation.) You can then click Apply Design Template and select a template name from the Apply Design Template dialog box. Notice the different effects that are created when you apply different templates.

TIP

> **Search for a Specific Template**
> To search for a particular template, on the toolbar in the Apply Design Template dialog box, click Tools and then choose Find. Specify your search criteria and then click Find Now.

Creating a New Template

To create a custom look for future presentations, you can create your own template based on changes you've made to a presentation's color scheme and its title and slide masters. (Later in this chapter, you'll learn how to change the color scheme and the title and slide masters.) It's not a bad idea to model your template on an existing one. When you apply the template, the color scheme, background items, and text formatting will be the same as those you've used in the presentation.

To create a template, follow these steps:

1 Open or create a presentation that you want to use as the basis for a template.

2 Make any changes to the presentation that you want to save in the new template.

NOTE

> All the existing text, clip art, and links will be saved in the template unless you remove them now.

3 From the File menu, choose Save As.

4 Browse to find the folder in which you want to save the template. If you save your template in the same place as the standard PowerPoint templates, your template will be listed with the others in the Apply Design Template dialog box. These are typically stored in \Program Files\Microsoft Office\Templates\Presentation Designs.

5 In the Save As Type box, select Design Template.

6 In the File Name box, type a name for the template and then click Save.

III

Fine-Tuning the Presentation

Changing the Color Scheme

Every template you apply contains a color scheme that provides the various parts of a presentation with a coordinated set of eight default colors. The most distinctive design element of the presentation is the background, so the first color in the color scheme is the background color. The other seven colors effectively complement the background color and are applied to text, charts, and other objects that appear against the background. Whenever you choose a command that allows you to change the color of an object, such as the Font command, you can display the default color scheme by clicking the arrow next to the Color box. Figure 11-2 shows the default color scheme displayed in the Font dialog box.

FIGURE 11-2.

The default color scheme in the Font dialog box.

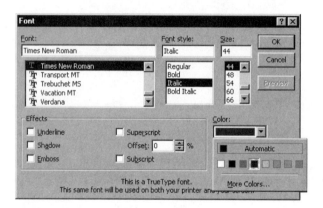

Changing the colors in the color scheme can be enough to dramatically transform the look. When you modify the color scheme, you can apply the revised scheme to the entire presentation. If you apply the color scheme to all slides in a presentation, the new colors are applied to every object in the presentation as well. The only exceptions are objects to which you have assigned specific colors. For example, if you have selected a special color for certain words in a slide title, the color remains even when you change the overall color scheme.

SEE ALSO

For more information about transferring color schemes, see "Copying Color Schemes Among Slides," page 273.

As always, you can save a modified color scheme for future use. After you've carefully matched your organization's standard colors, for example, you can save the color scheme in a template and distribute the template to coworkers. That way, every presentation delivered by a representative of your organization can have the uniform look you want. In addition, if you've modified the color scheme for one presentation, you can copy the color scheme directly to another.

NOTE

You cannot save a color scheme in its own file. Because a color scheme is always part of a template, to save the revised color scheme, you must save the template with a new name.

SEE ALSO

For more information about working with speaker notes and handouts, see "Printing Handouts and Notes Pages," page 366.

PowerPoint also allows you to use a different color scheme for speaker's notes and handouts by revising the color schemes of their masters. The revised color schemes of the notes and handouts have no effect on the overall color scheme applied to the presentation.

Selecting a Standard Color Scheme

The easiest way to change the color scheme of a presentation is to select one of PowerPoint's standard color schemes, all of which were created by professional artists.

To select a predefined color scheme, follow these steps:

1 Open the presentation whose color scheme you want to modify.

2 From the Format menu, choose Slide Color Scheme.

3 Click a different color scheme.

4 Click Apply to All to apply to every slide or click Apply to apply to the current slide.

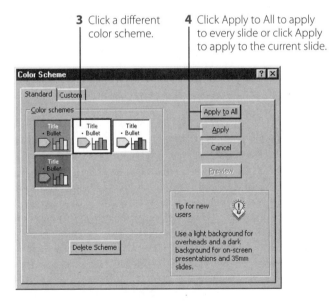

NOTE

If you previously applied a color to a specific element in your presentation, that element will not be affected by the new color scheme.

III

Fine-Tuning the Presentation

Add Your Custom Color Scheme to the List

If you create a custom color scheme, you can add it to the Standard Color Scheme list. To do this, in the Color Scheme dialog box, click the Custom tab. Then click the Add As Standard Scheme button. Now your custom color scheme is always available for selection on the Standard tab.

Creating a Custom Color Scheme

Occasionally, the standard color schemes won't quite work for your presentation. You might want to vary the brightness or the shade of one or more colors, or you might want to select a different set of colors entirely. If this is the case, you can create a custom color scheme. You'll probably want to first select a template for your presentation that has a color scheme similar to the one you want to create.

To create a custom color scheme, follow these steps:

1 Have a presentation open on your screen.

2 From the Format menu or the shortcut menu, choose Slide Color Scheme. In the Color Scheme dialog box, click the Custom tab, shown below. Table 11-1 on page 284 provides more information about the eight color scheme colors listed in the Color Scheme dialog box.

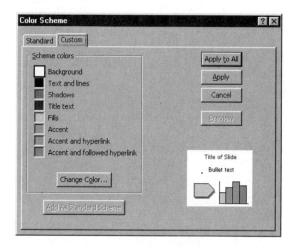

3 To change one of the eight scheme colors, double-click its box or click the box once and then click Change Color. For example, to change the fill color, double-click the Fills box to open the Fill

Color dialog box, and then click the Standard tab. The Fill Color dialog box displays dozens of colors and several shades of gray from which you can select a new color. (Note that the current color is shown in the Current color box.)

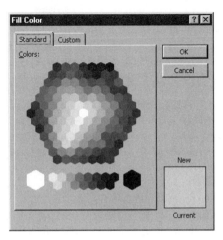

4 Select a color by clicking it and then click OK. If you don't see the color you want, click the Custom tab.

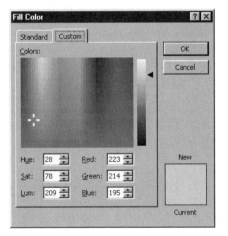

You can use the two color boxes in the upper half of the Custom tab to select a color. You can use the large box on the left to select the general color (the *hue*) and the intensity of the hue (the *saturation level*). As you click or drag the crosshair elsewhere across the color and intensity matrix, the color in the New color box changes. The numbers in the edit boxes also change to indicate the numeric values of the color.

The vertical strip to the right of the color box has a triangular marker that indicates how much black or white is mixed with the color (the *luminance* of the color). Click or drag the triangular marker up or down the strip to change the luminance of your color.

TABLE 11-1.   The Color Boxes in the Color Scheme Dialog Box

Color Box	Description
Background	The color applied to the background of the slides. The background color can be shaded in a template from light to dark or dark to light, and, on selected slides, it can be superseded by a different background color that you select.
Text And Lines	The color applied to bulleted text and to text blocks typed onto the slides with the Text Tool. Also used for lines and arrows drawn with the Line Tool and as the outline color for AutoShapes and objects drawn with the other drawing tools.
Shadows	The color applied to shadows created with the Shadow command.
Title Text	The color applied to slide titles and subtitles.
Fills	The color used to fill AutoShapes and objects drawn with any drawing tool. Also the color used to fill the first series in a graph.
Accent	The color used as a second color in graphs, org charts, and other added elements.
Accent And Hyperlink	The color used as a third color in graphs, org charts, and other added elements. Also used for hyperlinks (jumps to other slides, presentations, or Internet addresses on pages).
Accent And Followed Hyperlink	The color used as a fourth color in graphs, org charts, and other added elements. Also used for hyperlinks that have already been used on pages.

The edit boxes contain numeric values for the hue, saturation, and luminance (*HSL*) and for the red, green, and blue (*RGB*) of the color. You can use the HSL and RGB numbers to specify an exact color. For example, you can record the numbers of a color you like in one color scheme and then enter the numbers in another color scheme to reproduce the same color. (You can enter either the three HSL numbers or the three RGB numbers—you don't need both sets.)

5 On the Custom tab, click or drag the crosshair in the large box to the general color you want, and then drag the marker on the vertical strip to brighten or darken the color. Check the New color box in the lower right corner of the tab to see the new color.

6 When you're satisfied with the new color, click OK to return to the Color Scheme dialog box. You can click Preview to see how the new color will appear in the presentation. (You may need to drag the Color Scheme dialog box to one side to preview the presentation.)

7 Follow steps 3 through 6 to change any of the other Scheme Colors. Then click Apply To All to apply the color scheme to the entire presentation. Or click Apply to apply the scheme to just the current slide.

After you create a custom color scheme, you can add it to the presentation as a standard scheme. This way, if you change one or more slides to another color scheme, you can always return the slides to the custom color scheme you created.

To add a custom color scheme as a standard scheme, follow these steps:

1 From the Format menu or shortcut menu, choose Slide Color Scheme. In the Color Scheme dialog box, click the Custom tab. The custom color scheme appears on the tab.

2 Click Add As Standard Scheme. PowerPoint copies your custom color scheme to the Standard tab.

> **NOTE**
>
> You can remove a custom color scheme you have added as a standard scheme. In the Color Scheme dialog box, click the custom color scheme and then click Delete Scheme.

PowerPoint's Color System

Although PowerPoint provides a broad palette of colors from which to choose, it does not follow the commonly used color matching systems for selecting and specifying colors, such as the Pantone or Trumatch system. To match a color, such as the dominant color in your company's logo, you must go through the trial-and-error process of selecting a color, sending it to your color output device, examining the output, and then adjusting the color in PowerPoint. The process can be time-consuming, because most output devices produce colors that are lighter or darker than they appear on your screen. In addition, the number of colors you see on the screen and the precision with which they are displayed depend on the color capabilities of your hardware. Even the brightness control on your monitor affects how a color looks. When you do find the correct color, you might want to make note of its HSL or RGB number so that you can reproduce it later.

Editing the Title Master or Slide Master

Like the template and color scheme, the title and the slide masters are other elements you can modify to make global changes in a presentation. Changes you make to the title master affect only the slides you add with the Title AutoLayout; changes you make to the slide master affect all other slides in the presentation. Both masters contain:

- A background color that can have various special effects applied

- A scheme of fonts and text formatting for the slide titles and bulleted text

- An optional group of graphic objects placed on the background and arranged to form a design

The title and slide masters give the presentation an overall look and consistency by setting the design of the background and text. They also save you from the tedium of formatting each slide individually. This section discusses how to open the title master and the slide master and how to customize their background color and shading, title and text, and background design.

Opening the Title Master or Slide Master

To display the title master so that you can edit it, follow these steps:

1   Make sure that a title slide is displayed. To determine whether the current slide is a title slide, on the Formatting toolbar, click Common Tasks and then click Slide Layout. The Slide Layout dialog box shows which layout is selected. Click Cancel to return to your slide.

2   Hold down Shift and then click the Slide View button in the lower left corner of your screen.

The title master for the current presentation appears, as shown in Figure 11-3.

FIGURE 11-3.

The title master.

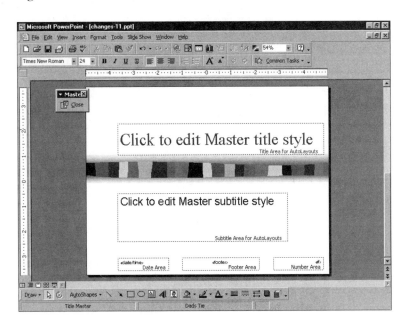

To display the slide master, follow these steps:

1   Make sure that a slide other than the title slide is displayed. If you're unsure, on the Formatting toolbar, click Common Tasks and then click the Slide Layout. Check which layout is selected. Click Cancel to return to your slide.

2   Hold down Shift and click the Slide View button. Or, from the View menu, point to Master and then choose Slide Master.

The slide master for the current presentation appears, as shown in Figure 11-4 on the next page.

FIGURE 11-4.

The slide master.

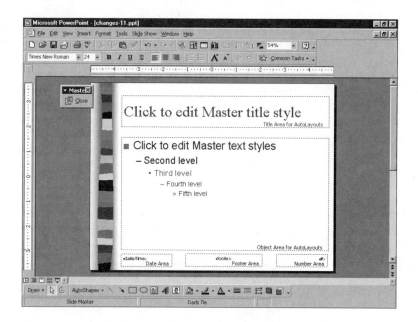

You can open the title master or slide master with any slide displayed. From the View menu, point to Master and then choose Title Master or Slide Master. Using the menu commands, you can easily switch between the title master and slide master without having to change the slide currently displayed. If a design template is not applied to the presentation, the Title Master command is not available.

As you can see, the title master or the slide master temporarily takes over the screen. A new Master toolbar also appears containing two buttons—a Slide Miniature icon button to display a small version of the slide, and a Close button to close the master and toolbar. If you do not see the Master toolbar, from the View menu, point to Toolbars and then click Master.

To return to your presentation, click the Close button on the Master toolbar. Or click the Slide View button.

Altering the Custom Background

Although the color scheme supplies a background color for a presentation, you can modify the background color when you change the slide background for the master. Modifying the background color on a master is similar to modifying the background color in the color scheme.

You can also make other changes to the master's background. For instance, you can set a shading for the background color and then lighten or darken the shading. You can also apply patterns, textures, or a picture to the background.

To change the fill color of the master's background, follow these steps:

1 Be sure that the master is displayed on your screen.

2 From the Format or shortcut menu, choose Background. The Background dialog box appears.

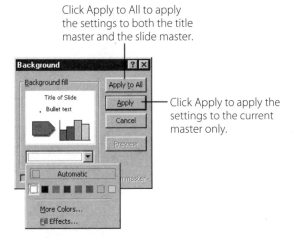

Click Apply to All to apply the settings to both the title master and the slide master.

Click Apply to apply the settings to the current master only.

3 Use the controls in the drop-down list to select a different background color. The current background appears in the drop-down list box. To change to a background color that complements the color scheme, select Automatic or one of the eight colors that appear in the drop-down list. To select a different color, choose More Colors and then click the Standard tab.

There are a variety of other ways to change the appearance of the background, including its shading, pattern, and texture. You can even insert a picture for a "watermark" effect.

TIP

Preview the New Background

You can click the Preview button in the Background dialog box to preview the new background. After you click Preview, you can drag the dialog box aside to see more of the background. If you're not satisfied with the background, the Background dialog box is still on the screen, so you can select a different setting.

III

Fine-Tuning the Presentation

You can change the master background without even opening the title or slide master. From the Format menu, choose Background. Specify the color, texture, pattern, or picture you want for the background and then click Apply To All. The new background is applied to all slides in the presentation, and the title and slide masters are updated to reflect this new background.

Applying a Gradient

You can shade the background of a title master or slide master using one color, two colors, or a preset color scheme. To apply shading to the background, follow these steps:

1   Be sure that the master is displayed on your screen.

2   From the Format or shortcut menu, choose Background.

3   From the drop-down list on the Background dialog box, select Fill Effects.

4   On the Fill Effects dialog box, be sure that the Gradient tab is selected. Under Variants, four standard gradients using the current color are shown.

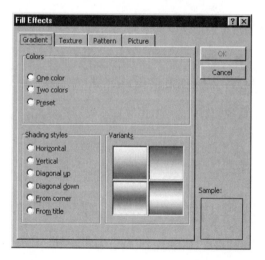

To select a different background color altogether, select the One Color, Two Color, or Preset options. Then use the drop-down lists to select a color or preset color scheme. You can also select More Colors to specify a different color in a standard or custom color scheme. If you are using just one color, you can use the scroll bar under the Color drop-down list to vary the intensity of the shading.

If you want the gradient to be drawn in a direction that's different from what you're seeing under Variants, choose an option under Shading Styles. For example, to create a background shade that runs vertically, click Vertical as the shading style.

5 Under Variants, choose one of the variations of the gradient that contains the colors and shading style you have specified. If you want the gradient to move from dark to light, click the variant that shows a transition from dark to light. Other variants allow you to shade the background from light to dark, from light to dark to light, or from dark to light to dark.

Applying a Texture

Yet another way to change the background of the title master or the slide master involves applying a texture. Applying a texture can change the overall "feel" of your presentation. You can choose from several textures, such as medium wood, white marble, cork, and paper.

To apply a texture to the background, follow these steps:

1 Be sure that the master is displayed on your screen.

2 From the Format or shortcut menu, choose Background. The Background dialog box appears.

3 From the drop-down list, select Fill Effects.

4 Click the Texture tab of the Fill Effects dialog box.

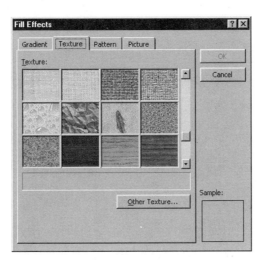

5 Use the scroll bar to view all the available textures. Click the one you want.

Figure 11-5 shows a slide that has been formatted with a textured background.

FIGURE 11-5.

This slide includes the Water Droplets texture as its background.

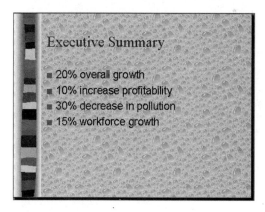

Applying a Pattern

Rather than shade the background, you can apply a pattern made up of two colors. PowerPoint offers more than 48 patterns and many colors to choose from.

To apply a pattern to the background, follow these steps:

1 Be sure that the master is displayed on your screen.

2 From the Format or shortcut menu, choose Background. The Background dialog box appears.

3 From the drop-down list, select Fill Effects.

4 Click the Pattern tab of the Fill Effects dialog box.

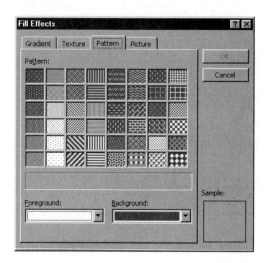

5 Click the texture you want to use.

The patterns shown are composed of the foreground and background colors displayed in the Foreground and Background boxes. You can select a different pattern and different foreground and background colors to create the combination you want.

Inserting a Picture

(?) SEE ALSO

For more information about inserting pictures, see Chapter 13, "Placing Photos and Clip Art on Slides," page 331.

You can insert a picture in the background of either the title or the slide master.

To insert a pattern in the background of a master, follow these steps:

1 Be sure that the master is displayed on your screen.

2 From the Format or shortcut menu, choose Background. The Background dialog box appears.

3 From the drop-down list, select Fill Effects.

4 Click the Picture tab of the Fill Effects dialog box.

5 Click the Select Picture button to browse and choose a background picture stored on your computer. PowerPoint will scale the picture to fit the entire background area of the slide.

Bright, bold pictures work well on title slides, such as the one in Figure 11-6. Because text will be displayed over the picture on other slides, you may want to choose something simple rather than complex. A muted version of the title slide picture often works well.

FIGURE 11-6.
Pictures enhance your presentation.

III

Fine-Tuning the Presentation

Formatting the Title Master or Slide Master

With the background set the way you want, you can turn your attention to the appearance of text in the presentation.

Figure 11-7 shows the title master of the Notebook template. As you can see, the title master displays text in five areas indicated by dashed boxes: the title, subtitle, date, footer, and number areas contain sample text for you to format. When you change the formatting of the sample text on the title master, only the formatting on the title slide changes. To change the formatting on the remaining slides, change the formatting of the text of the slide master.

FIGURE 11-7.

A sample title master.

As shown in Figure 11-8, the slide master looks similar to the title master, but instead of a subtitle area, it contains an object area for AutoLayouts. The object area for AutoLayouts holds sample text at each of the five bulleted text levels. When you change the formatting of the sample text on the slide master, the formatting of the text on every slide—except for the title slide—changes accordingly.

FIGURE 11-8.

A sample slide master.

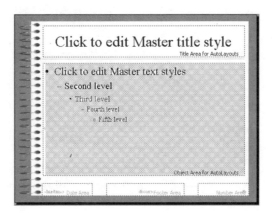

The initial colors of the text in the title, subtitle, and object areas are determined by the colors of the color scheme. For example, the Title Text color of the color scheme sets the title area text color, and the Text And Lines color of the color scheme sets the object area and subtitle area text color. But changing the color of the sample text on the master overrides the color scheme. Even when you change the actual color scheme, the text colors on the title master or slide master are applied rather than the color scheme's text colors.

? SEE ALSO

For more information about formatting text, see "Formatting Text in Slide View," page 96.

- To change the appearance of the slide titles or subtitles, format the text in the title or subtitle area by selecting the text and then using buttons on the Formatting toolbar or commands from the Format or shortcut menu. To change the font and color of the title, for example, click the title to select it, click the right mouse button to display the shortcut menu, choose the Font command, and then select options in the Font dialog box.

- To change all instances of a particular font to another font, choose the Replace Fonts command from the Format menu.

- If you want to make uniform changes to all the bulleted text in a presentation, drag across all the text in the slide master, to select all the bulleted text, and then use the text formatting commands.

? SEE ALSO

For more information about formatting bullet styles, see "Changing the Bullet Shape, Color, and Size," page 106.

- To change the formatting of the bulleted text at only one of the indent levels, select the text at that level and then make a formatting change. For example, to change the font used by bulleted text lines at the second level, select the text Second Level, as shown in Figure 11-9, and then use the text formatting commands to make the changes you want. Even if you just click somewhere in the level, any formatting changes will be applied to all bulleted text at that indent level.

FIGURE 11-9.

To change the formatting of the bulleted text at the second level, select the level and then use the text formatting commands.

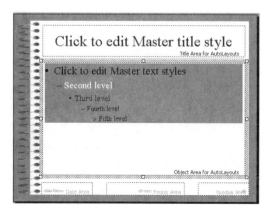

■ To change the style of bullet used at a particular level, click in the text of that level. Then from the Format menu, choose Bullets And Numbering. On the Bulleted tab, select the bullet shape, size, and color you want.

Format Bullet Levels

Although you can apply different formatting to the text at each level, try not to deviate too much from the formatting of the first level. Otherwise, you might end up with a jumble of formatting. Consider using the same font for each level, but make them distinctive by varying the size.

Creating a New Background or Modifying the Existing Background

You can create your own background design or modify an existing one by using PowerPoint's drawing tools to place graphic objects on the background of the title or slide master. Professional artists can do wonders with simple drawing tools, creating entire scenes like those found in the templates that come with PowerPoint. If your artistic skills are not strong, you might prefer to add a few simple geometric shapes to the background. A line or two, or a row of small shapes that you create with the AutoShape tool, can look quite nice.

Rather than compose a background design of your own, you can make minor modifications to the background objects in one of the templates. Simply by moving some of the existing objects, duplicating objects, or changing the objects' positions, you can create a new background design with a unique look. Figure 11-10 shows a slide with a floral graphic added to the Nature template.

FIGURE 11-10.

A custom background design.

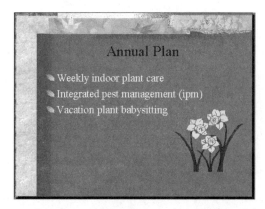

NOTE

> Any graphic objects that are already a part of the title master or slide master have been grouped into a single object. If you want to work with the individual objects, first select the group of objects and then choose Ungroup from the Draw menu. *You'll learn more about grouping and ungrouping objects in "Grouping Objects," page 322.*

SEE ALSO

For more information about using Power-Point's drawing tools, see "Drawing and Formatting the Basic Shapes," page 304.

Text annotations, clip art, and scanned pictures saved as bitmapped files are other elements you can add to the background of the title master or slide master so that they appear on every slide. You'll learn more about how to add these elements to slides (and master backgrounds) in Chapters 12 and 13.

Adding a Header or Footer

PowerPoint makes it easy to add three special text elements to the background of every slide: the date, the time, and the slide number. You can display these elements when you display the presentation in a slide show or print the presentation as slides, handouts, or notes pages. To add a header or footer to your presentation, from the View menu, choose Header And Footer. The Header And Footer dialog box appears with the Slide tab active, as shown in Figure 11-11.

FIGURE 11-11.

This Header And Footer dialog box specifies that the date, slide number, and footer text be displayed on each slide.

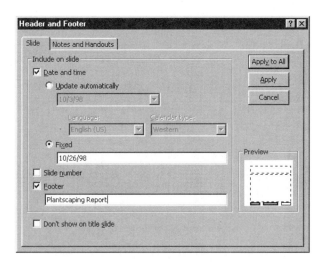

To add the date or time, select the Date And Time check box. If you want the date and time to be automatically updated each time you display or print your presentation, select the Update Automatically option. If you want to enter a fixed date that doesn't change, select the Fixed option. The format of the date and time is determined by the format you select in the corresponding drop-down list or the format you type in the edit box. The Preview window shows the placement of the options you select.

To add the slide number, select the Slide Number check box. To add standard text to every slide, select the Footer check box and type the text you want in the corresponding edit box. If you don't want the date, time, slide number, or footer text to appear on the title slide, select the Don't Show On Title Slide check box.

When you are satisfied with your choices, click Apply To All to add the header or footer to the entire presentation. Or, click Apply to add the header or footer to the current slide only.

If you want to add a header or footer to your notes or handouts, in the Header And Footer dialog box, click the Notes And Handouts tab, and then select the options you want. Click Apply To All to apply the header or footer to the entire presentation.

You can position the date, time, slide number, and footer text anywhere on the slides. To reposition one of these elements, first open the title or slide master and select the frame that contains the element you want to move. Then drag it to a new location.

NOTE

You can change the header and footer in the title master or slide master. In this case, you can't change the header or footer to just one slide when working in the title master or slide master. Any header or footer changes you make are applied to all the slides in the presentation.

TIP

Track Versions with Date and Time
You might want to use the date and time to keep track of versions (while the presentation is in the draft stage, for example), and then remove them when you're ready to display or print the final presentation. To remove the date and time, simply choose Header And Footer from the View menu, click the Slide tab, and clear the Date And Time check box.

Inserting the Slide Number, Date, or Time on Selected Slides

While you can add the date, time, or slide number as a header or footer on any slide, you can also add this information in other locations on one or all slides in your presentation. To do this, follow these steps:

1 Move to the slide to which you want to add the date, time, or slide number.

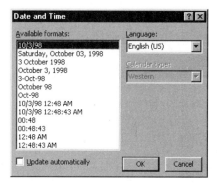

The Text Box button

2 On the Drawing toolbar, click the Text Box button.

3 With the Text Box tool, draw a text box in the slide.

4 Click inside the text box.

5 From the Insert menu, choose Date And Time or Slide Number. If you choose Date And Time, select a format in the Date And Time dialog box.

You can start numbering slides at a number other than 1. From the File menu, choose Page Setup, and then change the number in the Number Slides From box. Changing the starting slide number is helpful when the presentation you're creating is a continuation of a presentation in another file.

The changes you have learned about in this chapter are broad in scope and they affect an entire presentation. They allow you to govern the overall appearance of a presentation and to customize its look. In the next two chapters, you'll learn to use the PowerPoint drawing tools to add and modify graphic objects on a slide, and how to add existing photos and clip art to your presentation.

III

Fine-Tuning the Presentation

CHAPTER 12

Drawing in PowerPoint

You don't have to be an artist to create professional-looking graphics in Microsoft PowerPoint. No matter what your artistic ability, you can use the program's drawing tools to add simple graphic shapes to slides. You can enclose an area within a rectangle, for example, or add a sunburst shape that contains a message like "Special!" or "New!" You can even combine individual shapes to create a more elaborate diagram or map. PowerPoint's commands for editing shapes are also easy to use. You can resize, rotate, and flip graphic objects, combine individual objects into a grouped object, and even create three-dimensional objects with perspective.

In this chapter, you'll learn how to use the drawing tools on the Drawing toolbar to add graphic objects to a slide and how to modify individual objects or groups of objects. In the next chapter, you'll learn how to add ready-made images to your presentation.

Setting Up the Drawing Area

In Slide view or Normal view, you can turn on two built-in PowerPoint features that can help you position items with accuracy. PowerPoint's rulers, which run along the top and down the side of the presentation window, measure distances from the horizontal and vertical centers of the slide. In addition, two movable guides—dashed lines that cross the slide horizontally and vertically—allow you to line up objects with great precision against measurements on the rulers or against each other. Figure 12-1 shows both the rulers and the guides.

FIGURE 12-1.

The rulers and the guides.

Rulers   Guides

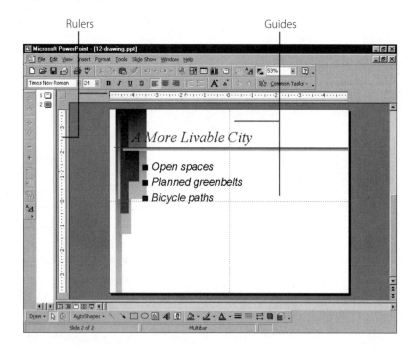

To view the rulers, choose Ruler from the View menu. To view the guides, choose Guides, also from the View menu. You can also choose both Ruler and Guides from the shortcut menu that appears when you position the mouse pointer on the slide background and click the right mouse button.

Dashed markers on the rulers track the movement of the mouse pointer to help you "eyeball" the position of the pointer as you draw and edit objects. The fixed, unchangeable zero point of the rulers is the exact center of the slide. To position objects on a slide more accurately, move the guides by dragging them. For best results, click the guide where it extends into the slide's margins; otherwise you'll select one of the slide's objects instead. As you drag a guide, an indicator on the guide shows the guide's horizontal or vertical distance from the ruler's zero point. For example, to place an object that must extend one inch (1.00) to the left of the slide's center and two inches to the right, you can drag the vertical guide one inch to the left of the slide's center, as measured by the ruler. Next, you can draw the object from the guide to approximately two inches to the right of the slide's center, and then drag the guide to the exact two-inch mark. Finally, you can adjust the right edge of the object to align with the guide.

Create More Guides

If two guides are not enough, you can replicate a guide by holding down Ctrl and dragging a copy of the guide off the original guide. You can then use the new guide just as you would use the original.

You can also use numerical measurements in a dialog box to position objects precisely on the slide. *You will learn about this later in the chapter in "Moving, Resizing, and Scaling Objects," page 323.*

The Drawing Toolbar

The basic set of drawing and editing tools is located on the Drawing toolbar at the bottom of the PowerPoint Slide view or Normal view window.

- You can click the button of a drawing shape, such as a line, rectangle, or oval, and then draw the shape in the slide.

- You can click the AutoShapes button and use the AutoShapes menu to choose from a set of pre-drawn shapes.

- You can format the shape with the formatting buttons, changing the color or style or other aspects of the shape.

- You can click the Draw button and use the Draw menu to edit shapes.

Figure 12-2 shows the Drawing toolbar.

FIGURE 12-2.
The Drawing toolbar.

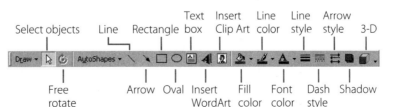

III

Fine-Tuning the Presentation

Drawing and Formatting the Basic Shapes

 SEE ALSO

For more information about color schemes, see "Changing the Color Scheme," page 280.

On the Drawing toolbar, you'll find a button for each of the basic shapes you can add to a slide. Shapes have an outline and a fill area whose default colors are determined by the current color scheme. To review or change the presentation's color scheme, from the Format menu, choose Slide Color Scheme, and then click the Custom tab. The color scheme's Text And Lines color sets the outline color, and the Fills color governs the interior color. Because the color scheme controls these colors, any change to the color scheme also changes the colors in shapes you've drawn. However, if you have individually formatted the line or fill color of an object, the object retains its unique colors regardless of the dictates of the color scheme.

Lines and Arrows

A line or arrow is the easiest drawing you can create. A straight line simply connects two end points.

To add a straight line or arrow to a slide, follow these steps:

The Line button

1 On the Drawing toolbar, click the Line or Arrow button.

2 Position the mouse pointer where you want the line to start.

3 Hold down the left mouse button and drag to where you want the line to end.

The Arrow button

4 Release the mouse button. A line appears between the start and end points. When you draw an arrow, the arrowhead points in the direction toward which you draw.

 TIP

> **Draw a Straight Line**
> To constrain the line to exactly horizontal, vertical, or diagonal, hold down Shift while dragging to draw the line.

When you hold down Ctrl as you drag, the first end point becomes the center of the line, and the line radiates outward in opposite directions from the first end point as you drag.

To change the appearance of the line, click the line to select it, and then click one of the formatting buttons on the Drawing toolbar, as shown in Figure 12-3. You can use the formatting buttons to change the appearance of lines, arrows, and other objects you've drawn.

FIGURE 12-3.

The formatting buttons on the Drawing toolbar.

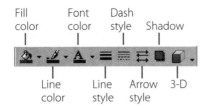

The Line Color button displays the currently selected color. To choose a different color, click the down arrow next to the button. You can choose one of the eight basic colors of the current color scheme. Or click More Line Colors to choose other colors in the Colors dialog box.

To change the thickness of the selected line, click the Line Style button and then choose one of the displayed line styles. To set the line weight in quarter-point increments, click the Line Style button and then choose More Lines. On the Colors And Lines tab in the Format AutoShape dialog box, change the setting in the Weight edit box.

The Arrow Style button works similarly to the Line Style button. Choose an arrow style or click More Arrows for more choices in the Format AutoShape dialog box.

The Shadow and 3-D buttons apply a shadow and 3-D effect to a line, but these effects are more suited to shapes like rectangles and squares. They will be covered later in the chapter, in "Adding a 3-D Effect," page 318.

② SEE ALSO

For more information about creating custom colors, see "Creating a Custom Color Scheme," page 282.

For more options while changing the appearance of a line, you can double-click the line. The Colors And Lines tab of the Format AutoShape dialog box appears, as shown in Figure 12-4 on the next page. In the Color drop-down list, the eight colors of the color scheme are shown at the top, along with any other colors you have applied to the objects in the presentation. If you don't like any of the eight colors, you can select one of the other standard colors on the palette, or click More Colors to choose or create one of your own.

In the Style drop-down list, you can select from more than a dozen preset line weights or double and triple line combinations. You can use the Dashed drop-down list to change the solid line style to a dashed or dotted line. Use the Begin Style, End Style, Begin Size, and End Size drop-down lists to change the arrowhead appearance at one or both ends of the line.

III

Fine-Tuning the Presentation

FIGURE 12-4.

The Colors And Lines tab of the Format AutoShape dialog box.

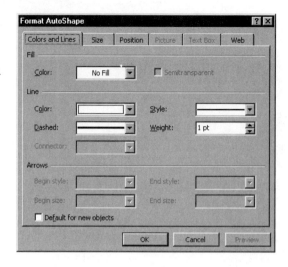

If you want every line you create to have the style you just specified, select the Default For New Objects check box at the bottom of the Colors And Lines tab.

After you specify the changes you want, click OK.

Copy Formatting from One Object to Another

To copy the formatting of an existing object to a new object, click the object with the formatting you want to copy. On the Standard toolbar, click the Format Painter button, and then click the new object.

Rectangles and Squares

You can use the Rectangle button on the Drawing toolbar to draw a rectangle or square. As you'll see, drawing a rectangle is almost as easy as drawing a line.

To draw a rectangle or a square, follow these steps:

The Rectangle button

1   On the Drawing toolbar, click the Rectangle button.

2   Position the mouse pointer at the location for one corner of the rectangle or square.

3   Hold down the left mouse button and drag diagonally to the opposite corner of the rectangle or square.

4   Release the mouse button. A rectangle or square appears in the size and shape you dragged, displaying the line and fill colors of the current color scheme.

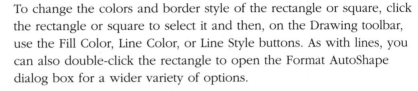

Draw a Perfect Square
To draw a perfect square rather than a rectangle, hold down Shift while dragging.

To have a rectangle grow outward from the first point you click, hold down Ctrl while you drag. To have a square grow outward from the first point you click, hold down both Shift and Ctrl while you drag.

The Fill Color
button

To change the colors and border style of the rectangle or square, click the rectangle or square to select it and then, on the Drawing toolbar, use the Fill Color, Line Color, or Line Style buttons. As with lines, you can also double-click the rectangle to open the Format AutoShape dialog box for a wider variety of options.

The Line Color
button

To add a more interesting fill to the rectangle or square, click the Fill Color button on the Drawing toolbar and then choose Fill Effects. These special fills, which allow you to add shading, a texture, a pattern, or a picture, are covered later in this chapter, in "Applying Special Fills to Objects," page 314.

The Line Style
button

You can also add a shadow or 3-D effect to a rectangle or square. These two special effects are covered later in this chapter in "Adding a Shadow," page 317 and "Adding a 3-D Effect," page 318.

Ovals and Circles

In the same way as you use the Rectangle button to draw rectangles or squares, you can use the Oval button on the Drawing toolbar to draw ovals or circles.

To draw an oval or a circle, follow these steps:

The Oval
button

1 On the Drawing toolbar, click the Oval button.

2 Position the mouse pointer at the location of one corner of an imaginary rectangle that would enclose the oval or circle.

3 Hold down the left mouse button and drag to the opposite corner of the imaginary rectangle.

4 Release the mouse button. An oval or circle appears, displaying the line and fill colors of the current color scheme.

Draw a Perfect Circle
To draw a perfect circle rather than an oval, hold down Shift.

III

Fine-Tuning the Presentation

To have an oval grow outward from the first point you click, hold down Ctrl while you drag. To have a circle grow outward from the first point you click, hold down both Shift and Ctrl as you drag.

To change the colors and border style of the oval or circle, select the shape, and then click the formatting buttons on the Drawing toolbar. You can also double-click the oval and make changes in the Format AutoShape dialog box.

As with rectangles, ovals and circles can also have shadows and 3-D effects. These two special effects are covered later in this chapter in "Adding a Shadow," page 317 and "Adding a 3-D Effect," page 318.

AutoShapes

PowerPoint's AutoShapes are familiar and frequently used shapes, such as arrows and stars. They are generally more complex than those on the Drawing toolbar, and many of them have an adjustment handle, which allows you to adjust their most characteristic feature. For example, a cube has an adjustment handle that you can drag to adjust the depth of the cube. An arrow's adjustment handle changes the shape of the arrowhead.

To draw an AutoShape, follow these steps:

1 On the Drawing toolbar, click the AutoShapes button.

2 From the menu, point to the type of shape you want and then click the shape you want to draw.

3 On the slide, position the mouse pointer where you want the AutoShape to begin, hold down the left mouse button, and then drag the AutoShape into place.

4 If the AutoShape has an adjustment handle, as shown below, drag the adjustment handle to adjust it to the size and shape you want.

Drag this adjustment handle.

An AutoShape can be filled and outlined, just like any other object you draw. You can also move, resize, copy and paste, and duplicate an AutoShape. You'll learn how to do this later in this chapter in "Moving,

Resizing, and Scaling Objects," page 323, and "Cutting, Copying, and Duplicating Objects," page 323.

> **Resize an AutoShape without Stretching It**
> To resize an AutoShape proportionally, without stretching it out of shape, hold down Shift as you drag one of the shape's corner handles.

Curves and Freeforms

With options in the Lines category of AutoShapes, you have the freedom to draw curved and straight lines—even combinations of the two—along with some fairly complex objects.

To draw a curve or freeform, follow these steps:

The Curve
button

The Freeform
button

1 On the Drawing toolbar, click the AutoShapes button.

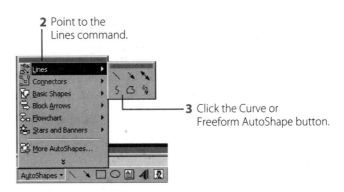

2 Point to the Lines command.

3 Click the Curve or Freeform AutoShape button.

4 Position the mouse pointer on the slide where you want to position the beginning of the shape.

5 Click the first point of the shape. For a curve, as you click succeeding points in the shape, the line curves. For a freeform shape, the lines are straight. If you want curved lines between points in a freeform, hold down the mouse button and drag the lines. The pointer changes to a pencil shape, and the lines curve as you drag.

6 Move the pointer to the next point for the shape and click again.

7 Repeat moving the pointer and clicking until you have completed the entire shape.

8 Click once near the starting point of the shape to close the shape. Or double-click at any point to end the shape as it is and leave it open.

III

Fine-Tuning the Presentation

To force a straight line between two points, hold down Ctrl when you click the second point. To constrain a straight line segment to exactly horizontal, vertical, or diagonal, hold down Shift as you move the mouse pointer.

 TIP

> **Correct a Shape While Drawing**
> As you draw a curve or freeform shape, you can remove previous points you've added by pressing Backspace.

Scribbles

The Scribble button

With scribbles, you can draw anything you want on a slide. It's just like doodling on a piece of paper. To add a scribble, click AutoShapes on the Drawing toolbar, point to Line, and then click Scribble. Position the pointer on the slide where you want to start the scribble, hold down the mouse button, and just draw.

You can reshape a curve, freeform, or scribble by editing its points. You'll learn to reshape objects later in this chapter in "Reshaping a Line by Editing its Points," page 319.

Connectors

Connectors are lines and curves whose ends are attached to other drawn objects. After you've added a connector between two objects, you can move the objects and they remain connected. Connectors are very helpful when you draw flowcharts and schematics, for example.

To add a connector, click AutoShapes on the Drawing toolbar and then point to Connectors. Click one of the nine connector styles.

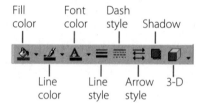

As you pass the mouse pointer over drawn objects on the current slide, you see connection points appear at the edges of the objects. Click a point on the object you're connecting from, and then click a point on the object you're connecting to, as shown in Figure 12-5. You can add more than one connector between two objects, and you can move the end of a connector to a different connection point on an object just by dragging it there.

FIGURE 12-5.

Click connection points on two objects to add a connector.

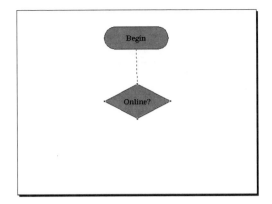

PowerPoint supplies three types of connectors: straight, elbow, and curved. To change connector types, right-click a connector and then choose a different type on the shortcut menu. Elbow and curved connectors show yellow diamonds along their paths. You can drag these diamonds to reshape the connectors. For example, you can reshape a connector after you've moved one of the objects to which it is attached. You can also reshape the connector automatically, joining the two closest points on the objects. To reroute a connector automatically, select the connector, click the right mouse button, and choose Reroute Connectors from the shortcut menu.

Adding Text to an Object

You can add text to the interior of any drawn object (except the Line shapes) by clicking the object and then typing. Because the text becomes an integral part of the object, when you move the object, the text moves too.

If you try to enter more than a few words, however, the text may overrun the borders of the object, as shown in Figure 12-6.

FIGURE 12-6.

The text in this object has overrun the object's borders.

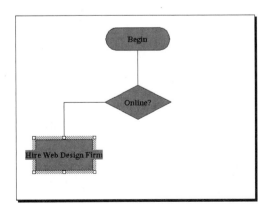

To wrap the text within the object, follow these steps:

1 Click the object to select it.

2 From the Format menu, choose AutoShape.

3 In the Format AutoShape dialog box, click the Text Box tab.

4 Select the Word Wrap Text In AutoShape check box.

5 Click OK.

The newly wrapped text fits within the left and right borders of the object, as shown in Figure 12-7.

FIGURE 12-7.

The text in this object wraps neatly within the object.

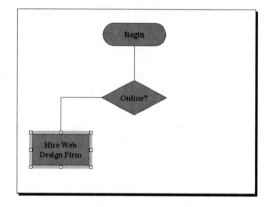

If you select the Resize AutoShape To Fit Text check box in the Format AutoShape dialog box, the object adjusts to the text rather than the other way around.

The Increase Font Size button

The Decrease Font Size button

To keep the text from overrunning the top and bottom borders of the object, you can open the Text Box tab in the Format AutoShape dialog box and select the Resize AutoShape To Fit Text check box. Or you can reduce the text size. To make minor adjustments to the size of the text in the object, drag across the text to select it and then, on the Formatting toolbar, click the Increase Font Size button or the Decrease Font Size button. Or press Ctrl+Shift+> to increase the font size or Ctrl+Shift+< to decrease the font size.

Switching Shapes

You can replace one shape with another. You can convert a star to a sunburst, for example, or a rectangle to an oval. To do this, follow these steps:

1 Click the shape you want to replace.

2 On the Drawing toolbar, click Draw and then point to Change AutoShape.

3 Point to the AutoShape type and then click a new shape.

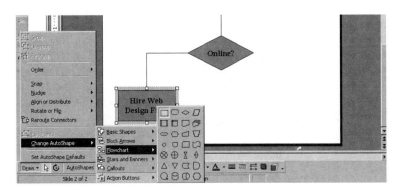

The new shape retains the original shape's positioning, size, and formatting.

Editing Objects

Up to this point, you've learned how to change the format of your drawn objects by changing fill and border color and the border style of objects. PowerPoint provides other editing options as well, such as adding a shadow or 3-D effect to an object. These options are discussed in this section.

Selecting Objects

Before you can make changes to a graphic object in PowerPoint, you must always first select the object. If you want to make the same change to more than one object, you can select multiple objects at once.

To select a single object, simply click the object. To select more than one object, do one of the following:

The Select Objects button

■ Hold down Shift as you click each object. (To deselect one of the selected objects, click the object again while holding down Shift.)

■ On the Drawing toolbar, click the Select Objects button, and then drag a selection box around the objects. Only objects that are completely enclosed by the selection box are selected. For example, Figure 12-8 on the next page shows a selection box that will select two of the five objects (flowchart symbols and their connectors) on a slide.

III

Fine-Tuning the Presentation

FIGURE 12-8.
Two of the five
objects on this
slide are selected.

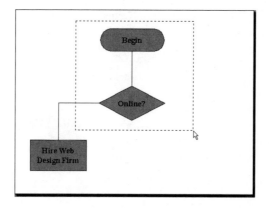

To select all the objects on a slide, choose Select All from the Edit menu or press Ctrl+A. All objects on the slide, including titles, bulleted text, and graphs, are selected.

After you select multiple objects, any changes you make will affect all the selected objects.

Applying Special Fills to Objects

When you learned how to add basic shapes earlier in this chapter, you also learned how to use options on the Drawing toolbar to change the fill and line colors and styles of a selected object. Special options also let you create objects filled with a color shading, objects filled with a pattern or texture, or objects filled with a picture.

Filling an Object with Shading

Shadings in objects add richness and depth and can give the appearance that the objects have been illuminated from the side, top, or corner. Combined with shadows, shadings can create an impressive three-dimensional effect.

To add shading to an object, follow these steps:

1 Select the object.

2 On the Drawing toolbar, click the down arrow next to the Fill Color button.

3 Select Fill Effects. The Fill Effects dialog box appears.

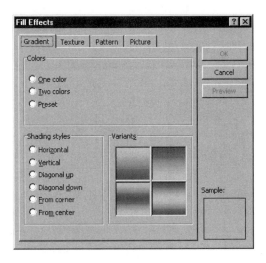

4   On the Gradient tab of the dialog box, select a Shading Style and one of the Variants, which depict how the shading progresses from light to dark color, dark to light color, and so on.

5   To change the color of the shading, select one of the color options at the top of the dialog box, and then fine-tune the color by selecting options in the corresponding drop-down list. If you select the One Color option, you can also use the scroll bar in the Colors section to make the shading darker or lighter. To use one of PowerPoint's ready-made color schemes, click the Preset option and then select a scheme from the Preset Colors drop-down list.

Filling an Object with a Texture, Pattern, or Picture

Adding texture to an object can give the object a whole new feel. PowerPoint provides many different textures to choose from, including oak, green marble, canvas, tissue paper, and even sand.

To fill an object with a texture, follow these steps:

1   Select the object.

2   On the Drawing toolbar, click the down arrow next to the Fill Color button.

3   Select Fill Effects.

4   In the Fill Effects dialog box, click the Texture tab.

III

Fine-Tuning the Presentation

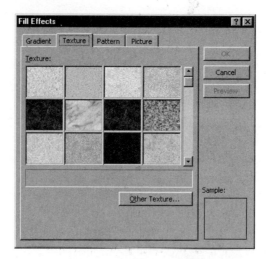

5 Select any of the textures shown or click Other Texture to select a different texture stored in a file on disk.

? SEE ALSO

For more information about working with different Gradient, Texture, Pattern, and Picture tabs in the Fill Effects dialog box, see "Altering the Custom Background," page 288.

Rather than fill an object with a solid or shaded color, you can fill it with a pattern made up of two colors. PowerPoint offers a number of patterns and a wide variety of foreground and background colors to choose from.

To fill an object with a pattern, click the Pattern tab in the Fill Effects dialog box. On the Pattern tab, shown in Figure 12-9, the patterns are composed of the colors displayed in the Foreground and Background boxes. You can select a different pattern and different foreground and background colors to create the combination you want.

FIGURE 12-9.

The Pattern tab of the Fill Effects dialog box.

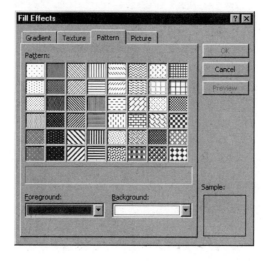

Use the Picture tab in the Fill Effects dialog box to select a picture file to place within an AutoShape. You might need to resize the AutoShape to see the entire picture, because you cannot resize the picture.

Filling an Object with a Semitransparent Color or the Background

You can set the fill color for a shape as translucent rather than fully opaque. This way, you can see other objects through the AutoShape. To fill the object with a translucent or semitransparent color, follow these steps:

1 Select the object.

2 From the Format menu, choose AutoShape. Or, double-click the object.

3 In the Format AutoShape dialog box, click the Colors And Lines tab.

4 Select the Semitransparent check box.

To fill the object with the same color as used in the slide background, follow these steps.

1 Select the object.

2 On the Drawing toolbar, click the down arrow next to the Fill Color button.

3 Select No Fill. The object becomes completely transparent, and shows the background or anything else layered behind it. Or click the color of the background to fill the object with the color used in the slide background.

Adding a Shadow

You can add a shadow behind objects and determine the shadow's color, direction, and size. You can add a shadow to any object you've drawn and to any text you've added to a slide.

To add a shadow, select the object, and then click the Shadow button on the Drawing toolbar. From the Shadow palette, shown in Figure 12-10 on the next page, choose the shadow style you want.

III

Fine-Tuning the Presentation

FIGURE 12-10.

The Shadow palette.

The Shadow
button

To alter the color, direction, and size of the shadow, select the shadowed object, and then click the Shadow button on the Drawing toolbar. Choose Shadow Settings. The Shadow Settings toolbar appears, as shown in Figure 12-11. Use the buttons on this toolbar to turn the shadow on or off, nudge the shadow in any of four directions, and change the shadow color.

FIGURE 12-11.

The Shadow
Settings toolbar.

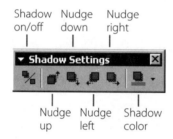

The Semitransparent Shadow option on the Shadow Color palette causes the shadow to be translucent.

 TIP

Create Consistent Graphics

To create a slide that makes visual sense, apply the same shadow to every object on the slide, even the title of the slide.

Adding a 3-D Effect

You can give certain AutoShapes, such as the basic shapes, block arrows, and callouts, a full three-dimensional effect that imparts to them the appearance of depth. To add or vary the 3-D effect for these objects, select the object and then click the 3-D button on the Drawing toolbar. From the palette of preset 3-D styles, select a style to display the object at a certain tilt and depth.

NOTE

Adding a 3-D effect to a shape removes any shadow the shape might have had.

The 3-D
button

For more control over a 3-D effect you have added, select the object with the 3-D effect and then click the 3-D button on the Drawing toolbar. Choose 3-D Settings; the 3-D Settings toolbar appears, as shown in Figure 12-12. Use the buttons on this toolbar to fine-tune the 3-D effect.

FIGURE 12-12.

The 3-D Settings toolbar.

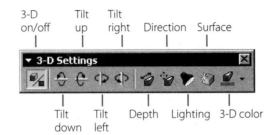

- The 3-D On/Off button turns the 3-D effect on or off.

- The four Tilt buttons rotate the object in 3-D space.

- The Depth and Direction buttons increase the apparent depth of the object and the direction the object faces.

- The Lighting button allows you to choose the side from which the light shines. Choose the white cube in the center to have the light appear to come directly from in front of the slide. You can also choose three light intensities: Bright, Normal, and Dim.

- The Surface button allows you to change the surface texture of the object, which affects how much light is reflected off the object.

- The 3-D Color button allows you to change the color of the 3-D surface.

Reshaping a Line by Editing its Points

Lines, curves, arrows, and freeform shapes can be stretched, rotated, moved, and copied, but to change their shape, you'll need to edit their points. You can think of all these objects as multiple segments joined end to end. The points where segments are joined can be moved to reshape the object. Figure 12-13 on the next page shows the difference in the selection highlight when a shape is clicked versus when a shape's points are ready to be edited.

FIGURE 12-13.

Two versions of a selected shape.

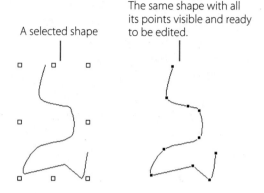

A selected shape

The same shape with all its points visible and ready to be edited.

To see the points of a line, arrow, curve, or freeform shape so that you can edit it, select the object, click the right mouse button, and then choose Edit Points from the shortcut menu. Edit the points of the object in one of the following ways:

■ Drag any of the points to a new position.

■ Add new points by pressing Ctrl and clicking between existing points.

■ Add a point by clicking between two points and dragging.

■ Delete a point by clicking the point with the right mouse button and then choosing Delete Point from the shortcut menu.

■ To close the first and last points of the object with a straight line, click the object with the right mouse button and then choose Close Curve from the shortcut menu.

A point can also be one of four styles. The style affects how the ends of the segments join that point. To change the point style, right-click the point itself and then choose an option on the shortcut menu. The four point styles are as follows:

■ The Auto Point is the default, and it has segments on either side whose direction and length cannot be changed manually except by dragging the point.

■ You can modify the segments on either side of a Smooth Point by dragging either of the handles that appear adjacent to the point, as shown in Figure 12-14. Dragging either handle changes the segments equally, but in opposite directions.

FIGURE 12-14.
Drag either handle to reshape a Smooth Point.

Drag either handle.

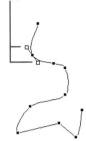

- When you change a point to a Straight Point, you'll find that you can drag either handle independently to reshape the segment on one side of a point only.

- Choosing Corner Point creates a corner whose angle can be changed when you drag either handle.

You can change a curved line segment between points to a straight line segment, and vice versa. Click the line segment with the right mouse button and then, from the shortcut menu, choose Straight Segment or Curved Segment.

After you finish editing points, click elsewhere on the slide or choose Exit Edit Points from the shortcut menu.

Transferring Object Formats

After you finish modifying the appearance of an object, you can transfer, or copy, the object's format to another object by using the Format Painter button on the Standard toolbar. Simply select the object whose format you want to copy, click the Format Painter button and then select the object to which you want to transfer the format. If you double-click the Format Painter button, the format will be copied to all subsequent objects you select until you press Esc or click the Format Painter button again to turn it off.

Set an Object Format as the Default
After you've formatted an object, you can save it as the default for shapes of that type. To do this, select the object. On the Drawing toolbar, click Draw and then choose Set AutoShape Defaults.

III

Fine-Tuning the Presentation

Arranging Objects

In addition to providing tools and commands that change the look of one or more objects, PowerPoint provides several features that allow you to arrange objects on slides in a wide variety of ways. You can:

- Group objects permanently or temporarily to keep them together while you move or reformat them

- Cut and copy objects

- Move, nudge, resize, and scale objects

- Rotate and flip objects

- Change the layering order of objects from front to back

- Line up objects with respect to each other and evenly space out objects by distributing them

Grouping Objects

If you frequently make changes to more than one object at a time, you might want to combine the objects in a group. The objects are then treated as a unit, and any changes you make affect the entire group. For example, you can select the group and then move all the objects as a unit or modify the fill color so that all the objects in the group change simultaneously.

To group objects, first select them, using either the Shift key or the Select Objects button on the Drawing toolbar. On the Drawing toolbar, click Draw and then click the Group button. When the objects are grouped, one set of handles surrounds the group, as shown in Figure 12-15.

FIGURE 12-15.

A group of objects has one set of handles.

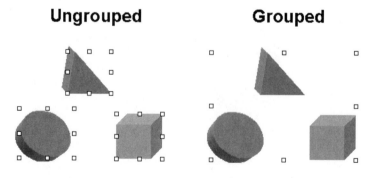

Ungrouped   **Grouped**

After you group objects, you can ungroup them. Select the group, click Draw on the Drawing toolbar, and then click the Ungroup button. The Regroup button puts a group back together after it's been ungrouped.

Cutting, Copying, and Duplicating Objects

You can cut, copy, and paste graphic objects as you would any object on a PowerPoint slide by using:

- The Cut, Copy, and Paste buttons on the Standard toolbar

- The Cut, Copy, and Paste commands on the Edit menu or the shortcut menu

- Their keyboard equivalents (listed on the Edit menu)

Not only can you cut and copy objects from one slide to another, but you can cut and copy objects from one presentation to another. The easiest way is to open two presentations side by side in Slide view, cut or copy the object from one presentation, and then paste it in the other.

The fastest way to duplicate an object and simultaneously position the duplicate is to hold down Ctrl and drag a copy of the object into position. You can also select the object and then choose Duplicate from the Edit menu. Or press Ctrl+D. You can then drag the object into position.

 TIP

> **Undo Drawing Actions**
> Remember, you can undo most of the commands discussed in this chapter by clicking the Undo button on the Standard toolbar or by choosing Undo from the Edit menu.

Moving, Resizing, and Scaling Objects

To move an object, place the mouse pointer on the object, hold down the left mouse button, and then drag the object to a new location. To move an object horizontally or vertically, hold down Shift while you drag.

To move objects just a little, you can nudge them. On the Drawing toolbar, click Draw, point to Nudge, and then choose Up, Down, Left, or Right. The selected object moves a small increment in the direction you specified. Sometimes a little nudge is all you need.

Select and Nudge an Object with the Keyboard
To use the keyboard to nudge an object, press Tab until the object you want to move is selected, and then press the Left, Right, Up, or Down arrow key to move the object in small increments.

To help you position an object, you can use the Snap commands. On the Drawing toolbar, click Draw, point to Snap, and then choose To Grid or To Shape. Then, as you drag the object, it will automatically jump to the nearest horizontal and vertical ruler marking or align with the nearest edge of an adjacent object, if one is near. To turn off Snap To Grid temporarily and drag an object freely on a slide, hold down Alt as you drag. The object will move smoothly without little jerks as it jumps from ruler marking to ruler marking.

To resize or reshape an object, drag one of the object's handles in the direction you want. If you want to maintain the proportions of the object, hold down Shift while you drag a corner handle. If you want the object to grow out from its current center, hold down Ctrl while you drag a corner handle.

Rather than drag objects into position, you can set object placements and sizing very precisely on the Size and Position tabs of the Format AutoShape dialog box. Double-click the object you want to resize and then click the Size tab. Under Size And Rotate, enter the precise dimensions you want in the Height and Width boxes. You can also resize or reshape the scale or proportion an object. Under Scale, enter a percentage in the Height and Width edit boxes. To double the size of an object, for example, enter 200 percent in both the Height and Width boxes under Scale. Keep in mind that objects can be scaled no larger than the size of the slide. When you select the Lock Aspect Ratio check box as well, the Width setting changes to equal any new Height setting, and vice versa.

Use the Position tab in the Format AutoShape dialog box to position the top left corner of the object relative to the top left corner or the center of the screen.

Rotating and Flipping Objects

You can rotate a single object or a group of objects around its center, and you can rotate multiple selected objects, each around its own center.

To rotate a single object or group of objects, follow these steps:

1 Select the object, as shown below.

The Free Rotate
button

2 On the Drawing toolbar, click the Free Rotate button.

3 Place the mouse pointer on a corner handle of the object or group and then drag the handle left or right around the center of the object or group.

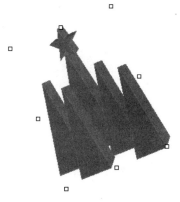

 TIP

> **Rotate Objects with Precision**
> For more precision while rotating, click a handle and drag the pointer away from the object before dragging in a circle around the object.

If you select multiple objects, each object rotates around its center when you rotate any one of the objects. In Figure 12-16 on the next page, the objects were not grouped before being rotated, and each object has rotated around its own center.

III

Fine-Tuning the Presentation

To turn rotating off, click the slide background or click the Free Rotate button again.

FIGURE 12-16.

Ungrouped objects rotate around their own centers.

You can rotate an object exactly 90 degrees to the left or right. Select the object and then click Draw on the Drawing toolbar. Point to Rotate Or Flip and then choose Rotate Left or Rotate Right.

To create a mirror image of an object, you can flip it.

1 Select the object you want to flip.

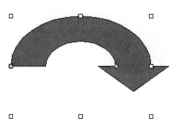

2 On the Drawing toolbar, click Draw, and then point to Rotate Or Flip.

3 Click Flip Horizontal or Flip Vertical. The object shown below was flipped horizontally.

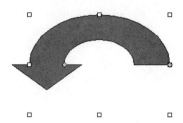

Ordering Objects

When any objects on a slide overlap, you can change their order in the stack of overlapping objects. You can move an object one level higher or lower in the stack, or send an object to the top or bottom of the stack.

To move an object one level higher or lower in a stack, select the object. On the Drawing toolbar, click Draw and then point to Order. Click Bring Forward or Send Backward. If you want to move an object to the very top or bottom of the stack, choose Bring To Front or Send To Back instead.

Figure 12-17 shows two versions of a simple drawing. On the left, the "C" triangle in the center is layered in the back. On the right, the "C" triangle is moved to the front with the Bring To Front command.

FIGURE 12-17.

The triangle has been moved forward one layer with the Bring To Front command.

Aligning Objects

You can line up objects with respect to each another. Select the objects, click Draw on the Drawing toolbar, and then point to Align Or Distribute. There are six alignment commands you can use for vertical and horizontal alignment. The objects align with the object that is farthest out. That is, right-aligned objects align with the object farthest to the right. On the Align Or Distribute submenu, if you choose Relative To Slide, the objects align with the far edge of the slide. Figure 12-18 on the next page shows three objects before and after the Align Center command is chosen.

III

Fine-Tuning the Presentation

FIGURE 12-18.
Three objects before
and after being
centered.

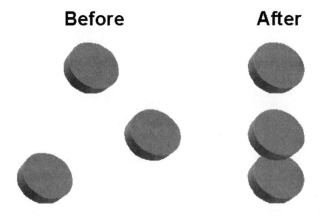

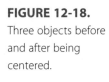 **TIP**

Add Align Commands to a Toolbar
The commands on the Align Or Distribute menu are available as toolbar
buttons that you can drag to any toolbar. *For information about customizing
a toolbar, see "Customizing Toolbars," page 510.*

Distributing Objects

You can space selected objects evenly on a slide. Select the objects.
On the Drawing toolbar, click Draw, and then point to Align Or Distribute. Choose Distribute Horizontally or Distribute Vertically, depending
on whether you want the objects spread out across the slide, or down
the slide as shown in Figure 12-19. If you choose Relative To Slide, the
slides will also be evenly spaced across or down the entire slide.

FIGURE 12-19.
Objects before and
after being distributed.

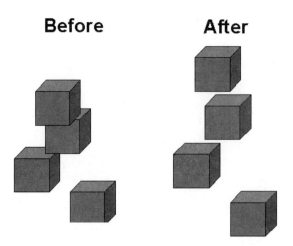

Saving a Drawing for Use in Another Presentation

One method you can use to save your most valuable drawings, such as logos, is to copy and paste the drawings into a special presentation. When you need a particular drawing, you can open the presentation, copy the drawing, and then paste it into a new presentation.

? SEE ALSO

For more information about importing files to the Clip Gallery, see Chapter 13, "Placing Photos and Clip Art on Slides," page 331.

Another method is to add the drawing to PowerPoint's Clip Gallery. You can copy and paste the objects into a drawing application such as Microsoft PhotoDraw or Microsoft Paint and then save the drawing as its own file. Then you can import the file to the Clip Gallery, where you'll always have access to the objects from within PowerPoint.

In this chapter, you learned how to create pictures by drawing them. In the next chapter, you'll learn how to import photos and clip art that have already been created and stored in files or in PowerPoint's Clip Gallery.

III

Fine-Tuning the Presentation

CHAPTER 13

Placing Photos and Clip Art on Slides

W ords and charts may tickle the thought processes, but an image settles deep in long-term memory where you want your message to remain. The power of an image, whether it's a photo or a clip art cartoon, is its ability to tell a story at a glance, so never hesitate to incorporate images that are relevant to your story.

This chapter looks at acquiring images and selecting clip art, placing them on slides, and then formatting these images to look exactly the way you want.

Adding a Photo to a Slide

Sometimes you can create a presentation using the photos you have on hand. At other times you'll need to review a presentation and determine which slides would be enhanced by an image. Then you can set out to find suitable pictures.

The photo files that you bring into a presentation can come from a variety of sources. You can shoot your own presentation-ready pictures with a digital camera and obtain ready-to-use picture files. Or, if you don't have a digital camera, you can use any camera, even a point-and-shoot disposable, to capture images on a roll of film. After your photos are developed at a local one-hour shop, you can use an inexpensive scanner to scan them into files that you place on slides. But if you'd rather use professionally taken pictures, you can buy photos from a stock photo library. For a fee, of course, the companies that offer these are only too happy to license images to you on a CD or let you download pictures directly from their Web sites.

Aside from the basic suitability of an image, just about any digitized photo that has been stored in a photo file, such as a .jpg, .tif, or .bmp file is usable for a presentation. Unless you want to do some fancy photo manipulation in an image editing program such as Microsoft PhotoDraw or Adobe PhotoShop, you can import photos onto a slide exactly as they are. When you get them on the slide, you can change their size and even tweak their brightness levels and contrast within PowerPoint.

Shooting Photos with a Digital Camera

Although some say that digital cameras can never replace film, they can be ideal for capturing a quick image of a person, product, or location and enhancing a presentation with real, see-it-for-yourself photos. Digital cameras replace a time-consuming, three-step process (take the pictures, have the film developed, and scan the photos) with a quick two steps (take the pictures and transfer them to the computer).

Most common digital cameras shoot photos at a standard 72-dpi (dots per inch) resolution. The main difference between camera models, besides the quality of the lens and color-capturing apparatus, is the size of the pictures they take. Inexpensive, entry-level digital cameras capture images that are 640 pixels wide by 480 pixels tall. Mid-range, "mega-pixel" cameras (under $1,000) capture images that are 1024 by 768 pixels in size. (Some even go to 1280-by-1024 pixels.) High-end, professional digital cameras ($5,000–$15,000) can take images containing even more pixels.

Large pictures are better for printing on a color printer or manipulating in a photo editing program because the extra pixels provide more detail. Even if you cut out and blow up a smaller portion of the picture, that portion will still have enough pixels to show a detailed image. But large pictures can actually be a drawback in PowerPoint because the resolution of a PowerPoint slide shown on the screen is only 96 dpi; so large pictures are too big for a typical slide. They have to be reduced in size, which decreases their resolution and therefore reduces the amount of detail they show.

To understand the relationship between the resolution of the pictures and their size on the screen, you have to consider just a few numbers. Here's a quick run-through. The default size of a slide in an on-screen presentation is 10 inches wide by 7.5 inches tall. Because Power-Point's display is fixed at 96 pixels per inch, that's 960 pixels across by 720 pixels down. In other words, a picture that is 960 pixels by 720 pixels in size just fills a default slide.

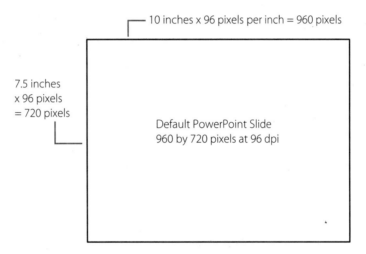

Because you probably want to leave room for a title at the top of the slide and some margin on the left, right, and bottom, the usable area for a photo on a typical slide is somewhat smaller—only about 6 2/3 inches wide by 5 inches tall. At 96 dpi, that translates to photo dimensions of only about 640 by 480 pixels.

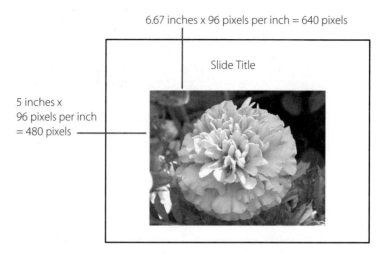

6.67 inches x 96 pixels per inch = 640 pixels

Slide Title

5 inches x
96 pixels per inch
= 480 pixels

Now consider the size of the images that you normally get from a digital camera. If your mid-priced camera captures pictures at 1024-by-768 pixels at 72-dpi resolution, the pictures, when you first import them, will be quite a bit larger than a PowerPoint slide.

1024 pixels x 72 dpi = 14.22 inches wide.

768 pixels x 72 dpi = 10.66 inches tall.

That's far larger than the 6 2/3 by 5 inches that you want for the photo, so you must reduce the image in PowerPoint to about 47 percent of its former size, which reduces it from 14.22 by 10.66 inches to 6.66 by 5 inches.

As you scale a picture down using PowerPoint's image scaling controls, from 1024-by-768 pixels to 640-by-480 pixels, the scaling process discards pixels, which causes the image quality to deteriorate somewhat. The greater the original size of the image, the more you must reduce it in PowerPoint and the more the onscreen quality suffers.

That may lead you to wonder whether you should still go out and buy the most expensive digital camera you can afford just to take photos for a PowerPoint presentation. If you plan only to use the photos in an on-screen presentation exactly as you've taken them, the answer is no. But the realities are that you are likely to want to use the images in other programs, you almost certainly will print them out, and you might even want to crop out a portion of a photo and blow it up on the screen. Then you'll be happy to have the extra detail that additional pixels provide.

Size of a 96-dpi slide
at 960 by 720
(10 by 7.5 inches)

Size of a 72-dpi photo
at 1024 by 768
(14.22 by 10.66 inches)

Target size of photo
(6.67 by 5 inches)

Consider what happens when you crop out the center portion of two different photos of the same subject; one taken with a camera that shoots pictures at 640-by-480 pixels and another taken by a camera that shoots pictures at 1024-by-768 pixels. When you crop out the center of a 640-by-480 photo to isolate a subject, you are left with an image that is 320-by-240 pixels. When you crop out the same center of the larger photo, you get an image that is 512-by-384 pixels. To fit the smaller image into a 640-by-480 space on a slide, you must increase its size by 150 percent. That makes each pixel in the image 150 percent larger so that only 48 pixels fit an inch. In other words, the resolution has decreased from 72 dpi to 48 dpi. To fit the larger image to the same space, you actually must reduce its dimensions, by a relatively minor 6 percent. That makes the pixels a little smaller so that more of them will fit an inch. In this case, the resolution actually increases from 72 dpi to more than 76 dpi. That's a relatively imperceptible increase, but the difference between 48 and 76 dpi is more visible. The smaller pixels in the 76-dpi image show more detail and make the picture look less "pixelated" or blotchy. Figure 13-1 on the next page shows detail from the same picture at both 48 and 76 dpi.

III

Fine-Tuning the Presentation

FIGURE 13-1.

Detail from a photo
at 48 dpi (left) and
76 dpi (right).

Choose a Digital Camera that Stores Photos as JPEGs

Some digital cameras store images in a file format that is proprietary to the manufacturer of the camera. To use these images in PowerPoint, you must use the software that comes with the camera to translate them to a file format that PowerPoint can import, such as BMP, TIF, or JPG. To avoid that extra step, choose one of the many popular cameras that store photos in JPEG format (JPG files). PowerPoint can directly import JPEG images, without any need for translation.

Inserting Digital Camera Photos in PowerPoint Slides

To add a photo that you've taken with a digital camera to a slide, you usually insert a graphic file that you have already transferred from the camera to the computer. Use the software that comes with the camera to transfer the files to a folder on your system. Then follow these steps:

1 From the Insert menu, choose Picture.

2 From the Picture submenu, choose From File.

3 In the Insert Picture dialog box, navigate to the file that contains the picture and select the file.

4 Click Insert.

The photo appears on the current slide, ready to be resized, moved, or formatted.

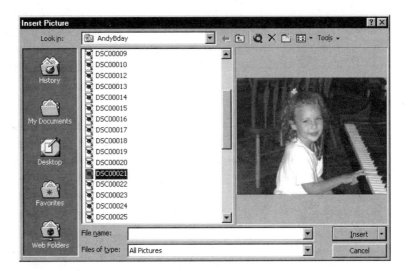

Downloading Photos Directly from a Camera

If your camera comes with a TWAIN driver, PowerPoint enables you to download images directly from the camera. If your camera provides a TWAIN driver, the driver will be installed when you set up the software for the camera.

1   From the Insert menu, choose Picture.

2   From the Picture submenu, choose From Scanner or Camera.

3   In the Insert Picture From Scanner Or Camera dialog box, select your camera from the Device drop-down list. If your camera does not appear on the list, it does not have a TWAIN driver installed in Windows.

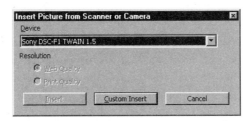

4   Click Custom Insert. A dialog box for your camera opens with controls you can use to select an image to download.

5   Use the controls in the dialog box for your camera to select an image to download. The image appears on the current slide.

Scanning Photos

Like a digital camera, a scanner converts an image to digital data, but it reads an existing photo into a file. The most popular type of scanner is a flatbed scanner, which sits on a desktop and reads photos that you place upside down on a glass plate under a hinged lid.

Before you can scan, of course, you must install the scanner and the software that comes with it. Usually, this requires plugging the scanner into the computer and running the scanner software's setup program. Because Windows includes scanning software for a number of popular scanner models, it might be able to detect the scanner and install the appropriate software automatically.

Using PowerPoint's Built-In Scanning Software

PowerPoint's built-in scanning software simplifies the task of scanning a photo directly onto a slide. It gives you two choices of quality and one button to push. For more control over your scanning, you can also switch over to the scanning software that comes with your scanner.

To scan a photo, follow these steps:

1 From the Insert menu, choose Picture.

2 From the Picture submenu, choose From Scanner Or Camera.

3 In the Insert Picture From Scanner Or Camera dialog box, choose your scanner from the Device list, if it's not already selected.

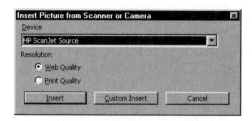

4 Click Web Quality or Print Quality to choose low resolution (96 dpi) or medium resolution (150 dpi).

5 Click Insert to begin the scan. After the photo is scanned, it appears on the PowerPoint slide.

NOTE

You can use PowerPoint's built-in scanning software if the manufacturer of your scanner has provided a TWAIN driver for Windows. Only devices that have installed TWAIN drivers appear on the Device list in step 3 above. The TWAIN driver is usually installed in Windows automatically when you set up the software that comes with the scanner.

Choosing Web Quality at step 4 scans the photo at 96 dpi, the preferred resolution for an image on a Web page. Choosing Print Quality, instead, scans the photo at 150 dpi, a higher resolution that is more suitable for printing.

SEE ALSO

For information about JPEG compression, see "How JPEG Files Work Their Magic," page 343.

After a photo is scanned, PowerPoint's scanning software compresses it using JPEG compression, a sophisticated data compression scheme developed especially for images. This greatly reduces the amount of image data in the PowerPoint file, but it also reduces the quality of the image somewhat because JPEG removes some color information from the picture as it compresses it.

Using the Scanning Software for Your Scanner

For more options while scanning, you can use the scanning software that comes with your scanner. Using your scanner's software rather than the module built into PowerPoint lets you make more choices about the resolution and number of colors in the scanned photo and about whether to perform color adjustment or image sharpening as the image is scanned.

Depending on the model of your scanner, you may be able to start the scanning software by clicking its shortcut on the Start menu. If a shortcut is not available on the Start menu, you can start a scan from within PowerPoint by following these steps:

1   From the Insert menu, choose Picture.

2   From the Picture submenu, choose From Scanner Or Camera.

3   In the Insert Picture From Scanner Or Camera dialog box, choose your scanner model from the Device list, if it's not already shown.

4   Click Custom Insert. This starts the scanning software for your scanner. Figure 13-2 on the next page shows the scanning software for a Hewlett-Packard scanner.

III

Fine-Tuning the Presentation

FIGURE 13-2.

The scanning software for a Hewlett-Packard scanner.

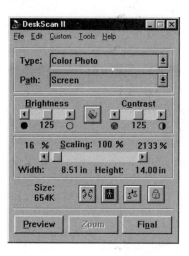

Your scanning software may give you exact numeric choices for resolution, such as 100 dpi or 200 dpi, or it may offer more vague options such as low, medium, and high or faxing, filing, and printing. It's up to you to determine what real numbers these options correspond to, and the software's online help or printed documentation may help. Options for color are usually black and white (2 colors), grayscale (256 gray shades), 256 colors, thousands of colors, or millions of colors.

The choice you make for resolution depends on your ultimate plans for the photos. If you want to use them only within PowerPoint, you can choose a low resolution because PowerPoint displays photos only at 96 dpi, the resolution limit for most monitors and computer projectors. In other words, 96 dpi is the fixed resolution that PowerPoint uses to display images because there's no point in trying to display an image at a higher resolution when the monitor or projector is unable to show the extra sharpness. If you are given the choice, select a low resolution (usually 72 or 100 dpi) or select exactly 96 dpi to obtain an image that is ideal for use in PowerPoint.

If you also plan to use the photos in a printed publication, you should choose a higher resolution, such as 200 dpi or even 300 dpi. The pages you print will show finer detail because most printers have a print resolution of 600 dpi or greater. But be aware that when you insert high-resolution images in PowerPoint, they will be displayed at 96 dpi. Figure 13-3 shows the same photo on two slides. The image on the left was scanned at 100 dpi and the image on the right was scanned at 300 dpi. Notice that the images look identical because they are both displayed on the screen at 96 dpi.

FIGURE 13-3.

72-dpi scan at left.

300-dpi scan at right.

The drawback to scanning an image at a higher resolution is that it produces a much larger image file. A photo that is 4-by-6 inches scanned at 72 dpi can produce a 300- to 600-kilobyte file. The same photo scanned at 300 dpi can produce a file that is larger than five megabytes. Inserting large image files in PowerPoint causes your presentation files to grow in size dramatically. In addition, larger files take longer for PowerPoint to work with. They are slower to display or change, particularly if you are using a computer without a great deal of memory.

If you are not planning to print the presentation, the best solution might be to scan photos twice, once at a higher resolution for use in other programs, and once at a lower resolution for use in PowerPoint. Insert the low-resolution versions in PowerPoint and save the high-resolution versions for use in programs like Microsoft Publisher.

Another detail you need to consider when scanning photos is the number of colors that you get in the output file. Some scanning software specifies the number of colors in an image by its bit depth—256-color pictures are 8-bit, images with thousands of colors are 16-bit, and images with millions of colors are 24-bit.

You'll get the best quality by using 24-bit images with millions of colors. You'll get excellent quality with thousands of colors or 16-bit images, plus the file sizes will be smaller. 256-color images, in still smaller files, show deterioration in color changes that are subtle. In photos with a sky background, for example, you may see bands of color (light blue, medium blue, dark blue) rather than a smooth transition from light to dark blue.

III

Fine-Tuning the Presentation

Choosing a File Format for the Scanned Image

If, in addition to bringing the images you scan directly into PowerPoint, your scanning software lets you save them in files, it may give you a choice of file format to use, such as BMP, TIF, or JPG. In addition, it may give you the option to compress the images and, if you choose JPG, perhaps even set the compression level. Here's a rundown on some of the most popular graphics file formats. There's no reason to use any format other than these.

- **BMP**, the file format used by Windows, is convenient because you can view images in Windows Paint and preview images in Windows Explorer when you view the contents of a folder as a Web page (choose As Web Page from the View menu in Explorer). On the other hand, BMP files are usually uncompressed, so they are very large and consume vast amounts of disk space. BMP is fine if you don't need to move the presentation to a different computer or if you plan to save a presentation as Web pages, during which the images are compressed anyway.

- **TIFF** (.TIF), Tagged Image File Format, is a cross-platform graphics file format (you can view TIFF images on both the PC and the Macintosh without having to convert them), and it offers a version that includes compression (called LZW compression). In other words, when you save the file, you can choose either an uncompressed TIFF format or the LZW-compressed TIFF format, which gives you a much smaller file. TIFF files, like BMP files, are easily read by PowerPoint so you can place them directly on slides. TIFF files, like BMP files, give great visual results, and the compressed form (LZW) produces a smaller presentation file that can be moved among computers more easily.

- **JPEG** (.JPG), (an abbreviation for Joint Photographic Experts Group), is most popular for storing photographic images because its high compression yields a small file. A 300-kilobyte TIFF file can become as little as 19 kilobytes when saved as a JPEG file. Because small JPEG files can be transmitted quickly over the Internet, they're used often for photos on Web pages. The drawback to JPEG files is that they discard some of the color information in a photo during compression. This is called *lossy* compression as compared with the *lossless* compression of BMP and TIFF files. Because of their compression, JPEG files show compression artifacts, such as blurring and color blotches. However, when you save an image as a JPEG file, you can reduce the deterioration in

JPEG images by choosing a low compression level in the options that you get in most scanning software.

- **PNG** (pronounced "ping," and short for Portable Network Graphics) is a relatively new file format that is becoming more prevalent with the advent of Microsoft Internet Explorer 5.0, which can display PNG files. PNG files use an effective, and lossless, compression scheme, just like BMP and TIF files, but they are better suited for use on the Web because they can be progressively rendered. In other words, they appear to gradually come into focus as they are received over the Internet. Because all the Office applications can read PNG files, they're an appropriate format for transferring images among the applications.

How JPEG Files Work Their Magic

In an uncompressed bitmapped file, such as a BMP file, each pixel in an image is represented by one byte of data in the file. Bitmapped files are large because a 640-by-480-pixel image is 480 rows of 640 pixels each. That's 307,200 bytes. When a file is saved as a JPEG image, groups of pixels of a similar color are averaged into a single value. For example, a group of pixels that represents one of the flesh tones in a picture of a face or that represents one of the blue colors in a picture with a sky background is averaged to a single color. This averaging of groups of pixels reduces the number of colors in the image, removes detail, and produces some blurriness and color blotching.

Downloading Photos

Stock photo companies such as Photodisc, Adobe Image Club, and Corbis let you license photos from their extensive libraries of professionally photographed images. Each company has a Web site you can visit to search for and select a relevant photo. After paying a license fee for use of the photo, you can usually download the image directly from the company's Web site. If you'd rather not download the image, you can have a CD sent to you.

Inserting a Photo That Is Already on Your System

You may have access to a library of relevant photos on your system. Perhaps all the photos that you need for a project are already categorized neatly in folders on your company's server. If the photos you need are simply waiting for you, you can easily use drag-and-drop editing to place them right onto slides and avoid using commands on the Insert menu. To drag a photo, open Windows Explorer (click My Computer) and navigate to the folder that holds the photos. Select a photo and drag it right onto a slide in the PowerPoint window.

Alternatively, you can click Insert on the menu, choose Picture from the Insert menu, and then choose From File on the Picture submenu. In the Insert Picture dialog box, navigate to the photo file, select it, and then click Insert.

Drop a Photo Into a Clip Art Placeholder

To create a perfect bulleted text and photo slide every time, create a new slide and choose one of the slide layouts that has both bulleted text and clip art. Then insert a photo file or drag a photo file from an Explorer folder onto the slide. After the photo is on the slide, you can drag it to the clip art placeholder. The photo will be sized to fit the placeholder neatly.

Formatting a Photo

To move the photo, you can simply drag it to a new location on the slide. To resize a photo while maintaining its proportions, drag one of its corner handles in the desired direction. To stretch a photo, drag one of the side rather than corner handles.

To obtain much more precision when sizing a photo, use the controls on the Format Picture dialog box. From the Format menu, choose Picture to open the dialog box. Then click the Size tab, shown in Figure 13-4.

FIGURE 13-4.

The Size tab of the Format Picture dialog box.

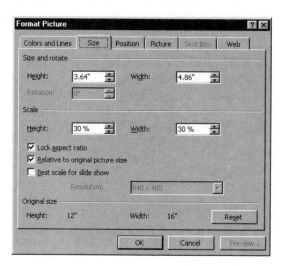

On the Size tab, the Height and Width controls allow you to enter an exact size for the image. The two Scale controls let you resize an image by entering a percentage instead. To double the size of an image, for example, you'd enter 200 percent in both the Height and Width controls. If the Lock Aspect Ratio check box is checked, you only need to enter a percentage in one of the controls. The other control is set to the same percentage; the picture is resized proportionately. After you resize an image, the Scale controls show the current scale of the photo unless you uncheck the Relate To Original Picture Size check box. Then the percentages shown revert to 100 percent, and any further scaling changes are based on the current photo size, not the original size. Regardless of the changes you make, the original size of the image remains visible at the bottom of the dialog box, and you can always return a photo to its starting point by clearing the Lock Aspect Ratio check box and clicking the Reset button.

How to Stop Waiting for Photos to Show Up on the Screen

Photos take somewhat longer to draw than other objects on a slide. Therefore, you might want to draw a box on the slide to use as a temporary placeholder for a photo while you create and format other elements of the presentation. When the presentation is otherwise complete, you can import the photo.

Creating a Background Using a Photo

By switching to the Slide Master before you insert a photo, you can place the photo on the background of every slide in a presentation except the title slide. First, choose Master from the View menu and then choose Slide Master from the submenu. Then use Insert Picture to place the photo on the Slide Master. If you want to place the photo behind the presentation text, select the photo and choose Send To Back from the Draw menu's Order submenu. The figure below shows a photo on presentation slides 1 through 4. To place a photo on the background of the title slide, choose Master and then Title Master from the View menu and follow the same procedure.

Adjusting a Picture

After you insert a photo, you can use the controls on the Picture toolbar to brighten or darken the image or to give it more or less contrast.

III

Fine-Tuning the Presentation

Using Image Control, Brightness, and Contrast

With Image Control on the Picture toolbar, you can show a color picture as a grayscale image, a black-and-white image, or a watermark, which is a pale version of the image that is suitable for a slide background. Any changes you make to the photos with the controls on the Picture toolbar only affect how the picture looks in PowerPoint. The original photo file on disk is not affected.

To open the Picture toolbar and gain access to its controls, right-click a photo and choose Show Picture Toolbar from the shortcut menu.

To change how the photo is displayed, click the Image Control button on the toolbar and choose Grayscale, Black & White, or Watermark from the menu that appears. The default, Automatic, shows the picture exactly as is. Grayscale shows a color image in shades of gray, making a color photo look like a black-and-white image. Showing an image as grayscale gives you a good impression of how it will look when printed on a black-and-white laser printer. Black & White chooses a mid-level color in the image and displays anything brighter as white and anything darker as black. It's a quick-and-dirty artistic effect you might like. Watermark reduces the contrast of a picture to produce a pale, washed out translation. You can then use the picture as a background and even superimpose text on it. Figure 13-5 shows the effects of the various image control options available on the Picture toolbar.

FIGURE 13-5.

The effects of the Image Control options.

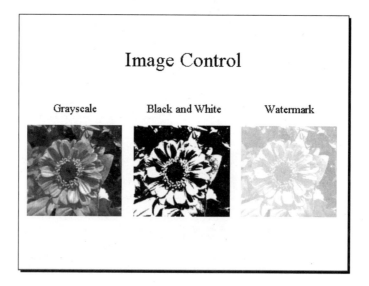

To adjust the brightness or contrast of a picture, click the More Contrast, Less Contrast, More Brightness, and Less Brightness buttons on the

Picture toolbar until you're satisfied with the appearance. Adding a little contrast can make pictures more vivid when you display slides in a darkened room with a computer projector. Remember, though, you aren't modifying the original photo, only the version of the photo that is displayed in PowerPoint.

Cropping an Image

Cropping a picture is like using scissors to cut away the parts of a photograph that you want to remove, but you can only make straight cuts across or down the image. To use the crop tool, select the photo and click Crop on the Picture toolbar. Then place the mouse pointer (which looks like the cropping icon on the toolbar) on one of the handles surrounding the image and drag the handle toward the center of the picture, as shown in Figure 13-6. To display only the left half of a picture, for example, drag the right side handle halfway across the image to the left. You can drag other handles to close in on the part of the picture you want to display. When you're finished, click anywhere outside the image.

You can restore parts of a photo that have been cropped by using the Crop tool again to drag the handles back out to the edges of the image.

FIGURE 13-6.

Cropping a photo.

You can also crop a photo using the controls on the Picture tab of the Format Picture dialog box. Right-click the picture and choose Format Picture to open this dialog box. The four Crop From boxes allow you to enter exact cropping measurements. For example, you can crop in one inch from the left by entering *1″* in the Left box.

III

Fine-Tuning the Presentation

Changing the Frame Around an Image

The Line Style button on the Picture toolbar lets you select from any of the standard black, single, double, or triple borders to frame the image. To design your own border and even choose a different color, choose More Lines from the bottom of the Line Style display, which takes you to the Colors And Lines tab of the Format Picture dialog box. Choose a color for the line, whether it should be dashed, and then select a style and weight.

Choosing a Color to Become Transparent

A new feature in this version of PowerPoint allows you to choose part of a photo to become transparent. This allows you to pull the subject of a picture out of the normal rectangular box that all pictures appear in. For example, you can isolate someone's face from a portrait and have just the face appear to float on a PowerPoint slide. Figure 13-7 shows an example of this.

FIGURE 13-7.

The color surrounding the face has been made transparent.

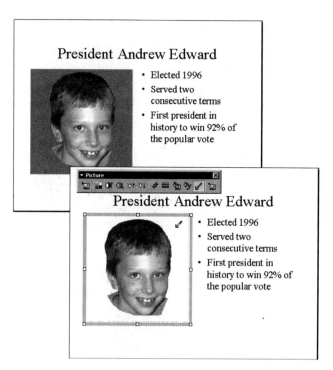

For this feature to work, the subject that you want to isolate in a photo must be surrounded by a single, uniform color. Because that's rare to find in a photo, you probably need to work on the photo in an image editing program, such as Microsoft PhotoDraw, to replace all the pixels in the photo, except those of the subject, with a single color. You also need to be sure that the color of those pixels does not appear anywhere within the subject area of the photo, or those pixels will be removed, too, leaving see-through holes in your subject. Choose a peculiar color that you can't find anywhere in the part of the photo that you want to keep.

One way to accomplish this in most photo editing programs is to draw an irregular shape around the subject area of the photo and then fill the shape with a color. Microsoft PhotoDraw allows you to cut out an area of a photo and move it to a new picture. You can then place that cutout on a rectangular background filled with a color that's not in the photo.

After you insert a photo that has had the pixels you do not want replaced with a single color, open the Picture toolbar and click the Set Transparent Color button. Then click anywhere in the colored part of the rectangle, and all the pixels of that color will immediately disappear, leaving behind only the part of the picture you want.

Resetting a Photo

To remove all the changes to a photo that you've made in PowerPoint, click the Reset Picture button on the Picture toolbar. The picture will revert to the way it was when you first inserted it in PowerPoint.

Getting Art from the Clip Gallery

The Clip Gallery is a shared Microsoft Office component that offers a selection of clip art, pictures, sounds, and motion sequences, such as animations or videos. You can use it from any Office program to select a clip. You can even use it to store clips you've created or gathered, such as the photos for a project. With the Clip Gallery, they'll be readily available to you for any document, spreadsheet, or presentation.

Choosing Clip Art

If you know that you'll want to add clip art when you create a new slide, you can select one of the two AutoLayouts that come with clip art placeholders. Figure 13-8 on the next page shows these two AutoLayouts. After you select one of the AutoLayouts, you can double-click the placeholder to open the Clip Gallery for browsing.

III

Fine-Tuning the Presentation

FIGURE 13-8.

The two AutoLayouts with clip placeholders.

AutoLayouts with clip art placeholders

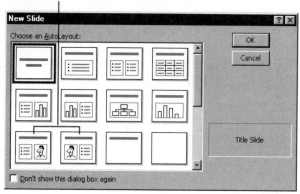

If you want to add clip art or a photo to an existing slide that does not have a clip art placeholder, display the slide in Slide view and then do one of the following:

- Click the Insert Clip Art button on the Drawing toolbar.

- From the Insert menu, choose the Picture command, and then choose Clip Art from the Picture submenu.

The Insert Clip Art dialog box appears, as shown in Figure 13-9. This is the same dialog box you see when you double-click a clip art place-holder on a slide. Although in that case, it's called the Microsoft Clip Gallery dialog box.

FIGURE 13-9.

The Insert Clip Art dialog box.

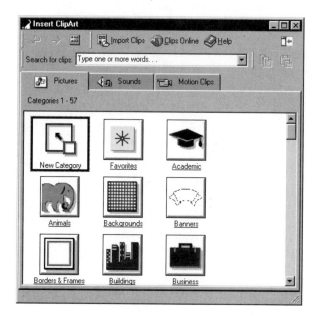

An alphabetized list of clip art categories appears in the dialog box preceded by a New Category button, which you can click to start a new category, and a Favorites category, where you can store the images you use most often. To browse for a suitable image, click an appropriate category and then scroll through its selections. To see a clip's keywords, its dimensions, and its file type, move the mouse pointer onto an image and pause without clicking.

To quickly move a clip onto a slide, click the clip once and then click the Insert Clip button on the pop-up toolbar. To see a larger version of the clip in its own window, click the clip once and then click the Preview Clip button on the shortcut menu. To return to a display of all the categories so you can choose a different category of images, click the All Categories button on the toolbar.

Just before you finalize a particular clip, you may want to have the Clip Gallery show you clips that are similar in theme, just in case there's a clip that might be a little better. Click a clip and choose Find Similar Clips from the shortcut menu. You can then either click Find Best Matching Clips or click one of the keywords displayed. The Clip Gallery displays a few more images that are close in nature, so even if you don't find a better clip, you'll be reassured that you've chosen the most appropriate clip in the Gallery.

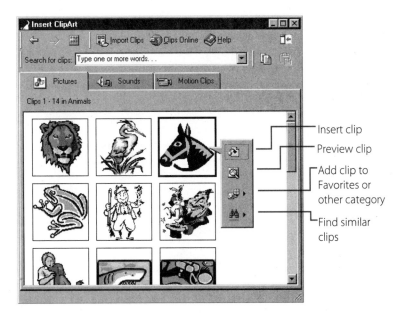

Insert clip

Preview clip

Add clip to Favorites or other category

Find similar clips

Drag an Image from the Clip Gallery

You can select a clip from the Clip Gallery and drag it right onto a slide. You can't use the drag-and-drop feature if you clicked a clip placeholder on a slide to open the Clip Gallery, though.

When the clip art you've selected is on the slide, you can drag it to move it or drag a handle to resize it. As with all pictures, drag a corner handle to maintain the clip art's proportions or hold down the Ctrl key and drag a corner handle to stretch or shrink the picture from the center out.

Creating a Background Using Clip Art

To add a clip art image to the background of every slide in a presentation, add the picture to the Slide Master background. First choose Master from the View menu and then Slide Master from the submenu. Then open the Clip Gallery, select the image you want, and click Insert Clip. After you add a picture to the Slide Master, you can place the picture behind the text of the presentation by selecting the clip art object and choosing Send To Back from the Draw menu's Order submenu (on the Draw toolbar).

Finding Clip Art in the Clip Gallery

Each picture in the Clip Gallery is associated with keywords that you can use to search for images. To search for a picture in the Clip Gallery, enter a search word in the Search For Clips text field and press Enter. You can also pull down the list to choose from among the searches you've already made.

Enter a search word here.

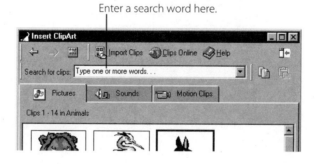

For example, to find a clip art image that shows a sailboat, enter "sailboats" in the Search For Clips text field. You can also enter more abstract terms, such as "leadership." The Clip Gallery has a sophisticated keyword matching system, so even though you've entered "leadership," it finds an image that has the keyword "supervise." Figure 13-10 shows the Clip Gallery after a search for the keyword "boats."

FIGURE 13-10.

The Clip Gallery dialog box after a search for the keyword "boats."

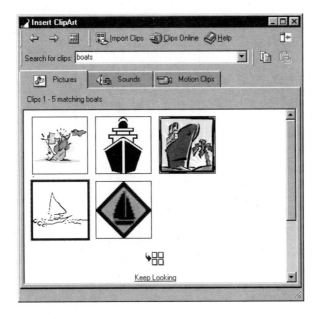

Replacing a Clip Art Selection on a Slide

After you add a picture from the Clip Gallery to a slide, you can replace the picture by double-clicking it. When the Microsoft Clip Gallery dialog box reopens, you can select a replacement picture. You can also select the picture, click the right mouse button, and choose Replace from the Clip Object submenu on the shortcut menu.

Recoloring Clip Art

The clip art from the Clip Gallery has a preset combination of colors that may clash with the color scheme of your presentation. To recolor a clip art picture so that it displays colors that match the color scheme in your presentation, select the clip art, click the right mouse button, and then choose Show Picture Toolbar from the shortcut menu. Although using the Picture toolbar is quick and convenient, you can find dialog box equivalents for the toolbar buttons by choosing Picture from the Format menu. Figure 13-11 on the next page shows the Picture Toolbar and its buttons.

III

Fine-Tuning the Presentation

FIGURE 13-11.

The Picture Toolbar.

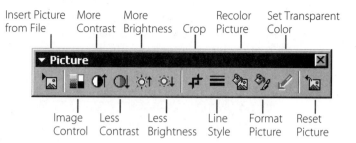

After you've summoned the Picture toolbar, click the Recolor Picture button. In the Recolor Picture dialog box, shown in Figure 13-12, find the original color that you want to change in the picture, and select a new color from the adjacent drop-down list of colors. To change only the background and fill colors in the picture without changing the colors of the lines, select the Fills option before changing colors.

FIGURE 13-12.

The Recolor Picture dialog box.

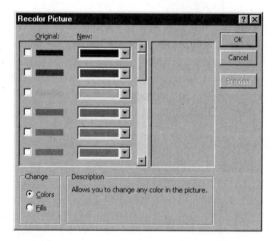

When you open a color drop-down list, you can select one of the eight colors in the current color scheme or you can select More Colors to make the full palette of colors available. Keep in mind that when you select a color in the color scheme, you gain two advantages:

- The colors in the picture match the colors used throughout the presentation

- The color scheme attached to the presentation controls the colors in the picture, so if you change color schemes, the picture will recolor accordingly

If you select a color from the More Colors dialog box instead, the color remains fixed even when you change the color scheme. As a result, the color might clash with the new color scheme's colors.

You can recolor as many of the colors in the picture as you want. Then click Preview to see the results. When the new colors are satisfactory, click OK.

Adding Clip Art and Photos to the Clip Gallery

The Clip Gallery comes with a substantial number of images, but you may have clip art pictures on your system that have been installed with other software or that you've purchased separately. You also might have photos you've scanned or taken with a digital camera. By adding the images that are already on your system to PowerPoint's Clip Gallery, you can retrieve them all from one central place.

To add an image, choose Insert Clip Art to open the Clip Gallery, click one of the existing categories and then click the Import Clips button on the toolbar in the Clip Gallery. You can also click New Category and then create a new category. In the Add Clip To Clip Gallery dialog box shown in Figure 13-13, find and select the file to add and click Import.

FIGURE 13-13.

The Add Clip To The Clip Gallery dialog box.

The Clip Import options, at the bottom of the Add Clip To Clip Gallery dialog box, let you either copy or move the images to the Clip Gallery; you determine whether the image remains at its original location after it is added. By choosing the third option, Let Clip Gallery Find This Clip In Its Current Folder Or Volume, you can add a image to the Clip

III

Fine-Tuning the Presentation

Gallery without duplicating it in the Gallery. The Clip Gallery goes to the image's original folder and gets a copy of the image whenever you need it. This avoids unnecessary duplication and conserves disk space.

Using the Clip Gallery as a Photo Album for your Digital Photos
Rather than buy special software to organize the photos you take with your digital camera in a photo album, you can use the Clip Gallery. Create folders on your disk to categorize your photo files by date or subject. Also add corresponding categories in the Clip Gallery. You can then add the images in the folders to the categories in the Clip Gallery, choosing Let Clip Gallery Find This Clip In Its Current Folder Or Volume. When you want to browse your photo album, open the Clip Gallery from any Office application and select one of the categories you've created for your photos.

After you select a clip, the Clip Properties dialog box opens, as shown in Figure 13-14. On the Description tab of the dialog box, enter a short description of the clip and then, on the Categories tab, select additional categories under which you want the image filed. On the Keywords tab, add keywords for searching by clicking the New Keyword button. You can click Preview to see the image in a preview window or click OK when you've finished adding categories and keywords. The image is added to the Gallery in the category you've chosen.

FIGURE 13-14.
The Clip Properties dialog box.

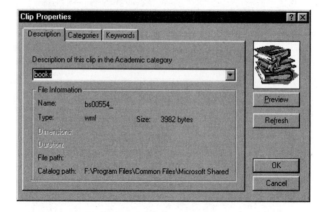

Drag files into the Clip Gallery
The drag-and-drop feature also works when you want to add clips to the Clip Gallery. You can drag clips from the desktop or from folders directly onto category buttons in the Clip Gallery.

Images that you add to the Clip Gallery are stored as part of your Windows user profile. Therefore, each person who uses the machine and starts Windows with a different user name and password will see different images. The images for each user are stored in a folder with the following pathname: \Windows\Profiles*username*\Application Data\Microsoft\Media Catalog.

⭐ **TIP**

> **Checking the Categories and Keywords of a Clip**
> You can check and change the description of a picture, move it to another category in the Clip Gallery, or create a new category to put it in by pointing to the picture in the Clip Gallery and clicking the right mouse button. Choose Clip Properties from the shortcut menu to make changes or choose Delete Clip to remove the picture from the Clip Gallery (but leave the original on the disk). You can also rename or delete entire categories by right-clicking a category on the category display and then choosing either Rename Category or Delete Category.

Periodically, you may want to update the previews shown in the Clip Gallery. Any changes to the original pictures on disk will be reflected in the Clip Gallery. To update an image, select it, click the right mouse button, choose Clip Properties, and then click Refresh on the Description tab of the Clip Properties dialog box.

⭐ **TIP**

> **Adding Photos by Dragging**
> The fastest way to add images to the Clip Gallery is to open the folder containing the clips, open the Gallery, and then drag the files from the folder onto one of the category icons in the Clip Gallery.

Updating the Clip Gallery from the Web

Microsoft has established a Web site called Clip Gallery Live from which you can download new clips. To reach this site, connect to the Web as you normally do and then click the Clips Online button on the toolbar of the Clip Gallery. Your Web browser opens and takes you to the Clip Gallery Live Web site. Select clips from the Web pages and choose Download there to add the images to the Downloaded Clips category of your Clip Gallery.

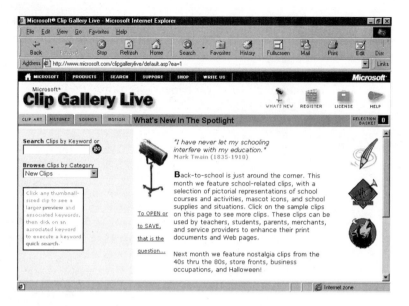

Importing an Image from Another Application

You may want to add a particular graphic to a presentation but not maintain it in the Clip Gallery. Perhaps the graphic is customized for a special presentation and it will never be used again. To directly import a graphic from a graphic file, follow these steps:

1   In Slide view, choose Picture from the Insert menu.

2   Choose From File from the Picture submenu.

3   Select a graphic file in the Insert Picture dialog box shown in Figure 13-15. You can search for a picture by entering a file name or property in the appropriate text boxes near the bottom of the dialog box and clicking Find Now.

4   Click Insert to place the graphic on the current slide.

PowerPoint can import graphic files of two types: *vector* and *bitmap*. Vector files are produced by drawing and graphing programs, and they contain an arrangement of individual objects—circles, rectangles, lines, filled areas, and text characters, for example. A bitmapped file contains a picture that is composed of a pattern of dots, much as newspaper photos are composed of tiny dots.

FIGURE 13-15.

The Insert Picture dialog box.

Because vector files contain objects, they can be edited easily. You can ungroup a vector file and then remove or resize an individual object to change the picture and leave other objects that are underneath untouched. Most clip art is provided in vector format so that it can easily be edited and resized to fit any need. Bitmapped files can be edited, too, but not as easily as vector files. To erase part of a bitmap, you must erase the dots, leaving a hole in the picture. Parts of objects that appeared to be behind the object you've erased are erased, too. But with their many dots, bitmaps can represent a photographic picture accurately, which is why software that you use with a scanner generates a bitmapped version of a photograph rather than a vector file. Therefore, if you intend to place a scanned image in a presentation—a photograph of a person or a scanned logo, for example—you must always import a bitmapped file.

Table 13-1 on the next page identifies graphic file types you can import.

 NOTE

> You can only import file types for which you've installed a graphic filter. The Microsoft Office applications share the same graphic filters, so if you installed a graphic filter when you installed Word or Excel, for example, you can use the same graphic filter in PowerPoint.

The files you learned to add in this chapter appear on slides whether you print them, view them on overheads, or broadcast them in a presentation delivered on the Web. The multimedia file types that you will learn to add in the next chapter impart sound and motion to PowerPoint slides. They come to life only when the presentation is seen in a slide show in a face-to-face meeting or online presentation.

III

Fine-Tuning the Presentation

TABLE 13-1.   The Graphic File Types You Can Import

File Format	Type
Windows Bitmap (.BMP)	Bitmap
Windows Metafile (.WMF)	Vector
Windows Enhanced Metafile (.EMF)	Vector
Computer Graphics Metafile (.CGM)	Vector
Encapsulated PostScript (.EPS)	Vector
Tagged Image File Format (.TIF)	Bitmap
PC Paintbrush (.PCX)	Bitmap
Macintosh PICT (.PCT)	Bitmap
Micrografx Designer/Draw (.DRW)	Vector
CompuServe GIF (.GIF)	Bitmap
AutoCAD Format 2-D (.DXF)	Vector
CorelDRAW! (.CDR)	Vector
DrawPerfect (.WPG)	Vector
Kodak Photo CD (.PCD)	Bitmap
Lotus 1-2-3 Graphics (.PIC)	Vector
Portable Network Graphics (.PNG)	Bitmap
True Vision Targa (.TGA)	Bitmap
Windows DIB (.DIB)	Bitmap
HP Graphics Language (.HGL)	Vector
Portable Network Graphics (.PNG)	Bitmap
JPEG (.JPG)	Bitmap

Printing Pages
and 35-mm Slides

S omehow printing always seems to be the hard part about using a computer. You work so hard to create a look on the screen, but on your printouts, the darks are too dark and the lights are too light. And once you've printed overhead transparencies in landscape orientation, you can't get audience handouts in portrait orientation without murmuring incantations.

Well, PowerPoint solves these problems by taking care of all the portrait-to-landscape, overhead-to-slide, and screen-to-paper conversions behind the scenes so that you can concentrate on expressing yourself.

In this chapter, you'll learn how to tell PowerPoint exactly what type of output to generate, whether it's a set of overheads from your slides or audience handouts with up to nine slide miniatures per page. You'll also learn to print the speaker's notes you've entered on notes pages and print the presentation to a file that you can give to a service bureau to produce 35-mm slides.

Setting Up the Pages

The first step in creating printed output or 35-mm slides is to check the current page setup. The page setup determines the size and orientation of the slides you've created. You may be wondering why you don't change the page setup before starting a presentation. The answer is that you can, but you don't have to. You can leave the default setting, which displays the presentation properly in a slide show and on regular pages or landscape overheads printed on 8½-by-11-inch pages, and change the page setup only if you need to print 35-mm slides or custom pages with odd heights and widths.

When you change the page setup, PowerPoint does all the work to resize and reorient the material on slides to fit the new page size and orientation. For example, you can create landscape slides for a screen show, which have a horizontal orientation, and then switch to portrait slides if you need a vertical printout for a printed report. In most cases, PowerPoint adjusts everything on your slides so well that you'll think you've been creating portrait slides all along.

To check the page setup, choose Page Setup from the File menu. In the Page Setup dialog box, shown in Figure 14-1, you see options for setting the slide width and height, the starting slide number, and the orientation for slides or for notes, handouts, and outline printing.

FIGURE 14-1.
The Page Setup dialog box.

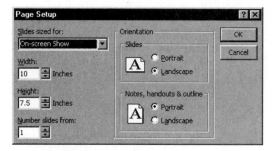

Slide Size

From the Slides Sized For drop-down list in the Page Setup dialog box, select one of the six preset slide sizes (On-screen Show, Letter Paper, A4 Paper, 35-mm Slides, Overhead, Banner), or select Custom and then set a custom width and height in the Width and Height boxes.

> **NOTE**
>
> When you select the Custom option, the default settings for the Width and Height are set to the printable area of the page for the current printer.

Slide Numbering

? SEE ALSO

For more information about numbering slides, see "Inserting the Slide Number, Date, or Time on Selected Slides," page 299.

In the Page Setup dialog box, the number shown in the Number Slides From box sets the slide numbering that appears both on the slides and in the slide number indicator at the bottom of the PowerPoint window. Keep in mind that before the number is actually displayed on a slide, you must enter the page number symbol on the slide by choosing Header and Footer from the View menu and then clicking Slide Number on the Header and Footer dialog box, or by adding a text box to each slide, or a particular slide, and choosing Slide Number from the Insert menu.

You can start numbering slides from any number. For example, to set the number of the first slide in the current presentation to 10, type *10* in the Number Slides From box or click the up arrow at the right end of the box to increase the setting to 10.

Slide Orientation

You can set two different orientations: one for slides and one for notes, handouts, and outline pages. With these settings, you can print speaker notes and audience handouts in portrait orientation even when you print slides in landscape orientation.

 TIP

Adding Master Embellishments

Slides, handouts, and notes pages have master slides that you can embellish with a header and footer, text, slide number, and graphics. To open one of the masters, hold down the Shift key as you click a view button. For example, to open the slide master, hold down the Shift key as you click the Slide View button. To open the handout master, hold down the Shift key and click the Outline View button or Slide Sorter View button. To open the notes pages master, you must point to Master on the View menu and then choose Notes Master from the submenu. To return to one of the standard views, click a view button without pressing the Shift key.

Printing Pages

To begin the printing process, make sure the presentation you want to print is displayed in PowerPoint, and then choose Print from the File menu or press Ctrl+P. The Print dialog box opens, as shown in Figure 14-2 on the next page.

FIGURE 14-2.

The Print dialog box.

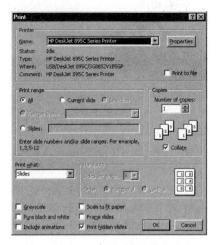

To use the default printer settings you've chosen on the Print tab of the Options dialog box (available on the Tools menu), click the Print button on the Standard toolbar.

The name of the printer that's currently selected is displayed at the top of the Print dialog box. To print the presentation on a different printer, select a printer from the Name drop-down list. If you want to transport a presentation file to another system for printing, select the Print To File check box, which prints the presentation to an output file on disk.

To access additional options for the printer that's currently selected, click the Properties button at the top of the Print dialog box.

The Print Range options let you print all the slides, the current slide, or a selection of slides in the presentation. To print the entire presentation, click the All option. To print only the slide shown in the current view, click the Current Slide option. To print selected slides, click the Slides option and enter the corresponding slide numbers in the Slides box. You can separate nonconsecutive slides with commas and separate the first and last number of a range of slides with a hyphen. You can even combine nonconsecutive slides and ranges of slides by using both commas and hyphens. For example, to print slide 3 and also slides 6 through 8, you can enter 3,6-8 in the Slides box.

Another way to select the slides to print is to switch to Slide Sorter or Outline view and hold down the Shift key or the Ctrl key as you click each slide or slide icon. When you open the Print dialog box, click the Selection option in the Print Range section to print only the selected slides.

To print a portion of an outline, select the portion and then choose Print. In the Print Range options, click the Selection button. Only the text you've selected prints.

You can increase the number in the Number Of Copies box to print multiple copies of the slides. If you print more than one copy, you can also select the Collate check box to print properly sequenced sets of slides rather than multiple copies of the first page followed by multiple copies of the next page, and so on. Printing collated copies can take considerably longer because the computer must resend each page to the printer several times rather than send the page once and have the printer churn out multiple copies.

The default setting for the Print What option is Slides, but you can also select Handouts, Notes Pages, or Outline View from the drop-down list.

The Special Print Options

The options in the Print dialog box let you make important changes to the way the presentation prints, although the defaults work well in most cases. Each of these special options is described here:

- The Grayscale option converts the colors on slides to shades of gray that are best suited for printing on black-and-white laser printers that can produce gray shades. Although Windows converts colors to gray shades when you print color slides to a black-and-white printer, PowerPoint chooses the best grays to give printouts an optimal look. When you choose the Grayscale option, the background of the slide does not print on a black-and-white printer, such as a laser printer. To print the background, turn off the Grayscale option.

  When you let PowerPoint choose gray shades, some objects might not appear the way you'd like them to. For example, a dark object might no longer be visible against a dark background. You can adjust the color of an individual object by selecting the object and using the Colors And Lines command on the Format or shortcut menu. If you want to change the color of a text selection, use the Font command on the Format menu.

- The Pure Black And White option converts all colors in the presentation to either black or white. Use this option when you need to print to a printer that cannot print gray shades.

- The Scale To Fit Paper option properly scales the slides to fit the printed page even if the slides have been set up for a different page size. For example, to print a slide that you sized for 35-mm slides (in the Slide Setup dialog box) on an 8½-by-11-inch page, you can use the Scale To Fit Paper option.

- The Frame Slides option prints a narrow frame around each slide. This option is useful if you want to display your slides as overheads.

- The Print Hidden Slides option prints slides that you have hidden using the Hide Slide command on the Slide Show menu. If the presentation contains no hidden slides, the option is unavailable.

Figure 14-3 shows two versions of a color slide printed on a laser printer. The left page was printed with both the Grayscale and Pure Black And White options turned off, and the right page was printed with the Grayscale option turned on.

FIGURE 14-3.

A page printed with two different print options: plain (left) and Grayscale (right).

Printing Handouts and Notes Pages

To print audience handouts, choose Print from the File menu or press Ctrl+P, and then select Handouts from the Print What drop-down list in the Print dialog box. The Handouts options on the Print dialog box allow you to print two, three, four, six, or nine slides per page. The Horizontal setting runs the slides in order across the page. The Vertical setting runs them down the page instead. The orientation of the handouts is determined by the Orientation setting in the Page Setup dialog box shown earlier. Figure 14-4 shows a handout page with three slides per page, leaving the audience members plenty of room to jot down notes about each slide.

FIGURE 14-4.

A handout page with three slides on the page.

To print notes pages, select Notes Pages from the Print What drop-down list. As with handouts, the orientation of the notes pages is determined by the Orientation setting in the Page Setup dialog box.

Printing the Outline

To print the presentation outline just as it appears in Outline view, select Outline View from the Print What drop-down list box in the Print dialog box. The outline prints with as much detail as is currently displayed in Outline view. Collapsed entries do not print. Figure 14-5 on the next page shows an outline as printed.

III

Fine-Tuning the Presentation

FIGURE 14-5.

A printout of an outline.

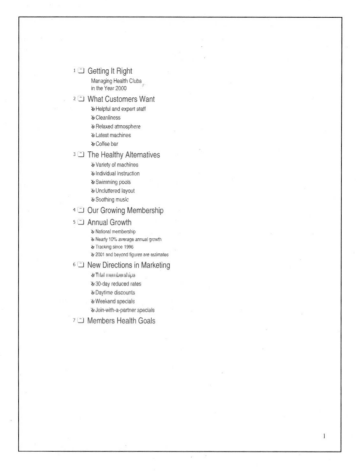

The outline that PowerPoint prints is useful, but not very pretty. To give an outline formatting that is suitable for a printed document, you should send it to Microsoft Word, where you can use Word's text formatting options. To send an outline to Word from Outline view, choose Send To from the File menu and choose Microsoft Word from the submenu. On the Write-Up dialog box, click Outline Only and then click OK. The outline appears in Word and the text has the same formatting as it does on the slides of the presentation.

Creating 35-mm Slides

If you're lucky enough to have a film recorder attached to your system and the Windows printer driver for the film recorder, you can select the film recorder as your printer and then print to the film recorder as if you were printing to any other printer. The film recorder creates an image of each slide on 35-mm slide film. To get final 35-mm slides, you only need to have the film developed into slides. You may need to refer to the documentation for the device for special instructions on using it with a Windows-based application such as PowerPoint.

Most people do not have expensive film recorders at hand, however. Instead, they rely on a service bureau that takes a PostScript file generated from PowerPoint and feeds it into a film recorder. Many service bureaus provide overnight service, returning the developed 35-mm slides by next-day delivery. A local service bureau may even provide same-day service. Because PowerPoint is so popular and commonly used, any service bureau should be able to provide you with instructions for generating a suitable file from your presentation and delivering it to them.

PowerPoint comes with software that makes it especially easy to use Genigraphics as your service bureau. When you install PowerPoint, you can also install the Genigraphics Wizard, which automatically creates a PostScript file that Genigraphics can accept. The Wizard takes your order, generates the file, and sends it to Genigraphics by modem or over the Internet.

To create an order, choose the Send To command from the File menu and then choose Genigraphics to activate the Genigraphics Wizard, shown in Figure 14-6.

FIGURE 14-6.

The first page of the Genigraphics Wizard.

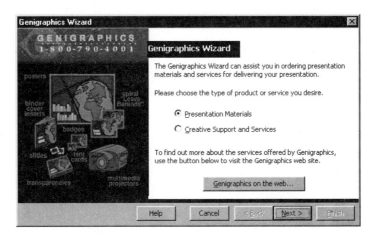

The Genigraphics Wizard prompts you for the type of products or electronic services you need in addition to your mailing and billing information. You can use the wizard to send your request electronically or save it to a file to send later either by disk or modem.

In this chapter, you learned to produce a paper copy of a presentation, or a version on 35-mm slides. In the next chapter, you learn to produce an electronic version of a presentation, a slide show that displays on the screen with television-like transition effects, multimedia elements like sound and video, and animated slides that will surely capture the attention of an audience.

PART IV

Performing with PowerPoint

CHAPTER 15

Making Lively Slide Shows

The most rudimentary slide show simply reveals one slide after another. But by setting transition effects so that slides replace each other with cinematic special effects, you can easily jump to a higher level of sophistication in your presentations. You can even go a step farther by creating fully animated slides with text and graphics that glide into place or fade from view. And the crowning touch is be to enhance a presentation with a full audio soundtrack, such as a voiceover, sound effects, and a full musical score with audio cuts from your favorite CD.

Of course, you don't have to go full Hollywood; you can add only as much pizzazz as you want. But whether it's a little animation or a fully staged spectacle you're after, you'll learn about it in this chapter.

Basic Slide Transitions

The first step toward converting a sequence of slides to a slide show is to assign a transition effect for the switch from one slide to the next. Transitions are special effects that you add to slides to make them show up in animated ways. PowerPoint has twelve basic transitions and several variations of each, so you can keep an audience guessing.

To start, you can see how a show looks without transition effects by moving to the first slide and clicking the Slide Show button at the bottom of the presentation window, shown in Figure 15-1, or choosing Slide Show from the View menu. The first slide stays on the screen until you click the mouse button, press the Spacebar, or press the Enter key to go to the next slide. Each slide simply replaces the previous slide the same way a set of photographic slides display with a carousel projector. To end the show, press Esc.

FIGURE 15-1.
Slide Sorter View button.

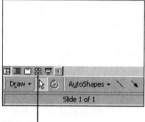

Slide Sorter View button

To begin assigning transition effects, switch to Slide Sorter view, where you can work with and preview effects. To switch to Slide Sorter view, click the Slide Sorter View button or select Slide Sorter from the View menu.

TIP

Don't Overdo It

Transition effects are undoubtedly snazzy, but they could end up detracting from the content of your presentation if you use too many different effects during a slide show or set them all to Slow to heighten the drama. Instead, it's best to use Fast for the transition speed whenever possible, and use one effect repeatedly, changing effects only for new segments of a presentation.

In Slide Sorter view, you can assign transitions by selecting them from the Slide Transition Effects list box on the Slide Sorter toolbar, shown in Figure 15-2.

FIGURE 15-2.

The Slide Sorter toolbar.

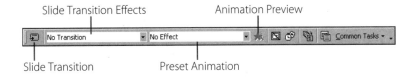

To assign a basic transition effect to a slide, click the slide and then select an effect from the Slide Transition Effects drop-down list. If you watch carefully, you'll see an instant preview of the transition right in Slide Sorter view. If you miss the preview, repeat it by clicking the small transition effect icon just below the slide. Figure 15-3 shows this icon. You can also click the Animation Preview button on the Slide Sorter toolbar.

FIGURE 15-3.

Click a Transition Effect icon to preview the transition effect applied to the slide.

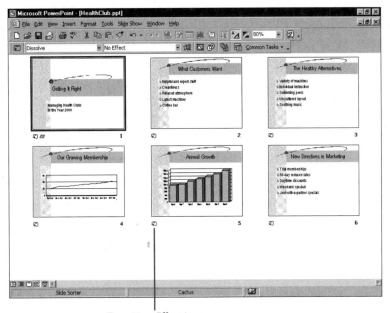

Transition Effect icon

To apply a single effect to all the slides, choose Select All from the Edit menu or press Ctrl+A and then select an effect from the Slide Transition Effects drop-down list. To apply the same transition effect to only a certain number of slides in sequence, select the slides and then select an effect. Remember, you can select more than one slide by holding down the Ctrl key as you click each slide, by holding down the Shift key and clicking the first and last slides in the sequence, or by drawing a selection box around a group of slides using the mouse pointer.

A Special Effect for Slide Titles

If you select the same transition effect for all the slides in a slide show, you might consider using a different effect for the title slides of each segment of your presentation. Simply select all the title slides, and then select a different effect from the Slide Transition Effects drop-down list.

The Slide Transition button

For more options for transition effects, you can click the Slide Transition button on the Slide Sorter toolbar, to the left of the Slide Transition Effects box. This opens the Slide Transition dialog box, shown in Figure 15-4, in which you can select not only a transition effect but also a speed for the effect and the amount of time you want the slide to remain on the screen. (Another way to open the Slide Transition dialog box is to select one or more slides and choose Slide Transition from the Slide Show menu, or click the right mouse button and choose Slide Transition from the shortcut menu.)

FIGURE 15-4.

The Slide Transition dialog box.

The default Advance option on the Slide Transition dialog box, On Mouse Click, requires you to click the left mouse button to advance to the next slide. If you'd rather have the show advance automatically, select the Automatically After check box and enter a time in minutes and seconds.

In the Slide Transition dialog box, you can also add sound transitions by selecting sounds from the Sound drop-down list. You must have a sound card and speakers installed (or at least headphones) to hear them, but most new computers come with sound cards built in.

In the Sound drop-down list you'll find a selection of stock sounds that come with PowerPoint, such as applause, drum rolls, and chimes. To play your own sounds that you've saved as .wav files on your hard disk, scroll to the bottom of the list and click Other Sound. Then you can browse your hard disk to find your own sound files. After you select a sound, it plays only once unless you select the Loop Until Next Sound check box to make it run continuously throughout the show (or at least until you reach a new sound on the next slide). You can also select Stop Previous Sound from the Sound drop-down list to stop a looping sound from a previous slide.

After you've made selections in the Slide Transition dialog box, click Apply to apply them to the selected slides, or Apply To All to apply them to the entire slide show.

How to Create a Graceful Ending

To create a graceful ending to a slide show, you can add a black slide to the end by choosing Options from the Tools menu and selecting the End With Black Slide option on the View tab of the Options dialog box. Take heed, however— if you don't include the black slide, PowerPoint will reappear after the last slide, and you'll be faced with the sudden glare of menus, buttons, and toolbars.

Adding Multimedia Files to Slides

You can add sounds (audio and music) or motion clips (video and animations) to a slide the same way you add a photo or clip art picture. In a slide show, these multimedia elements play automatically.

Adding a sound places an icon on a slide in Slide view. To hear the sound while you are still in Slide view, you can double-click the icon. Adding a motion clip displays the first frame of the clip. To start the clip playing in Slide view, you can double-click the first frame. (Animated GIF files, a common and easy-to-create form of animation, play only when you view them in a slide show.)

The Microsoft Clip Gallery offers a number of sound and motion clips for your use. You can also record your own clips, collect them from others, or download them from the Web. In addition, your organization might have a set of clips (company radio spots, theme songs) stored in files in a shared resource on the server from which everyone can borrow.

Inserting a Clip from the Clip Gallery

To add a multimedia selection from the Clip Gallery, click the Insert menu and choose Movies And Sounds. On the Movies And Sounds submenu, choose either Movie From Gallery or Sound From Gallery. Depending on your menu selection, the Microsoft Clip Gallery opens to either the Motion Clips tab or the Sounds tab.

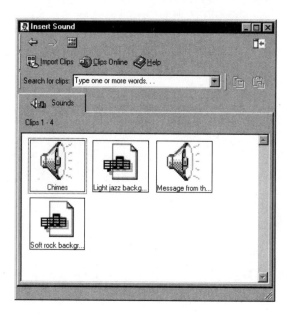

To choose a clip, click the clip in the Clip Gallery and then click the Insert Clip button on the pop-out menu, as shown in Figure 15-5. You can also drag a clip from the Gallery directly onto a slide. To see a clip's duration, file size, and file type in the Gallery, place the mouse pointer on the clip and pause without clicking. A small box shows the information.

As you insert a clip, PowerPoint displays a dialog box to ask whether you want the clip to play automatically in the slide show. If you click Yes, the clip plays whenever you turn to or go to the slide during a slide show. If you click No, you must click the clip on the slide to play it.

Instructing PowerPoint that you want a clip to play automatically gives you a rudimentary working show, but you can use a custom animation to determine precisely the order in which the clips you've added will play. *You learn to set custom animations in "Animating Slides," page 385.*

FIGURE 15-5.

The Clip Gallery.

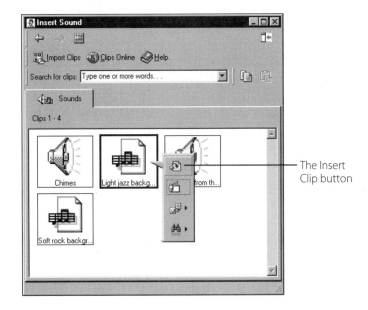

The Insert
Clip button

If you'd rather not get into the nitty-gritty of a custom animation, which
allows you to control the individual objects on a slide, you can use
some simple options in Slide view to determine how and when multimedia files are played. To see these options, select the icon or media
clip in Slide view and then choose Edit Movie Object or Edit Sound
Object from the shortcut menu. In the Movie Options dialog box,
shown in Figure 15-6, you see the total playing time for the clip and
options to loop (or repeat) the movie until stopped and to rewind the
movie after it has played. In the Sound Options dialog box, the only
available option is to loop the sound.

FIGURE 15-6.

The Movie Options
dialog box.

Adding Sounds from Files

To add a sound from a file on your hard disk, point to Movies And
Sounds on the Insert menu, and then choose Sound From File from the
submenu. Use the options on the Insert Sound dialog box to navigate
to the folder in which you've stored sound files, and then double-click

a sound file. PowerPoint asks whether you want the sound played automatically. Click Yes to have the sound start when you reach the slide during a slide show. Click No if you'd rather use a custom animation later to time the start of the sound in relation to the other objects on the slide.

⭐ **TIP**

Audition a Sound

Before you double-click a sound on the Insert Sound dialog box, you can audition it by right-clicking the sound file name and choosing Play from the shortcut menu.

The standard file format that holds recorded sound files on a PC is a .wav file, but PowerPoint can import and play a number of other sound file formats. These are listed in Table 15-1.

TABLE 15-1.   The Sound File Formats that PowerPoint Can Play

File Extension	Type	Description
.wav	Microsoft Waveform file	Windows format for sound files
.aif, .aiff	Audio Interchange File Format	File format used for sound on Amiga, Atari, SGI, and Macintosh computers
.aifc	Audio Interchange File Format	Compressed version of .aif or .aiff file.
.au	Sun/NeXT/DEC Audio file	File format used for sound on Sun/NeXT/DEC computers

Playing Sound Segments

PowerPoint does not give you the option to use only a segment of a sound file. It can only play the complete sound just as it was recorded into the file. But you can trim a sound file down to just the segment you want by using the Windows Sound Recorder accessory to cut off portions at the beginning or end of a .wav file.

To open the Sound Recorder, point to Accessories on the Start menu. The Sound Recorder is most likely located in the Entertainment category. If you can't find the Sound Recorder anywhere on the Start menu, use Find on the Start menu to search for the file sndrec32.exe.

Converting Other Sound File Formats

You can find a number of sound file format converters on the Internet—one example is Awave at *http://hem.passagen.se/fmj/fmjsoft.html*. These utilities can convert just about any recorded sound file to a .wav file that you can use in PowerPoint.

Open the .wav file in the Sound Recorder and play it a few times so you know the portion that you want to extract. Move the slider to the approximate starting position for the segment in the file and press Play. You can try again, adjusting the slider a bit each time and using the Position indicator (shown in hundredths of a second), until you've found the exact starting point for the sound. From the Edit menu, choose Delete Before Current Position. Now you can find the end of the segment using the same technique and then choose Delete After Current Position from the Edit menu. Save the remaining sound as a new .wav file. Now you can insert the new file in a PowerPoint slide.

Adding MIDI Music from Files

If you want to play an audio clip from a cassette tape or a radio program, you need to record it into a .wav file and then put that file on a PowerPoint slide. But if you want live music produced by the music synthesizer on your sound card, or even a synthesizer keyboard that you have hooked to your company, you must insert a MIDI file in a slide.

Unlike .wav files, which store recorded music, MIDI files (.mid or, less commonly, .rmi) store music data that is played back by a music synthesizer. (No, you don't need a rack of keyboards and a longhaired musician in the room when you give a presentation.) Most newer computers have MIDI synthesizer chips built into their sound systems, so you only need to connect speakers or hook up to the room's sound system.

You can treat MIDI files just like .wav files. When you insert a .mid file in a slide, you can set it to play and loop automatically. In fact, the icon for a .mid file on a slide looks just like the icon for a .wav file.

There are some real advantages to using MIDI files rather than recorded music in .wav files. First, .mid files are very small. More than a minute's worth of music can fit into a .mid file that is only a few kilobytes long. MIDI files download quickly, so they are suitable for Web presentations. You can also obtain public domain .mid files from a number of sources on the Web. Search for MIDI using any of the Web's popular search engines to find them. And if you have a good-quality sound card, you probably have a fine MIDI synthesizer in your system, too, so the quality of the music your sound card can create will be impressive.

To add a MIDI file to a slide, point to Movies And Sounds on the Insert menu, and then choose Sound From File on the submenu. Navigate to the folder in which you have .mid files saved, and then double-click a .mid file name. A dialog box opens to ask whether you want the sound to play automatically. If you click Yes, the sound will play when you turn to or go to the slide in the presentation. If you click No, an icon appears on the slide, but the sound does not play unless you double-click the icon.

MIDI icon

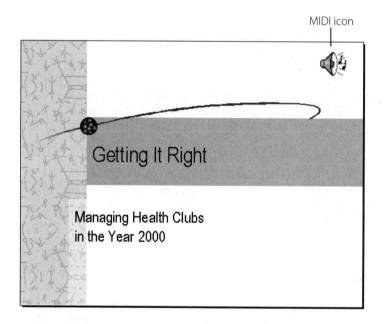

Hiding the MIDI Icon

Unfortunately, the MIDI icon you see in Slide view after you insert a MIDI file (the small speaker) appears on a slide even in a slide show. To hide the icon, you need to create a custom animation for the slide. In the Custom Animation dialog box, you can choose to hide the icon when the MIDI file is not playing.

Adding CD Audio Soundtracks

To play a music selection from a CD, you can insert a CD audio track in a slide. PowerPoint will play the music track you want from the CD during the slide show. You can choose not only the selection from the CD by track number but also a segment of the selection by entering the starting and ending points from the start of the track in seconds.

To insert a CD audio selection, point to Movies and Sounds on the Insert menu, and then choose Play CD Audio Soundtrack on the Movies and Sounds submenu. You do not have to insert the CD in the CD-ROM drive, but if you do insert a CD and the Windows CD Player starts playing the CD, be sure to stop it and close the CD Player before continuing. The Movie and Sound Options dialog box appears, as shown in Figure 15-7.

FIGURE 15-7.

The Movie and Sound Options dialog box.

In the Track boxes of the Movie and Sound Options dialog box, enter a Start and End track number. You can also enter a point during the tracks, in seconds, at which the playing should start and end. The dialog box displays the total playing time of the music you have selected if you have the audio CD in the CD drive.

When you enter the appropriate numbers and click OK, PowerPoint asks whether you want the sound played automatically in the slide show. Click Yes to have the sound played when you turn to or go to the slide during the presentation. Click No if you plan to set a custom animation to determine when the sound should play in relation to other inserted objects on the slide. You can always double-click the CD audio icon on the slide to play the sound during a slide show.

Adding Video and Movies from Files

To add a motion clip from a file on your hard disk, point to Movies And Sounds on the Insert menu, and then choose Movie From File from the submenu. Use the options on the Insert Movie dialog box to navigate to the folder in which you've stored movie files, and then double-click a movie file. PowerPoint asks whether you want the movie played automatically. Click Yes to have the movie start when you reach the slide during a slide show. Click No if you'd rather use a custom animation later to time the start of the movie in relation to the other objects on the slide.

 TIP

Audition a Movie

Before you double-click a movie on the Insert Movie dialog box, you can audition it by right-clicking the movie file name and choosing Play from the shortcut menu.

The standard file format that holds recorded movie files on a PC is an .avi (Audio Video Interleaved) file, but PowerPoint can import and play a number of other movie file formats. These are listed in Table 15-2.

TABLE 15-2. Recorded File Formats that PowerPoint Can Play

File Extension	Type	Description
.cda	CD audio track	CD audio file format
.dat	MPEG movie file	Extension used for some MPEG files
.m1v	MPEG movie file	Extension used for some MPEG files
.m3u	MPEG URL	MPEG file reference in e-mail
.mov	Apple QuickTime	Apple Macintosh movie file format
.mp2	MPEG movie file	Extension used for some MPEG files
.mpg	MPEG movie file	Moving Pictures Experts Group file

Adding Animated Images

Animated GIF files are small files that display a sequence of image frames. They're relatively easy to create and they're very popular. Nearly all the animations you see on the Web are made with animated GIFs. In fact, if you are using PowerPoint to create Web pages, you should use animated GIFs for animations because they play properly in most Web browsers.

PowerPoint does not provide a tool for creating animated GIFs, but you can download from the Web a number of inexpensive shareware programs that help you create animated GIFs.

Inserting an animated GIF is just like inserting any movie file. You can use all the same procedures described in the previous section, "Adding Videos and Movies from Files." Unlike .avi files, though, animated GIFs play only in slide shows. You can't preview them in Slide view.

"Animating" Slides

The bulleted text on text slides and the graphic objects you've added can appear either all at once or sequentially during a slide show. To have the items "build" on a slide, you must assign animations to them.

In Slide Show view, you can quickly assign preset animations to text slides to have the title and individual bulleted items appear in sequence with a fancy, animated effect. Some of these animations even provide sound effects. To create this effect, select one or more text slides with bulleted items and then choose an animation from the Preset Animation drop-down list on the Slide Sorter toolbar or from the Preset Animation selections on the shortcut menu.

For more control over the animations on a slide, or if you want to animate the graphic objects on a slide as well, you must use a custom animation that you apply in Slide view. Double-click the slide to return to Slide view so you can set the custom animation there.

In Slide view, deselect all objects on the slide, if necessary, by clicking the background of the slide. Then choose Custom Animation from the Slide Show menu. The Custom Animation dialog box appears, as shown in Figure 15-8 on the next page.

FIGURE 15-8.

The Custom Animation dialog box.

Click here to animate objects. Slide preview

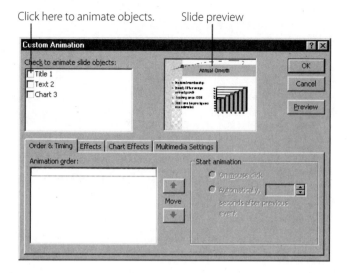

In the Custom Animation dialog box, you see a list of the objects on the slide that can be animated. Each is accompanied by a check box. To animate an object, select its check box. As you select objects to animate, you establish an animation order, which appears as the Animation Order list on the Order & Timing tab of the dialog box, as shown in Figure 15-9. To reorder the list, select an item and click the up or down arrow buttons next to the list.

FIGURE 15-9.

The Animation Order list.

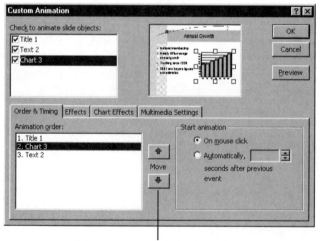

Select items on the list and reorder them by clicking the arrow buttons.

Now that you've set the order of the animations, you can determine when each animation will begin. You can select an object in either list

IV

Performing with PowerPoint

in the Custom Animation dialog box and choose an option in the Start Animation section on the Order & Timing tab. The default is to animate the object when you click the mouse (On Mouse Click), but you can also animate the object a number of seconds after the previous event or after the appearance of the slide if no previous animations have been set up.

Next, you will want to choose an animation effect for each text object. Click the Effects tab in the Custom Animation dialog box and select a text object on the list. You will see that the object you select in the object list appears selected in the slide preview, as shown in Figure 15-10. You can choose an entry animation for the text and a sound to play when the object appears. In the After Animation section, you can also choose whether the object is given a new color or is hidden after the animation.

FIGURE 15-10.

Text object is selected both in the list and in the slide preview.

Object is selected both in list and in preview.

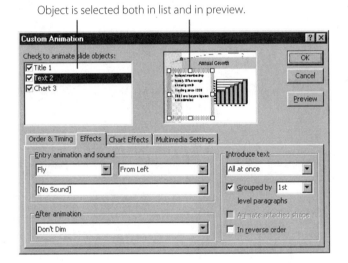

You can also make selections in the Introduce Text section of the Effects tab. The text can appear All At Once, By Word, or By Letter. The best way to see these options is to select each one and then click Preview in the Custom Animation dialog box. In the preview, you won't be able to see the Grouped By Paragraph Level options, though. If you turn on grouping by selecting the check box next to Grouped By, you can determine how much text will appear when you advance the slide show. Grouping text by the first level paragraphs, for example, brings in the first level bullet point and all the text below it at lower levels. Grouping by the second level brings in the first level text and the first bullet of the second level. You would have to click again to bring in the next second level text item.

The last two options in the Introduce Text section let you bring in text items in reverse order. If the text is within an AutoShape, choose whether the AutoShape should animate with the text or whether the shape should already be visible when the text arrives in animation.

 TIP

> **Previewing a Slide's Animations**
>
> To preview a slide's animations, turn to the slide in Slide view, and choose Animation Preview from the Slide Show menu. A small window appears to demonstrate the animation.

 TIP

> **Quickly Changing the Animation Settings of an Object**
>
> By clicking an object in Slide view before selecting Custom Animation from the Slide Show menu, you'll find that the object has already been selected in the Custom Animation dialog box. You can immediately make changes on the Effects tab.

Using the Animation Effects Toolbar

You can display the Animation Effects toolbar, shown in Figure 15-11, by clicking the Animation Effects button on the Formatting toolbar. (Or choose Toolbars from the View menu, and select the Animation Effects option.) You can then use the toolbar buttons to animate individual objects. Keep in mind, however, that in order to use most of the buttons on the Animation Effects toolbar, you must be in Slide view and you must first select an object on the current slide, such as a title or bulleted text. When you have time, explore these buttons further. You'll have a blast sending bullets flying and dropping in titles out of thin air.

FIGURE 15-11.
The Animation Effects toolbar.

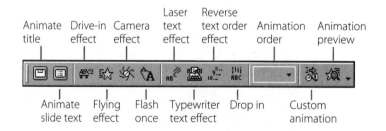

"Animating" Charts

When a chart resides on a slide, you can animate some of the elements within a chart. For example, you can have the bars of a bar chart appear one after another. To set the animation effects for a chart, select the

IV

Performing with PowerPoint

chart on the slide object list in the Custom Animation dialog box and then click the Chart Effects tab.

On the Chart Effects tab, shown in Figure 15-12, choose a setting for Introduce Chart Elements, and make sure Animate Grid And Legend is selected if you also want the chart's background elements to animate. Chart elements have fewer entry animation effects available, but you can still choose from a number of effects on the Chart Effects tab. You can also choose a sound to play when the chart element appears. The After Animation setting goes into effect only after the entire chart has displayed.

FIGURE 15-12.
The Chart Effects tab of the Custom Animation dialog box.

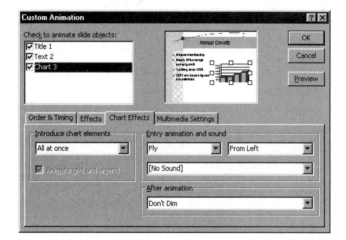

Playing Multimedia Elements

Multimedia elements on slides, such as sound and movie clips, appear on the object order list as Media items.

You can change the way a media item plays by selecting the media item on the slide object list and then clicking the Multimedia Settings tab of the Custom Animation dialog box, shown in Figure 15-13 on the next page. You can have the slide show pause until the media clip has completed (this option is particularly useful for playing a video clip) or keep the slide show running while the music or narration continues. If you select Continue Slide Show, you can designate whether the clip should stop at the end of the current slide or after a specified number of slides have been shown. By clicking More Options, you can get to options that let you loop a media clip, rewind a movie clip after it is played, or play a CD audio track or segment.

FIGURE 15-13.

The Multimedia Settings tab of the Custom Animation dialog box.

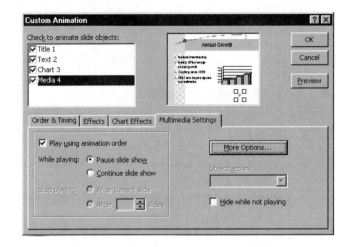

To prevent the clip's icon from displaying on the screen during a slide show, click Hide While Not Playing. The clip or its icon still appears in Slide view, but it is not visible during the actual slide show.

Hiding Slides

The Hide Slide button

To hide one or more slides during a slide show, select the slides in Slide Sorter view, and click the Hide Slide button on the Slide Sorter toolbar or choose Hide Slide from the shortcut or Slide Show menu. A slash appears through the slide number in Slide Sorter view to indicate that the slide is hidden. Although the hidden slide continues to display in Slide Sorter view, it does not appear during a slide show unless you call it up.

To show a hidden slide during a slide show, press H when you are viewing the previous slide during the presentation. You can also move the mouse pointer over the current slide, and when the pop-up button shown in Figure 15-14 appears in the lower left corner of the slide, click the button to display the pop-up menu, also shown in Figure 15-14. Next choose Go from the pop-up menu and then click Slide Navigator or By Title. The slide number of a hidden slide is shown in parentheses, but you can still select the slide to display it.

To unhide a hidden slide, select the slide in Slide Sorter view and click the Hide Slide button again or choose Hide Slide again from the shortcut or Slide Show menu.

FIGURE 15-14.

The slide show pop-up menu and button.

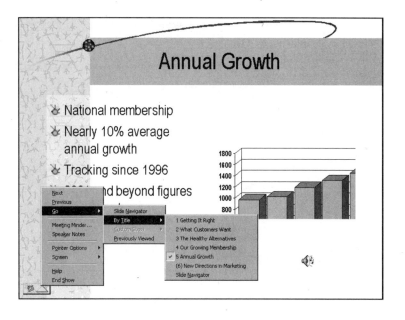

IV

Performing with PowerPoint

Making Slide Shows Interactive

What could be better than a slide show with fancy transitions and animation effects? A slide show that lets viewers control what they see and when they see it! PowerPoint's Action buttons and Action settings let you add buttons to your slides that viewers can click to jump to any slide in the slide show, play a video, play a sound, jump to a Web page or even start another software application. Of course, you can use Action Buttons to control the slide show when you are the presenter, but the command's real power lies in its ability to let your viewers move through a slide show or a presentation you've posted on the Web at their own pace and in their own order.

To add an Action button to a slide, follow these steps:

1 Switch to Slide view.

2 Choose Action Buttons from the Slide Show menu.

3 Click a button on the pop-out menu of buttons shown in Figure 15-15 on the next page.

 TIP

Assigning Actions to Other Slide Objects

You can give any object on the screen, such as a text block, a picture, or an Auto-Shape, its own action settings. Simply select the image or graphic object in Slide view, and choose the Action Settings command from the Slide Show menu.

FIGURE 15-15.
The Action Buttons
menu.

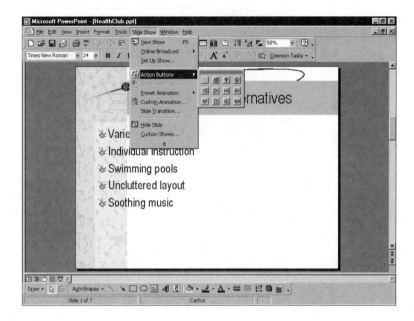

4 Use the mouse pointer to draw a rectangle on the slide the position and at the size of the button you want. When the button appears, you'll see the Action Settings dialog box shown in Figure 15-16.

FIGURE 15-16.
The Action Settings
dialog box.

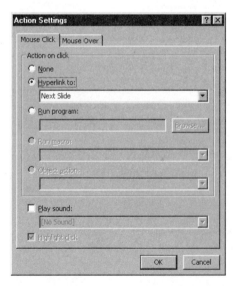

5 Select one of the Mouse Click options, such as Hyperlink To, and then choose an option for the action from the drop-down list. All the Mouse Click options are listed in Table 15-3.

TABLE 15-3. The Mouse Click Options

Option	Effect
Hyperlink To	Allows viewers to move to a specific slide, custom show, Internet URL (Web page address), or to another Power-Point program or a file from a different program
Run Program	Allows viewers to open a different application when they click the button
Run Macro	Lets viewers run a Visual Basic for Applications macro
Object Action	Allows viewers to play, edit, or open a media clip or under-lying application when they click the button
Play Sound	Allows viewers to click a button to play a sound

When you select the Hyperlink To option, shown in Figure 15-17 on the next page, you must also specify the destination you want viewers to move to by selecting one of the options from the Hyperlink To drop-down list. If you select the Slide option on the list, the Hyperlink To Slide dialog box appears. You can then select a specific slide, even if it's hidden. If you select URL, you must enter a full Internet or intranet address, such as *http://www.microsoft.com* or *http://WebServerName/ folder/HTMLfile*. When you select the Play Sound option, you must also select a sound to be played from the drop-down list. When you select the Run Program option, you must enter the full pathname for the application you want viewers to open. For example, enter the path for a Microsoft Word document that you want viewers to read or print. When you select the Object Action option, you must also select an action from the Object Action drop-down list. For example, select Edit to allow viewers to edit the underlying data for a Microsoft Excel chart.

A second tab in the Actions Settings dialog box, labeled Mouse Over, allows you to assign actions to buttons when the viewer moves the mouse pointer over them. You might want to have a voice tell someone to "Go ahead and click here" when he or she moves the mouse over a button, for example.

★ TIP

Adding Supplemental Information on Hidden Slides
You can supply your viewers with additional information that they see only if they want to by creating a slide with the information, hiding the slide, and then making the slide the target of an interactive object on another slide.

FIGURE 15-17.

The Hyperlink To options.

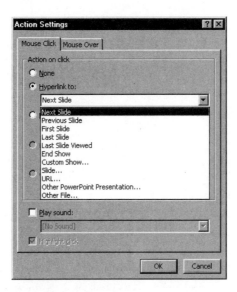

Adding Drill-Down Documents

If you have data in another Windows application that can support an assertion you've made in a presentation or provide additional information, you can embed the data as an object on a slide so that it appears as an icon. During the slide show, you can then double-click the icon to "drill down" to the information and display the data in its original form. For example, you can embed a Microsoft Word document or a Microsoft Excel spreadsheet as a *drill-down document* (a document you can double-click to open). In fact, you can embed any file created by a Windows application that can act as an OLE server or an OLE object application. Most Windows applications can provide OLE objects for use in PowerPoint.

To embed an existing object, first choose Object from the Insert menu, and when the Insert Object dialog box appears, select Create From File and click the Browse button. In the Browse dialog box, select the file you want and then click OK. When you return to the Insert Object dialog box, select the Display As Icon option and click OK. The object appears on the current slide as an icon that you can double-click to open and work with the original object. Figure 15-18 shows an embedded Excel object on a slide.

When you double-click the object, the application opens in its own window. Certain applications let you drag files from the Windows Explorer to a PowerPoint slide. You'll have to test your application to see if it supports this feature.

FIGURE 15-18.
An embedded Excel object represented by an Excel icon.

Creating a Slide Show with Branching

By embedding one PowerPoint presentation as a drill-down object in another PowerPoint presentation, you can branch to that presentation from within another slide show. The embedded presentation can provide detailed information on a topic covered by the main presentation. By adding embedded PowerPoint presentations, you can also create an interactive training or informational presentation in which the viewer can select particular topics to review. To embed a PowerPoint presentation, follow the procedure described in "Adding Drill-Down Documents" on the opposite page, but select a PowerPoint presentation as the object you want to embed.

You can also break off sections of a slide show to use as custom slide shows. Each section can contain slides that pertain to a certain audience. As you run the main slide show, you can choose to continue at any point with a custom show. You can even use custom shows to provide additional slides based on questions or feedback from your audience.

To create a custom show, choose Custom Shows from the Slide Show menu. In the Custom Shows dialog box, click New. In the Define Custom Show dialog box, shown in Figure 15-19 on the next page, enter a name for the custom show. Then select the slides you want in the custom show and click Add. When all slides are added, click OK and then choose Close to close the Custom Show dialog box.

To branch to a custom show during a slide show, you can click the button at the lower left corner of the current slide and choose Go from the pop-up menu. Choose Custom Show and then select the show name. You can also choose to display a custom show by choosing its name on the Set Up Show dialog box.

FIGURE 15-19.
The Define Custom Show dialog box.

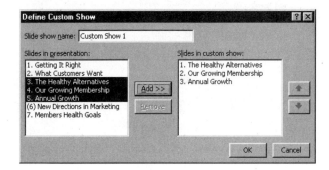

Adding Annotations

During a presentation, you'll want to direct your energies and persuasive charms toward delivering your grand vision rather than detailing the minor technicalities in your graphs. Fortunately, you can leave the wherefores and the gotchas to helpful little notes that appear in text boxes alongside the other text and graphic objects on the slides. Figure 15-20 shows a typical, useful text annotation.

FIGURE 15-20.
A text annotation can add important information to a slide.

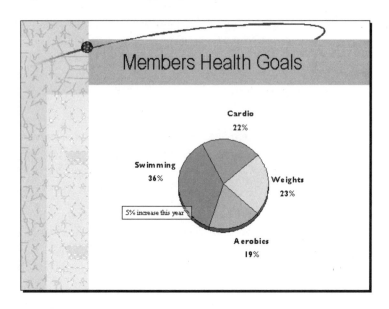

In this section, you'll learn how to add text annotations as well as how to add speaker notes to slides in Normal and Notes Pages views. While text annotations are designed to be seen by the audience, only the individual delivering the presentation sees the speaker notes. On the top half of a speaker's note page, the presenter sees a reduced version of the current slide. On the bottom half of the page, the presenter sees typed notes about the slide—points to make while the slide is on the screen and supporting information to mention, if necessary.

Adding a Text Annotation

The Text Box button

The main difference between entering text in a text placeholder and adding text as a text annotation is in how you get started. To enter the main body text of a slide, such as bulleted text lines, you can simply click a *Click to add text* placeholder and begin typing. To create a text annotation, you must use the Text Box button on the Drawing toolbar, and then type in an annotation.

To comment on the contents of a slide, you can add as many text boxes as you see fit, and you can move and copy them just like any other objects. But you might want to limit your use of text boxes to one every few slides to avoid cluttering the presentation or giving the impression that the exceptions to the rule are the rule.

NOTE

> As an alternative to text boxes, you can group comments, restrictions, exemptions, exclusions, and other technicalities on a subsequent slide, so they won't break the flow of your presentation. The subsequent slide can even be hidden so that you can display it only if necessary during a slide show.

To add a text box and enter a text annotation, follow these steps:

1 In Slide view, display the slide to which you want to add a text box.

2 Click the Text Box button on the Drawing toolbar.

3 Position the mouse pointer where you want the text box to appear, hold down the left mouse button, and drag out a rectangle. If you plan to type a short one- or two-word label, you can simply click the slide to add a small text box. The text box shown on the next page was created by dragging.

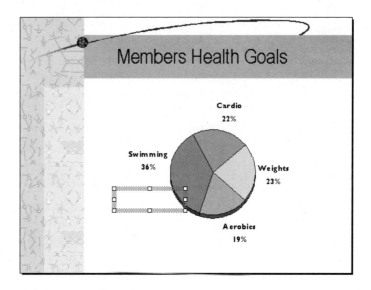

4 Type the text of the annotation. As shown below, the box grows vertically, if necessary, to accommodate the text you enter.

If you simply click and then type a long note, the text box extends horizontally and eventually goes off the slide. To reformat the text in the text box, you need to turn on word wrap for the text box.

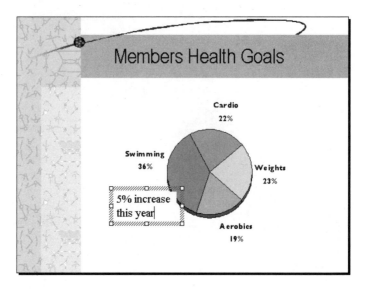

5 Click elsewhere on the slide to complete the text annotation or click the Text Box button again to add another text box.

IV

Formatting a Text Annotation

? SEE ALSO

For more information about formatting text, see Chapter 5, "Creating Slides in Slide View," page 87.

You can format a text annotation by adding formatting to the text box either before or after you actually enter the text. As is always the case when you format text, you can use the buttons on the Formatting tool-bar or the commands on the Format or shortcut menu to format the text in a text box. As you know by now, before you can format existing text, you must select it. To select part of the text in a text box, drag across it with the mouse. To select the entire text box, click the border of the text box. Unless you select specific characters to format, all text in the text box is reformatted.

In addition to changing the appearance of the text in a text box, you can also change its position within the text box by choosing Text Box from the Format menu or double-clicking the border of the text box. Then click the Text Box tab, and select the appropriate options in the Format Text Box dialog box shown in Figure 15-21. These options let you set the text anchor point (position of the text within the box), change the box internal margins (distance from the box to the text inside), fit the boundaries of the text box to the text, turn word wrap on or off, and even rotate the text by 90 degrees.

FIGURE 15-21.

The Text Box tab of the Format Text Box dialog box.

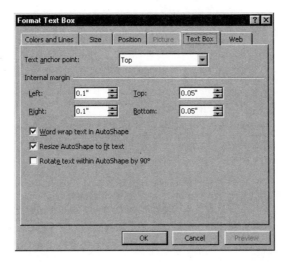

Moving, Resizing, and Formatting a Text Box

PowerPoint is very flexible when it comes to moving, resizing, and formatting text boxes. For example, you can move a text box to any location on a slide, even if it obscures other text or objects. You can also increase or decrease the size of the text box to accommodate more or less text. And if you're interested in changing the text box border or fill, PowerPoint offers a variety of options. To move a text box, follow these steps:

1 Position the mouse pointer on the border of the text box between two handles.

2 Drag the box to a new location on the slide.

To resize a text box, simply drag one of its handles.

> When you finish typing text in a text box, you can press Esc and then press the arrow keys to adjust the position of the text box incrementally.

Whether you present an electronic slide show, create printed output or 35-mm slides, the default settings display only the text of a text box. The box itself does not appear because its fill and border are not formatted. To format the fill and border, you can select the text box, and then click the Fill Color button and the Line Color button on the Drawing toolbar. You can also click the Shadow On/Off button to add a shadow and give the box some depth or click the 3-D button to give the box perspective and light-source shading. And you can use the Line Style and Dashed Lines buttons to change the style of the text box border. To change the color of the text, you can click the Font Color button on the Drawing toolbar.

The Colors And Lines command on the Format menu opens the Format Text Box dialog box and displays the Colors And Lines tab so that you can select the Fill Color and Line Color options you want to use. On the Colors And Lines tab of the Format Text Box dialog box, shown in Figure 15-22, use the Color drop-down list in the Fill section to select a

FIGURE 15-22.

The Format Text Box dialog box.

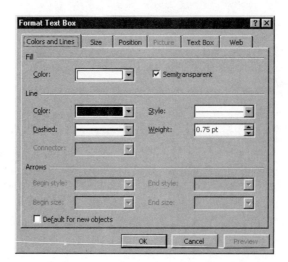

fill color or effect (Gradient, Texture, Pattern, or Picture). Use the Color drop-down list in the Line section to select a line color or pattern, and then use the Style, Dashed and Weight drop-down lists to change the appearance of the surrounding line. To format any new text boxes you create (in the current presentation) with the options you specify on the Colors And Lines tab, select the Default for New Objects check box.

TIP

How to Use a Shape Other than a Box

To create a text annotation with a more interesting shape, you can place an AutoShape on a slide, and then enter text in the AutoShape. To add text, click the AutoShape with the right mouse button and choose Add Text from the shortcut menu. To get really fancy, you can also add a text annotation to a clip art selection. *For more information about AutoShapes, see "AutoShapes," page 308. For more information about using clip art, see Chapter 13, "Placing Photos and Clip Art on Slides," page 331.*

Duplicating a Text Box

Duplicating a text box creates a second text box with the same formatting as the original. First format both the original text box and its text, and then select the original text box and choose Duplicate from the Edit menu or press Ctrl+D. After the duplicate text box appears on top of the original text box, you can drag the duplicate to a new position, select the text inside by dragging across it, and type replacement text. Another option is to hold down the Ctrl key and drag the text box to create a duplicate.

Adding Text as a Comment

Rather than add a text box annotation, which becomes visible on the slide, you might choose to add a comment instead. Comments are useful when everyone in a workgroup is checking a presentation on the network before it is released for delivery. The comments appear like yellow sticky notes on slides. When each comment is created, PowerPoint automatically adds the name of the person creating the comment. Comments can be easily hidden from view so they do not appear when the presentation is given.

To add a comment, choose Comment from the Insert menu. Type your comment after your name, which appears within the comment box. You can also record a spoken comment by choosing Movies And Sounds from the Insert menu after starting a comment.

To hide a comment, select the comment and click the Show/Hide Comments button on the Reviewing toolbar that opens when you insert a comment. The Reviewing toolbar is shown in Figure 15-23.

FIGURE 15-23.

The Reviewing toolbar.

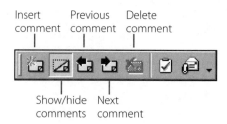

Adding Speaker Notes

Every slide in the presentation can have a special type of output called speaker notes or *notes pages*. On a notes page, you see two objects: the slide on the top part of the page and a text placeholder on the bottom part. The notes page for each slide is an integral part of the presentation, and it is stored in the same file. You can enter slide notes in Normal view, as shown in Figure 15-24.

Any indication of the presence of notes page text appears only in Normal view. But when you print the presentation, you can choose to print the notes pages.

To enter a note, click the *Click To Add Notes* placeholder below the slide image. Then begin typing in the placeholder as if you were typing text in a word processing program. The text will automatically wrap at the right edge of the text box. To start a new paragraph on the notes page, press Enter.

To see and modify how the notes pages will print, you can choose Notes Page from the View menu. In Notes Page view, you can use the buttons on the Formatting toolbar or the commands on the Format menu or the shortcut menu to format the notes page text before or after you type it. Again, if you want to format existing text, you must select the text first. You can also use the Line Spacing command on the Format menu to add line spacing within paragraphs or to add space before or after each paragraph. Figure 15-25 shows an enlarged view of a completed notes page where the notes text was formatted with bullets.

FIGURE 15-24.

You can enter notes
in the lower pane in
Normal view.

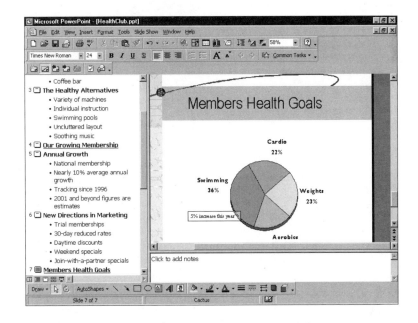

FIGURE 15-25.

Notes Page view.

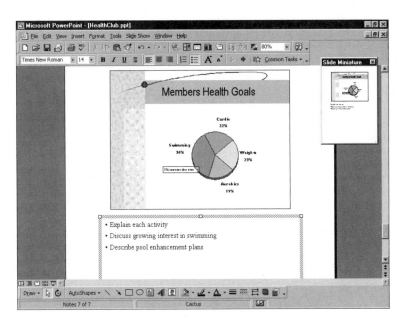

> **NOTE**

When you use spelling checker to check the spelling in your presentation it
also checks the spelling in notes.

? SEE ALSO
For information about printing notes pages, see Chapter 14, "Printing Pages and 35-mm Slides," page 361.

To enter speaker notes for the next slide in the presentation, click the Next Slide button or press the Page Down key. To return to the previous slide, click the Previous Slide button or press Page Up.

After you enter text on the notes pages of a presentation, you should resave the presentation to be sure the text is stored as part of the presentation file.

In this chapter, you learned how to create slide shows with transition effects, multimedia elements, and custom animations. In the next chapter, you'll learn how to give your slide shows in person, on a corporate intranet, or even over the Internet.

CHAPTER 16

Web Publishing and Collaboration

W hat would a presentation be without PowerPoint slides? But one-way delivery of information in a stand-up presentation is being supplanted by two-way information sharing in offices and organizations around the world as networking and the Internet create workgroups composed of both office mates and geographically scattered collaborators. To serve these team efforts, Microsoft PowerPoint 2000 has adopted a new role as a platform for communication and participation. Everyone in a workgroup can contribute to the development of a PowerPoint presentation that's been posted on a central Web server. They can not only view the presentation but also offer their views. This chapter takes a close look at the possibilities for using PowerPoint for both information delivery and information exchange on a Web.

Understanding the Possibilities

To understand the new capabilities of PowerPoint 2000 in Web publishing and collaboration, consider these real-world scenarios.

The Utopian Ideal

You work among a team of sophisticated PC users in an enlightened organization. The computer at your desk is connected to the department's Web server, which allows your team and others working collaboratively on projects to set up and maintain Web pages. Your department's Web server is connected, in turn, to the larger, organization-wide network, which also employs Internet technologies for communication and collaboration. This lets everyone else in the organization, or at least those who are given the authorization, reach your workgroup's Web server and browse your workgroup's Web pages with a recent Web browser, preferably Microsoft Internet Explorer 5.0 or later.

NOTE

In this scenario, and throughout this book, a Web is information on a network that you can view in a Web browser. That Web might be on the globe-spanning Internet, which is accessible by everyone who connects to the Internet. Or it might be on a closed, company-wide intranet, which is accessible only to those within the organization.

Someone in your group (you're reading this, so it's probably you) creates a PowerPoint presentation to introduce a new project, propose an idea, report an achievement, or herald some other development in your workgroup. Before you release the presentation by placing it on the company-wide Web site, you post it for review in a staging area by saving it as a Web page on the server that's accessible only to those in your workgroup.

Over the course of the day, all those who have something to say (and perhaps a few who don't) browse the slides in a Web browser and contribute comments to an online discussion about the presentation. This lets the participants read, consider, and react to the contributions of others. Those people who have been given the authorization to modify the presentation open the Web pages right in PowerPoint on their own desktops and attach pithy little comments or make important tweaks to the data. Your department's graphic artist (remember, this is a utopian vision), opens the Web presentation in PowerPoint and applies a stunning, new visual design with a custom design template and lots of relevant art. Before the day is out, you reopen the presentation from the Web server and, working again in PowerPoint, review each page and incorporate the most significant ideas from your colleagues into a presentation that's truly a product of the best of many minds.

You save a copy of the PowerPoint presentation on your system and move the Web presentation to a folder that everyone in the organization can access on the organization's intranet. Those who don't go looking for your presentation see it during the presentation broadcast that occurs across the company network during the company meeting. The project is approved, the organization reinvents itself in a new model and quickly emerges from niche player to market leader. At the annual stockholder's meeting, held online, your presentation is broadcast across the Internet and it becomes a global phenomenon soon after, when it's made available on the organization's Internet site.

A More Likely Scenario

Your organization is a little strapped for resources, but you do the best with what you have and create a personal Web site on your own computer that others can access through the company intranet.

Making the presentation available isn't hard because you install the Microsoft Personal Web Server on your computer, create a Web folder for everyone to access, and save the presentation in the folder as a Web page. You send out e-mail that contains a hyperlink to the Web page and you also print out a few copies and route them around the office for those who haven't quite gotten the hang of all this Web stuff.

After a few days, you collect the feedback you've received through office e-mail and intra-office memos, and you incorporate the best suggestions into a final PowerPoint presentation. This time, you save the presentation as a Web page and send it via e-mail it to the haggard and overworked Web Administrator. Within a matter of weeks, your presentation is posted on the organization's Web site so that everyone can share the value of your ideas. The project is eventually approved, the company reinvents itself, and you know the rest. Everything just requires more steps and takes a lot longer.

The Old-Fashioned Way

Just to put these newfound possibilities in perspective, here's how you might accomplish something similar without PowerPoint's Web capabilities: You create a presentation and print it as a set of pages to pass around to the others in your team. Your colleagues consider what they see without the benefit of knowing what others think, scribble barely intelligible notes on the pages, and return them for your analysis and interpretation. Then you have, oh no, a *meeting* and actually discuss the presentation page by page. You make some changes to the presentation and the process repeats itself. Sooner or later, everyone's signed off on the presentation and you get to deliver it during a speech at the company meeting some time the following quarter. Time marches on but eventually, your organization becomes a real player out there.

Although the scenarios above are fictitious, they're not far from the truth. PowerPoint's Web presentations make possible a new form of communication and collaboration that forward-thinking organizations can put at their disposal.

What Is a Web Presentation?

A Web presentation is a PowerPoint presentation that has been saved as a Web page and posted on a Web site on the Internet or on a company's internal network. Those who need to gain access to it can view the presentation by using their existing Web browser. They have no need to own PowerPoint or install a special viewer program to play a slide show, and they don't have to obtain the slide show on diskette or download the .ppt file from a network file server.

The ease with which others can both reach and view a slide show enhances your ability to use PowerPoint to communicate. But, in addition, PowerPoint's new Web features open an entirely new arena of participation and collaboration on presentations. Anyone who is granted access to a Web presentation posted on a company intranet or on the Internet can contribute to its development, so a PowerPoint presentation becomes a platform for a group effort on a project, proposal, report, business plan, or other form of collaborative work.

Specifically, anyone viewing a Web presentation in a browser can contribute to a discussion about the presentation, adding their comments to a public record of written messages and responses. Those who use PowerPoint and who are also given the authorization by the file permissions set up on the Web server can open the Web presentation in PowerPoint and work with it as though they had the original PowerPoint file. They can attach comments to slides, modify text and graphics, and then save a revision of the Web presentation without having to modify the original PowerPoint file.

What Do You Need to Publish Presentations?

The degree to which you can take advantage of Web presentations depends primarily on the capabilities of the network to which you have access.

If You're Connected to a Web Server on Windows NT Server or Windows 2000 Server

If you are a member of an organization that uses Web technologies on its internal network (a TCP/IP network) and if your workgroup, department, or entire company uses the Microsoft Internet Information Server 4.0 (IIS) Web server on the Microsoft Windows NT Server or Windows 2000 Server operating system, you have the best of all worlds. From your computer running Microsoft Windows 95, Windows 98, or Windows 2000, you can:

- Create a Web folder on the server, where you can easily save Web presentations and make them available to others on the company intranet or across the Internet

- Assign permissions to the Web folder so you can determine who has access to view a presentation and who can also modify the presentation

- Enable others to open Web presentations with their own copies of PowerPoint and add comments or edit slides

- Start discussions so that others can contribute their feedback about a presentation

These same capabilities apply to you if you are a small office or home office with a Web site on a Web server that is connected to the Internet. If the IIS server is hosted by an Internet Service Provider (ISP) using a Windows NT or Windows 2000 Web server, or if you have your own dedicated connection to the Internet and your own IIS Web server running on Windows NT Server or Windows 2000 Server, you can do everything listed above.

If You Are Part of a Workgroup on a Peer Network using Windows 95 or Windows 98

You can still give others access to your Web presentations if your organization uses Internet technologies on an internal network and you are connected to other Windows 95 and Windows 98 users in a peer network with no central Windows NT or Windows 2000 server.

To make your presentations available, you save them on your hard disk and use Microsoft Personal Web Server (available at no additional charge on the Windows 98 CD or on the Microsoft Web site at *http://www.microsoft.com/windows/ie/pws/*) to set up your own Web server.

In a network with no server, you can make presentations available only on your own computer. In other words, you can publish to a Web server on a computer running Windows 95 or Windows 98 only from the copy of PowerPoint that is running on that machine. The reason: a computer running Windows 95 or Windows 98 can't offer the Web server security features of a computer that is running Windows NT Server or Windows 2000 Server. Although you probably know the others in your workgroup or peer group, the information on your computer becomes vulnerable when you dial in to the Internet or connect to a larger network.

If you're part of a peer group using Windows 95 or Windows 98, you can:

- Create a Web folder on your machine, where you can easily save Web presentations and make them available to others on the network or in your workgroup

- Restrict access to the presentation by giving it a password

- Enable others to open your Web presentations with their own copies of PowerPoint and add comments or edit slides (they can't save the presentation back to your computer, though)

Software You Need

If you're connected to a centrally managed Web server on an organization's intranet, the Web server probably has everything you need to publish Web presentations and create and participate in collaborations. To confirm this, check with the system administrator or Information Services department to make sure you have access to a Microsoft Internet Information Services (IIS) Web server on a computer that is running Windows NT Server or Windows 2000 Server and has the Office Server Extensions installed.

The Office Server Extensions is a set of software that comes with Microsoft Office that the system administrator installs on a computer running the Windows NT Server operating system and the Internet Information Server 4.0 Web server. The Office Server Extensions enable the Web server to provide the Web publishing and collaboration services, such as Web folders and discussions, to users of Microsoft Office 2000 who connect to the server.

On your own machine, you must have Microsoft Office 2000 installed. The standard Office 2000 installation also installs Office Server Extensions support for both Web discussions and Web publishing. If you perform a custom setup, make sure that Office Server Extensions Support, listed under Office Tools in the list of features to install, is set to Run From My Computer.

If you're connected to a network without a central Web server, you must set up a Web server on your own machine. If you're using Windows 98, you can install the Microsoft Personal Web Server. The installation files are in a folder named "add-ons" on the Windows 98 CD and the setup program is in a subfolder named "pws." If you are using Windows 95, you can download the Microsoft Personal Web Server from the Microsoft Web site.

Setting up the Personal Web Server gives you a Web address (called a Uniform Resource Locator, or URL) on the network. You can give this URL to others so they can access the Web presentations you save on your computer.

Knowing What to Expect in a Web Presentation

The surprising fact is that viewing a Web version of your presentation in the Internet Explorer Web browser is very much like viewing the presentation as a slide show in PowerPoint. Most elements and effects on slides—text items, charts, graphic objects, photos, sounds, video clips, transitions, and animations—appear to viewers just as you intended for them to be seen. That should be reassuring if you thought you'd have to make major concessions to create a version that can be viewed on a Web.

What You Can't Do in a Web Presentation

Unfortunately, though, not every slide show feature works properly in Web presentations. The following PowerPoint slide show features are not carried over to Web presentations:

Formatting

- The Shadow and Embossed font formatting effects don't work.

- A Web browser that is not running on a Windows-based operating system may substitute other fonts for the fonts you selected for a presentation, so your text layouts may not appear exactly as you created them.

Animation

- The By Word and By Letter Introduce Text options don't work. Instead, whole paragraphs appear.

- Chart Effects don't work.

- AutoShapes and their attached text are animated together.

- GIF animations do not play if they are grouped together.

Action Settings

- The Run Macro option does not work.

- Highlight Click and Highlight When Mouse Over don't work.

- Object Action options don't work.

- A hyperlink to a custom show won't play the show.

Other Slide Show Features

- Linked and Embedded objects don't play.

- Sound plays only on the current slide. It does not continue playing when you move to another slide.

- The Play Sound option doesn't work if the object is also formatted as a hyperlink.

- The shortcut menu commands don't work.

- The Backspace key takes you to the last slide viewed, not to the previous slide.

- You can't run individual custom shows.

- The Update Automatically check box does not work for dates and times.

Despite these differences, the primary distinction between a Web version of a presentation that's viewed in Internet Explorer and a typical Power-Point slide show is in who's running the show. A typical PowerPoint slide show is given by a presenter who controls the pace and advances the show from slide to slide. In a Web version of a presentation, the viewer usually controls the show. Therefore, a Web presentation is often more like an unattended presentation, which requires on-screen controls that viewers can use to navigate from slide to slide. By default, PowerPoint provides navigation controls that include a list of slide titles that appear in a separate frame to the left of each slide and Next Slide/ Previous Slide buttons that appear in a frame below each slide, as shown in Figure 16-1. A viewer can click any slide title to jump to that slide or click the Next Slide or Previous Slide buttons to move through slides one by one.

FIGURE 16-1.

A Web version of a presentation includes a list of slides to the left and a navigation bar below the slides.

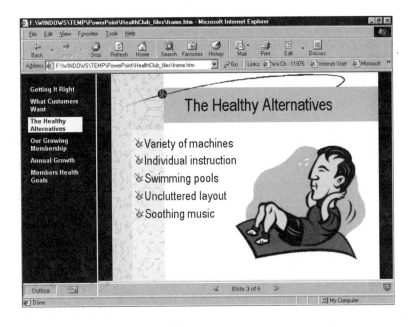

When you save a presentation as a Web page, PowerPoint generates a set of HTML files and, by default, puts them in a supporting files folder. If you create a link to the file fullscreen.htm in the support files folder, the Web page opens as a full screen in Internet Explorer. If you have also given the slides timings, the slides will advance automatically according to their timings.

For Those with Older Versions of Internet Explorer

Although it's true that anyone using a recent version of Internet Explorer (4.0, 5.0, or later) can see your presentation almost exactly as you meant it to be seen, those using earlier versions of Internet Explorer (3.01 and earlier) suffer a few limitations. In earlier browsers, slides appear at a fixed size on the screen (users of Internet Explorer 4.0 and later see slides that resize to fit the browser window). In addition, users of older browsers cannot see the transition and animation effects that you've given to slides. Instead, slides follow each other without fades, dissolves, wipes, or any other transition that is faithfully reproduced in later browsers. Users of older browsers also cannot see movies, hear sounds, or view a presentation full screen. And finally, although clicking a slide title in the slide title list still takes you to the appropriate slide, passing the mouse over the titles won't highlight them in reverse video in the list of slide titles.

If you're working in a controlled environment, such as within an organization in which everyone uses the latest available version of Internet Explorer, you can go all out and take advantage of every slide show trick. But if you plan to post a presentation on a Web site, you should take care to save a Web version that everyone can view. In "Saving a Presentation As a Web Page," on page 415, you learn to set options that save a presentation in a format that's appropriate for your anticipated viewers.

For Those Using Netscape

Users of any version of Netscape Navigator will see the same results as those who use Internet Explorer 3.0 and earlier. Slides appear at a fixed size on the screen and they are static, that is, they display no transition or animation effects, and they also do not play sounds or movies. Netscape users are also unable to display a presentation full screen.

For Those Using Macintosh Web Browsers

Those using Macintosh Internet Explorer 4.5 will see what the Netscape or Internet Explorer 3.0 user sees: slides at fixed sizes and static pages without transition or animation effects. Users of earlier browsers will not see the presentation slides accurately. Some text and graphics may be missing, and the graphics that the user can see may be of poor quality.

Publishing a Presentation as a Web Page

After you complete a presentation, you can save it in Hypertext Markup Language (HTML), a format that Web browsers can read and display. You don't have to know anything about HTML or about creating Web pages. You simply use the Save As Web Page command to save a set of files that are ready for your Webmaster or Web Administrator to make available on an intranet or on the Internet as a Web page. You can also make them available yourself on your own machine or your department's Web server if Microsoft Personal Web Server is installed on a computer running Windows 95 or Windows 98 or if Internet Information Server 4.0 is installed on a computer with Windows NT Server or Windows 2000 Server installed.

An HTML version of a presentation contains a complete record of everything in the presentation: every slide, text element, graphic, chart, media file, transition effect, and animation. You can reopen the HTML version of the presentation in PowerPoint and work with the presentation exactly as if you had opened the original PowerPoint file (the .ppt file). In fact, if you've saved a PowerPoint presentation in HTML, you do not need to also save a copy as a standard PowerPoint file using the regular Save or Save As commands on the File menu. In fact, by having two versions of the presentation, you run the risk of losing track of where to find the latest changes to the slides. But, saving a presentation as a standard PowerPoint file saves everything in a single file, which can be easier to move, manage, archive, back up, and e-mail to others. An HTML version of a presentation, in comparison, is a set of files that you must be sure to keep together.

Previewing the Presentation in a Web Browser

Another step you'll want to take before saving the Web presentation is to preview its appearance in a Web browser on your system. Although this step is optional, it gives you the chance to review the slides and ensure that they look as you expect. When you preview a presentation, you can save yourself any possible embarrassment, because previewing a Web presentation in a Web browser is similar to previewing a slide show before giving it in front of an audience.

NOTE

This procedure previews the presentation in the default Web browser on your system. You should make sure the default browser is the same browser type for which you have targeted the Web pages.

To preview the presentation in your browser, choose Web Page Preview from the File menu. Your default Web browser opens and displays the HTML version of the presentation. If everything looks right, you're ready to save the presentation as a Web page.

Saving a Presentation As a Web Page

To save a presentation as a Web page, open it in PowerPoint and then, from the File menu, choose Save As Web Page. A special version of the Save As dialog box opens, shown in Figure 16-2 on the next page.

You may want to change the page title that is shown in the Save As dialog box. This title is taken from the opening slide of the presentation. To enter a new page title, click the Change Title button, type a new name, and click OK.

In the Save As dialog box, PowerPoint also offers an HTML file name that it acquires from the regular name of the PowerPoint file you've saved. It substitutes the three-letter extension .htm, which tells Windows that the file is an HTML file that it should open with a Web browser.

FIGURE 16-2.

When you click Save As Web Page, a special version of the Save As dialog box opens.

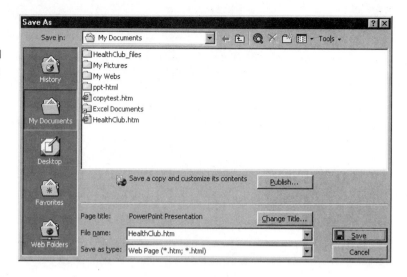

If you make no other changes in the Save As dialog box and click Save, you will have a Web page that uses PowerPoint's default settings. PowerPoint creates an HTML version of the complete presentation, saves it in the default folder for saved PowerPoint files, and opens it immediately in your Web browser.

If you look in the default folder, you'll find the .htm file for the Web presentation and a supporting subfolder, which has "_files" added to its name. In other words, if the .htm file is named NewProducts, you'll find a NewProducts_files subfolder within the folder in which you've saved NewProducts. (If you're using a language version of Microsoft Office 2000 other than English, the word "files" is replaced by the equivalent word in the current language.) The supporting subfolder contains files that hold all the bits and pieces that comprise the Web page, such as graphic bullets, background textures, pictures, and navigation bars. The .htm file and the files in the supporting "_files" folder are essential to the Web page version of the presentation, so if you need to move a Web presentation to another folder on your system or to another computer, be sure to move both the .htm file and the supporting folder together.

Saving a Portion of a Presentation as a Web Presentation

For more control over the Web presentation you save, you can click the Publish button on the Save As dialog box. This opens the Publish As Web Page dialog box, shown in Figure 16-3, which gives you the option to select a portion of a presentation to save and customize the Web presentation for a specific browser type.

FIGURE 16-3.

The Publish As Web Page dialog box.

 NOTE

If you save only a portion of a presentation as a Web page, make sure you also save the entire presentation to another Web page or in a standard PowerPoint file (a .ppt file) or you will lose the slides that are not include in the Web presentation.

SEE ALSO

For more information about choosing certain slides for custom shows, see "Creating a Slide Show with Branching," on page 395.

In the Publish What section of the Save As Web Page dialog box, you can select a range of slides to save in the Web presentation. If you've already selected certain slides and listed them in a custom show, you can select the custom show as the set of slides you want in the Web page. If the presentation includes speaker's notes on notes pages, you can click the Display Speaker Notes check box to see the notes on the slides.

Targeting Users of Specific Browsers

In the Browser Support section of the Save As Web Page dialog box, you can target a particular browser version. Choosing Microsoft Internet Explorer 4.0 Or Later (High Fidelity) generates a show that offers the best graphic fidelity, fastest performance over the Web, and smallest file size, which contributes to faster performance. But you can't always count on all your viewers having the Microsoft browser or having the latest version of the browser.

Optimizing a Web Presentation for Internet Explorer 3.0 or Netscape Navigator Users

If your expected audience uses a combination of Internet Explorer versions 5.0, 4.0, and 3.0, or any version of Netscape Navigator greater than 3.0, you should optimize the presentation for Internet Explorer 3.0 and Netscape Navigator 3.0. To do this, choose Microsoft Internet Explorer Or Netscape Navigator 3.0 Or Later in the Browser Support section of the Save As Web Page dialog box.

Optimizing a Web Presentation for Web TV Users

If your expected audience will use Web TV to browse the presentation, you should set the Target Monitor Screen Size to 544 x 376. To do this, click the Web Options button on the Publish as Web Page dialog box and then click the Pictures tab in the Web Options dialog box. From the Screen Size drop-down list, choose 544 x 376.

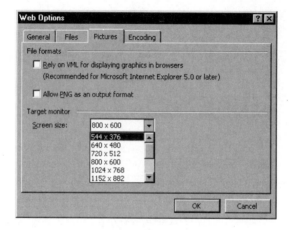

When you're ready to save the file as a Web page, choose Microsoft Internet Explorer Or Netscape Navigator 3.0 Or Later in the Browser Support section of the Save As Web Page dialog box.

Optimizing a Web Presentation for Users of a Variety of Browsers

When you don't know the type of Web browser your expected audience will be using (when viewers may use different versions of the Microsoft, Netscape, and Web TV browsers), you can choose the third option in the Browser Support area of the Publish As Web Page dialog box, All Browsers Listed Above (Creates Larger Files). This creates two versions of the presentation in the supporting folders file. One version is suitable for Microsoft Internet Explorer 4.0 or later and the other is suitable for Internet Explorer 3.0 or Netscape Navigator. The presentation detects the browser version being used by the viewer and displays the version that is most suitable for the browser.

Changing the Advanced Web Presentation Options

For greater control over the appearance and functioning of Web presentations, you can click the Web Options button on the Publish As Web Page dialog box to open the Web Options dialog box.

Displaying Slide Navigation Controls

On the General tab of the Web Options dialog box, shown in Figure 16-4, you can decide whether the slides will be accompanied by slide navigation controls, contained in an outline pane to the left that lists the slide titles and a navigation pane below that shows forward and back buttons. Your viewers can click these slide titles and navigation controls to jump from slide to slide. You'll need to use slide navigation controls unless you've placed hyperlinks on pages so users can click buttons, text links, or linked graphics to move to other slides. Figure 16-5 shows the title slide of a Web presentation both with navigation controls and without.

FIGURE 16-4.

The General tab of the Web Options dialog box.

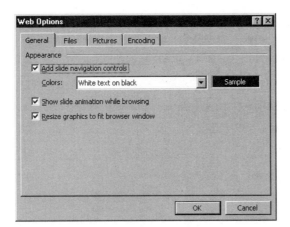

FIGURE 16-5.

The title slide of a Web presentation both with (left) and without (right) slide navigation controls.

On the General tab, you can also choose from among a small set of color options for the slide titles.

Showing Slide Animation

The Show Slide Animation While Browsing option, also on the General tab of the Web Options dialog box, enables any transition effects between slides and animation effects on slides that you've created in PowerPoint. Remember, though, these animations are visible only to those who use Internet Explorer 4.0 or later.

Resizing Graphics to Fit Browser Window

When the Resize Graphics To Fit Browser Window option is turned on in the Web Options dialog box, the slides in a Web presentation automatically adjust to fit the Web browser window in Internet Explorer 4.0 or later as you make the window larger or smaller. You can see an example of this in Figure 16-6.

FIGURE 16-6.

The size of slides can adjust when you change the size of the Web browser window.

Web presentation in browser window

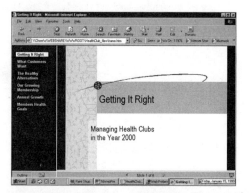

Resize Graphics To Fit Browser Window turned off

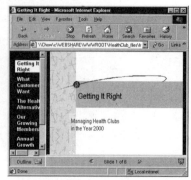
Resize Graphics To Fit Browser Window turned on

Most people don't change the size of their browser window during a presentation, but different users may have various Windows desktop size settings, so using this option creates a Web presentation that neatly fits the user's browser, no matter how large it is.

Determining the File Names and Locations

The Files tab of the Web Options dialog box, shown in Figure 16-7, offers options that let you fine-tune how the files for a Web presentation are handled.

FIGURE 16-7.
The Files tab of the Web Options dialog box.

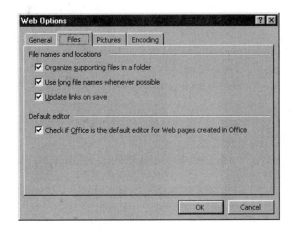

Leaving selected the Organize Supporting Files In A Folder option ensures that all the supporting files for a Web presentation are placed together in a folder so they're easier to find, move, and back up. This is shown in Figure 16-8. When this option is turned off, all the supporting files are saved in the same folder as the .htm file.

FIGURE 16-8.
When supporting files are organized in a folder, a Web presentation consists of a .htm file and a supporting files folder.

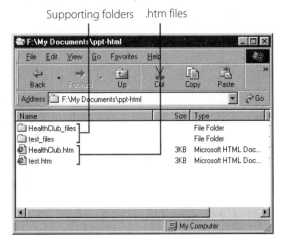

If you will host a Web presentation on a server that requires file names of eight characters or less, you should turn off the Use Long File Names Whenever Possible option.

Because a slide in a Web presentation can be composed of many elements that are linked to the slide, such as graphic bullets and background pictures, you should leave the Update Links On Save option turned on. This causes PowerPoint to update and verify all the links and helps avoid missing graphics.

If you install another program designed for creating Web pages, that program may open when you try to open a saved Web presentation. Leaving the Default Editor option on the Files tab selected allows PowerPoint to check whether it is the default program that is registered in your copy of Windows to reopen Web presentations. If it is not, a dialog box will ask whether you want to restore the association between Web presentations and PowerPoint.

Changing How Pictures Display

The options on the Pictures tab of the Web Options dialog box, shown in Figure 16-9, determine how PowerPoint will treat graphics in Web presentations. If you can be sure that Web presentation viewers will be using Internet Explorer 5.0 exclusively, you can take advantage of the Rely On VML For Displaying Graphics In Browsers option, which offers better-quality graphics in smaller file sizes. Small files translate to faster transmission over an intranet or the Internet, so the graphics on slides will appear faster and without the tradeoff in quality that is usually required to ensure adequate speed.

FIGURE 16-9.

The Pictures tab of the Web Options dialog box.

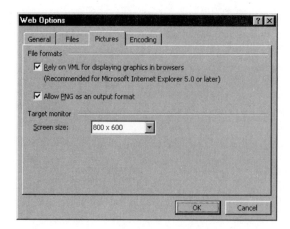

The first option, Rely On VML For Displaying Graphics In Browsers, allows PowerPoint to use the Vector Markup Language (VML) to represent the graphics on slides in HTML files. Rather than send the images on Web pages as graphics files, which are large and slow to transmit, PowerPoint sends the graphics as short and quickly transmitted VML instructions. At the receiving end, Internet Explorer 5.0 interprets these instructions and recreates the graphics in the user's browser.

The second option, Allow PNG As An Output Format, gives PowerPoint permission to use the Portable Network Graphics (PNG) file format for graphics rather than the conventional JPEG and GIF formats that are used in Web pages. PNG files represent graphics in small files without loss of clarity, as is common in JPEG files, and they can display transparency on Web pages, which is the key attribute of GIF files. Internet Explorer 4.0, 5.0, and later can display PNG files.

The Target Monitor option on the Pictures tab lets you optimize a Web presentation for screens set at any of several standard sizes, such as 640 x 480 or 800 x 600. If your viewers will see the presentation using Internet Explorer 4.0 or later, the slides will dynamically resize to any browser size, but if viewers will be using other browsers, such as the Web TV browser, the slides will be at a fixed size. This setting allows you to determine that fixed size.

Changing the Encoding Options

If the Web presentation contains text in a language other than English, you can change the language for which the Web page is targeted on the Encoding tab of the Web Options dialog box. The Save This Document As list presents a long list of encoding choices. The default choice is Western European (Windows), but you can choose Unicode if you know that all users will be using a recent Web browser version.

Using Web Folders

If Web folders are supported by the Web server you can use, they make publishing a presentation to the server as easy as copying a file to a folder on your hard disk. If the Web server to which you want to publish a presentation does not support Web folders, you must use the File Transfer Protocol (FTP) to transfer the HTML files of the Web presentation to the Web server. This is a more involved process, but it's covered later in this chapter, in "Saving a Web Presentation to a Web Server Using FTP," on page 428.

What Are Web Folders?

A Web folder is a special link to a folder that is on the company Web server, your departmental Web server, or the personal Web server on your own system. A Web folder can even link to a folder on a Web site on the Internet hosted by an Internet Service Provider.

After you've set up a Web folder so that it points to the proper folder on the Web server, you can publish a presentation to the server just by saving it in the Web folder. You don't have to worry about saving HTML files in a certain way, gaining authorization to access a Web site, or using a special technique to copy files to particular folders on the server with long and obscure addresses.

Adding Web Folders

If you work in a large organization, you may find that you have one or more links to Web folders that were set up by the system administrator. To check whether you have Web folders set up on your computer, open My Computer and double-click the Web Folders icon. If you see icons in addition to the Add Web Folder icon, as shown in Figure 16-10, you already have Web folders. Each icon represents a folder to which you can publish Web presentations. Web folders also appear in the Network Neighborhood window when you double-click Network Neighborhood on the Windows desktop.

FIGURE 16-10.

Web Folders listed in My Computer.

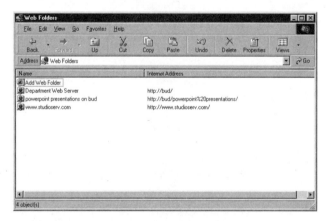

If you see only the Add Web Folder icon, you must add a Web folder to gain access to its capabilities. To add a Web folder, you need to know the Web address, or URL, of the folder to which you can publish presentations. A URL is an address such as this: *http://www.studioserv.com* or *http://DepartmentWebServer/Presentations/*. Your system administrator or Webmaster can give you this information. Once you know the URL to use, you can follow these steps to add a Web folder:

1 Open My Computer.

2 Double-click the Web Folders icon.

3 Double-click the Add Web Folders icon to open the Add Web Folder wizard.

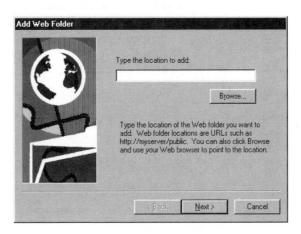

4 On the first page of the Add Web Folder Wizard, type the URL of the Web folder in the Type The Location To Add box, or click Browse and navigate to the folder using your Web browser. When you get to the folder in the browser, click in the Type The Location To Add box to transfer the URL.

5 Click Next to move to the next step of the wizard. The Add Web Folder Wizard confirms that the folder is available and that you have authorization to use it. If a password is required to access the folder, you are prompted to enter it.

6 Type a name for the Web folder in the Enter The Name For This Web Folder box.

7 Click OK. The new Web folder appears in the Web folders list.

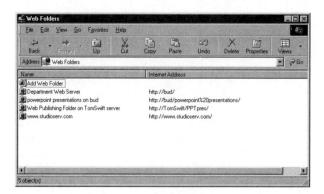

You can also add a new Web folder from within PowerPoint when you are ready to save a presentation for the Web. To add a Web folder from within PowerPoint, follow these steps:

1 From PowerPoint's File menu, choose Save As Web Page.

2 In the Save As dialog box, click the Web Folders button.

3 Click the Create New Folder button on the toolbar.

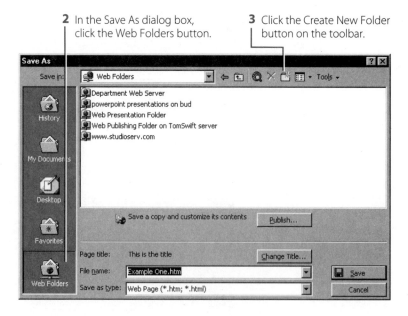

4 Use the Add Web Folder wizard as you did in steps 4–7 of the procedure above.

To check the contents of the Web folder, you can double-click it in the Web folder list.

> **NOTE**
>
> You can copy, rename, and delete files in Web folders just as you copy, rename, and delete the files in any folder in Windows Explorer.

Saving a Presentation to a Web Folder

After you've added a Web folder, or if a Web folder has already been set up on your computer, publishing a presentation to it is as easy as saving a file to any folder on your hard disk.

To save a presentation to a Web folder, follow these steps:

1 From PowerPoint's File menu, choose Save As Web Page.

2 In the Save As dialog box, click the Web Folders button.

3 Double-click the Web folder that you want to open.

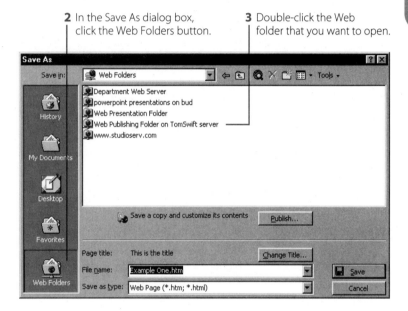

At this point, you might notice a delay while PowerPoint confirms the availability of the Web folder across the network and opens it.

4 Click the Publish button if you want to change the publishing options for the presentation or just click Save to save the presentation.

The presentation is saved as a Web page and the page (actually, the set of files that make up the page) is transferred to the Web folder. If the Open Published Web Page In Browser option is turned on, your Web browser opens, reads the Web page you've just uploaded, and displays the first slide of the presentation.

If you've already saved a presentation to a folder on your hard disk, you can publish it to a Web folder by opening the Web folder in Windows Explorer and then dragging the presentation from the folder on your hard disk to the Web folder. Remember, though, that a complete Web presentation consists of an .htm file accompanied by a folder that contains the additional files for the page. In other words, if you saved a presentation as ProjectX.htm, you must copy both ProjectX.htm and the folder named "ProjectX_files" to the Web folder.

Managing Presentations in Web Folders

Managing presentations after you've copied them to Web folders is as easy as managing presentations in folders on your hard disk. You can open two Web folders and drag a Web presentation from one folder to the other. Be sure you drag both the .htm file and the files in the support folder, though. You can also select a Web presentation in a Web folder and delete it by pressing the Delete key.

Saving a Web Presentation to a Web Server Using FTP

The whole concept of Web folders is for you to avoid having to use a special program to transfer a Web presentation to a Web server. But if the Web server you use does not support Web folders, you can still save a presentation to a Web site by using the standard method of transferring files to and from a Web server: File Transfer Protocol, or FTP.

To reach a Web server easily using FTP, you can add the Web server to a list of FTP servers in PowerPoint. Then you can select the FTP server as the destination when you save a presentation as a Web page. PowerPoint automatically uses FTP to transfer the presentation from your machine to the appropriate place on the Web server. To use FTP, you must know the Web address of the server and folder to which the Web presentation files should be saved. You must also know the user ID and password that will grant access to the server.

To add a Web site to the list of FTP servers and then save the presentation to it, follow these steps:

1 Connect to the network on which the FTP server resides. If the network is the Internet, connect to the Internet.

2 Open the presentation in PowerPoint.

3 From the File menu, choose Save As Web Page.

4 Click the down arrow next to the Save In list and then choose Add/Modify FTP Locations from the Save In list.

5 In the Add/Modify FTP Locations dialog box, enter the Web address of the FTP site in the Name Of FTP Site box.

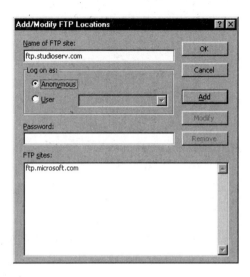

6 If you are not required to enter a password to access the FTP site, click Add to add the site to the list of FTP sites, and then click OK. If you must enter a password, click User to enter your user ID, and in the Password box, enter a password. Then click Add to add the site to the list of FTP sites and click OK.

7 In the Save As dialog box, double-click the name of the FTP server you've added. PowerPoint connects to the FTP server and displays the folders on the server.

8 Double-click a folder to open it and then proceed with the saving process as though you were saving the Web presentation to a Web folder.

Working with a Presentation Offline

To save a presentation as a Web page on a Web server, you must connect to the server. To view the presentation, you also must connect to the Web server. But if you use Internet Explorer 5.0, you can connect to a server and make a Web presentation available offline. This allows you to continue to view the presentation and even make changes to it after you've disconnected from the server.

Making a Web presentation available offline allows you to copy a presentation to a laptop computer and then take it with you on the road. You can give the presentation and even update it as you travel. Later, when you reconnect to the server, you can synchronize the version of the presentation on your computer with the version on the server to be sure that the latest iteration is located on both machines.

Making a Presentation Available Offline

When you're ready to make a presentation available offline, you can select a particular presentation to be replicated or you can select an entire Web folder. The object you select is copied to your computer so it is available after you disconnect.

To make a folder or presentation available offline, follow these steps:

1 Open My Computer and double-click the Web Folders icon.

2 Double-click the Web folder that contains the presentation that you want to make available offline.

3 Click the folder or the Web presentation in the folder with the right mouse button.

4 From the shortcut menu, choose Make Available Offline.

The folder and its contents, or the Web presentation you've selected, is replicated. During the replication, which may take a few minutes, you see the Synchronizing dialog box shown in Figure 16-11.

FIGURE 16-11.

The Synchronizing dialog box shows the progress as a Web folder or presentation is synchronized between the server and your computer.

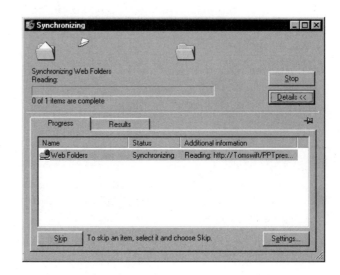

> **NOTE**
>
> When you make a Web presentation available offline, be sure to select both the .htm file for the presentation and the supporting files folder. In other words, to make the Web presentation named Profits.htm available offline, be sure to select both Profits.htm and the Profits_files folder before you choose Make Available Offline.

Working on the Presentation Offline

After you've made a Web presentation available offline, you can view it in Internet Explorer 5.0 and then open it in PowerPoint by following these steps:

1 From the File menu of Internet Explorer 5.0, choose Work Offline.

2 In the Address box in Internet Explorer, enter the full Web address of the Web folder or Web presentation as though you were still connected to the Web server.

  The Web presentation opens in Internet Explorer and the Internet Explorer title bar reads "Working Offline."

3 From the File menu, choose Edit In Microsoft PowerPoint For Windows.

The Web presentation opens in PowerPoint and is ready for editing.

Synchronizing the Presentation Automatically

When you first make a presentation available offline, the default synchronization schedule is established. The presentation will be synchronized when you log on to the network and when your computer is idle for a designated interval, but you can change the settings that determine how and when the synchronization will occur.

As the presentation is first being synchronized to your computer (when you first choose to make it available offline), you can click Settings in the Synchronizing dialog box to begin altering the schedule for synchronization. If you have already made a presentation available offline, you can begin altering the synchronization schedule by pointing to Programs on the Windows Start menu, pointing to Accessories, and then clicking Synchronize on the Accessories menu. In the Items To Synchronize dialog box, click Setup. Both methods open the Synchronization Settings dialog box, shown in Figure 16-12 on the next page.

FIGURE 16-12.

The Synchronization
Settings dialog box.

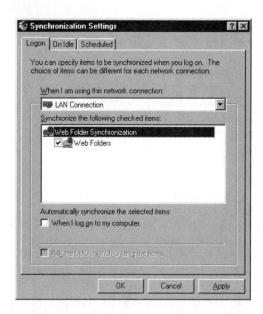

By changing the settings on the three tabs of the Synchronization
Settings dialog box, you can determine when synchronization will occur.

- To have the presentation synchronized each time you log on to
  the network, click Web Folders on the Logon tab and also click
  When I Log On To My Computer in the Automatically Synchronize
  The Selected Items section.

- To have the presentation synchronized when your computer is
  idle, click Web Folders on the On Idle tab and also click Synchronize The Selected Items While My Computer Is Idle. You can
  change this length of time by clicking the Advanced button on
  the On Idle tab.

- To have the presentation synchronized according to a daily,
  weekly, or monthly schedule, click one of the synchronization
  tasks listed on the Schedule tab and then click Edit. The options
  on the four tabs of the Daily, Weekly, or Monthly dialog box let
  you set a precise synchronization schedule. You can delete these
  default schedules and create your own by clicking Add on the
  Scheduled tab. The Scheduled Synchronization Wizard takes you
  through the steps of establishing a synchronization schedule.

Synchronizing the Presentation Manually

To synchronize a presentation manually, follow these steps:

1 Open My Computer and double-click Web Folders.

2 Double-click the Web folder that contains the presentation you want to synchronize.

3 Right-click the presentation (.htm) file and click Synchronize on the shortcut menu.

4 If the Resolve File Conflicts dialog box opens, which means both the version on the Web server and the version on your computer have been modified, do one of the following:

- To save both versions of the presentation, the one on the Web server and the one on your computer, click Keep Both Versions. Save The Version On My Computer To the Network As and then enter a new name for the presentation.

- To replace the version on the Web server with the version on your computer, click Keep Only The Version On My Computer. Replace The Network Version.

- To replace the version on your computer with the version on the Web server, click Keep Only The Network Version. Replace The Version On My Computer.

Collaborating with Others on a Presentation

Placing a Web presentation on a Web server enables each member of a workgroup to gain access to the presentation when it's convenient. It also enables members of a workgroup to participate in the development of a presentation and share information about a presentation topic in a collaborative forum called a discussion.

Editing a Web Presentation Online

A PowerPoint presentation that you open with your Web browser is an HTML version of the presentation. When it was saved to the server, it was saved as a Web page. The remarkable thing about a Web presentation is that it contains the complete information PowerPoint needs to rebuild the presentation in PowerPoint as though you were using the original PowerPoint file. In other words, when you open a Web presentation in PowerPoint rather than in a browser, you can work with it exactly as the original creator of the presentation worked with it.

Because you can open a Web presentation and work with it in PowerPoint, you can edit the presentation and change its contents or appearance. You can also add comments to the presentation to leave notes for other viewers. After you finish working, you can save the presentation, and the HTML files will be returned to the Web server with the updates in place.

Opening a Web Presentation

To open a Web presentation, you can use two methods: you can open the Web presentation in PowerPoint directly, or you can browse the presentation and then open the presentation you're browsing in PowerPoint.

To open a Web presentation in PowerPoint, follow these steps:

1 From PowerPoint's File menu, choose Open.

2 In the Open dialog box, click Web Folders to see the list of Web folders that you can access from your computer, or if you know the Web address (URL) of the presentation on the Internet, enter it in the File Name box in the dialog box.

3 Double-click the Web folder that contains the Web presentation.

4 Double-click the .htm file for the presentation.

To open a Web presentation from your browser, follow these steps:

1 In your browser, open the Web presentation by entering its Web address.

2 From the browser's File menu, choose Edit Microsoft PowerPoint For Windows Presentation.

With either method, if the Web presentation is on a network Web server or an Internet Web server, it'll take a minute for PowerPoint to transfer the presentation from the server to your machine. As the presentation is transferred, you will see a Transferring File message. When the presentation is fully transferred, it opens in PowerPoint.

After you open a Web presentation in PowerPoint, you can add slides, move slides, add charts to slides, change the data in a chart, and insert comments in individual slides; in short, you can do anything to the presentation that PowerPoint allows.

To return the presentation to the Web server, you simply save it. The presentation is transferred back to the server where it becomes available to others in its revised form.

Participating in Discussions About a Presentation

An online discussion is a written conversation about a Web presentation that appears right along with the presentation when it's viewed in a Web browser. After someone starts a discussion and opens with a question or remark, anyone can contribute a response by entering it right in a separate window in the browser. Further responses from others are added to the thread until everyone who has something to say has added a comment. Each discussion has a subject that's created by the initiator of the discussion, but others can add additional discussions that have other subjects.

Unlike discussions in the other Microsoft Office applications, which can be tied to specific pages of a document, or items on pages, a discussion in a PowerPoint Web presentation is tied to the entire presentation, not to a particular slide.

To be able to create and participate in discussions about a Web presentation, you must be working with a Web presentation that is hosted on a Web server that has Windows NT Server or Windows 2000 Server and the Office Server Extensions installed. You can't use discussions if your presentation is hosted on a Web server on your own computer, so discussions are really the province of workgroups or departments that have a centrally managed Web server.

You can use almost any Web browser to start and participate in Web discussions, although the support for discussions is strongest in Internet Explorer 4.0 or later. If you use Internet Explorer 3.0, Netscape Navigator, or another browser, see "Participating in Discussions with Netscape Navigator or Internet Explorer 3.0," later in this chapter.

Starting a Discussion

To start a discussion, open the Web presentation in Internet Explorer and click Discuss on the toolbar. If you are asked for the name of the discussion server, enter the name that has been given to you by the system administrator. If one or more discussions are already started, you will see them in the Discussion pane that opens below the presentation pane, as shown in Figure 16-13 on the next page. This pane is accompanied by the Discussions toolbar. If no discussions have been started, the discussion pane does not open, but the Discussions toolbar is visible.

FIGURE 16-13.

The Discussion pane
and Discussion toolbar
appear below the
presentation pane in
Internet Explorer.

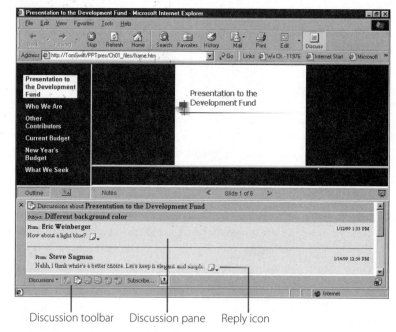

Discussion toolbar   Discussion pane   Reply icon

To add a new discussion, click the Insert Discussion About The
Document button on the Discussion toolbar. Type a discussion subject
and first message in the Enter Discussion Text dialog box that opens,
as shown in Figure 16-14. Then click OK.

FIGURE 16-14.

Enter a new discussion
subject and initial
message in the
Enter Discussion Text
dialog box.

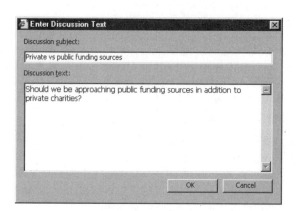

The discussion text you've entered appears in the Discussion pane
followed by a small yellow icon that others can click to reply to the
message, as shown in Figure 16-15. Because you're the originator of
the message, you can also edit or delete the message.

FIGURE 16-15.

Responses to a message appear indented below the message.

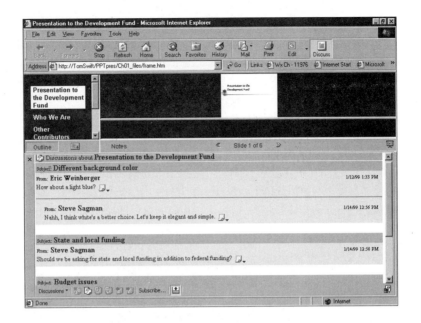

 TIP

> **Starting a Discussion from Within a Web Presentation in PowerPoint**
>
> You can also start a discussion when you've opened a Web presentation from a Web server right in PowerPoint. In PowerPoint, you open the Discussion pane by pointing to Online Collaboration on the Tools menu and then choosing Web Discussions on the submenu.

Contributing to a Discussion

If you open a Web presentation in Internet Explorer and the presentation has one or more discussions, the Discussion pane opens automatically and shows the discussions. Each discussion begins in a dark gray bar that identifies the discussion subject. The initial message falls immediately below and responses to it are indented underneath the message.

To contribute a comment to a discussion, click the yellow icon to the right of the message you want to answer and then choose Reply from the menu that appears. A new Enter Discussion Text dialog box opens and the subject is already entered. To enter a comment, type it into the Discussion Text box and then click OK. You contribution is indented below the message to which you are responding.

Filtering a Discussion

If many participants have contributed to a discussion, you can filter the discussion to see only the remarks added by a particular participant. You can also filter the discussion to see only remarks that were added within a certain time period, such as the last two days.

To filter a discussion, click the Discussions button on the Discussion toolbar and choose Filter Discussion from the drop-down menu. In the Filter Discussion dialog box, shown in Figure 16-16, choose a participant from the Created By drop-down list or a time interval from the Creation Time drop-down list. For example, to see only comments added by a participant named "John Smith," choose John Smith from the drop-down list.

FIGURE 16-16.

The Filter Discussion dialog box.

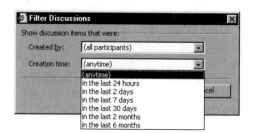

Participating in Discussions Using Netscape or Internet Explorer 3.0

If you use a version of Internet Explorer earlier than Internet Explorer 4.0 or if you are using Netscape Navigator or another Web browser, you can still participate in Web discussions, but you must use the Microsoft Office Server Extensions start page to add remarks. To access the start page, type the address of the Web server followed by msoffice in the Address box in the browser. If the Web server is http://WebServer, you should enter *http://WebServer/msoffice*.

The Discussions toolbar that appears in your browser might look somewhat different from the one shown in this book, but it will offer the same features.

In this chapter, you've learned to publish presentations on a Web site and use the new features of PowerPoint 2000 to collaborate on presentations with others in a workgroup. In the next chapter, you learn to deliver presentations you've prepared using traditional techniques and also to transmit presentations across networks or the Internet.

CHAPTER 17

Delivering Presentations

T he payoff for all your hard work comes when your slides go on display. Overhead projections and 35-mm slides look good enough, but they pale in comparison to electronic slide shows that can include sophisticated transition effects, animations, music, voice narrations, and even video clips.

To give such a presentation, you might think you need to bring along a small army of technicians and a truckload of computer equipment, but fortunately, that's far from the truth. The reality is that you might be able to arrive at a meeting room or conference hall with just a few disks or walk in with nothing but your notes and use the computer there to connect to a Web presentation back at your office. And if you're new to Microsoft PowerPoint 2000, you can dismiss one more notion: that everyone needs to gather and attend your presentation in person. With PowerPoint's online meetings and presentation broadcasts, you can deliver presentations to those who are around the company or around the world, and they can attend without ever leaving their desks.

Delivering a Slide Show in Person

Giving a presentation live, whether it's to a small group in a conference room or a large audience in an auditorium, is still the most popular to way to communicate your ideas. If you'll be giving a live presentation, you can run a show in a number of ways.

Running the Presentation from a Web Server

? SEE ALSO

For more information about saving a presentation as a Web page and setting up Web folders, see "Web Publishing and Collaboration," page 405.

If you will be presenting at a location in your company where you can access the company network, you might be able to run the presentation in a Web browser at the presentation site. You don't need to worry about bringing a computer and taking along the presentation, and you don't have to worry about whether you'll find PowerPoint installed and ready on the presentation computer.

Before the presentation, save the slide show as a Web page and note the address of the Web folder. (You might even send a link to the presentation by e-mail to someone at the presentation site, just as a backup.) When you get to the presentation site, open the browser on any computer connected to the network and enter the address of the Web presentation in its Web folder.

> NOTE

> Although the presentation can be run on any Web browser, it will look best if you run it in Microsoft Internet Explorer 4.0 or 5.0 and use Internet Explorer's full-screen view. In this view, attendees won't be able to detect that you're using a Web browser to display the show rather than the PowerPoint program.

If you need to deliver the presentation to another company or deliver it at a remote site, you still might be able to run the presentation in a Web browser if you can save the presentation to a Web server that can be reached over the Internet. When you arrive at the presentation site, use a client's computer to dial in to the Internet and run the presentation in a browser.

Running the Presentation from a Computer at the Presentation Site

If you can't be sure you'll find a computer at the presentation site with a browser and connection to the network or the Internet, you can take the presentation with you on a set of disks and install it on a computer at the presentation site. PowerPoint's Pack and Go Wizard helps you put everything on disks before you leave.

To use the Pack and Go Wizard, follow these steps:

1 In PowerPoint, open a presentation file on your computer or a Web presentation on a Web server.

2 Choose Pack And Go from the File menu.

 NOTE

If you did not install this feature when you installed Microsoft Office, you will be prompted to insert the Microsoft Office CD the first time you use the Pack And Go Wizard.

3 Click Next on the first page of the Pack And Go Wizard.

4 Choose Active Presentation on the second page of the wizard, and click Next.

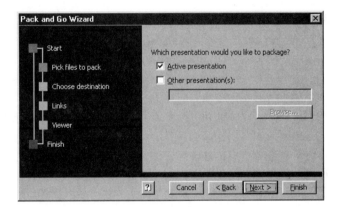

 TIP

Packing Multiple Presentations
To pack multiple presentations, click Other Presentations on the second page of the Pack and Go Wizard, click Browse, and then choose multiple .ppt files in the Select A Presentation To Package dialog box (hold down Ctrl as you click each file).

5 On the third page of the wizard, choose A:\ Drive as the destination for the file, and click Next.

6 On the fourth page of the wizard, click the options for the items you want included in the presentation, and click Next.

- Choose Include Linked Files to include Excel spreadsheets, Word documents, and other files that you've linked to the presentation.

- Choose Embed TrueType fonts to include the fonts that you've used to create the presentation. If you do not choose this option, the fonts on the destination computer that are closest to your fonts will be used.

7   On the fifth page of the wizard, choose Viewer For Windows 95 Or NT if you want to be able to run the presentation on a computer that does not have PowerPoint installed, and click Next.

> **NOTE**

If you did not install this feature when you installed PowerPoint, you will be asked to insert the Microsoft Office CD the first time you try to use the Viewer.

8   On the last page of the Wizard, click Finish to start the packing process.

The Pack and Go Wizard compresses the presentation and transfers it to a disk. If the presentation is too big to fit on a single disk, the wizard will prompt you to insert additional disks. Be sure to number these disks so you can insert them in the proper order when you install the presentation on the destination machine.

? SEE ALSO

For additional information about installing the PowerPoint Viewer, see "Installing the PowerPoint Viewer," page 443.

When you arrive at the location for the presentation, insert the first disk in the computer that you will be using, view the contents of the disk in Windows Explorer, and double-click the file pngsetup.exe. This installs the presentation and the viewer in a folder on the machine. To run the presentation, open the viewer in the folder by double-clicking Ppview32.exe. When the viewer opens, select the presentation file and click Show to begin the presentation.

Running the Presentation from Your Laptop Computer

To take a presentation with you on a laptop, you have quite a few choices. If the presentation is a standard PowerPoint file on your desktop computer or on the network, these are your options:

- You can Install PowerPoint on the laptop and take the .ppt file (the main PowerPoint file) with you. At the remote site, run the presentation in Slide Show view in PowerPoint, or right-click the .ppt file and choose Show from the shortcut menu to start the slide show without starting PowerPoint.

- You can install PowerPoint on the laptop and take a .pps file (a PowerPoint file that always runs as a slide show). At the remote site, double-click the .pps file, which starts the slide show in PowerPoint.

- You can install just the PowerPoint viewer without installing all of PowerPoint and take the presentation as a .ppt or .pss file. At the remote site, use the viewer to display the slide show exactly as you would if you were using Slide Show view in PowerPoint.

If the slide show is available as a Web presentation on a central Web server in your department or company and you can connect the laptop to the network, you have a few more choices:

- You can open the Web presentation in a browser on your laptop and then choose to edit it in PowerPoint. Once the presentation is open in PowerPoint, you can save it as a .ppt file or .pps file and take it with you.

- You can make the Web presentation available offline on your laptop, so you can run it in your browser after disconnecting from the network.

These options are covered in Chapter 16, "Web Publishing and Collaboration."

Creating a File That Always Runs As a Slide Show

You can save any presentation as a show file that always runs as a slide show. When you double-click this file in Windows Explorer, the show starts. When the show ends, PowerPoint also ends. You must have PowerPoint installed on the machine on which you'd like to run a PowerPoint show file.

To create a show file, choose Save As from the File menu. In the Save As dialog box, choose PowerPoint Show (*.pps) from the Save As Type drop-down list.

Installing the PowerPoint Viewer

When you install PowerPoint on your laptop, you can choose to install the PowerPoint Viewer as well, but if you know that you will not be editing a presentation on the road, you might want to install only the Viewer on the laptop to conserve disk space.

To install the PowerPoint Viewer, you can do either of the following things:

- Copy the contents of the following folder from the Microsoft Office 2000 CD to a folder on your hard disk: Pfiles\Msoffice\ Office\Xlators.

- Download the Viewer from the Microsoft Web site at the follow- ing address: *http://officeupdate.microsoft.com/downloadCatalog/ dldPowerPoint.htm?ShowType=Viewer*.

You can then open the folder on your hard disk and double-click Ppview32.exe to start the Viewer. To make it easy to start the Viewer, you might want to create a shortcut to it on your Windows desktop by dragging Ppview32.exe from the open folder to the desktop.

> **NOTE**

> The PowerPoint viewer cannot display picture bullets or automatic numbering on slides, two new capabilities of PowerPoint 2000. If you plan to use the viewer, avoid using these features on slides.

Setting Up the Slide Show

With the options in the Set Up Show dialog box, you can choose the type of show to run and how the show should proceed. The options you choose are saved with the presentation so they will be in effect no matter how you start the show. To open the Set Up Show dialog box, shown in Figure 17-1, choose Set Up Show from the Slide Show menu.

FIGURE 17-1.
The Set Up Show dialog box.

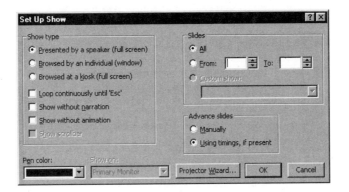

To run the entire show, select All in the Slides section of the Set Up Show dialog box. You can also enter a starting and ending slide in the From and To boxes. To run a slide show as an unattended demonstration (in a store window or building lobby, for example), click Loop Continuously Until 'Esc' in the Show Type section of the Set Up Show dialog box. The show will run as an ever-repeating loop that can only be interrupted when someone presses the Esc key. To make the Esc key unavailable, you can remove the keyboard and the mouse after you start the show and leave only the monitor and system unit.

In the Set Up Show dialog box, you can also choose to run the show without narrations and/or animations, and whether to advance the show manually or with the timings you established when you rehearsed the slide show timings. *You will learn about rehearsing a slide show in "Rehearsing Automatic Slide Show Timings," page 448.*

Special Show Types

PowerPoint offers three special slide show types, available in the Set Up Show dialog box. The first, Presented By A Speaker, is the traditional, full-screen slide show. The second, Browsed By An Individual, displays the show in an Internet Explorer-like window with navigation controls that make it easy for the viewer to move through the show. The third option, Browsed At A Kiosk, displays the show full-screen, but it also restarts the show after five minutes of inactivity and prevents the viewer from modifying the show. When you choose this option, Loop Continuously Until 'Esc' is selected automatically.

Setting Up a Computer Projector

If you will be using a computer projector to display a presentation to an audience, you can run the Projector Wizard, which helps detect your project and get it set up properly before the show.

To run the Projector Wizard, choose Set Up Show from the Slide Show menu, and then click Projector Wizard in the Set Up Show dialog box. The Projector Wizard starts, as shown in Figure 17-2.

FIGURE 17-2.

The Projector Wizard helps you connect a computer projector.

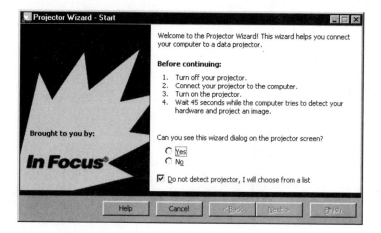

Controlling the Slide Show with the Mouse

We all like to control the show, but it's usually not as easy as Power-Point makes it. During a slide show, you can use the pop-up menu button and pop-up menu, shown in Figure 17-3, to control various aspects of the show. The button appears in the lower left corner of the current slide when you move the mouse pointer. You can then click the button to display the slide show pop-up menu.

The Next and Previous commands on the pop-up menu let you move forward or backward through the slides in your slide show. To move to a specific slide, choose Go and then Slide Navigator from the menu, and when the Slide Navigator dialog box appears, select a slide and click Go To. To display a hidden slide from any slide in the presentation, you have to use the Slide Navigator—hidden slide numbers appear in parentheses. To stop a slide show at any time during your presentation, simply choose End Show from the pop-up menu.

The remaining commands on the slide show pop-up menu let you access the Meeting Minder for note taking, open a Speaker Notes box

FIGURE 17-3.
The pop-up menu button and pop-up menu.

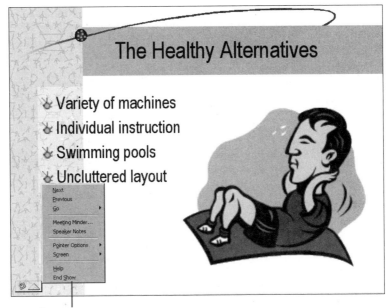

Pop-up menu

so you can view the notes for the slide, change the arrow pointer to a pen so that you can mark up slides (you can even change the color of the pen's "ink"), or hide the pointer altogether. You can also pause an automatic slide show or replace the current slide with a black screen (say, during an interruption in the proceedings).

⭐ TIP

Hiding the Pop-up Menu Button During a Slide Show
To hide the pop-up menu button during a slide show, choose Options from the Tools menu, and clear the Show Pop-up Menu Button option on the View tab of the Options dialog box. You can still access the pop-up menu by clicking the right mouse button during a slide show (unless you also clear the Pop-up Menu On Right Mouse Click option in the Options dialog box).

Controlling the Slide Show with the Keyboard

In addition to the slide show pop-up menu, you can use the keys listed in Table 17-1 on the next page to control various aspects of the show.

TABLE 17-1.   The Slide Show Keyboard Controls

Press This	To Perform This Action
Spacebar, Enter, Right arrow, Down arrow, Page Down, or N	Advance to next slide
Backspace, Left arrow, Up Arrow, Page Up, or P	Return to previous slide
Slide number+Enter	Go to slide number
B or period	Black screen/resume
W or comma	White screen/resume
Ctrl+A	Show mouse pointer as arrow
Ctrl+P	Show mouse pointer as pen
S or + (numeric keypad)	Pause/resume automatic show
H	Show/hide hidden slide
Ctrl+H	Hide pointer now
Ctrl+L	Hide pointer always
Tab	Go to next hyperlink
Enter (while hyperlink is selected)	Follow "mouse click" behavior of hyperlink
Shift+Enter (while hyperlink is selected)	Perform "mouse over" behavior of hyperlink
Esc	End show

Rehearsing Automatic Slide Show Timings

To create a slide show that proceeds on its own while you speak, you can simply enter the amount of time you want each slide to remain on the screen in the Slide Transition dialog box in Slide Sorter view. Another method, however, is to practice giving the presentation first and have PowerPoint record the length of time you keep each slide on the screen. You can then use PowerPoint's findings to determine the amount of time you need to display each slide. You can also get a good idea of the overall length of the show.

To enter the display time manually for each slide, first select the slide in Slide Sorter view and click the Slide Transition button on the Slide Sorter toolbar, or move to the slide in Slide view and choose Slide Transition from the Slide Show menu or the shortcut menu. In the Slide

Transition dialog box, enter the number of seconds in the Advance section's Automatically After box.

To record slide durations during a rehearsal of the slide show, click the Rehearse Timings button on the Slide Sorter toolbar or choose Rehearse Timings from the Slide Show menu. When the slide show begins, the Rehearsal toolbar shown in Figure 17-4 is displayed on the first slide.

FIGURE 17-4.

The Rehearsal toolbar.

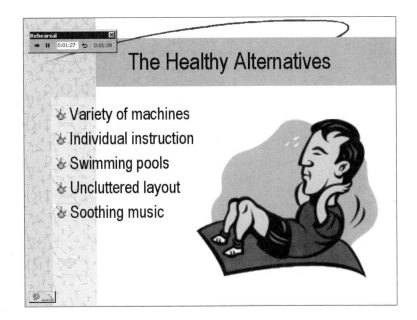

Practice giving the presentation, advancing the slides by clicking the Next button on the Rehearsal toolbar. As you speak, the elapsed time for the slide show is displayed on the right slide of the Rehearsal toolbar, and the elapsed time for the current slide is displayed in the middle. You can click the time for the current slide, enter a time, and then click the Next button to continue the show. You can also pause the slide show by clicking the button with the double vertical line, or you can click Repeat to repeat the current slide if you want to re-record the time for that slide.

After you complete the last slide, a dialog box shows the total length of the show and gives you the option to place the new timings in Slide Sorter view. If you click Yes, the timing for each slide appears under the slide in Slide Sorter view. To run the show with the timings, choose Slide Show from the View menu, select the Use Timings If Present option in the Set Up Show dialog box, and then show the presentation again.

TIP

> **Using Slide Timings in a Web Presentation**
>
> If you've recorded slide timings in a presentation and selected Use Timings If Present, you can create a presentation that automatically advances from slide to slide when it's viewed on the Web. To do this, use Internet Explorer 4.0 or 5.0 to open the file fullscreen.htm that is in the supporting files folder for the presentation. This opens the presentation in Internet Explorer's full-screen view and begins advancing the slides.

To remove slide timings, select one or more slides in Slide Sorter view, click the Slide Transition button on the Slide Sorter toolbar, and then clear the Automatically After option in the Advance section of the Slide Transition dialog box.

Marking Up Slides

To call special attention to a slide, or if you just don't know what to do with your hands during a slide show, you can use the mouse pointer to draw directly on slides. You can circle items, draw arrows, or add written comments, much as sportscasters do when drawing football plays on TV during a game.

To draw on a slide, you can either press Ctrl+P, click the pop-up menu button, or right-click a slide and choose Pointer Options from the pop-up menu. On the Pointer Options submenu, choose Pen to activate the pen pointer. Next press the left mouse button while moving the pointer on the slide to express yourself dramatically with scribbles. To clear everything you've drawn on a slide, press the E key (for erase) or choose Screen from the pop-up menu and then Erase Pen. When you're finished marking up your slides, choose Arrow from the pop-up menu or press Ctrl+A to return to the normal mouse pointer. Figure 17-5 shows annotations drawn during a slide show.

You can also change the color of the pen pointer's "ink" by choosing Pointer Options and then Pen Color from the slide show pop-up menu.

 TIP

> **Hiding the Mouse Pointer**
>
> During a slide show, if you want to hide the mouse pointer, whether it's an arrow or a pen, press Ctrl+H. To make the pointer reappear, press Ctrl+A.

FIGURE 17-5.

Annotations drawn during a slide show.

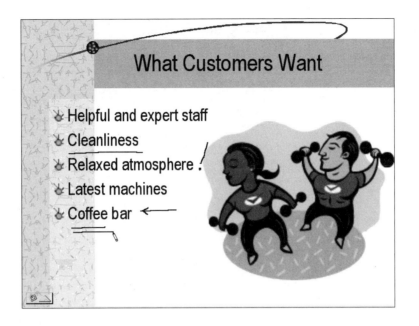

Showing a Presentation with Two Screens

If you are using Windows 98 or Windows 2000, you can use two graphics cards and two monitors to display a slide show on two screens. The audience can see what's on one monitor and you can view notes you've prepared ahead of time and take notes during the meeting in the Meeting Minder on the other monitor.

In the Set Up Show dialog box, choose the monitor on which to display the presentation by selecting it from the Show On drop-down list.

Managing the Meeting

Have you ever left a meeting without a list of the tasks everyone agreed to perform, and then had a hard time following up to see that things got done? Whether you are on the road, in a conference room down the hall, or at your desk, you can ensure more productive meetings by using Meeting Minder to make notes to yourself, create a list of action items, and take meeting minutes. When the meeting is done, clicking a button sends the minutes and action list to Microsoft Word, where you can edit and check spelling. Meeting Minder also sends notes to meeting attendees via electronic mail, using Microsoft Exchange or Microsoft Outlook.

Before you start a slide show, you can open Meeting Minder, shown in Figure 17-6 on the next page, by choosing Meeting Minder from the Tools menu. During a slide show, you can right-click and choose Meeting Minder from the shortcut menu.

FIGURE 17-6.

The Meeting Minder.

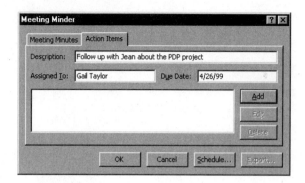

If you are displaying a slide show on your computer or projecting it on a screen or a large monitor, your audience sees the Meeting Minder window in addition to the slides. You can probably interrupt the slide show to record minutes and action items without distracting your audience too much, but this method doesn't work very well as a way of making notes to yourself. You are better off creating your notes in Notes Pages view and printing them out. If you are viewing a presentation using two computers, only you can see Meeting Minder when you open it, so you can check your notes without distracting other conference participants.

After you have opened Meeting Minder, you can type notes about the meeting on the Meeting Minutes tab. You can also enter action items for meeting attendees or others on the second tab of the Meeting Minutes dialog box. Enter the item and then click Add. You can close Meeting Minder and continue the presentation, and then open it again as necessary to record notes, minutes, and action items for other slides.

Another way to view minutes and action items is to export them to Microsoft Outlook or Microsoft Word. Exporting the minutes gives you a chance to polish them before distributing them to the meeting's attendees. Exporting action items puts them right into your group's shared information store. To export items, click the Export button in the Meeting Minder dialog box when the meeting is over. A second Meeting Minder dialog box appears, as shown in Figure 17-7, offering you two export options. If you select Post Action Items To Microsoft Outlook, the actions items for the presentation will be sent to Outlook. If you select the second option, Send Meeting Minutes And Action Items To Microsoft Word, PowerPoint exports your notes to a Word document and opens Word so you can edit your notes. Select the export option you want, and then click the Export Now button.

FIGURE 17-7.

The Meeting Minder
Export dialog box.

On the Action Items tab of the Meeting Minder dialog box, you can
also click Schedule to open an Outlook appointment form. In this
form, you can schedule a follow-up meeting and invite attendees.

If you enter any tasks on the Action Items tab during the meeting, Power-
Point displays a list of all the task assignments as the last slide in your
slide show or presentation conference. You can then check the list's
accuracy and remind everyone of their individual tasks before they leave
the meeting. Later, after you've had a chance to refine the list of action
items in Word, you can send it to everyone as electronic mail or as a fax.

Conducting an Online Meeting

With PowerPoint's online meetings, you no longer need to find a
conference room, schedule it, set up a computer, projector, and screen,
and make sure the coffee pot is full before you present a slide show to
your coworkers and superiors. With online meetings, you can use your
computer network to give a presentation to as many people as you
want, and they don't have to leave their offices!

An online meeting allows you to schedule a time for a "virtual" meeting,
designate which computers on the network will participate in the meeting, and then orchestrate the slide show from your desktop while you
use the telephone or your computer's sound system to talk with the
meeting's attendees. Everyone who connects to the meeting and has a
sound card installed and speakers or headphones will be able to hear
the presenter. Everyone connected will also be able to view the slide
show and make annotations on slides for everyone else to see. Participants can also type messages to each other in a chat window, speak to
each other if they have microphones connected to their computers, and
draw together on a shared whiteboard. The presenter controls the flow
of the show and switches from slide to slide as needed.

As the host, you prepare for the online meeting by scheduling a time
for the meeting, sending e-mail to participants informing them of the
time for the meeting, and gathering the computer names or addresses
of all the computers that will participate in the meeting.

TIP

> **What Happened to Presentation Conferencing?**
>
> Presentation conferencing, a feature of earlier versions of PowerPoint, has been replaced by online meetings and presentation broadcasting in PowerPoint 2000. Unlike presentation conferencing, which required that everyone in the conference have PowerPoint, online meetings and presentation broadcasts do not require that the participants have PowerPoint. Anyone who has Internet Explorer can view a presentation broadcast and anyone who has Microsoft NetMeeting, which comes with Internet Explorer, can participate in an online meeting.

Joining an Online Meeting

If your presence is desired in an online meeting, you will receive an e-mail invitation in Outlook or Exchange from the meeting organizer or a phone call from the individual to let you know when the meeting will occur. If you accept the invitation by clicking Accept in the e-mail message, a reminder is automatically added to your calendar. At the appropriate time, a reminder message will open, as shown in Figure 17-8. Click Join NetMeeting in the reminder to make yourself available for the online meeting. The NetMeeting window opens and awaits a call from the meeting organizer. If you will be attending the meeting over the Internet, connect to the Internet at this point. You must choose the same server as the person who will conduct the meeting so he or she can find your computer and send you an electronic call to join the meeting.

FIGURE 17-8.
An Outlook reminder message about an upcoming meeting.

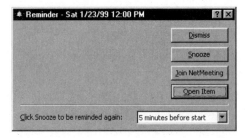

If you are not using Outlook or Exchange and if the organizer of the meeting informs you about the meeting with a phone call, be sure to start NetMeeting before the scheduled time for the meeting by choosing NetMeeting from the Windows Start menu. If the meeting will occur over the Internet, you must also connect to the Internet.

When the meeting organizer is ready to start the meeting, he or she will send a call to you and the other desired participants with an invitation to join the meeting. You can join the meeting by clicking Accept in the small Microsoft NetMeeting dialog box that opens, as shown in Figure 17-9.

FIGURE 17-9.

Click Accept to join the online meeting.

When the meeting starts, PowerPoint opens behind the Microsoft NetMeeting window with the presentation exactly as it appears on the meeting presenter's screen. You should minimize the Microsoft NetMeeting window so you can see the PowerPoint window.

Starting Your Own Online Meeting

Although you can initiate an impromptu meeting and spontaneously invite others to attend over the network, you probably will want to establish a scheduled meeting in advance and send out e-mail invitations to prospective attendees.

To schedule an online meeting, open the presentation that you want to deliver during the meeting and then point to Online Collaboration on the Tools menu. From the Online Collaboration submenu, choose Schedule Meeting. In the message dialog box that opens, shown in Figure 17-10, enter the message recipients and a subject for the message, such as "Invitation to join online meeting about Project X." Note that This Is An Online Meeting Using Microsoft NetMeeting is turned on by default and the presentation name is entered in the Office Document box.

FIGURE 17-10.

Fill out and send an e-mail message inviting others to attend your online meeting.

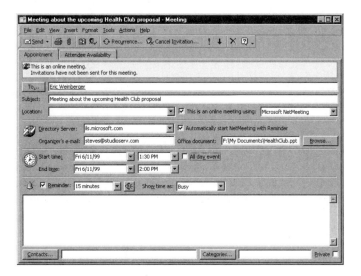

Invitation recipients can reply by clicking Accept in the e-mail invitation and at that point, a reminder will be added to their Outlook calendars.

When it's time to start the meeting, open PowerPoint again and open the presentation that you will deliver during the online meeting. If participants will be joining the meeting over the Internet, connect to the Internet. Point to Online Collaboration on the Tools menu and choose Meet Now from the Online Collaboration submenu. This opens the Place A Call dialog box shown in Figure 17-11.

FIGURE 17-11.

The Place A Call dialog box.

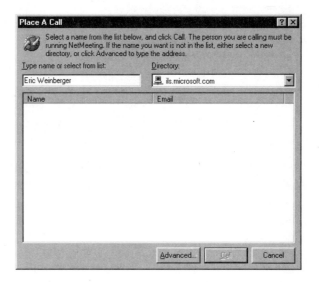

During an online meeting, the presenter's screen is sent to the participants exactly as it appears to the presenter. Before starting an online meeting, the presenter should set the Windows screen area or desktop size to the same size as the participants will use. If the presenter's screen is larger than any of the screens of the participants, the participants will see only part of the presenter's display. If you are the presenter, you can change the screen area by right-clicking the Windows desktop. On the Settings tab of the Display Properties dialog box, drag the Screen Area slider to the left to choose smaller dimensions, such as 800 x 600 pixels.

If you are connected to a corporate network, the default directory server should be listed in the Directory box in the Place A Call dialog box. If it is not listed, you can get the name of this directory server from your system administrator (on some systems, it won't be required). If you are connecting to the Internet for a meeting, you should select the Internet directory server to which your participants are connected.

The Place A Call dialog box shows a list of the names of people who are connected to the current directory server. To invite someone to the meeting, select a name from the list and click Call. When the first participant accepts, the Place A Call dialog box closes and the Online Meeting toolbar appears superimposed over the presentation, as shown in Figure 17-12. You can drag this toolbar down the screen and move it just below or next to the Drawing toolbar so it does not cover the presentation slides.

FIGURE 17-12.
The Online Meeting toolbar.

Participant list   Call participant

Remove participants

To invite more participants to the meeting, click the Call Participant button on the toolbar and then choose another participant to call. Continue in this fashion until everyone is present and accounted for. To remove a participant after the meeting is started, you can select a participant from the participant list and then click the Remove Participants button on the Online Meeting toolbar.

From now on, while the meeting is in progress, everyone attending the online meeting can see everything you do on the screen. To begin the presentation, you can switch to Slide Show view.

Conducting an Online Meeting

When you host an online meeting, you have several tools to help ensure that the meeting is productive. When you attend an online meeting, you can participate, but your role is limited.

Allowing Others to Edit Slides

When a meeting begins, the attendees see the same screen as you, but they are unable to control or edit the presentation. To make the presentation available to them for editing, you can click the Allow Others To Edit button on the Online Meeting toolbar. Any participant can then click the presentation to take control of it. While a participant has control of the presentation, that participant can switch from slide to slide in the presentation and edit the content of slides. In addition, the initials of the person in control appear next to the mouse pointer that everyone sees. To regain control of the presentation, you can click anywhere in the PowerPoint window or press the Esc key.

Opening a Chat Window

The host of an online meeting can turn on a chat window into which everyone can type comments during a presentation. When the presentation is completed, anyone who participated can then save the record of comments.

To open a chat window, click the Display Chat Window button on the Online Meeting toolbar. When the Chat window appears, anyone can type a message into the Message box and then press Enter or click the Send Message button. The messages from participants appear in the chat window.

The host might want to arrange the chat window below or beside the presentation window, as shown in Figure 17-13, so participants can enter comments as they watch the presentation.

FIGURE 17-13.

The chat window arranged beside the presentation window.

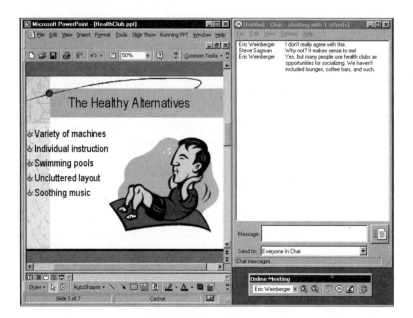

Opening the Whiteboard

As the host of an online meeting, you can also open a whiteboard during a presentation, which everyone can draw on, as shown in Figure 17-14. To open the whiteboard, click the Display Whiteboard button on the Online Meeting toolbar. Although it sounds counterintuitive, to allow everyone to draw on the whiteboard, you must turn off Allow Others To Edit.

FIGURE 17-14.

Everyone can draw shapes and add text to the whiteboard.

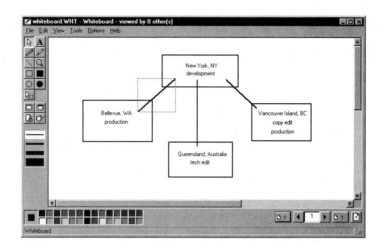

IV

Performing with PowerPoint

Participants can use the tools within the whiteboard to draw lines and shapes, add text, and point to objects on the whiteboard. Anything drawn by one person is seen by all the participants. As participants fill a whiteboard page, they can click the Add Page button to add new pages to the whiteboard. When finished using the whiteboard, each participant must close his or her own whiteboard window.

Sending a File to Participants

As the host of an online meeting, you can send a file to the participants in the meeting. To do so, you must reopen the Microsoft NetMeeting window by clicking NetMeeting on the Windows taskbar. On the Tools menu in the NetMeeting window, point to File Transfer, and then click Send File on the submenu. In the Select A File To Send dialog box, choose a file and then click the Send button. The file is transferred to a folder on the computers of all the recipients. The recipients designate this folder by selecting Options from the Tools menu and then clicking Change Folder on the General tab of the Options dialog box.

Ending an Online Meeting

To end an online meeting, click the End Meeting button on the Online Meeting toolbar and then click Yes in the small confirmation dialog box that appears. The presentation window closes on all the participants' screens. The participants must then exit NetMeeting themselves and disconnect from the Internet if the meeting was being held over the Internet.

Participating in an Online Meeting

As a participant in an online meeting, you can only watch the show until the host of the meeting relinquishes some control and allows others to edit the presentation. Although you can see the Online Meeting toolbar just as the host sees it, you cannot click its buttons or use its controls.

To take control of the presentation when the host allows you to, click in the PowerPoint window. Now everyone else connected to the meeting can see the changes to the presentation that you make on your screen. You can continue to edit slides until the meeting host regains control of the meeting.

To leave an online meeting before it has ended, click the Microsoft NetMeeting button on the Windows taskbar to reopen the NetMeeting window and click Hang Up. In the NetMeeting window, you can also see a list of all the current meeting attendees.

 # Broadcasting a Presentation Across the Network

While the participants in an online meeting get the chance to interact with one another and contribute to the development of a set of slides, the viewers of an online broadcast are purely passive. During a broadcast, a presenter delivers a presentation to those who tune in on the network or watch the presentation on the Internet. To view a broadcast presentation, viewers need only to have Internet Explorer 4.0 as their Web browser.

What You Need for a Presentation Broadcast

PowerPoint provides all the software you need to broadcast presentations to groups of up to 15 people on a small company network. If you need to broadcast a presentation to a larger group, or if you want to broadcast a presentation to an unlimited audience on the Internet, you must have Microsoft NetShow Server on a computer running Windows NT Server or Windows 2000 Server.

IV

Performing with PowerPoint

About NetShow Server

Microsoft NetShow Server is an add-on to Windows NT Server or Windows 2000 Server that is available at no additional cost. It allows you to configure, manage and deliver streaming video, audio, and animation content over the Internet or over a corporate intranet. System administrators can obtain NetShow Server from the Microsoft Web site at the following address: *http://www.microsoft.com/ ntserver/nts/downloads/recommended/mediaserv/default.asp*.

If you want to include audio with the presentation, such as the sound of your voice during the presentation, you must have a microphone and sound card installed in the computer from which you will be broadcasting. If you will be broadcasting video, you must have a video camera and video card installed.

Setting Up and Scheduling a Broadcast

When the presentation you want to broadcast is complete, and when you've determined a time for the broadcast, you should set up the presentation for the broadcast and send out broadcast announcements by e-mail. The e-mail you send out by scheduling a broadcast will include a link that viewers can click to tune in to the broadcast in Internet Explorer when it's time. If the viewers use Outlook, the e-mail also schedules a reminder in the Outlook calendar that will pop up at the appropriate time and give them the opportunity to click a button in order to view the broadcast.

Prior to setting up the presentation, you must create and share a folder for the broadcast. The broadcast files will be housed in this folder and retrieved from it by the broadcast viewers. It's best to share a folder on a separate server that everyone can reach instead of setting up a folder on your hard disk, which would mean that everyone would be accessing these files during the presentation, and that could slow the operation of your machine.

Does a presentation broadcast folder already exist?

If you work in a large organization, you should check with your system administrator to see whether the administrator has already created and shared folders that you can use for broadcasting presentations and for saving recordings of broadcasts for later viewing.

To share a folder, navigate to the folder in Windows Explorer, right-click the folder, and then choose Sharing from the shortcut menu. Click Shared As in the Properties dialog box for the folder, and enter a name in the Share Name box. You can leave the Access Type set to Read Only and click OK to proceed.

If you want to record presentations to make them available to viewers later, you can create a second shared folder in which to store recorded broadcasts.

To set up the presentation for broadcast, follow these steps:

1   Open the presentation in PowerPoint.

2   On the Slide Show menu, point to Online Broadcast and then click Set Up And Schedule on the submenu.

 NOTE

If you did not install this feature when you installed PowerPoint, you will be prompted to insert the Microsoft Office CD the first time you choose Online Broadcast from the Slide Show menu.

3   In the Broadcast Schedule dialog box, make sure Set Up And Schedule A New Broadcast is selected and click OK.

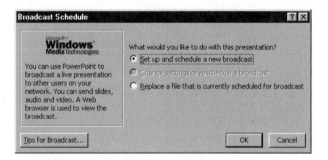

4   On the Description tab of the Schedule A New Broadcast dialog box, enter a title, description, speaker, and contact for the broadcast.

This information will appear on the lobby page that viewers see when they tune in just before a broadcast. You can preview this lobby page by clicking Preview Lobby Page in the Schedule A New Broadcast dialog box.

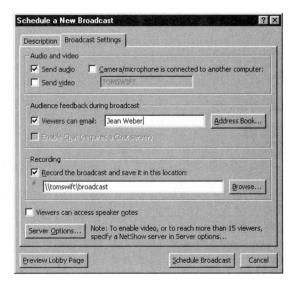

5 If this is the first time you've broadcast a presentation, click the Broadcast Settings tab. Otherwise, you can skip the rest of these steps.

6 In the Audio And Video section of the Broadcast Settings tab, select the Send Audio check box if you will be sending a live audio narration. Select the Send Video check box if you will be sending a live video signal, too.

7 If you want to show viewers the e-mail address of someone to contact during the broadcast, click Viewers Can Email in the Audience Feedback During Broadcast section of the dialog box, and enter the e-mail address of the contact or click the Address Book button and browse for the address.

8 If a Microsoft Chat Server is installed on your network, you can select the Enable Chat check box. This lets viewers communicate with each other during a broadcast by typing messages into a Microsoft Chat window.

9 If you want to record the broadcast so viewers can tune in and watch it later, select Record The Broadcast And Save It In This Location. Then enter the name of the shared folder name in which the broadcast should be saved or click the Browse button and browse to the folder. The folder name should be in this form: \\computername\sharedfoldername. For example, if the folder has the share name *SavedBroadcasts* on a computer named *Central*, the folder name is \\Central\SavedBroadcasts.

10 To let viewers see the speaker notes you've included in the presentation, select Viewers Can Access Speaker Notes.

11 Click Server Options.

12 In the Step 1 section of the Server Options dialog box that opens, enter the name of the shared folder you created for the broadcast, or click the Browse button and navigate to the folder. This folder name should be in the same format as the broadcast folder name: \\computername\sharedfoldername.

13 In the Step 2 section of the Server Options dialog box, select Use A Local NetShow Server On This LAN if you will broadcast to more than 15 viewers and you have a NetShow Server installed on the network. Enter the name of the NetShow Server in the Server Name box. Otherwise, select Don't Use A NetShow Server.

14 Click OK to close the Server Options dialog box.

Using a Third Party NetShow Service Provider

If you do not have a NetShow server but need to broadcast to a large audience, you can use a third party NetShow service provider on the Internet to broadcast your presentation. In the Server Options dialog box, select Use A Third Party NetShow Service Provider. A Web page will open in your browser with information about third party NetShow service providers.

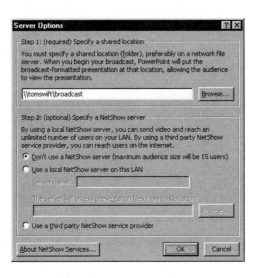

Now that you've set up the broadcast, you can schedule it so viewers will receive e-mail notices informing them about the upcoming broadcast.

1 In the Schedule A New Broadcast dialog box, click Schedule Broadcast.

PowerPoint checks to make sure that the folder you have designated for the presentation broadcast is valid and available. It also displays a reminder that you must use NetShow Server if you intend to broadcast the presentation to more than 15 viewers.

A new message opens in your e-mail program that contains information about the broadcast and a hyperlink that viewers can click to get to the broadcast.

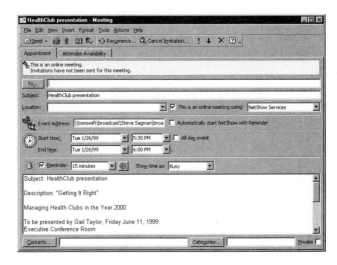

2 Enter the recipient addresses in the To box.

3 Enter the appropriate date and time for the broadcast in the Start Time and End Time boxes.

4 Click Send.

The message is sent to the addressees, who can reply with a notification that they will attend.

The broadcast schedule that you've established is now stored in the PowerPoint file. You can close the file and reopen it near the time of the broadcast. You can also schedule additional broadcasts for a presentation at different dates and times and for different groups of viewers.

When viewers click the link to get to the lobby page just before the broadcast begins, they'll see a countdown with the time remaining until the broadcast.

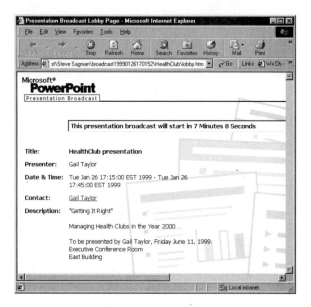

Rescheduling a Broadcast

The schedule for presentation broadcasts is saved in the PowerPoint file, so each file can have its own broadcast schedule. To reschedule a particular broadcast on the schedule, open the presentation in Power-Point, point to Online Broadcast on the Slide Show menu, and then choose Set Up and Schedule. In the Broadcast Schedule dialog box, choose Changing Settings Or Reschedule A Broadcast and click OK.

In the Schedule dialog box, shown in Figure 17-15, you see the current broadcasts that are scheduled for the presentation. Select a broadcast and click Reschedule. This opens the mail program again and starts a new message that you can send to recipients to update the scheduled time of the broadcast.

FIGURE 17-15.
You can reschedule presentation broadcasts in the Schedule dialog box.

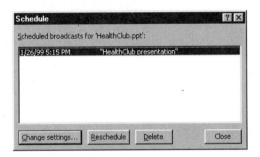

Beginning the Broadcast

If you are using Outlook, a reminder will open at the reminder time you scheduled for a presentation broadcast. Even though you will be the one giving this presentation, click View NetShow. PowerPoint will open the scheduled presentation, note that you are the one scheduled to do the presenting, and display a message that says *Do you want to broadcast this presentation?* Click Yes. The Broadcast Presentation dialog box opens, as shown in Figure 17-16.

FIGURE 17-16.
The Broadcast Presentation dialog box.

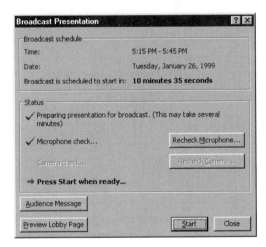

PowerPoint prepares the presentation for broadcast, saving the broadcast files to the folder you designated, and it then asks you to speak into the microphone so it can automatically adjust the input volume. It also displays a countdown timer that shows the remaining time until the scheduled start for the broadcast. At the precise time for the start of the broadcast, a new dialog box asks whether you want to start the broadcast. If you're ready, click Yes. If you need to delay the start of the presentation, click No. At this point, you might want to click Audience Message in the Broadcast Presentation dialog box and enter a new message for those who've tuned in for the broadcast such as "The presentation will begin in only five minutes." After you've entered the message, click Update. Viewers who are watching the lobby page and waiting for the presentation to start will see the new message replace the countdown timer.

Tuning In to the Broadcast Yourself
It's a good idea to have a second machine nearby that is tuned in to the presentation broadcast so you can see what viewers see on their machines.

Now you can begin giving your presentation. Speak into the microphone at a normal volume and control the presentation just as if you were giving the presentation before an audience in the room. Viewers who are tuned in will hear your voice and see the presentation slides advance.

At the end of the show, you will see the "End of slide show, click to exit" black screen. The viewers will not see this slide. Instead, they will continue to see the last slide of the presentation. When you click the mouse button to end the show, a dialog box opens to ask "End the broadcast?" If you click Yes, viewers are returned to the lobby page, where they see the message "This presentation broadcast has ended."

If you have chosen to record the broadcast, viewers will also see a Replay Broadcast button that they can click to watch the recording. Viewers can return to the lobby page for the broadcast at any time to replay the broadcast. Other viewers who are given the address (or who are sent a link by e-mail) can also visit the lobby page to see a presentation that they were unable to attend.

In this chapter, you've learned to share presentations with others. In the next chapter, you will learn to share information among the Microsoft Office applications as you develop a presentation.

PART V

Advanced PowerPoint

CHAPTER 18

18

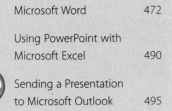
Using PowerPoint with Other Applications

lthough PowerPoint certainly stands on its own, it becomes even more powerful when combined with its partners in Microsoft Office 2000: Microsoft Word 2000, Microsoft Excel 2000, and Microsoft Outlook 2000. PowerPoint is the public voice of Office, telling the stories you write in Word and the numbers you crunch in Excel with professionally and consistently designed images.

Many of the common attributes shared by the Microsoft Office applications are perfectly obvious after you've used them a little. You'll notice the common menus, dialog boxes, toolbars, and even procedures that make it easy for you to switch from one application to another. You'll also find that the applications share spelling dictionaries, AutoCorrect word lists, drawing tools, and the Clip Gallery.

But below the surface of Office, a powerful technology called OLE (pronounced *olé*) gives the Office suite the capability to gracefully share information. For example, you can move objects such as text or numbers from one application to another just by dragging them from one window into another. And when you move an object between applications and then decide to edit the object, an OLE feature called *in-place editing* summons the menus, dialog boxes, toolbars, and procedures you used to create the object so you can make changes as though you were working in the original program. You can move a worksheet from Excel to PowerPoint, for example, and then choose to edit the object. Suddenly, Excel's menus and toolbars appear within PowerPoint's window. When you finish editing, PowerPoint's menus and toolbars reclaim the screen.

The drag-and-drop method is the key to transferring information among the Office applications. You can almost always select an item in one application and drag it to another application's window. And if you want a copy of the information to remain in the original application, just hold down Ctrl as you drag.

In this chapter, you'll learn how to select objects and drag them between applications. You'll also pick up a few points to keep in mind as you exchange information between the Office applications, as well as learning about menu alternatives you can use with other Microsoft Windows applications that do not support drag-and-drop procedures.

Using PowerPoint with Microsoft Word

In Chapter 4, you learned how to exchange outlines between Microsoft Word and PowerPoint, and in Chapter 16, you learned how to export meeting minutes and action item lists from PowerPoint to Word. But you can also exchange one paragraph or one picture with similar ease. Best of all, you can embed an entire PowerPoint slide show in a Word document, transforming a potentially drab report into a lively, stimulating presentation complete with special effects, sound, music, and perhaps even video.

Of course, you can embed individual multimedia elements in a Word document without using PowerPoint, but embedding them in a Power-Point presentation and then embedding the presentation in Word allows the multimedia objects and the presentation to be played together in a slide show within a Word document.

Transferring Word Text to PowerPoint

There are several ways to transfer text from Word to PowerPoint, depending on how you want that text to look and behave once it's there.

- You can copy text from Word and paste it into PowerPoint. You can then edit the text in PowerPoint as if you had typed it there to begin with.

- You can embed Word text in PowerPoint so you can edit it using Word menus and toolbars.

- You can link embedded text so that whenever it's changed in the original Word document, it's automatically updated in PowerPoint.

Copying and Pasting Word Text into PowerPoint

Suppose you have text you've already typed in Word that you want to use in PowerPoint. Rather than retyping the text, you can simply copy and paste it from Word to PowerPoint. Follow these steps:

1 In Word, select the text you want to copy.

2 From Word's Edit menu, choose Copy, or click the Copy button on the Standard toolbar.

3 Switch to PowerPoint by clicking any visible part of its window or by clicking its name on the taskbar.

4 Turn to the slide in which you want to paste the Word text.

5 Click where you want to paste the Word text. If you paste into an existing text placeholder, the pasted text adopts the existing font, size, and other style attributes of the PowerPoint text box. If you paste the text elsewhere on the slide, PowerPoint creates a new text box for the pasted text.

6 From PowerPoint's Edit menu, choose Paste, or click the Paste button on the Standard toolbar.

> **NOTE**

If you paste multiple paragraphs into a bulleted list placeholder, only the first paragraph is formatted as a bullet point. Select the other paragraphs and then on the Formatting toolbar, click the Bullets button.

V

Advanced PowerPoint

You can use the Copy and Paste commands in this fashion to make a simple copy of selected text and paste it into PowerPoint from Word and from any other application. Be aware, however, that this Copy and Paste method does not tie the text in PowerPoint to the original application. In other words, when you double-click text you've copied from Word, you are not returned to Word so you can edit the text.

Embedding Word Text in PowerPoint

When you *embed* Word text in PowerPoint, you are actually pasting a picture of the Word text, that is, the *object*, into your slide. When you double-click the Word object, the Word menus and toolbars appear so you can work with the text using Word tools.

To *embed* the Word text in PowerPoint, follow these steps:

1 In Word, select the text you want to embed in PowerPoint.

2 From Word's Edit menu, choose Copy, or click the Copy button on the Standard toolbar.

3 Switch to PowerPoint by clicking any visible part of its window or by clicking its name on the taskbar.

4 From PowerPoint's Edit menu, choose Paste Special (instead of Paste).

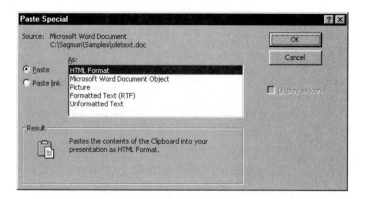

5 In the Paste Special dialog box, be sure that the Paste option (not Paste Link) is selected.

6 In the list, select Microsoft Word Document Object. The Word text is inserted in its own text box on the slide. If you want, you can move the text box to position it better on the slide.

SEE ALSO

For more information about editing the text, see "Editing Word Text in PowerPoint," page 477.

When you double-click this text, a miniature Word window opens and the toolbars and menus change to Word's. You can edit the text in the miniature window and then click outside the window to revert to PowerPoint's toolbars and menus.

Click to add title

It is necessary to hope…
for hope itself is happiness.
–Samuel Johnson

 TIP

Show Linked Word Text as an Icon
To place a Word icon that represents linked text in a PowerPoint presentation, select the Display As Icon check box in the Paste Special dialog box.

 SEE ALSO

For more information about the Paste Special dialog box, see "Linking a PowerPoint Slide to Word," page 484.

You can also *link* the embedded text to its original in the Word document. With a link, whenever the text is updated in the original Word document, it is automatically updated in the PowerPoint slide. To link embedded text, follow the same steps as to embed text described above, but in the Paste Special dialog box, select Paste Link instead of the Paste Special option. In this case, you cannot edit the text directly in PowerPoint; instead, you open and edit the text in Word. Changes you make in Word flow through to PowerPoint.

Dragging Text from Word to PowerPoint

You can embed text that you've already typed in Word with the drag-and-drop method. Rather than retype the text, you can simply drag it from Word to PowerPoint as easily as you drag it from place to place within a Word document.

V

Advanced PowerPoint

To drag text from Word to PowerPoint, follow these steps:

1 Open the Word and PowerPoint windows, and then arrange them so they share the screen and both are visible, even if one window overlaps the other.

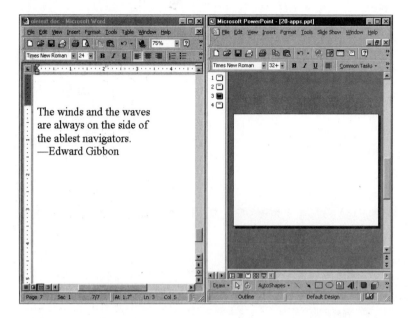

2 Make sure the slide in which you want to embed the Word text is displayed in the PowerPoint window and that Slide view or Normal view is active.

3 In Word, select the text—a sentence, a paragraph, even a table, or anything else you've created in Word.

4 While holding down Ctrl, place the mouse pointer on the selection, drag the selection to the current PowerPoint slide, and then release the mouse button. The text is copied from Word to PowerPoint. To move rather than copy the text, drag without holding down Ctrl. Either way, the text appears in the slide as an embedded object.

You can resize the Word object frame. If you drag one of the corner handles, you size the Word object proportionally according to its original dimensions. If you drag one of the center handles, you can stretch or compress the length or width of the embedded Word object. Figure 18-1 illustrates this distinction.

FIGURE 18-1.

You can resize embedded text from Word (top) by dragging one of the center handles (center) or one of the corner handles (bottom).

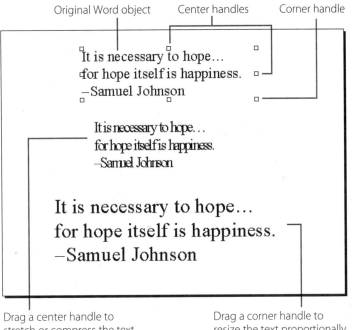

Drag a center handle to stretch or compress the text.

Drag a corner handle to resize the text proportionally.

Editing Word Text in PowerPoint

If you have copied and pasted text from Word into PowerPoint, you can edit the text in PowerPoint as if you had originally typed it there.

However, if the text is a Word object, you use the Word editing tools. Without leaving PowerPoint, you can work within a special editing window and use all the commands and controls as if you were actually in Word.

To edit a Word object in PowerPoint, follow these steps:

1 Double-click the Word object. Word's menus and toolbars replace those of PowerPoint, and a frame that represents a small Word editing window, complete with its own rulers, appears around the text.

2 Work within Word's editing window to make the editing or formatting changes you want. All of Word's commands and controls are available to you here.

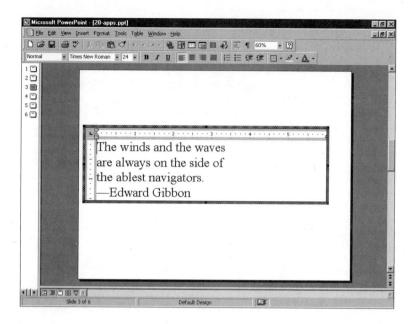

3 When you finish editing the text, click the PowerPoint slide outside the Word editing window. The window disappears, but the revised embedded text object remains with the changes you made, and PowerPoint's menus and toolbars reappear.

You can also edit the embedded text using Word's menus and toolbars by clicking the text with the right mouse button, pointing to Document Object, and then choosing Edit from the shortcut menu. The Word editing window appears. Again, when you finish editing, simply click outside the text picture to save your edits and return to the PowerPoint slide.

If you would be more comfortable editing the text in a separate Word window, you can use the right mouse button to click the embedded Word text object in PowerPoint. From the shortcut menu, point to Document Object, and then choose Open. The text opens in a full-screen Word window. After you edit the text, from Word's File menu, choose Update. Then, again from the File menu, choose Close & Return To *<Presentation>*.

Transferring PowerPoint Information to Word

Just as you can copy or drag text from Word to PowerPoint, you can transfer PowerPoint slides, graphics, and text to Word. You can copy and paste, drag, and embed and link information from PowerPoint to Word.

Send Your Entire Presentation Text to Word

You can copy the entire text (without the graphics) of your PowerPoint presentation to a new Word document. This can be useful if you're writing a report based on information you have in a presentation. Follow these steps:

1 From PowerPoint's File menu, point to Send To and then choose Microsoft Word. The Write-Up dialog box appears.

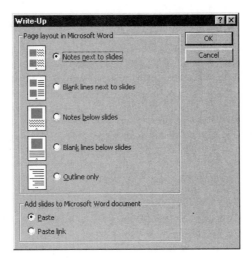

2 Select the Outline Only option, and then click OK. Word opens and the presentation's outline text is copied to a new document with a generic name as a Rich Text Format (RTF) document.

3 If you want to save the document under a name you choose, or as a Word document rather than RTF file type, from the File menu, choose Save As. In the File Name box, type the name you want. In the Save As Type box, click Word Document (*.doc).

Embedding a Slide in a Word Document

Because they're both part of the Microsoft Office suite, Word can use many of the same resources that PowerPoint enjoys. By using Word's Object command from the Insert menu, you can access Microsoft Graph as easily as you can from within PowerPoint, so you don't need PowerPoint to create a graph for a Word document. WordArt is also available in Word, so you can have fancy headings in memos as well as in a slide show. In addition, Word has its own powerful table functions, so you don't need PowerPoint's help there either.

But by dragging a PowerPoint slide to Word, you can place an image of the slide in a document, complete with a background design and a combination of foreground and background text and graphical objects. You can also copy and paste individual objects from a PowerPoint slide into a Word document using the Copy and Paste commands.

To drag a slide from PowerPoint to Word, follow these steps:

1 Arrange the PowerPoint and Word windows on the screen so that they are both visible.

2 In PowerPoint, make sure the slide you want to drag is visible in the Slide Sorter view.

3 In Word, make sure the page in which you want to embed the PowerPoint slide is visible.

4 In PowerPoint, place the mouse pointer on the slide and drag the slide from PowerPoint to Word. To copy the slide rather than move it, hold down Ctrl as you drag.

After the slide appears in Word, you can drag it within the Word window as you would a block of text. You can also drag a corner handle to resize the slide proportionally. By clicking the slide with the right mouse button, you can open a Word shortcut menu with commands that apply to the slide (see Figure 18-2). For example, you can add a border, shading, and caption to the slide, or frame the slide so that you can wrap text around it and use other techniques that apply only to framed elements.

FIGURE 18-2.

The shortcut menu for a slide dragged to a Word document.

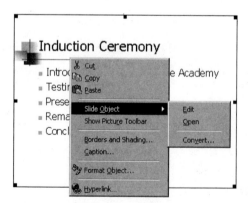

Also on the shortcut menu is the Slide Object command. When you point to Slide Object and then choose Edit, the menus and toolbars change to those for PowerPoint. You can edit the slide just as you would if you had opened PowerPoint yourself. After you finish, click the insertion point anywhere else in the Word document (outside the slide); the menus and toolbars change back to those of Word, and you can continue working with the rest of your Word document.

You can drag slides into many other Windows applications in the same way. However, for some programs, your slide won't budge. If this happens, use the Copy command instead. Follow these steps:

1 Have PowerPoint and the other application open.

2 In PowerPoint's Slide Sorter view, click the slide you want to copy.

3 From PowerPoint's Edit menu, choose Copy. Or, on the Standard toolbar, click the Copy button.

4 Switch to the other application's window by clicking on any visible part of its window or by clicking its name on the taskbar.

5 Select where you want the slide to be inserted.

6 Choose the other application's Paste command. The slide is embedded.

Embedding a PowerPoint Presentation in Word

In addition to embedding a single PowerPoint slide in a Word document, you can embed an entire PowerPoint presentation in a Word document. To do this, follow these steps:

1 Arrange the Word document window and the Windows Explorer or My Computer window side by side on your screen.

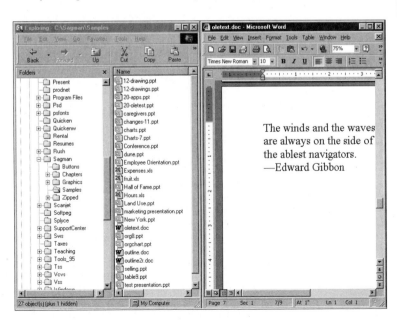

2 Hold down Ctrl and drag the presentation file icon from a folder into Word. The first slide of the presentation is the representative displayed in the Word document, as shown in Figure 18-3. You can click and resize the representative slide to any size you want.

FIGURE 18-3.

A presentation embedded in Word.

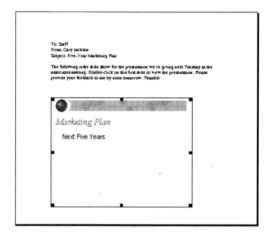

3 When you double-click the representative slide, the presentation opens and displays as a full-screen slide show. Press Esc to return to Word.

 TIP

Drag a Presentation from the Desktop into Word

You can also drag a presentation file stored on the Windows desktop into a Word document. Arrange the Word document window so that the presentation file icon on the desktop is visible. Drag the presentation file icon into the Word document where you want it to be embedded.

For another method, follow these steps:

1 Arrange Word and PowerPoint side by side on your screen.

2 Open the presentation and switch to Slide Sorter view.

3 Select the entire presentation by choosing Select All from the Edit menu or by pressing Ctrl+A.

4 Drag any one of the selected slides to Word while holding down the Ctrl key.

All the slides of the presentation are copied to Word. The first slide of the presentation appears as the presentation's representative in Word. You can click and resize the representative slide to any size you want.

When you double-click the slide, the presentation displays as a full-screen slide show. You can move around in the presentation using either the mouse or the keyboard.

- To move to the next slide, click the current slide. Or press the Spacebar, Down arrow, or Page Down key.

- To move to the previous slide, press the Up arrow or Page Up key.

- To return to the Word document, press Esc or click the last slide.

To edit the presentation embedded in Word, right-click the slide displayed in Word and then, from the shortcut menu, point to Presentation Object and choose Edit. The Word toolbar and menus change to those of PowerPoint, and an object frame appears around the slide. Make the changes you want to any slide in the presentation. When you're finished editing, click outside the object frame to leave the presentation. Remember that the changes you make to the presentation in Word exist only within the Word document. The original presentation is not changed unless you link it.

? SEE ALSO

For more information about linking Power-Point information to a Word document, see "Linking a PowerPoint Slide to Word," page 484.

You can also create a brand-new slide show for your Word document without ever leaving Word. To create a new PowerPoint presentation or a single slide from within Word, follow these steps:

1 In the Word document, position the cursor where you want the new presentation to be inserted.

2 From the Insert menu, choose Object. The Object dialog box appears.

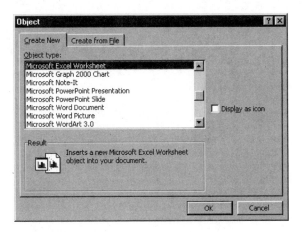

3 In the Object Type list, select Microsoft PowerPoint Presentation or Microsoft PowerPoint Slide, and then click OK. The Word toolbar and menus change to those of PowerPoint, and an object frame appears around the new slide.

4 Create the new slide or presentation. If you want to use a design template, on the Format menu, click Apply Design Template.

5 When finished, click outside the object.

> If you want to display only the PowerPoint icon in the Word document and not a slide, in the Object dialog box, select the Display As Icon check box. In this case, the new slide or presentation appears. Create it, and when finished, from the PowerPoint File menu, choose Close & Return To *<Document>*. The slide or presentation is represented by the PowerPoint icon in the Word document. Double-click the icon to display your presentation.

Linking a PowerPoint Slide to Word

If you want to include an existing PowerPoint slide in a Word document and make sure that it reflects any changes you make to it in PowerPoint, you can link the slide. When you link, the slide is actually stored in the originating PowerPoint presentation rather than in the destination Word document. Only a representation of the slide is displayed in Word. When you double-click the representation in Word, the slide appears, just as if you had embedded it. But because you have linked the slide, any changes you make to it in PowerPoint are reflected in the representation in Word.

The advantage to linking the slide is that you don't have to update the slide twice—once in PowerPoint and again in Word. The disadvantage is that you can't move the Word document to another computer without also moving the PowerPoint file. If you move the Word document without moving the PowerPoint file to the same destination, Word cannot find the PowerPoint data when you ask for it. Only when you fully embed a slide or presentation as described in the previous section can you transport the document along with its data.

You can link an existing PowerPoint slide or presentation to a Word document in one of two ways: by using the Insert Object command or by using the Paste Special command.

To link an entire PowerPoint presentation using the Object command, follow these steps:

1 In Word, position the cursor where you want the linked presentation to be inserted.

2 From the Insert menu, choose Object. The Object dialog box appears.

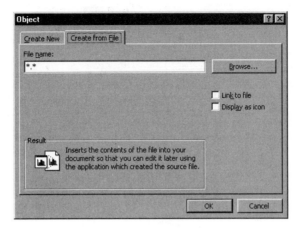

3 Click the Create From File tab.

4 In the File Name edit box, type the name of the presentation you want to link. Or click the Browse button to find the presentation, and then click Insert to return to the Object dialog box.

5 Select the Link To File check box, and then click OK. A representation of the contents of the file is shown in the Word document. Changes to the source file will be reflected in the Word document.

You can also link individual slides of an existing presentation to a Word document. To link a slide from a PowerPoint presentation using the Paste Special command:

1 Open the presentation containing the slide you want to link and switch to Slide Sorter view.

2 Select the slide you want to link.

3 From the Edit menu, choose Copy or click the Copy button on the Standard toolbar.

4 Switch to Word and click the insertion point where you want the slide to appear.

5 From Word's Edit menu, choose Paste Special. Word's Paste Special dialog box appears.

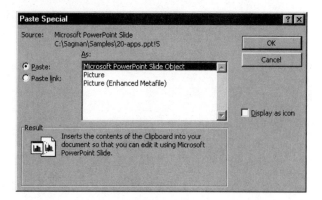

6 In the Paste Special dialog box, select the Paste Link option, and then click OK. The slide is linked into the Word document.

To edit a linked slide or presentation, use one of the following methods:

■ Click the slide once with the right mouse button. From the short-cut menu, point to Linked Slide Object and then choose Edit Link.

■ Select the slide. From Word's Edit menu, point to Linked Slide Object and then choose Edit Link.

In either case, PowerPoint appears, displaying the source presentation. Make the change, and then save the presentation. As soon as you save the presentation, your changes are reflected in the linked presentation in the Word document. Even if Word is closed, the changes appear the next time you open the Word document that contains the linked slide.

If you want, you can prevent changes to a linked slide from flowing through to Word. You might want to do this if you want more control over when changes to the linked slides are updated in your Word document. Follow these steps:

1 From the Edit menu in Word, choose Links. The Links dialog box appears.

2 If there is more than one link in the document, in the Links dialog box, select the link you want to change.

3 At the bottom of the dialog box, select Manual rather than Automatic as the Update option. To prevent the slide from being updated even when you use the Update Now command, you can also select the Locked option.

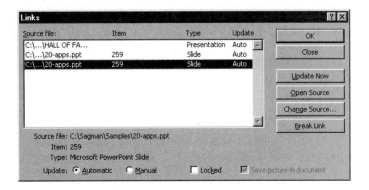

To manually update the links in your Word document, select the slide in Word. From the Edit menu, choose Links. In the Links dialog box, click Update Now. Click Close to close the Links dialog box. Or select the slide and then simply press F9.

Other options in the Links dialog box are:

- Open Source, which opens the presentation in PowerPoint for editing

- Change Source, which allows you to link a different object from another application

- Break Link, which severs the link and leaves a static picture of the slide in Word that cannot be edited or updated in PowerPoint

Inserting a PowerPoint Hyperlink in a Word Document

In addition to inserting a PowerPoint slide in Word, you can create a hyperlink in Word to a PowerPoint presentation. The title of the first slide appears as a hyperlink in the Word document.

To create a hyperlink, follow these steps:

1 In PowerPoint's Slide Sorter view, select the slide you want represented as the first slide seen in the hyperlink.

2 From the Edit menu, choose Copy. Or, on the Standard toolbar, click the Copy button.

3 In Word, click the insertion point where you want the hyperlink to be inserted.

4 From the Edit menu, choose Paste As Hyperlink. The hyperlink name appears in the Word document as the underlined slide title.

V

Advanced PowerPoint

When you click the hyperlink, the PowerPoint slide show opens, starting with the selected slide. You can move back and forth through the entire presentation. The Web toolbar also appears, so you can move forward or backward, or go to other web sites.

5 To return to the Word document, press Esc. A message asks whether you want to end the slide show. Click OK.

Transferring a Graphic to Word

Because Word and PowerPoint share the same Clip Gallery, you can open Clip Gallery to get a duplicate of a picture you used in Power-Point. However, you can also transfer a drawing, picture, or other graphic you used in PowerPoint to a Word document. This is particularly useful if you created an original drawing or modified a drawing or picture from Clip Gallery in a presentation, and you want to use it again in your Word document.

To transfer a graphic from a PowerPoint slide to a Word document, follow these steps:

1 Arrange the PowerPoint and Word windows side by side on the screen.

2 In PowerPoint, make sure you're in Slide View or Normal View and the graphic you want to transfer is visible.

3 In Word, make sure the location in the document where you want to insert the graphic is visible.

4 Hold down Ctrl and drag the graphic from PowerPoint to the location you want in Word.

If you need to edit the graphic, you can double-click it. Word's drawing tools, which work just like PowerPoint's drawing tools, are made available.

Using Word to Format and Print Notes Pages and Handouts

You can use PowerPoint to print handouts that have blank lines for audience notes. However, there are certain situations in which Word can provide more effective documents based on your presentations. For example:

- Print handout sheets based on your notes pages.

- Print your notes pages with blank lines.

- Include the handouts for a slide show in a Word report or training manual.

If you want to create any of these types of documents, follow these steps:

1 From the PowerPoint File menu, point to the Send To command, and then choose Microsoft Word. The Write-Up dialog box appears.

2 Choose one of the five layout options in the Write-Up dialog box. You can always change the formatting and layout once you have the information in Word.

3 Choose whether to paste or link the slides and notes to Word by clicking the Paste or Paste Link option. If you link the slides, any changes you make in the original slide show are also made in the Word document.

4 Click OK to begin the write-up to Word.

Figure 18-4 shows the result in Word when you select the Blank Lines Next To Slides option. The first column contains the slides. The second column contains blank lines for hand-written notes about the slide.

Advanced PowerPoint

FIGURE 18-4.

The layout for these handouts is Blank Lines Next To Slides.

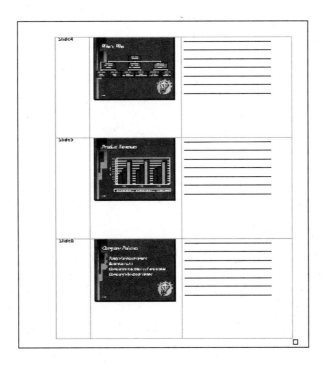

Using PowerPoint with Microsoft Excel

If you have numeric data, you are likely to accumulate it, calculate it, and analyze it in a spreadsheet program such as Microsoft Excel. You'll be glad to know that you can communicate between PowerPoint and Excel as easily as you can between PowerPoint and Word. In fact, you can create an Excel worksheet from within PowerPoint, drag a worksheet from Excel to PowerPoint, or drag a PowerPoint slide or presentation to an Excel worksheet using the same techniques you use with Word.

Transferring an Excel Worksheet to PowerPoint

You can create and insert a new Excel worksheet in PowerPoint. You can also embed an existing Excel worksheet in PowerPoint.

Creating a New Excel Worksheet within PowerPoint

You can create and embed a new Excel worksheet in a PowerPoint slide. To do this, follow these steps:

1 From the PowerPoint Insert menu, choose Object.

2 Be sure that the Create New option is selected.

3 Under Object Type, click Microsoft Excel Worksheet.

4 If you want the worksheet to be displayed in the slide as an Excel icon, select the Display As Icon check box.

5 Click OK. A worksheet frame opens on the current slide.

While you are entering data in your new embedded worksheet, Excel's menus and toolbars appear in PowerPoint and a framed worksheet window overlaps the PowerPoint slide, as shown in Figure 18-5. Using Excel commands and procedures, enter your data in the worksheet within the worksheet frame.

When you finish the worksheet, resize the worksheet frame to be sure that just those cells you want included are visible within the worksheet frame. Click outside the frame. PowerPoint's menus and toolbars reappear, and a picture of the Excel worksheet is displayed on the slide, as shown in Figure 18-6.

You can resize the object frame further at this point. If you drag one of the corner handles, the worksheet object is resized proportionally according to its original dimensions. If you drag one of the center handles, you can stretch or compress the length or width of the worksheet object.

FIGURE 18-5.

While you work on the embedded worksheet, the Excel menus and toolbars are available.

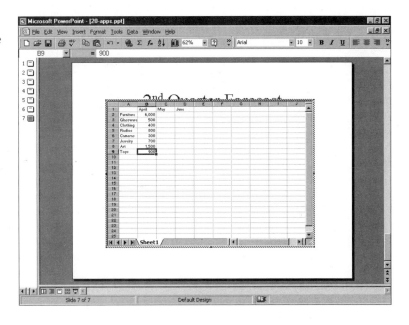

FIGURE 18-6.

The Excel worksheet is displayed on the PowerPoint slide.

Drag a corner handle to resize proportionally.

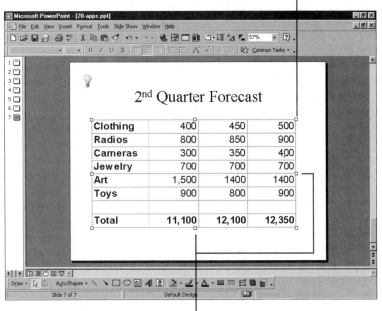

Drag a side handle to stretch or compress the length or width.

Embedding an Existing Excel Worksheet in PowerPoint

You can embed an entire Excel worksheet in PowerPoint, just as you can embed Word text. To do this, drag the worksheet file icon from any folder onto the open PowerPoint slide. The worksheet appears on the current PowerPoint slide as an embedded object.

You can also drag any part of an existing worksheet onto a slide. To do this, follow these steps:

1 Open the Excel and PowerPoint windows, and then arrange them so they share the screen and both are visible.

2 Make sure the slide in which you want to embed the Excel worksheet is displayed in the PowerPoint window and that Slide view or Normal view is active.

3 In Excel, select the worksheet range you want to move or copy.

4 Place the mouse pointer on the selection border until the pointer changes to an arrow, and then drag the border of the range to move the worksheet from Excel to the current PowerPoint slide. To copy rather than move the worksheet, hold down Ctrl as you drag. The worksheet range appears in the slide as an embedded object.

Figure 18-7 shows a range of numbers in Excel and the same range copied to PowerPoint with drag-and-drop editing. You can move and resize the worksheet by dragging its handles.

FIGURE 18-7.

An Excel worksheet that has been copied to PowerPoint with drag-and-drop editing.

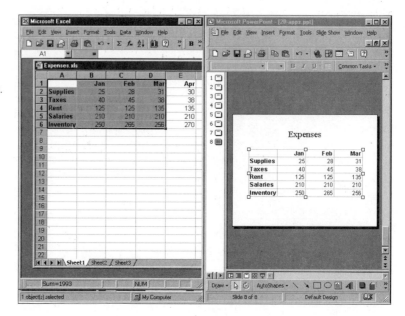

Modifying an Embedded Worksheet

To edit the worksheet, simply double-click it. Or click it with the right mouse button and then from the shortcut menu, point to Worksheet Object and choose Edit. Excel's menus and toolbars appear in place of those of PowerPoint, and the worksheet is surrounded by a frame. After you finish editing the worksheet, click outside the frame.

If you prefer, you can open the worksheet in an entirely separate Excel window. Use the right mouse button to select the worksheet object, and then from the shortcut menu, point to Worksheet Object and choose Open. When you finish editing in the Excel window, choose Update from Excel's File menu. Then, again from the File menu, choose Close & Return To *<Presentation>*.

TIP

Crop a Worksheet

You can crop a worksheet on a PowerPoint slide. Right-click the worksheet object and then, from the shortcut menu, choose Show Picture Toolbar. On the Picture toolbar, click the Crop button. The mouse pointer changes to a cropping icon. Place the cropping pointer on one of the worksheet picture's resizing handles, and then drag the handle inward to reduce the width or height of the picture.

Linking an Excel Worksheet to PowerPoint

You can link the worksheet embedded in PowerPoint to its original in Excel. With a link, whenever the data is updated in the original Excel worksheet, it is automatically updated in the PowerPoint slide. To link an embedded worksheet, you can use either the Object command from the Insert menu or Paste Special from the Edit menu. With the Object command, you can create link an entire new worksheet. With the Paste Special command, you can link a range of cells from an existing worksheet.

To link an Excel worksheet using the Object command, follow these steps:

1 From the PowerPoint Insert menu, choose Object.

2 Select the Create From File option.

3 In the File edit box, type the name of the Excel worksheet you want to link, or click the Browse button to locate it.

4 Select the Link check box, and then click OK.

V

Advanced PowerPoint

To link an Excel worksheet using Paste Special, follow these steps:

1 Open the worksheet in Excel, and then select the data you want in the slide.

2 From the Excel Edit menu, choose Copy. Or, on the Standard toolbar, click the Copy button.

3 Switch to PowerPoint's Slide view and, from the Edit menu, choose Paste Special.

4 In the Paste Special dialog box, select the Paste Link option and then click OK.

The worksheet appears in PowerPoint. If you make subsequent editing changes to the worksheet in Excel, the changes will flow through to the linked PowerPoint presentation when you resave the Excel file. If you make changes to the Excel file when the linked presentation is closed, the changes will appear the next time you open the presentation.

Remember, when you link an Excel worksheet to a PowerPoint presentation and you move the presentation to another system, you must also move the Excel worksheet.

Displaying a PowerPoint Slide or Presentation in Excel

? SEE ALSO

For more information about these procedures, see "Transferring PowerPoint Information to Word," page 478.

You can embed and link a single slide or presentation from PowerPoint in an Excel worksheet, following the same procedures you use to display a PowerPoint information in Word. Remember, you can:

■ Drag a single slide from PowerPoint's Slide Sorter view to Excel.

■ Select all the slides in PowerPoint's Slide Sorter view and then drag the entire presentation to Excel.

■ Insert a hyperlink in an Excel worksheet to a PowerPoint presentation.

■ Transfer a graphic from PowerPoint to Excel.

★ TIP

> **Proportionally Resize a Slide**
> After you drag a slide to Excel, you can resize the slide's width and height proportionally by dragging one of its corner handles.

If you've dragged a single slide to Excel, double-click the slide to open it in the PowerPoint window for editing. If you've dragged an entire presentation to Excel, double-click its representative slide to start the presentation. You can then control the slide show as if you were displaying it in PowerPoint's Slide Show view.

To edit an entire presentation embedded in Excel, select its representative slide, click the right mouse button, point to Presentation Object, and then choose Edit.

Sending a Presentation to Microsoft Outlook

Using Microsoft Outlook 2000, you can send and receive presentations to and from others in your workgroup and beyond. You can:

- Send a slide as the body of an e-mail message.

- Send a slide or entire presentation as an attachment to an e-mail message.

- Route the presentation to others.

- Post the presentation to a public folder that is accessible to everyone on your network.

To do any of these things, first be sure that Outlook is set up on your computer, and that you are connected to your network's mail server. Then, any time you want to send, route, or post presentations to others on the network, from the File menu, point to Send To, and choose the mail command you want to use.

In this chapter, you learned how to exchange information between PowerPoint and other applications. In the next chapter, you'll learn how to automate PowerPoint operations by programming with Visual Basic for Applications.

V

Advanced PowerPoint

CHAPTER 19

Customizing PowerPoint

Y ou have plenty of control over how PowerPoint works. You can customize the way PowerPoint looks, change many of its defaults, and even circumvent some of the steps that it would otherwise have you follow in its quest to guide you through the process unharmed.

In this chapter, you'll learn how to customize PowerPoint from top to bottom, changing the defaults for everything from the blank presentation to the composition of the toolbars. Once you've demonstrated your total domination over the program, you can truly be considered a PowerPoint master.

Creating a Default Presentation

When you select Blank Presentation from the PowerPoint dialog box or the General tab of the New Presentation dialog box, PowerPoint loads a default, blank presentation. You can't make any changes to this presentation, but you can create a new, custom default template that will apply the formatting and design elements you want in new presentations. With such a custom template, you can always apply such elements as a corporate standard background design, your corporate logo, and special text to each new presentation.

? SEE ALSO

For more information about changing the template, slide background, color scheme, or slide master, see Chapter 11, "Changing the Look," page 275.

First you'll need to customize a presentation. Start a new presentation or open an existing presentation, and then change any or all of the following elements, as needed:

- The template attached to the presentation

- Any graphic objects on the slide background, such as logos

- Special text on the slide background, such as the date, time, and slide number

- The color scheme

- The formatting of the slide master

- The Set Up Show dialog box options

> NOTE

Only the formatting changes you make to the slide master (and not special formatting of individual slides) are saved with the default presentation.

? SEE ALSO

For more information about using graphics, see Chapter 12, "Drawing in PowerPoint," page 301.

When you have finished customizing the presentation, you're ready to save it as your new standard presentation template. To do so, follow these steps:

1 From the File menu, choose Save As.

2 In the Save As dialog box, choose Design Template (*.pot) from the Save As Type drop-down list.

3 In the File Name box, type a name for the standard presentation, such as *Default Presentation*.

4 Click Save.

To start a new presentation with the default template you've designed, choose New from the File menu and then select the template on the General tab of the New Presentation dialog box.

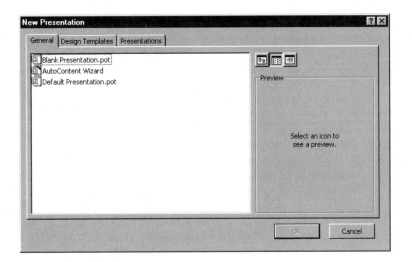

Add Templates to the General Tab

To add presentations to the General tab of the New Presentation dialog box, simply place copies of the presentations in the Templates folder, which resides within the Microsoft Office folder. Do not place them in any of the folders that are within the Templates folder, though, such as Presentation Designs, because then they will not appear on the General tab.

Changing the Start-Up Defaults

The basic operating defaults for PowerPoint are stored and set in the Options dialog box, available through the Options command from the Tools menu. The Options dialog box contains six tabs, each of which is reviewed here.

The View Options

You can use the options on the View tab, shown in Figure 19-1 on the next page, to change what you see as you work in PowerPoint and what your audience sees during slide shows.

- You can clear the Startup Dialog check box to skip the Power-Point dialog box that appears whenever you start the program. When you opt to skip this dialog box, PowerPoint loads the default presentation and displays the New Slide dialog box, in which you can select an AutoLayout whose placeholders you'll fill with text, charts, and graphics. When you skip the PowerPoint

Advanced PowerPoint

dialog box, you do not see the option to use the AutoContent Wizard to start a presentation, and you get whatever formatting is applied to the default presentation. But you can always use the AutoContent Wizard later by selecting it on the Presentations tab of the New Presentation dialog box. You can also select a template by choosing Apply Design Template from the Format menu or the Common Tasks toolbar. You might find it handy to skip the PowerPoint dialog box if you almost always use the same presentation design or when you have the presentation's content worked out, such as when you use PowerPoint to prepare presentations that vary only slightly.

FIGURE 19-1.

The View tab in the Options dialog box.

■ Clear the New Slide Dialog check box to skip the New Slide dialog box that normally appears when you choose to add a new slide. Instead, you jump straight to a new Bulleted List AutoLayout. To select a different layout, you can always choose Slide Layout from the Format button or hold down Shift as you click the New Slide button. This might be the ideal setup if you frequently create presentations that consist of series of text slides. The first slide of a new presentation is a title slide, and successive slides are bulleted list slides, unless you choose otherwise when you add each slide.

■ The Status Bar and Vertical Ruler check boxes show or hide the Status bar along the bottom of the PowerPoint window and the vertical ruler along the left side of the window. Clearing the Vertical Ruler check box lets you see more of the presentation window. If you've selected the Vertical Ruler check box but still do not see the ruler, choose Ruler from the View menu.

- When the Windows In Taskbar check box is selected, each Power-Point presentation you open is represented by a different button on the Windows taskbar. If you prefer to have just one button for all open PowerPoint presentations, clear this check box.

- The check boxes under Slide Show let you set options for actions during slide shows.

  - The Popup Menu On Right Mouse Click check box allows the menu to appear when you click the right mouse button during a slide show.

  - The Show Popup Menu Button check box shows the popup menu button during slide shows. You can click this button to bring up the popup menu.

  - The last check box, End With Black Slide, adds a black screen to the end of a slide show to provide a graceful ending.

The General Options

You can use the options on the General tab, shown in Figure 19-2, to change how you interact with PowerPoint.

 SEE ALSO

For more information about adding sounds to slide shows, see "Adding Multimedia Files to Slides," on page 377.

- The Provide Feedback With Sound To Screen Elements check box allows you to add sound to events that occur while you are working in PowerPoint, such as selecting menu options and closing dialog boxes. This has nothing to do with the sounds you add to slide shows. To change the feedback sounds, use the Sounds function in the Windows Control Panel.

FIGURE 19-2.

The General tab in the Options dialog box.

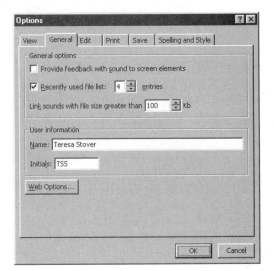

Advanced PowerPoint

- The Recently Used File List setting determines the number of presentation names that appear on the File menu. You can choose up to nine entries, that is, nine presentations to which you can quickly return without having to browse through your file structure. Remember, another way to return to recent presentations is to by click the Windows Start menu and then point to the Documents. The Documents menu lists the last fifteen documents you have opened in Windows.

- The Link Sounds With File Size Greater Than setting keeps the presentation file from becoming excessively large when you add sounds for slide shows. Sounds with file sizes over the size you designate with this option are linked to the presentation but stored in separate files. If you move the presentation to another computer, you also need to copy these files to keep the links intact.

- User Information contains the name or initials that will appear on notes you add to the presentation with the Comment command from the Insert menu.

- If you click the Web Options button, the Web Options dialog box opens, shown in Figure 19-3. This dialog box presents a new set of Web publishing options. Use this dialog box to set the appearance, file name and location, default editor, picture file format, monitor screen size, encoding, character sets, and fonts for use in Web presentations on the web. *For more information about these attributes of Web presentations, see Chapter 16, "Web Publishing and Collaboration," starting on page 405.*

FIGURE 19-3.

The Web Options dialog box.

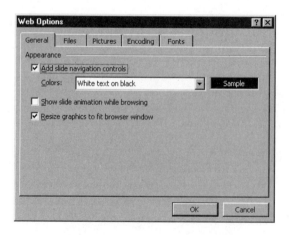

The Edit Options

Use the options on the Edit tab, shown in Figure 19-4, to change how text is handled.

FIGURE 19-4.

The Edit tab in the Options dialog box.

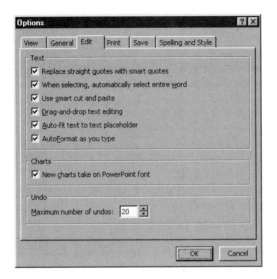

- The Replace Straight Quotes With Smart Quotes option enters typographically correct quotation marks (opening and closing) when you type a passage of text enclosed in quotation marks.

- When Selecting, Automatically Select Entire Word selects the entire first and last words of a text passage, even if you don't drag the mouse pointer across the beginning of the first word and the end of the last word.

- Use Smart Cut And Paste ensures that spaces are adjusted when you cut and paste text so that one space appears before and after the text.

- Drag-And-Drop Text Editing lets you use your mouse to select text and then move and copy text by dragging it to a new location.

- The Auto-Fit Text To Text Placeholder option ensures that if you enter a large amount of text into a text placeholder, the font size will automatically be reduced to try to accommodate the text. If you never want the font size to change this way, and instead let the text expand beyond the boundaries of the text box, clear this check box.

V

Advanced PowerPoint

■ The AutoFormat As You Type option applies automatic formats such as numbered listed or bulleted lists to your text while you're typing.

■ Under Charts, the New Charts Take On PowerPoint Font check box converts fonts in charts inserted from another presentation to 18-point Arial. Clear this check box to maintain existing font settings in charts.

■ Maximum Number Of Undos determines how many actions you can reverse. Clicking the Undo button on the Standard toolbar reverses your most recent action. (You can also choose Undo from the Edit menu or press Ctrl+Z.) To undo the action before that one, you can click the Undo button again, and so on. When you have clicked the Undo button the maximum number of times, PowerPoint will not reverse any more actions.

The Print Options

Use the settings on the Print tab in the Options dialog box, shown in Figure 19-5, to change settings for printing presentations.

FIGURE 19-5.

The Print tab in the Options dialog box.

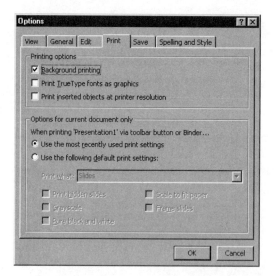

■ If the Background Printing check box is selected, you can continue to work on a presentation while another presentation is printing. Otherwise, the Print Status dialog box appears each time you print, tying up your computer until the printer has finished.

■ Print TrueType Fonts As Graphics sends TrueType fonts to your printer as graphic images instead of downloading the actual font.

If text is missing from printed slides, select this check box to try to resolve the problem.

■ Print Inserted Objects At Printer Resolution prints objects at the printer's resolution rather than the resolution you have selected for them to display in a slide show.

■ The Options For Current Document Only determine the print settings that are to be used when you click the Print button on the Standard toolbar.

The Save Options

The settings on the Save tab in the Options dialog box, shown in Figure 19-6, change what happens when you save a presentation.

FIGURE 19-6.

The Save tab in the Options dialog box.

■ Allow Fast Saves resaves any changes to slides at the end of the existing file, rather than resaving the entire presentation. The result is faster saving, but larger file sizes. After you complete a presentation, you can clear the Allow Fast Saves check box and save the presentation again. This reduces the size of the file on disk.

■ Select the Prompt For File Properties check box to display the Properties dialog box whenever you save a presentation.

■ The Save AutoRecover Info Every _ Minutes option saves a recovery file on the disk at the interval you select. This is useful if your computer stops working or the power fails as you create a presentation. If disaster strikes, you will be prompted to recover a recent version of the presentation the next time you start PowerPoint.

- Save PowerPoint Files As gives you the option to save the current presentation in a file that is compatible with an earlier version of PowerPoint. Use this option if you are in a workgroup that has computers with older versions of PowerPoint installed.

- Default File Location indicates the drive and folder in which your presentation files are stored by default. Whenever you click the Save As or Open command from the File menu, the Save In box shows the folder you specify here. (You can override this default by specifying a different location.)

The Spelling and Style Options

The settings on the Spelling And Style tab in the Options dialog box, shown in Figure 19-7, affect the checking behavior for spelling and style.

FIGURE 19-7.

The Spelling And Style tab in the Options dialog box.

- Clearing the Check Spelling As You Type setting will keep Power-Point from checking the spelling of text as you type it. With Hide Spelling Errors In This Document selected, PowerPoint still checks the spelling but does not display the wavy red lines under text that indicate misspelled words.

- Always Suggest Corrections determines whether the spelling checker suggests alternatives to a misspelled word. If you select this option, the spelling checker functions more slowly than if it simply has to point out spelling errors.

- Use the two Ignore check boxes if you want to avoid checking the spelling of words that are in uppercase or that contain numbers.

- The Check Style check box sets whether you want PowerPoint to check your presentation for style inconsistencies, as set up in the Style Options dialog box, shown in Figure 19-8. If you select the Check Style check box, click the Style Options button to set the styles you want checked. Styles include text case, end punctuation, font variety, text size, and legibility.

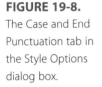

FIGURE 19-8.
The Case and End Punctuation tab in the Style Options dialog box.

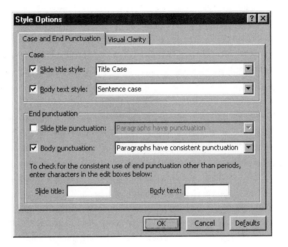

The Menu and Toolbar Options

Another set of options is available on the Options tab of the Customize dialog box. From the View menu, point to Toolbars, and then click Customize. Click the Options tab. Use this tab to set options for how you like your menus and commands to appear.

- The Standard And Formatting Toolbars Share One Row option indicates that the most frequently used commands on the Standard and Formatting toolbars will be showing and that they will be in one row, giving you more window space for your work. If you want them to appear in two separate rows, in their fully expanded rather than adaptive versions, clear this check box.

- The Menus Show Recently Used Commands First option indicates that the common commands and commands you've used recently show on a menu first. If you open a menu and then pause for a few seconds, or click the More Commands icon, the menu expands to show additional commands. If you prefer to see all available commands on a menu first, rather than use the adaptive menus, clear this check box.

■ The Show Full Menus After A Short Delay option indicates that the full menu will show after the menu is open for a couple seconds. If you prefer to not see the full menus until you click the More Commands icon, clear this check box.

■ The Reset My Usage Data button resets the menus and toolbars to their original settings, as if you haven't used any additional commands or buttons for the adaptive menus and toolbars.

■ Select the Large Icons check box if you prefer to see a larger version of your toolbar buttons.

■ The List Font Names In Their Font option lets you see what a font looks like in the Font drop-down list.

■ The Show ScreenTips On Toolbars option displays a small yellow tip containing the button name when you rest your mouse pointer over the button for a second or two.

■ The Show Shortcut Keys In ScreenTip option displays any applicable shortcut key, like Ctrl+S or Shift+F12 along with the button name in a ScreenTip.

■ Use the Menu Animations list to specify whether you want your menus to drop down with an unfolding or sliding animation effect. If you like both, choose Random. If you leave it at none, the menu appears instantly when you click it.

Customizing the Default Chart Type and Datasheet Settings

When you start a chart, Microsoft Graph always chooses a default chart type, but you can modify this style to obtain a standard chart design more suited to your needs.

To modify the default chart type, follow these steps:

1 Load Graph by clicking the Insert Chart button on the Standard toolbar. Or, from the Insert menu, choose Chart. Still another method is to double-click a *Double click to add chart* placeholder.

2 From the Chart menu, choose Chart Type.

3 In the Chart Type dialog box, select a Chart Type and Chart Sub-Type.

4 Click the Set As Default Chart button.

5 Click OK and then click Yes at the "Are You Sure?" prompt.

The next time you start a chart, the revised chart type will plot the data in the datasheet.

You can also customize some of the default settings for working with charts. To do this, follow these steps:

1 Start Microsoft Graph.

2 From the Tools menu, choose Options. The Graph Options dialog box appears.

SEE ALSO

For more information about charts, see Chapter 7, "Customizing Charts," page 155.

- The Datasheet Options tab provides two check boxes you can use to control the datasheet. The first option, Move Selection After Enter, determines whether the cell pointer moves to the next cell of the datasheet after you press Enter or whether it remains in the current cell. The second option, Cell Drag And Drop, turns drag-and-drop editing on or off within the datasheet window.

- On the Chart tab of the Graph Options dialog box, you can also specify whether empty cells of the datasheet should be omitted from the graph or plotted as zero. When empty cells are omitted, gaps may occur in the graph. The Chart Tips options determine whether Graph displays the name of a chart element and the value of a marker when you rest the mouse pointer over it.

NOTE

The Color tab of the Graph Options dialog box displays the colors used to fill the markers (Chart Fills) and the colors used for the lines and outlines (Chart Lines) of the graph. These colors are set by the current color scheme. You can override the colors of a chart by formatting its markers and lines directly. Because of this, you should not need to modify the colors on the Color tab.

V

Advanced PowerPoint

Setting the Drawing Defaults

To change the default fill color, line style, text style, shadow, and other effects of objects you draw using PowerPoint's drawing tools, follow this procedure:

1 Draw an object and apply settings for the fill color, line style, text style, and other attributes.

2 Click the object to select it.

3 On the Drawing toolbar, click the Draw menu, and then choose Set AutoShape Defaults.

Now the new default settings for color, style, and other attributes are applied whenever you draw any object.

Customizing Toolbars

As you've seen, PowerPoint's toolbars give you easy access to the most popular menu commands. But you may not find a toolbar button for every command you use frequently. Fortunately, you can customize the toolbars. You can add and remove buttons, move buttons from one toolbar to another, and create a custom toolbar containing your favorite toolbar buttons.

Displaying More Buttons on a Toolbar

If your Standard and Formatting toolbars share one row, you can display other buttons that are available on those toolbars by clicking the More Buttons button. A list of buttons that can be shown on that toolbar appear. If you click one of these buttons, it becomes a part of the regularly displayed toolbar.

From the More Buttons list, you can also choose Add Or Remove Buttons. A list appears which shows all buttons that are on the default version of this toolbar. These are the buttons that include the check-mark. To remove one of these buttons from the toolbar, click it. Other buttons are listed that you can add to the toolbar. To restore the original toolbar settings, click Reset Toolbar.

Displaying a Toolbar

The easiest way to display a toolbar is to click any visible toolbar with the right mouse button. On the shortcut menu that appears, the tool-bars accompanied by check marks indicate the ones that are already displayed. To display any other toolbar on the PowerPoint window, choose its name from the shortcut menu. Figure 19-9 shows the shortcut menu for toolbars. Or, from the View menu, point to Toolbars, and then choose from the toolbar menu.

FIGURE 19-9.

The shortcut menu for toolbars.

Likewise, to hide a toolbar you don't need on your window anymore, bring up the toolbar menu and click its name.

Adding and Removing Buttons

To add a button to a toolbar, make sure the toolbar you want to customize is visible, and then click it with the right mouse button. From the shortcut menu, choose Customize. Or, from the View menu, point to Toolbars, and then click Customize. The Customize dialog box appears.

On the Commands tab of the Customize dialog box, shown in Figure 19-10, is a list of categories that corresponds to the PowerPoint

FIGURE 19-10.

The Commands tab of the Customize dialog box.

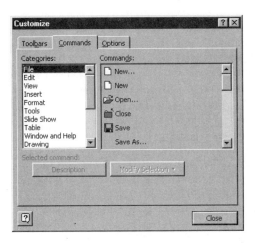

menus and toolbars, and a set of buttons that represents the commands in the selected category. Simply select a category, and then drag the command you want to any toolbar. You can drag as many commands from as many categories as you want, and you can drop the buttons in exact positions on the toolbars. For a description of any command, click the Description button. When you're finished adding buttons, click Close to close the Customize dialog box.

SEE ALSO

For more information about creating macros and assigning macros to buttons, see Chapter 20, "Automating PowerPoint with Visual Basic for Applications," page 515.

You can also create a macro and add it as a button on a toolbar. First create and save the macro. Then from the View menu, point to Toolbars, and click Customize. On the Commands tab, under Categories click Macros. A list of the macros you have created appears under Commands. Drag the name of the macro command to the toolbar. The macro name is added to the toolbar.

Removing a toolbar button is even easier. With the Customize dialog box open, simply drag the button off its toolbar. The button is always available in the Customize dialog box if you need it again.

TIP

> **Drag to Remove a Button**
> You don't have to open the Customize dialog box to remove a button from a toolbar. Simply hold down Alt and drag the button off its toolbar.

Moving Buttons Within and Between Toolbars

If you don't like the order of buttons on a toolbar or if you want to move a button to another toolbar, you can drag buttons within toolbars and between toolbars. You can drag a button up two positions in a vertical toolbar, for example, or drag a button from one toolbar to another. You can even create a custom toolbar, which starts blank, with no buttons. You can then drag your favorite buttons to it.

To move a button from one toolbar to another, hold down Alt and drag the button. To copy a button from one toolbar to another, hold down both Alt and Ctrl as you drag the button. A small plus sign appears next to the mouse pointer to indicate that you are copying rather than moving the button.

Creating a New Toolbar

To create a custom toolbar, follow these steps:

1 Right-click any visible toolbar and then choose Customize from the toolbar's shortcut menu. Or, from the View menu, point to Toolbars, and then choose Customize.

2 In the Customize dialog box, click the Toolbars tab, and then click New.

3 In the New Toolbar dialog box, type a name in the Toolbar Name box and click OK. A small, empty toolbar appears floating on your screen, as shown in Figure 19-11.

FIGURE 19-11.

The Custom toolbar floating on the Customize dialog box.

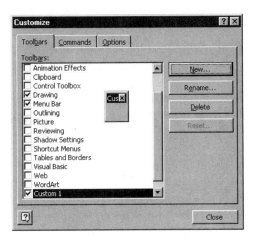

4 Drag copies of your favorite buttons or commands to the custom toolbar from the toolbars displayed on your screen or from the Commands tab in the Customize dialog box.

5 Reposition the toolbar by dragging it to one side of the PowerPoint window.

With that final bit of customization, you've done it. You've achieved the coveted status of PowerPoint guru. You're now ready to go out and present to the world!

CHAPTER 20

Automating PowerPoint with Visual Basic for Applications

You can make many tasks easier by having PowerPoint do them using its built-in programming language, Visual Basic for Applications (VBA). Simple VBA programs in PowerPoint can automate frequent tasks and handle chores that would otherwise require multiple steps.

All the applications in Microsoft Office 2000 share the VBA programming tools, which let you build automated business solutions with the Office applications. In fact, instead of buying customized applications, many companies use Office and VBA to fulfill their needs. For example, instead of buying a dedicated forms generator, a human resources department can program a business application in Word that automates and simplifies the process of filling in personnel review and evaluation forms. Similarly, you can use VBA in PowerPoint to create toolbar and menu commands that help you and those in your workgroup create standard presentations.

This chapter provides an introduction to programming automated solutions with PowerPoint.

What is Visual Basic for Applications?

A computer program is a cyborg version of a Miss Manners guide instructing the computer how to behave. For example, you can program a computer to display "Hello" on startup or "Bye" on exit. Computer programs are nothing more than a series of instructions (referred to as code) that control the computer.

VBA, which you use to create "code," is a modern version of the BASIC programming language, which was invented to teach programming to beginners. BASIC commands are essentially English commands, so you will find them easy to understand.

Before you start to create simple VBA programs, you should understand a number of procedures, which are the basis of this chapter. You should know how to:

- Use the macro recorder

- Run a recorded macro

- View (and eventually edit) a VBA macro

- Read VBA

- Use variables

- Get information from users

- Add your macros to custom toolbars and menus so that you can find them and run them easily

- Get your macro to make its own decisions

Recording Basic Macros

The first PC macros (shortened version of the term "macroinstructions") simply recorded a sequence of keystrokes, assigned them to a single keystroke, and then played them back. Microsoft redeveloped and extended this early concept of macros to create a fully programmable macro language for its Office suite. Microsoft later merged the idea of programmable macro languages with a bona fide programming language—BASIC—and VBA was born.

A macro language is a programming language built into an application that lets you automate a series of tasks by combining them into a single command. Macro recorders allow you to record the code necessary to automate such a series of tasks while you perform the task. You can then replay the macro when you want to perform that task again. Microsoft Excel, Microsoft Word, and Microsoft PowerPoint provide macro recorders.

How to Use the Macro Recorder

Although you have to be careful when using macro-recorded code wholesale, the code you get while recording a macro is a great starting point from which to expand.

How to Record a PowerPoint Macro

To use PowerPoint's macro recorder, follow these steps:

1 In PowerPoint, choose Macro from the Tools menu and then select Record New Macro. This opens the Record Macro dialog box, shown in Figure 20-1.

FIGURE 20-1.

In the Record Macro dialog box, you can name the macro you're about to record.

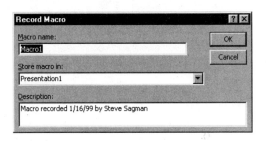

2 In the Record Macro dialog box, you can do the following:

- Change the name of the macro to something more descriptive.

- Select the template or presentation in which to store the macro. PowerPoint defaults to storing the macro in the current presentation.

- Enter a brief description of the macro.

3 Click OK in the Record Macro dialog box; PowerPoint displays the Stop Recording toolbar, which has one button: Stop Recording.

4 Perform the task in PowerPoint that you want to record.

5   After you finish recording the macro, click the Stop Recording button.

How to Run a Macro

When you run a macro, whatever you did when you recorded the macro happens again. In some cases, you might get an error message indicating that the macro can't perform the task it's trying to do. Often such errors occur because you're trying to redo something that's already been done. For example, you're trying to open a file that's already open or close a file that's no longer open. In such cases, make the necessary adjustment and then try running the macro again.

To run a macro that you have recorded:

1   Choose Macro from the Tools menu and then select Macros. This opens the Macro dialog box, as shown in Figure 20-2.

FIGURE 20-2.

In the Macro dialog box, you can run, edit, create, or delete macros.

2   Select the macro you recorded from the list and then click Run.

How to View (and Eventually Edit) a PowerPoint Macro

After you record a macro, you might want to look at it and eventually edit it. To look at (and change) a recorded macro:

1   Choose Macro from the Tools menu and then select Macros. This opens the Macro dialog box.

2   Select the macro from the list and then click the Edit button.

When you edit a macro, you're actually opening an application separate from PowerPoint called the Visual Basic Editor. (You may have noticed that Visual Basic Editor appears as an option on the Tools Macro submenu.) When you first edit a macro, the Visual Basic Editor is arranged in three windows:

- The macro itself appears in the large window on the right. To edit a macro, simply type in the macro window.

- At the upper left is the Project Explorer, which lets you manage the elements of your VBA project including such things as code and dialog boxes. If you don't see the Project Explorer, you can open it from the View menu.

- The Properties window lists information about the item that you are working with.

Because you can rearrange these windows, resize them, or close them, your Visual Basic Editor might not look exactly like the one pictured in Figure 20-3. To close the Project Explorer window, click the Close button in the upper right corner of the window.

FIGURE 20-3.

The Visual Basic Editor.

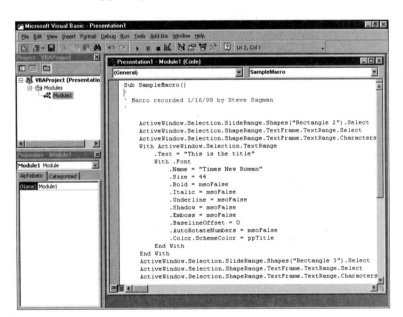

To close the Visual Basic Editor, choose Close And Return To PowerPoint from the File menu.

How to Read VBA

The best way to learn about VBA is to try recording some sample macros and then take a guided look at them to see what they mean. Later, you will learn to write some code from scratch. These code samples are short, so you can duplicate them easily and run them on your own computer.

First, try recording the following macro, named OpenExampleOne, which opens a PowerPoint presentation. Before you record the macro, start a new presentation, name it Example One, and save it in the C:\My Documents folder. Then close the presentation and start a new presentation.

To record the macro, follow these steps:

1 Start the macro recorder by choosing Macro from the Tools menu and choosing Record New Macro from the Macro submenu.

2 In the Record Macro dialog box, change the macro name to OpenExampleOne (without spaces between the words) and click OK.

3 From the File menu, choose Open.

4 Switch to the C:\My Documents folder, if necessary.

5 Select the presentation named "Example One," and click Open.

6 Click the Stop Recording button on the Stop Recording toolbar.

To see the macro you've just recorded, close Example One, choose Macro from the Tools menu, and then choose Macros. In the Macro dialog box, select OpenExampleOne and click Edit.

The macro should look something like this:

```
Sub OpenExampleOne()
'
' Macro recorded 6/12/99 by Steve Sagman
'

    Presentations.Open FileName:="C:\My Documents_
    \Example One.ppt", ReadOnly:=msoFalse
End Sub
```

 NOTE

In these code samples, the underscore (_) means that the current line of code continues.

To read the VBA code in the macro shown above, you need to understand a few things about macros. First, every macro you record is a *subroutine*. Subroutines are defined as instructions that perform specific tasks. Subroutines start with the keyword "Sub" followed by the name of the subroutine, in this case, the macro name and a set of parentheses, and all subroutines end with the phrase "End Sub," as shown below.

```
Sub NameOfThisSubroutine()
      Code
End Sub
```

Second, VBA code consists largely of objects—essentially, bundles of functionality—that you can manipulate in two ways:

- By setting or retrieving an object's properties (or characteristics)

- By using an object's methods (or procedures)

For example, PowerPoint presentations are objects. When you get a presentation's name through code, you get its Name property. When you open it through code, you use the Open method. The general syntax for manipulating objects is:

```
object.property or object.method
```

In any given line of code, you can either set a property or perform a method—you can't do both at once.

The sample code shown in the previous section (and repeated below) uses the Open method of the Presentations object (shown in bold). In this code, the first object is Presentation and the first action is a method, Open, as shown below:

```
Presentations.Open FileName:="C:\My Documents_
\Example One.ppt", ReadOnly:=msoFalse
```

The code following the Open method consists of the arguments (or additional information) that the method requires in order to do anything. In the sample code shown above, the first argument is FileName and the second is ReadOnly. Each argument is followed by a colon plus an equal sign (:=) and then the information the argument is to use. The information each argument uses is shown in bold.

```
Presentations.Open FileName:="C:\My Documents_
\Example One.ppt", ReadOnly:=msoFalse
```

The information that the FileName argument uses is fairly straightforward: It's the path and the file name of the presentation you want to open, enclosed in quotes. In VBA, all plain text must be enclosed in quotes so that VBA knows it's plain text rather than a misspelled object, property, method, etc. The information that the ReadOnly argument uses is quite a bit more obscure: It's a value (called an intrinsic constant) that's built into VBA and it equals False. The meaning of **ReadOnly:=msoFalse** amounts to this: Don't open this presentation in read-only mode.

About VBA Syntax

Here are two other things you need to know to read (and write) VBA:

- Each use of a VBA property or method and each VBA statement or function (programming terms for "command") is a single line of code (even though it might wrap onto more than one line for display purposes) that ends with a carriage return. For example, in the sample macro Presentations.Open FileName:="C:\My Documents\Example One.ppt", ReadOnly:=msoFalse is a single line of code that ends with a carriage return.

- Text that starts with an apostrophe (') indicates a comment line. (A comment is a note to yourself, which the macro ignores.) The default color for comments is green. The comment from the sample macro would be:

    ` ` Macro recorded 6/12/99 by Steve Sagman`

    Remember that the comment is considered to be a single line of code even though it wraps for display purposes. The comment ends with a carriage return after the word "Sagman."

> **NOTE**
>
> Do not break the use of a VBA property, method, statement, function, or comment into multiple lines by pressing Enter.

How to Extend the Useful Life of Your Macros

The problem with macro-recorded code is that it's hard-coded—in other words, it performs only the specific actions that you record. For example, the macro you recorded in the previous section can open only one file (Example One), and it can open this file only when it's located in C:\My Documents. To turn hard-coded code into code that's more widely usable requires two programming techniques: the use of variables and a way to get information from the people who run your macro.

How to Use Variables

Suppose television sets were hardwired to receive a single channel. You'd have to own three TVs just to watch the major networks. (Don't even think about cable.) Code that doesn't use variables is as inefficient as a TV that gets only one channel.

Variables are single-word names that store a particular type of data. The data might come from users or from another macro. Every programming language enables you to work with two general types of data—string data (text) and numeric data (integers). Some languages, such as VBA, support a variety of other types of data as well.

It's generally a good practice to declare variables—in other words, to list at the start of the program the variables used and the type of data each variable represents. You declare variables using the keyword "Dim" followed by the single-word name for the variable (such as FileToOpen) plus the data type (such as string).

For example, the following code specifies that the variable MyName is a string, sets the variable equal to "Sharon," and then displays that variable in a message box. The word "MsgBox" is a VBA function that opens a message box; the information that immediately follows the word MsgBox appears in the message box. Note that because MyName is a variable, the word "MyName" itself doesn't appear in the message box. Instead, the message box displays whatever MyName equals—in this case, "Sharon." (Note that variable names are not enclosed in quotation marks.)

```
Sub MyName()
    Dim MyName As String
    MyName = "Sharon"
    MsgBox Prompt:=MyName
End Sub
```

You can create a new macro and type the preceding code to test how variables work (and to see how to write code from scratch) by following these steps:

1   Open a new presentation.

2   Choose Macro from the Tools menu, and then select Macros.

3   In the Macro dialog box, type a single-word name for your new macro in the Macro Name box, such as MyName.

4   Click Create. This opens the Visual Basic Editor.

If the macro you just created is the first macro in the PowerPoint presentation that you're currently working in, the subroutine MyName will appear at the top of the macro window. Otherwise, it will probably appear below the other macros stored in the presentation. At this point, the subroutine consists of the following two lines of code:

```
Sub MyName()
End Sub
```

NOTE To adjust the macro window so that it displays only one macro at a time no matter how many macros are stored in a particular PowerPoint presentation, click the Procedure View button in the lower left corner of the macro window.

To add code to this subroutine, follow these steps:

1 Position the cursor on the blank line above End Sub.

2 Type the second line of code, which declares that the variable MyName contains a string (a.k.a. plain text).

```
Dim MyName As String
```

Notice that as you type, the Visual Basic Editor displays tips listing the options (alphabetically, of course) that might be correct in this context. For example, when you start to type the keyword "string," the Visual Basic Editor displays a list box (see Figure 20-4) that lists options that start with "s." After you type "str" the word "String" appears highlighted at the top of the listbox. Press Enter to insert "String" at your cursor.

3 Press Enter at the end of the second line of code, and then add the third line, which sets the variable MyName equal to "Sharon."

```
MyName = "Sharon"
```

4 Press Enter at the end of the third line of code, and then add the fourth line, which displays a message box with the name "Sharon."

```
MsgBox Prompt:=MyName
```

When you press the Spacebar after you finish typing "MsgBox," the Visual Basic Editor displays another tip with the complete syntax of the MsgBox function, as shown in Figure 20-5. Although it can take some time before you're comfortable reading tips such as this, one thing to remember is that arguments in bold text are required; arguments in nonbold text are optional. So the tip means this: The MsgBox function requires a single argument called Prompt, which tells it what to display. In this case it will display the text that the variable MyName contains.

FIGURE 20-4.

As you type, the Visual Basic Editor displays programming tips.

FIGURE 20-5.

When you type the keyword "MsgBox," the Visual Basic Editor displays the complete syntax for the MsgBox function.

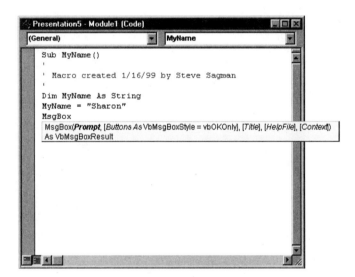

V

Advanced PowerPoint

At this point, you can run the macro in one of two ways:

- Return to PowerPoint and run it from the Macro dialog box.

- In the Visual Basic Editor, make sure the cursor is somewhere in the MyName subroutine, and then click the Run Sub/UserForm button on the Standard toolbar (see Figure 20-6 on the next page).

FIGURE 20-6.

The Standard toolbar of the Visual Basic Editor.

Run Sub/UserForm

When you run the macro, you should see the message box shown in Figure 20-7.

FIGURE 20-7.

The macro MyName displays a message box with the value of the variable MyName.

To change this macro so that it displays another name, simply type the name to display in the message box in the third line of code. For example, this line of code displays "Chuck" in the message box.

```
MyName = "Chuck"
```

This line of code displays "George Washington, first president of the United States" in the message box.

```
MyName = "George Washington, first president of the
United States"
```

To close the Visual Basic Editor, choose Close And Return To Microsoft PowerPoint from the File menu.

How to Get Information from People Who Run Your Macro

Although variables clearly make it easier to change the information that your macro uses, the subroutine presented above is still hard-coded. In other words, the only way to specify the name to display in the message box is for the programmer (that's you) to type as part of the code itself a new value for the MyName variable. However, it makes sense for the user (not the programmer) to indicate the name that the message box displays.

The simplest way to allow users to provide information to your macros is with an input box—a one-line dialog box in which people type text that your macro then uses. The InputBox function is similar to the MsgBox function in that it requires a single argument—Prompt—that, in this case, is used to tell users what information you need from them. The following macro asks users their name and then displays their answer in a message box.

```
Sub YourName()
    Dim YourName As String
    YourName = InputBox(Prompt:="What is your _
    name?")
    MsgBox Prompt:=YourName
End Sub
```

Notice that in this subroutine, the variable YourName is not set equal to plain text such as "Christine" or "Chuck." Rather, it's set equal to the result of the InputBox function. In other words, it's set equal to whatever users type in the input box. And this is the significance of the parentheses around the argument Prompt: These parentheses indicate that the function will return information to the program. If users type "Eric" or "Esmerelda" or whatever, the InputBox will return that information and store it in the variable YourName, which the MsgBox function can then display. Figure 20-8 shows the input box that this subroutine displays and the message box that results when the user types "Steve."

FIGURE 20-8.

Whatever users type in the input box (left) is displayed in the message box (right).

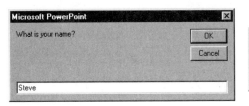 

Of course, the input box is the simplest way to get information from users. The more flexible and complex way to do this is to use a dialog box, which you create with the UserForms feature in the Visual Basic Editor. You can find instructions on how to use this feature in the Help file that comes with the Visual Basic Editor.

How to Create an Interface that Makes it Easy to Run Your Macros

Although you can run macros with the Run command in the Macro dialog box (see "How to Run a Macro," page xx), it's easier to run them from toolbars and menus, just as you would run any other PowerPoint command.

When you create a custom toolbar or add a custom menu to the menu bar, you're essentially doing the same thing: you're customizing Microsoft's toolbars. Toolbars can contain buttons, menus, or a combination of both.

How to Add a Macro to a Custom Toolbar

To create a custom toolbar and add a macro to it:

1 Choose Toolbars from the View menu, and then select Customize.

2 Click the toolbars tab in the Customize dialog box.

3 Click New.

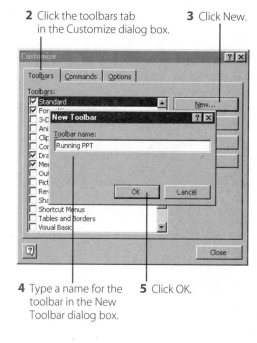

4 Type a name for the toolbar in the New Toolbar dialog box.

5 Click OK.

A new, blank toolbar appears. Move this toolbar away from the Customize dialog box so that it doesn't disappear behind it.

6 Choose the Commands tab in the Customize dialog box, and then select Macros from the Categories list box. The available macros appear in the Commands list, shown in Figure 20-9.

FIGURE 20-9.

When you select Macros from the Categories list on the left, the available macros appear in the Commands list on the right.

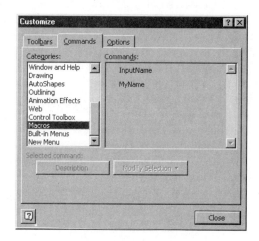

7   Drag the macros to add to the custom toolbar and drop them on the toolbar one at a time. The Figure below shows a custom toolbar with macros displayed as text buttons.

8   When you first add your macro to a toolbar, the macro's name appears on the toolbar. To add a graphic to the name, click the toolbar button with the macro's name, and then click the Modify Selection button in the Customize dialog box.

9   Select Change Button Image from the Modify Selection menu.

10   From the Change Button Image palette, click the graphic to use for your macro.

11   Click Close to close the Customize dialog box. Figure 20-10 shows a finished toolbar with graphic buttons representing your macros.

FIGURE 20-10.

This custom toolbar has both text and graphics.

How to Add a Macro to a Custom Menu on the Menu Bar

To add a custom menu to the menu bar, follow these steps:

1   Choose Toolbars from the View menu, and then select Customize.

2   Click the Toolbars tab in the Customize dialog box, and then select Menu Bar in the Toolbars list.

3   Click the Commands tab, and then select New Menu from the bottom of the Categories list box. When you do this, "New Menu" appears in the Commands list as well.

4   Drag "New Menu" from the Commands list to PowerPoint's menu bar. You can gauge the position of the new menu by the over-sized cursor that appears as you point with your mouse to various menu bar positions. In Windows, it's standard practice to add custom menus to the left of the Window menu.

5   Drop "New Menu" onto the menu bar, and then click it with the right mouse button.

6 Give the custom menu a new name (such as "Running PPT") by typing it into the Name box, as shown below, and press Enter.

To add a macro to your custom menu, follow these steps:

1 Select Macros from the Categories list box on the Command tab of the Customize dialog box.

2 Drag a macro from the Commands list to the new menu entry, and then, when the short, blank stub appears below, drag it onto the stub.

3 Click Close to close the Customize dialog box. The image below shows a finished menu bar with a custom menu for your macros.

Creating Advanced Macros that Make Their Own Decisions

In order to create more sophisticated macros—for example, macros that make their own decisions—you need to understand how to use control structures. Control structures determine the order in which code executes. Generally, macros run one line at a time, from beginning to end, unless this sequential flow is altered by events or control structures that cause the program either to execute code repeatedly or to execute code out of sequence.

- **Events** are "outside" elements that affect the computer program, such as a given amount of time passing, the user clicking a certain button, or the user opening a certain file.

- **Control structures** are techniques for processing "decisions" within the computer program itself. The most basic VBA control structure is If... Then... Else.

If... Then...Else

If... Then...Else is not only the most basic control structure, it's also the most intuitive because it means exactly what it says. The simplest form of this control structure executes code based on whether a certain condition exists. Here's the syntax:

```
If Condition1 Then
      Code1
End If
```

When a program executes this control structure, it first evaluates Condition1. If Condition1 is True, program execution continues with the first line of code in Code1. If Condition1 is False, Code1 is skipped and execution continues with the first statement following End If. For example, the code shown below works as follows: If x = 1, then the computer beeps; if x doesn't equal 1, nothing happens. Create this macro as described in the previous section, "What is a Variable?," using the following code. Use different values for x, and hear what happens.

```
Sub Example1()
      Dim x As Integer
      x = 1
      If x = 1 Then
             Beep
      End If
End Sub
```

> **NOTE** "Beep" is one of the simplest VBA statements: It does just what it says.

Two clauses, ElseIf and Else, allow you to add additional tests to your If... Then...Else control structures. Use these optional clauses to enable your code to take different actions depending on current conditions or user input. You see the syntax on the next page (the square brackets enclose optional parts of the control structure).

```
If Condition1 Then
     Code1
[ElseIf Condition2 Then
     Code2]
[ElseIf Condition3 Then
     Code3]
     .
     .
     .
[ElseIf ConditionN Then
     CodeN]
[Else
     CodeElse]
End If
```

When a program executes this control structure, it evaluates Condition1 first. If Condition1 is True, Code1 executes. When Code1 finishes, the program skips to the first statement following End If. If Condition1 is False, however, the program skips to the next ElseIf clause and evaluates Condition2. If Condition2 is True, Code2 executes and the program continues with the first statement following End If. If Condition2 is False, the program skips to the next ElseIf clause. The same process continues until one of three things happens:

■ An ElseIf condition is True (in which case, its block of code executes).

■ The program reaches the end of the control structure before a condition evaluates to True (in which case, none of the code inside the control structure executes).

■ The program encounters an Else clause.

An If...Then...Else control structure can have only one Else, which always appears as the last clause. Else clauses don't have conditions; they execute when all of the other conditions fail.

Here's a more complicated example using If...Then...Else. The code shown below works as follows: If x = − 1 and y = − 1, then the computer beeps; else if y = 0, then the computer does nothing; else if x or y equals any other number, the computer displays a message box with the word "Hi!" Again, create this macro as described in the previous section, "How to Use Variables," use different values for x and y, and watch the results.

```
Sub ExampleII()
      Dim x As Integer
      Dim y As Integer
      x = -1
      y = 0
      If x = -1 And y = -1 Then
            Beep
      ElseIf y = 0 Then
      Else
            MsgBox Prompt:="Hi!"
      End If
End Sub
```

Concatenation

Concatenation is a very big word for a simple and disproportionately powerful programming technique. Concatenation lets you combine a variable with plain text or one variable with another. To do this, put an ampersand (&) between the items to concatenate. For example, the following line of code concatenates the words "Your name is " with the information stored in the variable YourName. Note that the space after the words "Your name is " separates these words and the information in the variable with a single blank space.

```
"Your name is " & YourName
```

As you can see from this example, one thing that concatenation lets you do is provide more detailed feedback to users. The following VBA code provides an example of this. It uses the Date function to get the current date, assigns that date to the variable Today, concatenates it with two bits of plain text, "Today is " and a period (.), and displays the result in a message box. Instead of just displaying the date to users, you tell them what date you're displaying—that is, today's. "Date" is another of the simplest VBA functions.

```
Sub SampleConcatenation()
    Dim Today As String
    Today = Date
    MsgBox Prompt:="Today is " & Today & "."
End Sub
```

Comparison Operators

Comparison operators are symbols that allow you to compare expressions. The simplest comparison operator is the equal sign (=). Common comparison operators are listed below.

=	equal to
< >	not equal to
<	less than
>	greater than
< =	less than or equal to
> =	greater than or equal to

The following example uses an If... Then...Else control structure to check whether users have entered a valid number in the input box. If the number is valid, the program concatenates it with explanatory text and displays a message box. Otherwise, the program beeps and displays a message box informing users that they entered an invalid number. Since the InputBox function returns a string and the "greater than or equal to" operator requires a number, you must use the Val function to turn that string into a number.

> **NOTE**
>
> To use the Val() function, put the value (text or string variable to convert into a number) in parentheses after the keyword Val. For example, Val("10") = 10.

```
Sub ShowAnswer()
    Dim Answer As String
    Answer = InputBox("Enter a number_
    from 1 through 99:")
    If Val(Answer) <= 99 And Val(Answer) >= 1 _
        Then
        MsgBox Prompt:="You entered: " _
        & Answer & "."
    Else
        Beep
```

```
                    MsgBox Prompt:="You entered an invalid _
                    number."
        End If
End Sub
```

Using VBA to Automate Office Applications

In addition to automating routine tasks that you perform within PowerPoint, you can also automate the interaction of the Microsoft Office applications with VBA. For example, you can create a PowerPoint macro that will bring in numbers from Excel or enclose a PowerPoint presentation in a Word document.

To see how you can perform office automation with VBA, try following the procedure below to record a PowerPoint macro that will embed an Excel workbook in a presentation, add code to size the embedded object correctly, and allow users to type into an input box the path of the file to embed. Before continuing, make sure you have an Excel workbook with a short table suitable for displaying in a PowerPoint slide show.

1 In PowerPoint, move to a blank slide formatted in a way that's appropriate for displaying an Excel table—for example, use the Title Only AutoLayout. Don't select anything on the slide.

2 Choose Macro from the Tools menu, and then select Record New Macro. Name the macro InsertWorkbook.

3 Record the following: Choose Object from the Insert menu. This opens the Insert Object dialog box.

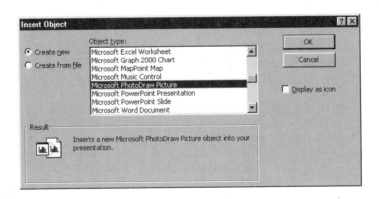

4 In the Insert Object dialog box, select the Create From File option.

5 Click Browse to open the Browse dialog box, which lets you select a file to embed in the active PowerPoint presentation.

6 After selecting an Excel workbook, click OK in the Browse dialog box. This returns you to the Insert Object dialog box.

7 Click OK to close the Insert Object dialog box and insert the selected file in the PowerPoint presentation.

8 Click the Stop Recording button.

After recording the macro, view it. Naturally, your macro will include the path information for the workbook you embedded rather than C:\My Documents\Sales Data.xls. The values indicating height, width, etc. may also differ. However, the basic structure of your macro will be the same as the one shown below.

```
Sub InsertWorkbook()
'

' Macro recorded 6/12/99 by Steve Sagman
'

ActiveWindow.Selection.SlideRange.Shapes._
AddOLEObject(Left:=120#, Top:=110#, Width:=480#, _
Height:=320#, FileName:="C:\My Documents\Sales _
Data.xls", Link:=msoFalse).Select
    With ActiveWindow.Selection.ShapeRange
        .Left = 201.875
        .Top = 218.375
        .Width = 316.125
        .Height = 103.25
    End With
End Sub
```

Unfortunately, this macro is unnecessarily verbose. To cut it back to a more manageable size, delete the following code:

```
With ActiveWindow.Selection.ShapeRange
    .Left = 201.875
    .Top = 218.375
    .Width = 316.125
    .Height = 103.25
End With
```

Your macro should now look (more or less) like the following:

```
Sub InsertWorkbook()
'
' Macro recorded 6/12/99 by Steve Sagman
'

ActiveWindow.Selection.SlideRange.Shapes._
AddOLEObject(Left:=120, Top:=110, Width:=480, _
Height:=320, FileName:="C:\My Documents\Sales _
Data.xls", Link:=msoFalse).Select
End Sub
```

> **NOTE**
>
> The arguments Width and Height in the above code set the workbook's size (in points). To resize the workbook manually, select it and then choose Worksheet Object from the Edit menu and select Edit. Resize the embedded object by dragging its edges, and then click anywhere off the object to stop editing it. To automatically display a greater portion of the embedded object when you insert it, increase the Height and Width values in the macro. Remember, however, that if you're running in VGA mode, the maximum width is 640 and the maximum height is 480.

If you move to another slide and run the macro you just recorded, it will insert the same Excel workbook in the active slide, which is referred to in code as the ActiveWindow. In some cases, the embedded workbook will appear misshapen. The following four lines of code—which you should insert immediately before the last line of code, End Sub—correct this problem by scaling the object to 100 percent of its original size.

```
With ActiveWindow.Selection.ShapeRange
    .ScaleHeight 1, msoCTrue
    .ScaleWidth 1, msoCTrue
End With
```

Your macro should now look (more or less) like the following:

```
Sub InsertWorkbook()
'
' Macro recorded 6/12/99 by Steve Sagman
'
```

```
ActiveWindow.Selection.SlideRange.Shapes._
AddOLEObject(Left:=120, Top:=110, Width:=480, _
Height:=320, FileName:="C:\My Documents\Sales _
Data.xls", Link:=msoFalse).Select

        With ActiveWindow.Selection.ShapeRange

              .ScaleHeight 1, msoCTrue

              .ScaleWidth 1, msoCTrue

        End With

End Sub
```

To display an input box where users can type the path of the Excel workbook to embed, add the following lines of code at the top of the macro after the comments:

```
Dim WhichWorkbook as String

WhichWorkbook = InputBox(Prompt:="Type the full _
path of the Excel workbook to insert into this _
presentation.")
```

Locate the hard-coded path for the Excel workbook and replace it with the variable WhichWorkbook. The FileName argument should now be as follows:

```
FileName:=WhichWorkbook
```

Your macro should now look (more or less) like the following:

```
Sub InsertWorkbook()
    '

' Macro recorded 6/12/99 by Steve Sagman
    '

        Dim WhichWorkbook As String

        WhichWorkbook = InputBox(Prompt:="Type the _
        full path of the Excel workbook to insert _
        into this presentation.")

        ActiveWindow.Selection.SlideRange.Shapes._
        AddOLEObject(Left:=120, Top:=110, Width:=480, _
        Height:=320, FileName:=WhichWorkbook, _
        Link:=msoFalse).Select

        With ActiveWindow.Selection.ShapeRange

              .ScaleHeight 1, msoCTrue

              .ScaleWidth 1, msoCTrue

        End With

End Sub
```

Choose Close And Return To PowerPoint from the File menu.

Move to another slide and run the InsertWorkbook macro. This time it displays an input box where you can type the path of the Excel workbook to embed.

For more information on creating automated solutions with PowerPoint, see:
- Online Help in Visual Basic Editor
- *Microsoft Office Developer's Handbook,* by Christine Solomon, published by Microsoft Press

V

Advanced PowerPoint

Index

About the Author

Stephen W. Sagman is the New York-based author of more than 20 books on the subjects of graphics, Microsoft Windows, business applications, and online communications, and he has contributed to several more. For Microsoft Press, he has also written *The Official Microsoft Image Composer Book* and *Microsoft PhotoDraw 2000 At a Glance.*

His books have sold well over a million copies worldwide, and they have been translated into Chinese, Dutch, German, Greek, Hebrew, Japanese, Portuguese, Russian, Spanish, Thai, and Turkish. His book Traveling The Microsoft Network, also published by Microsoft Press, was the recipient of the Award of Excellence from the Society of Technical Communication.

When he's not writing books, Steve runs Studioserv, a technical communications company that offers book editing and production, user documentation, software training, and user interface design (www.studioserv.com).

And when he's not writing or running his business, Steve plays jazz piano, sails his sloop *Offline*, and toils in the fertile loam of his garden.

He can be reached at:
steves@studioserv.com

Colophon

The manuscript for this book was prepared and submitted to Microsoft Press in electronic form. Text files were prepared using Microsoft Word. Pages were composed using Adobe PageMaker 6.52 for Windows, with text in Garamond and display type in Myriad. Composed pages were sent to the printer as electronic prepress files.

Cover Designer
Tim Girvin Design, Inc.

Interior Graphic Designers
Kim Eggleston
Amy Peppler Adams,
designLab

Layout Artist
Sharon Bell,
Presentation Desktop
Publications

Editor
Gail Taylor

Proofreader
Tom Speeches

Indexer
Audrey Marr